Nick Lucas

ALSO BY MICHAEL R. PITTS AND FROM MCFARLAND

Thrills Untapped: Neglected Horror, Science Fiction and Fantasy Films, 1928–1936 (2019)

Astor Pictures: A Filmography and History of the Reissue King, 1933–1965 (2019)

Western Film Series of the Sound Era (2009; paperback 2018)

RKO Radio Pictures Horror, Science Fiction and Fantasy Films, 1929–1956 (2015)

Western Movies: A Guide to 5,105 Feature Films, 2d ed. (2013)

Allied Artists Horror, Science Fiction and Fantasy Films (2011)

Columbia Pictures Horror, Science Fiction and Fantasy Films, 1928–1982 (2010)

Poverty Row Studios, 1929–1940: An Illustrated History of 55 Independent Film Companies, with a Filmography for Each (1997; paperback 2005)

Charles Bronson: The 95 Films and the 156 Television Appearances (1999; paperback 2003)

Horror Film Stars, 3d ed. (2002)

Nick Lucas
*The Crooning Troubadour
and His Guitar*

Michael R. Pitts

McFarland & Company, Inc., Publishers
Jefferson, North Carolina

LIBRARY OF CONGRESS CATALOGUING-IN-PUBLICATION DATA

Names: Pitts, Michael R., author.
Title: Nick Lucas : the crooning troubadour and his guitar / Michael R. Pitts.
Description: Jefferson, North Carolina : McFarland & Company, Inc., Publishers, 2023. | Includes bibliographical references and index.
Identifiers: LCCN 2023006583 | ISBN 9781476690674 (paperback : acid free paper) ∞
ISBN 9781476648514 (ebook)
Subjects: LCSH: Lucas, Nick. | Singers—United States—Biography. | Guitarists—United States—Biography. | Entertainers—United States—Biography.
Classification: LCC ML420.L925 P5 2023 | DDC 782.42164092 [B]—dc23/eng/20230214
LC record available at https://lccn.loc.gov/2023006583

BRITISH LIBRARY CATALOGUING DATA ARE AVAILABLE

ISBN (print) 978-1-4766-9067-4
ISBN (ebook) 978-1-4766-4851-4

© 2023 Michael R. Pitts. All rights reserved

No part of this book may be reproduced or transmitted in any form or by any means, electronic or mechanical, including photocopying or recording, or by any information storage and retrieval system, without permission in writing from the publisher.

Front cover: undated publicity photograph of Nick Lucas (author's collection)

Printed in the United States of America

*McFarland & Company, Inc., Publishers
Box 611, Jefferson, North Carolina 28640
www.mcfarlandpub.com*

Table of Contents

Acknowledgments viii
Preface 1

Biography 3
Discography 129
Songbooks and Song Folios 191
Songs 199
Sheet Music 201
Filmography 203
Radio 219
Television 229
Stage Shows 231

Bibliography 237
Index 241

To the memory of two of Nick Lucas' loyal fans,
Dennis Deas and Herbert Mecking

Acknowledgments

For their assistance in the preparation of this book, the author would like to thank the following: the Academy of Motion Picture Arts and Sciences (Anthony Slide), Accent Records (Scott Seely), the Altoona (Pennsylvania) Area Chamber of Commerce (James C. Caporuscio), the American Film Institute (Anne G. Schlosser), James Ashton, Ray Avery, Jim Bedoian, Len Bissell, Jr., BMG Music (Bernadette Moore), Johnny Bond, Bowling Green State University Libraries' Special Materials Collection (William L. Schurk), Bowling Green State University—Music Library and Bill Schurk Sound Archives (Patty Falk), Brian Boyd, Tim Brooks, Canadian Communications Foundation (Pip Wedge), Capitol Records (Pete Welding), Dick Carty, Country Music Foundation (Ronnie Pugh, Chris Skinker), Ken Crawford, Jr., Daleville (Indiana) Community Library, Dennis Deas, Ron Dethlefson, EMI Records of London; EMI Records Australia (Bill Robertson), Gibson USA (Carole Blackwell), Louis Harrison, Richard K. Hayes, Stan Hester, Barbara Hoover, John Jones, Larry F. Kiner, Gary Kramer, Bill Legere, David Lennick, William Corbert Leonard, the Library of Congress (Melissa Wertheimer, Samuel Brylawski, Katherine L. Wise, James R. Smart, Emily Sieger, Charles Sens), Jack Litchfield, Librato "Libby" Lucanese, Amelia Malcolm, Leonard Maltin, MCA Records (Steve Hoffman), Australian Consulate-General D.E. McFeat, Herbert Mecking, Don Miller, Mark Miller, Ken Murray, the National Library of Canada (Joan Colquhoun), the New York Public Library (Robert Kenselaar, Dorothy Swerdlove), James Robert Parish, Robert Perkins, James Roosevelt, Bruce L. Ross of the Santa Cruz Guitar Company, Paul Scriven, Thomas Edison National Historical Park (Leonard De Graaf), Toronto (Canada) Public Library (Karen Pearce, Brent Cehan), University of Southern California Performing Arts (Ned Comstock), Rudy Vallee, John S. Vasconi, Gerald F. Vaughn, Michael Weekes, Dr. Ray White, the Winnipeg (Canada) Public Library (Louise-Philippe) and York University (Katrina Cohen-Palacios, Rob Van Bliek).

Preface

When Col. Tom Parker introduced Elvis Presley to Nick Lucas on the set of *Love Me Tender* in 1956, he said, "Elvis, I want you to meet Nick Lucas. He's the best guitar player in the world."

It was Nick Lucas who almost single-handedly brought the six-string guitar to national popularity in the 1920s by replacing the banjo with the guitar, first in big-name orchestras and then on recordings. His was the first custom-made guitar that the Gibson Guitar Company made, from his specifications. He compiled a series of guitar instruction books that influenced generations learning and playing the instrument. His was the first line of custom guitar picks, resulting in a shape that is still in use today. He was also the first to compose songs specifically for the guitar and the first to record them.

Lucas considered himself a singer first and a guitar player second. By combining both efforts, he became one of the most popular entertainers of his time. He is considered one of the first, if not *the* first, crooners, with Brunswick Records billing him as "The Crooning Troubadour." His success in this field paved the way for others like Gene Austin, Johnny Marvin, Rudy Vallee, John Boles, Dick Powell, Seger Ellis, Oscar Grogan, Franklyn Baur, Bing Crosby, Dick Todd, Jack Miller, Chester Gaylord, Dick Robertson, Paul Small, Ozzie Nelson, Smith Ballew, Jerry Cooper and others. Since he was also the first Italian crooner, he opened the door for others of his ancestry, including Carmen Lombardo, Frank Sinatra, Vic Damone, Frankie Laine, Perry Como, Tony Bennett, Al Martino, Jerry Vale, Phil Brito, Dean Martin, Jimmy Roselli, Don Cornell, Steve Rossi, Sergio Franchi, Enzo Stuarti, Lou Monte, and many more. He is also credited as being one of the first band singers.

While becoming one of the top stars of vaudeville in the late 1920s and early 1930s, Lucas appeared on radio stations throughout the country, culminating in starring in several network radio shows in the 1930s. He continued to headline syndicated radio programs well into the 1950s. Paralleling his success on stage, he became one of the biggest record sellers of his time, reportedly selling over 80 million records, most of them for Brunswick between 1924 and 1934. He also had one of the longest recording careers, beginning with his making cylinders for Thomas Edison in 1912 and culminating in his last session in 1981.

Lucas appeared in three Broadway productions and two of the most successful early sound musical films, *The Gold Diggers of Broadway* and *The Show of Shows*, both 1929 releases by Warner Bros. From the former came his greatest record success, "Tiptoe Through the Tulips," that sold more than three million platters. Among the many songs he recorded that have become popular standards are "Painting the Clouds with Sunshine," "Sleepy Time Gal," "Bye Bye Blackbird," "Looking at the World Thru Rose Colored

Glasses," "In a Little Spanish Town," "I'm Looking Over a Four-Leaf Clover," "(Here Am I) Brokenhearted," "Among My Souvenirs," "The Song Is Ended," "My Ohio Home," "I'm Waiting for Ships That Never Come In," "Just Like a Melody Out of the Sky," "I'll Get By," "Coquette," "I've Got a Feeling I'm Falling," "Dancing with Tears in My Eyes," "Three Little Words," "You're Driving Me Crazy," "Lady Play Your Mandolin" and "Walking My Baby Back Home."

Lucas also had successful engagements in London and Australia. He was one of the most traveled entertainers in U.S. history with followers in all parts of the world. His fans included royalty such as the Prince of Wales and the Queen of Spain, politicians like Huey Long, Los Angeles Mayor Sam Yorty and New Jersey Congressman Peter Rodino, sports figures including boxers Jack Dempsey, Primo Carnera and Tony Galento, fellow entertainers Bing Crosby, Eddie Dean, Merle Travis, Gene Autry and Rudy Vallee—plus the many thousands, or even millions, who saw him in person in his 70-year show business career. He is also credited with having originated the intimate style of singing.

Even more important than his legion of show business accomplishments is the fact that Lucas was a nice, kind, friendly and generous human being. He made friends wherever he appeared and was much beloved by several generations. He was always willing to help others and made hundreds of benefit appearances for numerous charities and worthwhile causes. While one of the most talented musicians of his time, he had none of the affectations of stardom and easily related to people in all walks of life.

He died in 1982 at the age of 84 but Nick Lucas is still very popular today. His vintage records are collector's items, as are his songbooks and folios, guitars and guitar picks. His records have been put on compact discs, and his many film and video appearances are available on YouTube and elsewhere on the Internet, including the website www.nicklucas.com. Looking back on the many firsts in his career, his enormous talent and longevity in his chosen field, Lucas must be considered one of the 20th century's greatest entertainers.

Biography

Newark, New Jersey, a city steeped in Italian tradition, was where Nick Lucas was born on August 22, 1897, at 10 Gaslight Street. He was christened Dominic Antonio Nicholas Lucanese, the son of an Italian gardener who had come with his family from Ariana Di Pugla, Italy, seven years before. In 1886, his father Otto Maria Lucanese (born in 1859) married Bella Ermiania Luchese (Palmieri) (born in 1868) and they had nine children, five of whom lived to adulthood. In addition to Dominic (as Nick Lucas was called for many years), there was older brother Frank (born 1890) and sister Tessie (born 1894). Two younger brothers, Librato (born 1904) and Anthony (born 1908), rounded out the family.

In the 1900 Federal Census, Otto Lucanese is listed as Frisgela Lucaruse (Fugila Lucanese), living in a rented house on Garside Street in Newark's Ward 15. A day laborer, he could not read or write but spoke English. His household included his wife "Carmalia" (age 30) and children Frank (age eight), Theresa (six), Domenic (three), Nicolina (one and a half) and a boarder, day laborer Philip Highthetta (age 23). On his Social Security application, Nick Lucas listed his father's name as Ottomarina Lucas and his mother as Carmela Luchese, and his own birthday as August 24, not August 22, 1897.

Otto Lucanese was employed as a gardener for the Essex County Parks Commission in Newark, working mainly as a landscaper and tree surgeon. He made nine dollars a week. Although poor, the family managed to live comfortably. When Dominic was three years old, the family moved from Newark to the country, due to his father's health, and they rented a house in the small town of Silver Lake, on the boundary line of Newark. When the Lucanese family moved into the abode, it had no indoor plumbing; Otto remedied this inconvenience, in addition to digging a well to supply the family with water. All the family members pitched in to make life more comfortable; conservation and ingenuity were bywords, as they were with most immigrant families of that time. Dominic remembered his mother going daily to the local fish market for the family's evening meal and in those days, with a purchase, the fish dealer would give away ten pounds of tripe. His mother would prepare a tomato sauce to serve with the cooked tripe. Dominic thought the dish was delicious although at the time it was hardly considered a delicacy.

When Dominic was about four years old, his father told his older brother Frank, already an accomplished musician specializing in the accordion, to teach Dominic how to play a musical instrument. Too small to comfortably handle a guitar or banjo, Dominic was taught to play the mandolin. He strummed the instrument for hours to learn to play it, later recalling, "My mother used to take her sewing into the living room and keep an eye on me while I practiced." It was tedious work, but in later years he expressed gratitude to his mother and brother for the discipline they forced upon him. After four years of study and practice with the instrument, Dominic began to join Frank as he played at parties, christenings and weddings. They also went out "busking," which meant passing a hat around after a performance. This activity usually took place in saloons or streetcars and it meant a few extra dollars coming in to help with the family's expenses. By this time, there were nine children in the family, six brothers and three sisters, but two brothers and two sisters died at early ages. Being the oldest son, Frank was "the master of us all," according to younger brother Librato "Libby" Lucanese. He recalled that Dominic, even as a child, was very devoted to his family. "Nick always kissed my grandmother's hand before he left home to play," Libby said. "Nick was the most religious one in the family. So he thought it would bring him luck and it sure did. My grandmother would always bless him with a cross. He bought the big bell for our church when they built the new church. When he was a boy, he was always pressed and clean."

Regarding his early music training, Nick told Mark Humphrey in *Frets* (April 1980) magazine,

> [Frank] taught me music without any instrument, using the solfeggio system. Then he gave me a mandolin when I was nine or ten. Frank would drag me along, and we would play at Italian christenings and weddings. We even played on street corners and in saloons. I would pass the hat around. I was getting a lot of experience, because the Italian people, when they get to feeling good, like to dance all night long—especially the tarantella. We played for hours and hours, and my wrist got very tired, but I was getting great practical experience that paid off years later.

Frank graduated Nick to a guitar because he felt it went better with his accordion. "Working with him, I was learning all the time," Nick said. "You might play the same chords over and over again all night at a dance, and naturally you mastered them."

As a boy, Dominic walked three miles a day to Belleville School #4 in Newark and was a good enough guitar player to serenade the students each morning as they went to class. He sang in school programs and at Christmas and other holidays. School started at nine a.m. and he recalled having only enough time in the morning to get cleaned up, and have a cup of coffee and a piece of bread, before running to school, as he usually had been up until three or four a.m. with Frank making money for the family. His mother always put out fresh water for him to wash in, but one morning she forgot to empty the water from the night before, when she soaked bak-a-lah (codfish). A very sleepy Nick dashed himself with the water and ran immediately to school, as he was late. Once there, he noticed his classmates had a strong aversion to him. "I smelled like a fish store," he said. "And the teacher soon said to me, 'Dominic, leave the room and go home.'" He ran all the way home crying and told his mother what happened. She laughed and said, "Oh, *filia mia*. Oh, my dear son, I forgot to change the water." Dominic ended up not going to school for three days because it took that long for the fish odor to go away.

During his grammar school years, Dominic often became sleepy in class, especially in the afternoons, due to his late musical hours. Geography class seemed a good time for slumber and he would prop a book in front of himself so that it would appear that he was studying. Classmates sitting in back of him agreed to awaken him if the teacher came along or it appeared she would ask him a question. One day, Tony Paul, the boy behind him, forgot to wake Dominic as the teacher came around and found him not only sleeping, but also snoring. As punishment, he was sent to the principal's office. Dominic told the official about his late-night working activities and the necessity to make money for his family. The principal's one reproach was not to fall asleep in class again. After school, Dominic got even with Tony Paul by lacing him in a fight. During these years, Nick later said, "[I] did not get my proper rest but I was acquiring my musical education by working my way through grammar school."

On streetcars, Frank played the accordion and Nick the guitar and then, by passing the hat for nickels and dimes, they would make six to seven dollars per night. On one occasion, the boys worked various streetcars and ended up in Philadelphia – and did not know how to get home. Their father went to the police, who finally located the boys. Despite the expense, their father had to go to Philadelphia and rescue his wandering musicians. Apparently an all points bulletin was put out by the police for the boys as indicated in an item in the District of Columbia's *The Washington Times* (September 25, 1905): "The chief of police of Silver Lake, New Jersey, has requested Captain Boardman, chief of detectives, to look out for Frank and Dominic Lucanese, fourteen and ten [*sic*] years old respectively, who disappeared from their home in Jersey many weeks ago. Both lads are talented musicians, Frank with the piano and accordion, and Dominic the mandolin and the violin. The boys are said to have come to this city to play around hotels."

Brother Libby recalled that at the time, other musicians made fun of Dominic for playing the guitar instead of the banjo, which was the popular string instrument of the day. The young man obviously paid no attention to this and it helped him to develop his guitar style. Ironically, in the 1920s it was Nick Lucas who started the movement to replace the banjo with the guitar in bands and on records.

For about six years, Frank and Dominic continued to go out a minimum of three nights a week to perform in order to earn money for their family. In 1912, Frank joined a group called the Three Vagrants (they all dressed like hobos) and played various vaudeville circuits. The act consisted of Frank on the accordion with guitar and clarinet players rounding out the trio. Nick was able to see it a few years later and recalled that it was a "terrific act." The trio went on to record "The Mermaid"–"Sadness Waltz" for Columbia Records (E-3187) in 1920.

The year 1912 saw 15-year-old Dominic make his first recordings. Since he was well-known in the Newark area for playing various string instruments, some of his friends who were employed at the Edison Phonograph Company told him that Thomas Edison was looking for musicians to make test records. Prior to this time, Edison had issued a number of Hawaiian guitar selections on his Mexican Blue Amberol series recordings but the 1910 Mexican Revolution forced him to close his Mexico City recording laboratory. Now he was trying to find local talent. Dominic took a streetcar to Edison's East Orange, New Jersey, plant and there he recorded a number of test records on cylinders that were not intended for commercial release. Working during the recording process with Edison, he later recalled the inventor as a very nice man who was genuinely interested in the proper recording of string instruments. These cylinders marked the beginning of Lucas' 70-year recording career as he proved to be one of the few, if only, musicians to record from the cylinder era through acoustic and electrical recordings up to the multi-channel stereo discs of the 1980s.

In 1913, after Dominic graduated from grammar school, his father took him aside and told him he should make a choice as to whether to go to high school or learn a trade. His father said that the choice was his, and for him to do what he thought was best. He told his son, however, that a trade would be "something to fall back on when you become a man." The teenager decided to forgo further schooling in order to learn a trade. His father had a friend who was a foreman in a leather tannery and he gave Dominic a job. To get to work at the tannery, Dominic had to get up at five a.m. to catch the trolley. The job started at seven and continued until 5:30 p.m., with a half-hour lunch break at noon. Dominic would bring along his guitar (he had also mastered the mandolin, banjo and banjeaurine) and during the lunch breaks, he would play and sing a few songs for his fellow workers. Often they would ask him, "Why are you wasting your time here when you can play and sing like that? You are too young for such hard labor. You should go on the stage."

In an article with his byline in the September 2, 1926, *Oakland* (California) *Tribune*, Lucas wrote, "I always wanted a musical career. Since my earliest boyhood days, that has been my one supreme ambition. This was no easy matter, having old-fashioned parents who came from Italy with old world ideas that every bambino must grow up to be an artisan of some sort. Musicians to their mind meant little better than tramps." He noted that as a boy, besides playing his guitar at weddings and christenings, "Sunday was my big day. On Sunday mornings I used to sing in backyards and serenade the different tenants in the surrounding buildings. This gave me all the scope and early training possible and an insight into what the public wanted." From this he earned the money to buy a banjo.

At this time, Dominic was undecided as to whether he should stay at his factory job or venture into the music field. The deciding factor came when he fell in love with Catherine Cifrodella. Wanting to get married, he intensified his musical skills on the banjo and guitar and set out looking for a better paying job. After a couple of months, he gave up his two-dollar-a-day tannery job and obtained work at Johnson's Café, a Newark cabaret. He played the guitar and banjeaurine (a mandolin with a banjo head) with a trio that consisted of a piano player and violinist. He did two shows a night along with dance music between sets, and for this he was paid $20 a week. His working hours were from 8:30 p.m. to 2 a.m. and he stayed at this job for over two years, getting musical experience playing variety shows. He recalled to James Obrecht in *Guitar Player* (December 1980),

> So I played with this big orchestra—it consisted of three men [*laughs*], piano, violin and banjeaurine. We played the revues—like they had a soprano singer, a comic, a line of girls, and a male singer. The show lasted about two hours. Eventually they went haywire and put in a drummer. This was in Newark, and of course Newark is a short jump from New York. Naturally I got all the work in town because there were only a few musicians available who could qualify to play for these night clubs. You had to be a good faker and read quick. They'd say—play it in C, or play it in D, put it up in F, and put it down a key. And if you couldn't do that, the music didn't mean a damn thing. When I went to the Musicians' Union, I had to pass an examination so I could get my card. Of course, they don't do that today; you pay the initiation and you're in. I was at that club for two years, and this is where I got my experience. Towards the end there, I started doubling on guitar for waltzes and things like that.

When he got his first week's pay, he took the money home and put it under his pillow; the next day he gave his mother 15 of the 20 dollars he had earned. After getting a five dollar per week raise, Dominic and Catherine Cifrodella wed on August 22, 1917, his twentieth birthday. After their marriage, he continued to work at Johnson's Café for another six months and then transferred to the Iroquois Café where he was paid $28 a week.

Nick later told Dorothy Pisano in an article in the *Dallas Morning News* (December 21, 1928),

> Married life made me. Before I married, I did not know what I wanted to do with my life. I didn't even consider music as seriously as I should have. But when I met her, why, it just came to me right away that I had to try music, anyway. I had to do something different to make her happy and perhaps a little proud of me. I suddenly made up my mind, and right away I found myself financially able to claim her for my bride. Since that time she has been my best help all along the road. We are both of a romantic nature. We understand each other and each other's difficulties perfectly, and, well, you know, the luster of some things just doesn't wear off.

Catherine Cifrodella was born in April 1898 in Newark, the daughter of Nicholas and Cohunba Cifrodella. Her father, a grocer, migrated to the U.S. from Italy in 1890. Catherine had an older brother, Angelo (born 1893), and sisters Antonette (born 1896), Christina (born 1898) and Rose (born 1904). There is some question as to Catherine's birth year although both the 1900 and 1920 Federal Census lists it as 1897. Her tombstone gives it as 1898 while Nick told Johnny Carson in 1969 on *The Tonight Show* that she was 18 when they married in 1917, which would make it around 1899. The Social Security Death Index lists her birth as April 22, 1898.

Being a well-paid musician provided Dominic and his new bride a very comfortable living. The couple paid $35 a month for a three-room Newark apartment and they lived very nicely on his salary while he continued to learn his trade both as an instrumentalist and singer. By this time, he could read music. His tenor voice grew richer and finer with constant training. He could trace his singing ability to his mother: He said that the family was poor, "but [my father] loved music and he wanted us to have musical educations. He couldn't sing or play, but my mother, how she could sing!" Besides Dominic and Frank, younger brother Libby played the guitar and sang. Their youngest sibling, Anthony, was also a fine vocalist.

While working at the Iroquois Café, Dominic began using the professional name Nick Lucas, one that had been suggested to him by friends while was still in school. He felt Dominic Lucanese was too long for marquees and he liked the name Nick Lucas because it was shorter and more easily remembered, yet was still his own name, just abbreviated. He alternated between Nick Lucanese and Nick Lucas until he joined Brunswick Records as a solo artist in the mid–1920s; after that, he adopted the name Nick Lucas for good. A few years later, he made it his legal moniker. The 1920 Federal Census lists him as Nick Lucas and gives his profession as performer. The 1920 Newark City Directory gives his name as Nicholas Lucanes and lists him as an actor.

During his tenure at the Iroquois Club, Nick was heard by an agent who singled him out to organize a group to play for the Ziegler Sisters, a successful dance act. Nick put together "The Kentucky Five," since Southern names were the rage at the time due to the popularity of jazz bands. The group included Nick's Newark pal Ted Fio Rito, who stood up for him at his wedding, and Sammy Halperin, later special arranger and drummer for Paul Whiteman. To polish their act, the group leased the Central High School gymnasium in Newark and sponsored a dance, netting each of them about $10. The musicians then went to the 125th Street Theatre in New York City for a tryout, with all the major agents there to hear them. They were booked in vaudeville at the sum of $300 per week. As a specialty in the act, the violinist would play "Just a Little Love, a Little Kiss" and Nick would sing the chorus; this came off so well, it became a major part of the act and his big-time singing debut. Catherine was pregnant and stayed at home in Newark while Nick was on the road. From his weekly salary, Nick managed to send her $35 and he lived on the rest although he remembered it was not difficult since rooms were about a dollar a day and he dined in budget restaurants. For ten months, the Kentucky Five toured vaudeville's Interstate Circuit, which consisted of cities in Texas as well as New Orleans and locales in the eastern part of the country and Canada.

The Kentucky Five consistently got good reviews. *The Sioux City* (Iowa) *Journal* (January 11, 1918) wrote, "The 'Militaire Caprice,' which closed the act and the show, was accompanied without the aid of 'Old Glory,' but the audience enjoyed it, nevertheless." When the act appeared at the Orpheum Theatre in Canada's Vancouver British Columbia, *The Vancouver Sun* (January 29, 1918) opined, "The Kentucky Five are kings of syncopation and haunting melody. There was a swing and rhythm to their playing that filled the fight [sic] nighters with marked enthusiasm." *The Vancouver World* declared, "The 'jazz boys' are the embodiment of pep and ragedy [sic] harmony." *The Dayton* (Ohio) *Herald* (June 2, 1918) noted that the quintet was "said to be the jazziest of all jazz orchestras." When the act appeared at the Poli's Theatre in Bridgeport, Connecticut, that city's *Bridgeport Telegram* (July 26, 1918) declared, "Without a question the Ziegler Sisters and the Kentucky Five are snap." In Hazelton, Pennsylvania, the *Standard-Speaker* (September 10, 1918) stated, "It is a dancing and musical act out of the ordinary run of such efforts for the entertainment of the public," while the same city's *The Plain Speaker* (September 19, 1918) wrote of the act's second appearance at the Feeley Theatre, "The Ziegler Sisters and the Kentucky Five make a big act with grace and agility having a fine background in the Kentucky Five … a novelty offering of extraordinary merit and entertaining qualities." Between the two Hazelton stands, the act was at the Taylor Opera House in Trenton, New Jersey, where *The Trenton Evening News* (September 13, 1918) stated, "The Kentucky Five adds much to the success of the act in a musical way."

During the tour, Nick briefly returned to Newark to be with Catherine and on April 17, 1918, their daughter Emily Isabel Catherine was born. Since both parents wanted a girl, they were delighted with the new arrival.

Following the Kentucky Five's vaudeville run, Nick made his theatrical stage debut as part of a trio called the Three Chums, which included James Miller and Gill Mack. Cast as Signal Corps member Merrick, Nick (and the other trio members) sang "Buffalo Boys Come Back" in the melodramatic *The Crowded Hour*, presented at the Park Square Theatre in Boston in March 1919. The next month, it was at the Teck Theatre in Buffalo, New York. Back in Newark, Nick and Ted Fio Rito, along with Benny Krueger, Charlie Agnew and future composer Ralph Rainger, formed a group that played for student dances.

Nick next accepted a job with Vincent Lopez and His Peking Five at the Peking Café on 46th Street in New York City, the heart of the theater district. The club was patronized by the cream of Gotham society in addition to mobsters and racketeers, as Lopez was a very popular bandleader and a favorite with the elite. Besides the Lopez band, the club featured four chorus girls and an emcee-comic along with Nick singing some of the production numbers in the show. In between dance sets, Nick was sometimes asked by customers to join them. On Monday nights, usually a slow night, a man would come in with a party, buying drinks and tipping the band with a $100 bill. This man would tell Nick, "You've got a great voice. You should be on the stage!"

One of the man's young female companions also greatly admired Nick's singing. One evening, she asked Nick to have lunch with her. He told her he was married with an infant daughter. The girl was insistent: "That doesn't matter and there is no harm in a social date." Nick relented and accepted her invitation and she took him to a gourmet restaurant and insisted on paying the check. After they lunched together a few more times, Nick told her he was unable to see her any more. The woman became angry and said, "You'll be sorry for this." A few nights later, Nick received a telephone call and the party said, "I understand you've been going out with my girlfriend and I am coming down tomorrow to see you after you get through work." Frightened, Nick immediately contacted a friend from Newark who was known as "Little New Yorker"; he was one of the Mob. Nick told the gangster about the trouble and asked him to come to the club the next night. When he got off work the next morning at two a.m., Nick found two men waiting for him and his friend. The quartet went down the street to a small restaurant and there was the woman and a man who recognized "Little New Yorker." One of the mobsters told Nick, "I understand you have been going out with my girl and you have been taking money from her to support your wife and daughter." Nick replied that the woman was a liar, that she had never given him money nor had he asked her for any. At this point, "Little New Yorker" stood up for Nick and told the gangsters that Nick was an "honest working kid" and that "Nick would never do anything like that." The gangsters dropped the matter but warned Nick to "be careful who you go out with." Regarding the incident, Nick later recalled, "Needless to say, it was a close shave and I was very grateful to come out alive. I never realized I was having lunch with a gangster's moll."

After playing with the Vincent Lopez band for several months, Nick reteamed with Ted Fio Rito in Al Sarli's Band that played for several weeks in the spring of 1919 at Cicardi's Restaurant in St. Louis. Others in the group, that was sometimes billed as "Five Aces of Syncopation," were Frank Trumbauer (saxophone), Frank Quatrell (trumpet), Louis Salemme (violin) and Joe Zig (drums). For a time, Nick also played guitar and banjo at the Capri Inn, but after the Cicardi's engagement got going, he went onto the dance floor and serenaded the customers. Catherine and baby Emily joined him in St. Louis; they lived in a one-room apartment (with the bed in the wall) that cost $180 a month. Returning to New York City later in the year, Nick appeared in a musical revue staged at the Tokio Restaurant. The *New York Evening-Telegram* (September 27, 1919) reported the show headlined recording artist Julia Gerity, who was assisted by the Five Aces of Syncopation under the leadership of "Banjo Nick" Lucas.

Returning to Newark, Nick joined the Vernon Country Club Orchestra in 1919. The group originated in Vernon, California, and was sponsored in its New York City debut by popular bandleader Paul Whiteman. The banjo player for the aggregation became ill and had to return home; Nick auditioned for the job and stayed with the orchestra for nearly three years. Their first important engagement was at Reisenweber's Café on Columbus Circle, then one of the city's hottest nightspots. There were three different clubs in the café, one featuring the Original Dixieland Jazz Band, the second headlining Sophie Tucker, and the third featuring the Vernon Country Club Orchestra playing dance music. Nick recalled that the group quickly became "the sensation of New York City": They played at the posh club for a year before transferring across the street to the Boardwalk for another year's stay. There he also sang with the group, resulting in his appearing briefly in Lou Leslie's *Blackbirds* stage show.

While working with the Vernon Country Club Orchestra, Lucas also recorded with the group. In 1917, he made his first commercial recordings playing the mandolin with Earl Fuller's Jazz Band (which included Ted Lewis on clarinet) for Victor Records. In

1920, he was part of a group called the Vernon Trio that included George Gershwin on piano. They recorded two sides for Brunswick Records, the company for which Nick would later sell millions of records. Nick's recordings with the Vernon Country Club Orchestra initiated his steady work as a sideman on discs, usually playing the banjo. The records he did with the Vernon Country Club Orchestra were made in 1921 and issued on the Pathe Actuelle and Columbia labels. The next year, he and brother Frank teamed to record for Pathe Actuelle as the Lucas Novelty Quartet and the Lucas Ukulele Trio. In the summer of 1922, Nick recorded his own compositions "Picking the Guitar" and "Teasin' the Frets," the first guitar solos waxed in the U.S., for Pathe Actuelle. Their influence proved to be tremendous as they had a big impact on future guitar players like Eddie Lang and Merle Travis.

When Nick re-recorded "Picking the Guitar/Teasin' the Frets" for Brunswick Records in 1924, the company advertised it this way:

> There are two brilliant interpretations upon one record that will furnish to music lovers a new and pleasing music entertainment.... Nick Lucas reveals a most talented and captivating treatment. Clear toned, velvety and rich, his playing of these selections. Unusual harmonic revealments [sic] result when he strums weird chords, oddly balanced against the other. This is the kind of record that puts new life in the phonograph.

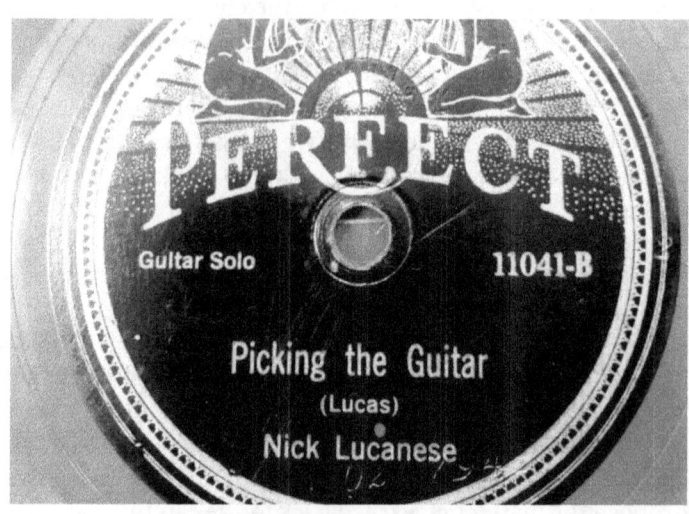

Label to "Picking the Guitar" (1922), Nick Lucas' first guitar record solo, issued on Perfect under his birth surname.

Label for "Teasing the Frets" on Brunswick in 1924.

A member of the Vernon Country Club Orchestra was alto saxophonist Don Parker, and with pianist Frank Banta, Nick played the banjo on records that were released on the Pathe Actuelle label as The Don Parker Trio. Nick left the Vernon group in the fall of 1921 and joined Sam Lanin's orchestra at the Roseland Ballroom at 51st Street and Broadway in New York City; in doing so, he signed a one-year contract for ninety dollars a week. The Roseland presented continuous dancing from 8 p.m. until 1 a.m. and two bands were provided for the entertainment. The Lanin group would do a set for about 20 minutes and then be relieved by a group led by Mal Hallett. This arrangement would continue throughout the evening. Among Nick's co-workers in the Lanin group were Miff Mole, Red Nichols, Arthur Fields, Rube Bloom and Jimmy and Tommy Dorsey. Lanin's band also made a number of phonograph records with Nick playing banjo; they were made in New York City for Gennett Records, a firm based in Richmond, Indiana. Occasionally vocalists Irving Kaufman, Cliff "Ukulele Ike" Edwards, Billy Jones and Ernie Hare were featured on these discs. Nick recalled that the recording sessions would run from 9 a.m. to noon and from 2 to 5 p.m. as it took about three hours to record two sides due to the wax cylinders that were used to make the record pressings. For his early records with Sam Lanin, Lucas was paid $20 per session.

Bailey's Lucky Seven was the name used by the Lanin group for the Gennett recordings, although these discs were also issued on other labels and the group was billed under several names. On Edison Bell Winner (a British label) and Westport, the group was called the Pavilion Players, Regent Orchestra, Diplomat Orchestra or Diplomat Novelty Orchestra, while Bailey's Lucky Seven was also used on releases by Starr (a Canadian label) and Apex. On Cardinal Records, they were called the Cardinal Dance Orchestra.

While doing these Gennett recordings with Lanin, Nick got the idea of substituting the guitar in place of the banjo. At the time, banjo and tuba players were placed far away from the recording apparatus because if they played too hard, the instruments would make the needle jump on the wax cylinder and the session would have to be redone. The banjo had a metallic tone when recorded and was also kept away from the recording device for this reason. One day Nick decided to bring his guitar to a recording session and Lanin asked, "What are you gonna do with that?"; he added that the guitar would not record properly. Nick suggested to Lanin the guitar be placed very close to the sound horn, or even under it, and the rhythm would be retained in the recording with none of

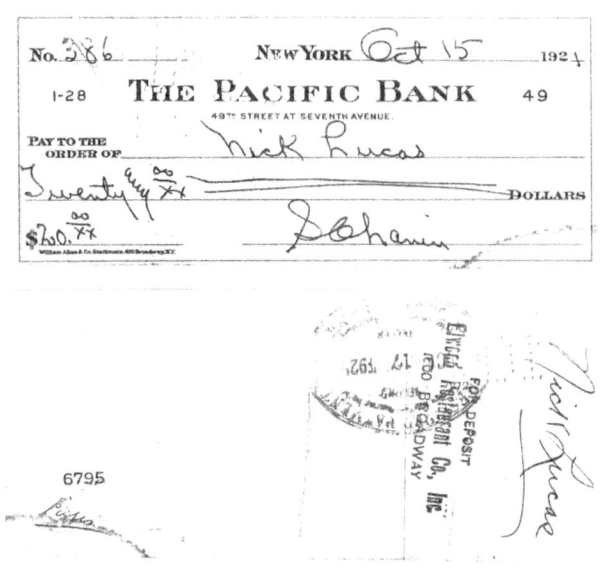

Copy of a check written to Nick Lucas by Sam Lanin for recording with Gennett Records as part of Bailey's Lucky Seven in 1921.

the worry of picking up the metallic sound of the banjo or causing the needle to jump. Lanin decided to give Nick's idea a try and it was very successful, thus making Nick the first musician to use the guitar on records with a big band. As a result, Lanin suggested to Nick he use the guitar, along with the banjo, in their live shows. After several performances, Lanin told him, "Leave the banjo and keep the guitar with the orchestra." In doing so, Nick set another precedent by being the first musician to replace the banjo with the guitar in a big-name band. At the time, the guitar was considered a pastime instrument, mostly played in homes, and was not thought suited for commercial use. Nick proved this conception false and his strumming the guitar in unusual rhythms, plinking grace notes and carrying the melody, brought the guitar to the attention of the bandsmen of the day. As a result, Nick soon found his services in great demand.

In the fall of 1923, Nick received a telephone call from Ted Fio Rito asking him to come to Chicago and join the Oriole Terrace Orchestra, which Fio Rito was fronting with Danny Russo. The band first gained attention while in Detroit at the Oriole Theatre and it getting ready to make its Chicago debut at the Edgewater Beach Hotel. Fio Rito, who was also a well-known songwriter, offered Nick $150 a week to join the band and told him, "We need you very, very badly." Liking the big increase in salary, Nick accepted the offer. Fio Rito asked him to find a novelty tune for the band since Paul Biese had a big success at the Edgewater with the song "Barney Google."

In the next few days, Nick began to talk with composers and song-pluggers he knew along New York's Tin Pan Alley and they came up with "Yes, We Have No Bananas," which Nick had recorded with Sam Lanin. He took the tune with him as he and his wife and daughter motored west to Chicago. The drive was not an easy one because there were no route numbers at the time and they had to go from town to town, asking directions at each stop. It took them four days to get from the Big Apple to the Windy City and Nick, upon arrival, immediately went into rehearsals for the Edgewater opening (the Oriole Orchestra, as it was now called, had a firm two-week booking). Nick played banjo and guitar with the band with Danny Russo as violinist and Ted Fio Rito on piano. The Oriole Orchestra's opening in Chicago was an "overnight sensation" and it stayed at the Edgewater Beach Hotel for nearly two years. During this time, Nick continued to take singing lessons.

Located in Chicago at Berwyn Avenue and Lake Michigan, the Edgewater Beach Hotel began operation in 1916. Besides offering rooms, it also had several restaurants, highlighted by its Marine Dining Room, in addition to the Yacht Club that was known for its cocktails. The hotel had a nine-hole golf course and a seaplane service, along with a 1200-foot private beach where bands played outside in warm weather on the Beach Walk, which was marble-tiled. In 1928, the Edgewater Beach Apartments complex opened and the hotel remained in operation until 1967.

Regarding Lucas' work with the Oriole Orchestra, *The Fort Wayne* (Indiana) *Journal-Gazette* (September 30, 1923) wrote, "An unusual attraction is the versatility of Nick Lucas. He is recognized as a peer among those who play stringed instruments. His ability with a banjo, guitar or ukelele [sic] has never been surpassed and the feats he performs are effectively novel. In addition to his prowess in drawing magic notes from the strings, Lucas possess a fine clear voice that lends an even brighter hue to many of the orchestra's dances." On top of playing at the Edgewater, the Oriole Orchestra maintained a touring schedule, mainly through Illinois and Indiana, and on October 5 and 6, 1923, the unit appeared at the Riverside Dance Palace in Indianapolis. In March 1924,

Nick was given a $350 harp guitar by a radio fan in Columbus, Ohio. Edgewater Beach Hotel manager William Denny presented him with the gift.

When the Oriole Orchestra moved outside the Edgewater in the summer of 1924, the *New York Clipper* (July 12, 1924) wrote, "Their opening on the beach walk of the hotel was attended by 4000 people.... They vocalize effectively in singles, duos, trios and quartets. This organization is by far the best musical and entertaining combination in and around Chicago.... Their routine is confined to classical and symphonic jazz that excels anything heard around here in some time."

At that time, Nick began making radio appearances on a Chicago station, WEBH, whose studio was located next to the Edgewater Beach Hotel. Between sets several times each evening, Nick took his guitar to the radio station and sang a song or two, later doing requests. For example, on October 14, 1924, he appeared in the 7 p.m., 9 p.m. and 11 p.m. time slots on WEBH. He began to build a following on the air and within weeks the station was deluged by hundreds of cards and letters from listeners all over the country who wrote to say how much they enjoyed his singing and guitar-playing. He stated in an article he wrote in the *Oakland* (California) *Tribune* (September 2, 1926), "I used to object strongly to singing songs to fill in on the radio, because I thought it was extra labor. After two or three programs were broadcast, I received a number of letters of appreciation of my work in broadcasting from people who liked my crooning and liked the way I played the guitar. Then I took advantage of this wonderful publicity field." He also broadcast weekly to Dr. Donald Baxter McMillan and his associates, who were at the North Pole.

In an interview with the *Santa Ana* (California) *Register* (September 13, 1927), Nick discussed his beginnings in radio. The article stated,

> When Lucas was not well known, he was asked to sing over the radio at Chicago. His services he was to render free of charge, he learned, so he decided not to do it. Broadcasting authorities at the station, WEBH, Chicago. urged him to appear at least once so he finally consented. Knowing nothing of the difference in ordinary singing and radio singing, Lucas was reprimanded for singing so loudly and was told to croon his songs. Radio listeners enjoyed the singing immensely and he received many letters after which his climb to success was made easier.

Regarding his singing, the article revealed, "Because he only sings love songs and because love songs awake memories in the hearts of both young and old, Nick Lucas ... has proved successful.... Each love song is a story in itself, Lucas said, and 'I tell the story with all my heart which is the reason it appeals to the public.'"

Radio stations were hungry for good talent in those days and Nick found a ready audience for his guitar solos and vocals. A number of entertainers would line up at the station each night, including the blackface comedy duo Sam 'n' Henry, who later dominated the airwaves as Amos 'n' Andy. There were no commercials and the radio station presented constant entertainment with Nick quickly becoming one of the medium's first name stars. "I was surprised at the distance that station covered," he later said of his newfound popularity on the ether. WEBH was owned by Eugene MacDonald, a friend of explorer Frederick Albert Cook, who at the time was on an expedition to the Arctic and who had become marooned in ice off Iceland. His ship was frozen for two months and the only outlet for communication to the outside world was the wireless. As a favor to MacDonald, once a week Nick would serenade the crew of the Cook expedition via the radio, noting he had a captive but appreciative audience. Regarding Nick's radio work on WEBH in Chicago, Edith Helleman wrote in her column "By Way of Diversion" in the *Forest Park* (Illinois) *Review* (January 10, 1925), "The wave length that carries one of Nick Lucas's songs must have a thrill of a lifetime, for when Mr. Lucas sings 'Forget Me Not, Means Remember Me,' a lot of things besides wave lengths get a thrill. Need we add, girls?"

Another activity for Nick at the time was promoting and singing his friend Ted Fio Rito's song compositions over the airwaves. These included earlier works like "Toot Toot Tootsie," "No, No Nora" and "When Lights Are Low" and current tunes such as "Charley, My Boy," "Alone at Last," "I Never Knew," "Sometime" and "Dreamer of Dreams," which Nick waxed as his first solo vocal recording for Brunswick Records.

While appearing with the Oriole Orchestra, Nick also recorded with the group on Brunswick Records and he did the vocal on the song "Oh! Mabel." The officials at Brunswick, one of the country's three largest recording companies along with Columbia and RCA Victor, began to notice Nick's big radio following plus his popularity with the Oriole aggregation. By this time, music publishers were placing his picture on sheet music in order to influence sales and on some of them he was dubbed "Nick Lucas—Chicago's Society Entertainer with the Oriole Orchestra." As a result, Brunswick signed Nick to make a solo record with an option for a one-year contract if the disc sold well. In November 1924, singing with his guitar as accompaniment, Nick recorded the Walter Donaldson composition "My Best Girl" backed by the Ted Fio Rito–Danny Russo number "Dreamer of Dreams." Within the next few months, the record became a big success and Nick was signed by Brunswick to the year's contract that paid him a royalty of one cent per disc sold plus a recording fee. The contract also called for renewal options on a yearly basis with annual increases in record royalties. "My Best Girl" sold in excess of a half million copies.

Brunswick Records was a branch of the Brunswick-Balke-Collender Company (BBC) that began making pianos in the mid–1850s and then went into manufacturing bowling equipment. It began recording and pressing phonograph discs in 1919 and expanded its operation in this field by purchasing Vocalion Records late in 1924. The company recorded all kinds of music, including popular, hillbilly and race records, and soon became one of *the* most successful labels.

When Ted Fio Rito heard about Nick's recording contract with Brunswick, he became angry; according to Nick, Fio Rito "wanted a piece of my action." He told Fio Rito, "Teddy, you are being very selfish about this. I have no contract with you, I work on a week-to-week basis, so let's be friends." With that, Nick gave his two-week notice and ended the phase of his musical career in which he served as an orchestra member and sideman musician. Fio Rito, however, never seemed to forgive Nick. As late as 1963, he told *Sacramento Union* columnist Bob McCarty that Nick "went south" with co-workers' tips and added, "Nick plugged my early songs like 'Charley, My Boy,' 'Toot Toot Tootsie' and 'No, No Nora' before Al Jolson came along. Nick would stroll through the room with his guitar and serenade but good and was tipped accordingly. Ten years later I found that the bigger bills wound up in his guitar and the four of us chopped up the chicken feed." At the time of Fio Rito's allegations, Nick told McCarty, "Bob, I'm not denying those bills wound up in my guitar but was it my fault that people tucked them in there?"

After leaving the Oriole Orchestra early in 1925, Nick went to work with pianist Hy Groves at the Tent Café in Chicago, located in the socialite district on the city's north side. During the six-days-a-week engagement, the duo was billed as "Society's Favorite Entertainers." While there, he met actress Fifi D'Orsay, who remained a close friend through the years, and the comedy team of Bert Wheeler and Robert Woolsey, who were starring in the "Ziegfeld Follies" (and later became popular movie stars at RKO). Wheeler was impressed with Nick's talents and told him he would be a big success if he could get a good manager. Nick "kind of laughed the idea off" but Wheeler went ahead and telephoned his own manager, Leo Fitzgerald, in New York City, then one of the most powerful agents in show business. The next day, Fitzgerald came to Chicago to meet Nick and the two made a handshake deal that lasted for nearly 15 years.

Now that Nick had a solo act with his guitar and vocalizing, a one-year Brunswick contract and a best-selling record under his belt, his future appeared bright. With Fitzgerald as his manager, there were no heights the singer-guitarist could not climb. Indeed, in the next five years he conquered vaudeville, recordings, Broadway, radio and motion pictures and in doing so made a name for himself in the annals of show business as one of its most important stars. At the age of 27, Nick was well on his way to becoming one of the biggest names in his profession.

Show business in the 1920s was in its golden age. Practically every town and city had one or more vaudeville theaters with weekly or split-week bill changes, giving the public the best in live entertainment and providing novices in the field a sounding board by which they could develop their acts and routines. Vaudeville was the most important entertainment venue of its time and many of the big names in show business prior to 1950 developed in this medium. By the mid–20s, the motion picture was reaching its apex in artistry and movie attendance was growing at a fast clip. Thanks to the major companies and a host of smaller ones, millions of records were sold annually in the U.S., costing between 50 and 75 cents each. Over one hundred million records were sold in the U.S. in 1927 and each of the major companies had one or more top-selling vocalists. Gene Austin became the big name at Victor, closely followed by Johnny Marvin, while Cliff "Ukulele Ike" Edwards was a big seller for Pathe and then Columbia. Brunswick had Al Jolson and Marion Harris. Vernon Dalhart sold millions of records via the majors plus a host of small labels under a score or more of pseudonyms. Dozens of musicals appeared on the Great White Way in the 1920s, producing some of that decade's great songs, along with the output from the writers of Tin Pan Alley. The Roaring Twenties provided the country with its richest period in cultural history and it was during the last half of the decade that Nick Lucas came to the forefront as one of the entertainment world's most popular artists. That he was able to do so in light of the stiff competition more than shows that he was not only an entertainer in the right place at the right time, but also that his extraordinary ability thrust him to the forefront.

In 1925, Leo Fitzgerald signed Nick to the Publix vaudeville circuit to appear in various locations in the Midwest, places that would give him good publicity and at the same time help enforce his image as a guitarist-crooner, something new and sensational at the time. When Nick joined Brunswick Records, it was not uncommon for entertainers to have an additional moniker. Gene Austin (who changed his surname from Lucas to his stepfather's last name of Austin in order to avoid confusion with Nick) was dubbed "The Whispering Tenor," and there were "Whispering" Jack Smith, Little Jack Little, Cliff "Ukulele Ike" Edwards, Wendell Hall, "The Red Headed Music Maker," and Art Gillam, "The Whispering Pianist," just to name a few. Brunswick dubbed Nick "The Crooning Troubadour," thus giving him the claim of being the first official crooner.

Even in this early phase of his career, Nick had several firsts to his credit: he was the first to replace the banjo with the guitar in recordings and in big name bands; he composed and recorded the first American guitar solos; he was probably the first recognized band singer; he was first to introduce the six-string guitar into popular music; and he became the first recorded crooner. Nick, though, did not like the title of "The Crooning Troubadour" and in later years he changed it to "The Singing Troubadour."

The January 15, 1925, issue of *Talking Machine World* noted the success of "My Best Girl" by Nick, "who is prominent because of his excellent banjo and guitar work as a soloist with the Oriole Orchestra. It is predicted that the vocal records by Lucas will prove quite a sensation. His style of singing and interpretation, along with his own guitar accompaniments, are different from any other works ever issued by the Brunswick Company." The article also noted that he was "quite a favorite with radio fans" and that Walter "Gus" Haenschen, music director of Brunswick laboratories, coached Nick; "[Lucas'] first record shows that this training has been of great value." Three months later, the same trade magazine said that Nick "has achieved fame" and "has enjoyed widespread demand ... [H]e is scoring in leading moving picture theatres and broadcasting stations of which he is now making a tour."

An article titled "Fame Thru Radio" appeared in the February 8, 1925, issue of *The Nebraska State Journal* (Lincoln, Nebraska), stating,

> Nick Lucas began broadcasting from a powerful station in Chicago. He had a voice that some described as sugary, florid, novel and vivid. Listeners-in immediately recognized a new style of singing. It was the crooning style and with his own guitar accompaniment and it was not long before thousands of radio fans looked forward to hearing a concert by the popular Lucas. Today, Lucas is one of the most popular Brunswick record artists. His first record, "Dreamer of Dreams" and "My Best Girl," has been a nation-wide sensation.

The Billboard (February 21, 1925) reported,

> Nick Lucas, "discovered" by the Brunswick Record Company following his broadcasting from a Middle West station, is selling reproductions of his peculiar style of singing in amounts undreamed of by Brunswick when they signed him exclusively. The crooning style, with his own guitar accompaniment, started on the records with a release of "My Best Girl" and "Dreamer of Dreams." That pressing sold out so quickly that two others were soon put out, "Somebody Like You" and "Because They All Love You." It is expected that the second will do even better than the first.

After his initial success with "My Best Girl," Nick was booked into the Chicago Theatre in Chicago, where he played between movie showings. He stayed at the theater, one of the largest and most important in the Windy City, for four weeks, and by the end of the run, his first solo record for Brunswick was selling so well he found bookings plentiful. Regarding his stand at the Chicago Theatre, *Variety* (December 17, 1924) reported,

> Nick Lucas first gained notice here as one of the better radio entertainers. His fine tenor voice and mandolin [sic] playing have been heard from many of the local broadcasting stations. Costumed as a Venetian troubadour, he sings two ballad numbers to his own mandolin [sic] accompaniment and plays a mandolin [sic] solo.... A moonlight effect is skillfully executed and as Lucas sings his final number, "Dreamer of Dreams," a full-sized gondola slides across the back of the stage.... Lucas has a soft, sweet tenor, particularly suited to such songs as he uses in this appearance. His voice and the remarkably fine setting made the picture a memorable one.

Leo Fitzgerald got requests from practically every major city for Nick to appear but the agent felt it best to nurture him along slowly, letting him get the feel of vaudeville while performing for smaller audiences before getting into big-time theaters. As a result of his Chicago stage success, he was booked for a tour of the leading picture houses and played in St. Louis, Des Moines, Indianapolis and other cities. His next major engagement was at Philadelphia's Earle Theatre, where he was a big success. From there, he was booked into the Palace Theatre in New York City, the mecca of vaudeville and the dream of every performer on the circuit. The Palace was the greatest showcase theater in the country because all the major bookers were housed in the same building and they would catch all the shows on Mondays; if the acts did well, they would be booked all over the country. Only the cream of the vaudeville crop played the Palace, with its two shows a day and eight bill acts.

The early tours deftly combined Nick's theater appearances while promoting his records. *Talking Machine World* (January 15, 1925) reported, "Brunswick dealers in Milwaukee did considerable advertising in connection with the appearance of Nick Lucas ... at the Milwaukee Theatre, during the week of December 27." The same trade journal quoted Milwaukee representative Carl Lovejoy in its April 11, 1925, issue: "Nick Lucas records continue to move well." The same issue noted, "Nick Lucas, popular Brunswick artist, made many friends among the trade in St. Paul, Duluth and Minneapolis on his recent tour here." The good publicity continued in the May 15, 1925, issue: "[Lucas] scored in an engagement at the Circle Theatre (Indianapolis).... The local Brunswick shop tied up the window display featuring his records." When he appeared in St. Louis in June, *Talking Machine World* related that his records "in a short time have become extremely popular." When Nick was at the Fox Theatre in Philadelphia that month, the same journal opined that he gave patrons "a treat in his guitar and vocal combination." While in Philly, he also entertained at the Kiwanis Club and appeared on many radio shows. Upon the release of Nick's second platter, "Somebody Like You/Because They All Love You," Brunswick announced, "Everybody went crazy over Nick Lucas' first Brunswick record—'My Best Girl.' Here's his second. It's just out, and a bigger hit than ever. Lucas and his magic guitar stir feet with craving for action. His unusual voice vibrates with a new kind of harmony."

The April 29, 1925, *Variety* reviewed the coupling of "Somebody Like You/Because They All Love You": "As a vocalist to his own guitar accompaniment, [Lucas] has met with wide favor, with the result he is 'canning' on his own, touring picture houses, etc. An insinuating yodel in his voice is the outstanding feature of his vocal work. The guitar interludes tend to clinch the good impression." In its July 20, 1925, issue, the same trade journal said of "Isn't She the Sweetest Thing?/By the Light of the Stars": "Nick Lucas is building a following from week to week during his picture house touring. His crooning vocal work to his own guitar accompaniment has a deadly effect on his audiences and the reaction in record sales is favorably noticeable as has checked up by the Brunswick sales department." *Variety* reviewed the same platter in its October 7, 1925, issue: "[Lucas]' does his stuff pretty on this release. Lucas is an expert song salesman, his guitar accompaniment making for a novelty musical background. Lucas' following has been growing apace...." In regards to the release "I've Named My Pillow After You/If I Can't Have You," Walter D. Hickman opined in the *Indianapolis Times* (May 27, 1925), "[O]f the two, the 'pillow' number is the best because it is filled with moonlight date night sentiment stuff which makes it a winner for both young and old.... This record will probably rival 'Dreamer of Dreams' as a best seller. Lucas has landed solid in the phonograph world. Understand that today he is Brunswick's best seller."

Nick felt he was not ready for big-time vaudeville when Leo Fitzgerald booked him into the Palace Theatre; he wanted to get more training and stage experience before tackling such a momentous task. To further complicate matters, he was given the headline spot on the bill, next to closing. As a result, he did "not do so well" in his Palace debut and the theater manager asked Fitzgerald to move him to the number four spot, the position of closing the first act. Again Nick did not go over well. The manager then asked to move him to number two spot, the act after opening; Fitzgerald declined the offer and had Nick relinquish his position on the Palace bill. *The Billboard* (February 27, 1925) reported that Nick "brought forth his pleasing lyric tenor voice and guitar in a spot wholly unsuited to his needs.... His style and songs are worthy of a hearing although not possessed of any definite kick."

Realizing he was not yet professionally prepared for the Palace, Nick and Fitzgerald took this setback well. Through William McCaffrey, a Midwest booker friend of Fitzgerald's, Nick appeared in a flash act in Cleveland. Here he was featured in a night club scene where he came on during the act and sang two songs and an encore, as the featured star of the scene, and he was a big hit. The star of the show, Margaret Young (sister-in-law of songwriter Richard Whiting), who also recorded for Brunswick, became ill during the run and theater manager John Royal asked Nick to take her place. He did so well as the headliner that Royal sent glowing reports about his performance to New York City bookers, who were quite surprised to hear of his phenomenal success

Advertisement for "Somebody Like You"/"Because They All Love You" (October 1925).

after the Palace episode. Nick felt that the Cleveland booking allowed him to get a "second wind"; this was aided by the solid reception he got in that city, which housed a large number of his fans from his Brunswick discs as well as from his days on Chicago radio. Nick also received a lot of encouragement from his friends after the Palace failure and this, coupled with his Cleveland success, breathed new life into his career.

Nick went back to the Chicago Theatre for another successful stand. As a result, he was booked all over the Keith-Orpheum Vaudeville Circuit and spent the rest of 1925 starring weekly and split-weekly in new towns and cementing his expertise in the vaudeville field. While appearing at the Rialto Theatre in Burlington, Iowa, the *Burlington Gazette* (April 7, 1925) took note of the fact he also appeared at a Lambs Club program: "He played and sang a half dozen selections ... charming his hearers with his melodies and causing them to readily understand the secret of popularity and no doubt financial success as an entertainer." When he appeared in Indianapolis in the spring of 1925, he was dubbed "Genius of the Guitar—Crooning Champion." That city's *Indianapolis Star* (April 27, 1925) wrote of his appearance at the Circle Theatre, "When listening to Mr. Lucas one feels a shock of surprise that our theatres are not full of crooning troubadours.... The songs Mr. Lucas sang ... were 'The Only One,' 'Dreamer of Dreams,' 'Hot Tamale Molly,' 'My Best Girl' and another one or two for good measure. He was very popular with the audience and was forced to give several encores." Nick was interviewed by Walter D. Hickman of that city's *Times* newspaper who reported in its April 29, 1925, edition:

> [Lucas] likes to glide over the [dance] floor with a companion to the strains of music. He is a good dancer. There isn't an ounce of up-stageness in Nick. When he is invited to a party, he does not refuse to take his guitar with him. Lucas has arrived at a position in life where he is generally sure of finding copies of his Brunswick records in every home.... The secret of his great success, he is always the human being.... In other words, there is no difference between the artist and Nick Lucas the man. And in that, I think, rests the secret of the great vogue of this man.

Nick told Hickman, "This may seem like stage talk, but my greatest ambition is to please my audience with every number regardless of whether I am on stage, in the air or on a phonograph record." While appearing at the Circle Theatre, Lucas entertained for the Broadcast Listeners Association of Indianapolis at the Severin Roof on May 1, 1925.

Appearing in *The Jazz Derby* revue at St. Louis' Grand Central Theatre, Nick "registered with a trio of selections" (*Variety*, April 15, 1925). The next week, he was in the same theater's *Sweetheart of Dixie* revue that was presented by Roy Mack, who directed Nick in Warner Bros. short films a decade later. Written by Larry Conley, the show also featured Thelma White, the Keller Sisters, Ed Lynch and James Dunn.

This was followed by a four-week stand at the Fox Theatre in Philadelphia and then at the Strand Theatre in New York City. During much of the late summer and fall of 1925, Nick appeared daily at the Silver Slipper in Atlantic City, New Jersey, and at night he headlined Philadelphia's Fox Theatre. In late July, it was announced that he had signed for an 18-week vaudeville tour that would take him from Denver to the West Coast. *Variety* (August 12, 1925) noted that Nick was "deferring picture house contracts to complete the entire season according to managerial demand." In September, it was reported he had cancelled his picture house and Silver Slipper bookings to appear in the Broadway production *Sweetheart Time*. The next month, however, he had engagements at the Lerner Theatre in Elkhart, Indiana, and the Regent Theatre in Bay City, Michigan, and he played for two weeks at the Addison Hotel in Detroit. When he returned to Indianapolis, that city's *Times* (November 16, 1925) reported, "Lucas is scoring even bigger at the Circle this week than he did on his first visit here some months ago." Of his appearance on radio station WFBM, the same newspaper stated, "Requests for selections by Nick Lucas, crooning singer, came in so rapidly that seven telephone operators and attaches could not handle them."

Also in the fall of 1925, Nick signed a long-term exclusive contract with music publishers Robbins-Engel for the publication of all his guitar solos, instrument books and song folios. The contract was for ten years and guaranteed him a minimum royalty income for that period. *Variety* (September 16, 1925) called the agreement "probably the longest term exclusive contract on record...." In January 1926, Robbins-Engel published his first songbook, *Nick Lucas' Comic Songs for Ukulele and Guitar.*

While he was on the road, Nick's wife and daughter remained in the family apartment in Newark. In those days, very good hotel rooms cost about five dollars a day and a good meal could he had for one dollar. Nick hired his brother-in-law to travel with him as his valet, to keep track of his luggage and instruments and make all the train connections that were required of his engagements. On occasion the brother-in-law was a bit slow and it was Nick who ended up looking after the train connections and other business. At one stop, Nick purposely let them miss a train as a lesson to his brother-in-law. It worked: After that, the young man was always prompt in getting Nick on the proper train for his next engagement. Nick later hired his school chum Tony Paul to handle all the traveling arrangements.

In its May 30, 1925, issue, *The Music Trade Review* reported that Frank Gibson, advertising manager for Gibson, Inc., stated that Lucas, who by then was using a Gibson-made guitar, "is probably recognized as the most prominent guitarist making records." The article noted that Nick "gained an enviable reputation over the radio and requests poured in for repeats when Lucas did his stuff on his Gibson guitar. Since he has

Cover of the songbook *Nick Lucas' Comic Songs for Ukulele and Guitar* (1926).

been recording for Brunswick and broadcasting from all the largest stations. Gibson has noticed a decided increase in the demand for the Gibson guitar in all sections where Mr. Lucas has played. Gibson representatives all over the country are cashing in on Gibson guitar sales by using Nick Lucas records for sales helps."

On July 6, 1925, in Kalamazoo, Michigan, Nick was given a tour of the Gibson Guitar factory. He wanted to see first-hand how guitars were made and he told Frank Campbell, who gave him the tour, that he attributed much of his success to his "wonderful instrument, and he is recommending it to all his friends in the profession" (*Talking Machine World*, July 11, 1925). Prior to this visit, Nick completed a successful engagement at the Strand Theatre in New York City. In an article debating whether radio helped the sale of popular songs, *The Billboard* (August 29, 1925) noted, "[T]here is the case of Nick Lucas, guitarist extraordinary, who owes all his success to the radio. Lucas' mellifluent crooning registered almost immediately with the tune-in 'bugs,' and he is now one of the biggest sellers on the Brunswick label, besides drawing big crowds nightly at an Atlantic City cabaret." The article also stated, "Nick Lucas is the writer of 'Underneath the Stars with You,' a mellow morsel of melody which [the] E.B. Marks firm is publishing."

When Nick made a tour of the West Coast on the Orpheum Circuit, *Talking Machine World* (October 15, 1925) reported that he was "playing to large and enthusiastic audiences.... [I]n cities in which he has appeared, record sales have shown a marked increase." By the end of 1925, Nick had seven Brunswick recordings on the market. The company advertised, "No vocal artist has ever been the universal favorite the [*sic*] Nick Lucas is.... If you don't know Nick—you should. He is a peculiar type of singer, called the crooning troubadour. His voice is very clear and mellow, with a wonderfully sweet tone. He pronounces his words so that you don't miss one, and best of all, he plays his own accompaniment on the guitar. Many wonder which is best, his singing or his playing." When he appeared in Fort Wayne, Indiana, in December 1925, the local Brunswick dealers announced, "We sold out of his records yesterday, as is usually the case Saturdays, but we have wired for more...." At the time, he had big sellers with "Isn't She the Sweetest Thing?/By the Light of the Stars," "I'm Tired of Everything But You/I Might Have Known" and "If You Hadn't Gone Away/Brown Eyes, Why Are You Blue?" Regarding the pairing of "I Might Have Known/I'm Tired of Everything But You," Walter D. Hickman (*Indianapolis Times*, October 7, 1925) wrote, "Here are two Nick Lucas numbers full of moonlight sentiment and guitar harmony. This record will not disappoint."

Within a year of his working for Brunswick Records, a major change took place in the recording process: Western Electric granted patent rights to its newly developed electrical recording process to Brunswick's rivals, the Columbia Phonograph Company and the Victor Talking Machine Company. To combat this move, Brunswick worked with General Electric, Radio Corporation of America and Westinghouse Electric to develop its own electrical recording process, called "Light-Ray." This not only resulted in better (easier) recording methods but also an improvement in sound. "Light-Ray" was introduced in the fall of 1925 by Brunswick but it took a couple of years before the process completely eliminated acoustic recordings. For playing its new electrically recorded discs, the Brunswick-Balke-Collender Company introduced a record-playing device, the Panatrope, also jointly developed with General Electric, RCA and Westinghouse Electric. Both RCA Victor and Columbia soon followed suit with their own players for electrical recordings. In November 1925, the Brunswick Panatrope debuted in New York City's Aeolian Hall to enthusiastic response. Several Panatrope models were manufactured, the lowest cost being slightly under $100. In 1926, because the Panatrope and its ilk could only play electrical recordings, Brunswick came out with a machine that would play both acoustic and electrical discs. It was manufactured in several different console models; prices for the new player ranged from $115 to $300. Over the coming years, Nick and other Brunswick recording artists took part in demonstrations of the Panatrope both on stage and at businesses that sold Brunswick records and players.

Nick made his Broadway debut in another flash act, this time in the musical comedy *Sweetheart Time*, produced by Rufus LeMaire. Mary Milburn and Eddie Buzzell were the featured players, with music by Walter Donaldson and lyrics co-written by Irving Caesar. It opened on January 19, 1926, with Nick appearing in the third act garden scene singing several songs, including "Sleepy Time Gal" which became a best-selling record for him on Brunswick. The play's slim plot had Buzzell as a young man who thinks he is dying. He meets a young woman (Milburn) who mistakenly thinks he's rich and how he is "cured" by a wild time in Paris. LeMaire first staged the show out of town as *Leave It to Me* but it had to be revised and recast with new numbers and dances added before it could reach Broadway. According to *Variety* (January 27, 1926), Lucas "went over for a sure hit. He is using all published numbers." *The Billboard* reviewer called Lucas "the outstanding feature of the show. He actually stops the story in the second act…. Lucas has a style of entertainment that appeals to a wide circle." Irene Dunne was an understudy in the production and Dorothy McNulty (later known as Penny Singleton) had a flashy dance number. Nick left the show on February 5, 1926: "Difference with management over the choice of his songs caused Lucas to give his notice" (*Variety*, February 3, 1926).

After only one year as a headliner, Lucas was a success in vaudeville, radio, Broadway and recordings. In the latter field, he followed his success on "My Best Girl" with "Because They All Love You." "I've Named My Pillow After You" (which he co-wrote), "Brown Eyes, Why Are You Blue?" and "Sleepy Time Gal." Regarding another of his Brunswick best

Advertisement for Nick Lucas singing "Sleepy Time Gal" that he introduced in the 1926 Broadway production *Sweetheart Time* and recorded for Brunswick Records.

sellers, "Isn't She the Sweetest Thing?/By the Light of the Stars," *Variety* opined, "Lucas is an expert song salesman, his guitar accompaniment making for a novelty musical background." In Australia, *The* (Adelaide) *News* (May 1, 1926) noted that Lucas' "quiet but effective style is gaining favor with each new issue...." In January 1926, Brunswick ran a newspaper advertisement that proclaimed, "The World's Three Greatest Entertainers Exclusively on Brunswick Records—Al Jolson, Nick Lucas, Wendell Hall." *Variety* analyzed the entertainer's career success in its July 27, 1925, issue:

> Nick Lucas is building a following from week to week during his picture house touring. His crooning vocal work to his own guitar accompaniment has a deadly affect on his audience and the reaction in record sales is favorably noticeable as has been checked up by the Brunswick sales department. Incidentally Lucas' rise to prominence is extraordinary considering only a few months ago he was an integral part of a Chicago dance organization until he took to solo radio work and thus was started on his theatre touring by himself."

The recording industry of the 1920s was different than in the decades that were to follow. Most single records then were packaged with both sides of a disc being potential best-sellers, unlike in later years when a "hit side" was usually backed by a lesser number. Naturally one song might be more popular than the other in the 1920s with the more successful tune becoming what is called a standard. For example, Brunswick packaged Nick's recording of "Sleepy Time Gal" with "I Found Someone to Love." Both were nice songs with good sales potential but it was "Sleepy Time Gal" that became the favorite and was one of the many standards Nick introduced on records in the 1920s. On the other hand, the coupling of "Isn't She the Sweetest Thing?/By the Light of the Stars" resulted in about equal popularity for both songs and still another best-selling platter.

In the mid–1920, Nick composed several popular songs, some of which he recorded for Brunswick. The 1925 tune "I've Named My Pillow After You" was written with Fred Rose and Billy Waldron; "I Might Have Known" (1925) was done with his friend and regular recording pianist Sam H. (Sammy) Stept. With Stept he also composed "I Found Somebody to Love" (1925), "Let Me Live and Love You Just for Tonight" (1926), "Underneath the Stars with You" (1927) and "Beside a Lazy Stream All the World Is Mine" (1928), the latter also with Bud Cooper. With Willard Thompson, he composed "When You're Lonely" in 1926. His picture also appeared on some of the sheet music for these tunes. As noted earlier, sheet music publishers began paying Nick to put his picture on their tunes in order to help sales. This practice continued into the 1970s with his picture appearing on dozens of sheet music covers, many on songs he recorded or promoted on stage and radio. He noted that sometimes his picture appeared on the sheet music for songs he never heard of or performed such as "Too Many Parties and Too Many Pals."

Another 1925 tune Nick composed was "If I Can't Have You," which he waxed for Brunswick, as did Kitty O'Connor on Columbia (429-D), James Doherty (Edison 5819) and Palala's Hawaiians (Vocalion 15115). "When You're Lonely" was also done by Danny Small and Harry Mays for Columbia late in 1927 but was not issued. "Beside a Lazy Stream All the World Is Mine" was recorded by the Frank Black Orchestra (Brunswick 3092) with the vocal by Harold "Scrappy" Lambert.

Making records before the late 1920s was not an easy task. When Nick began commercial recording in 1917, he soon learned that heavy-sounding instruments like the tuba and banjo could easily disrupt the fragile recording mechanism used to capture recorded sound on wax. When he began making solo records for Brunswick, the process had not improved to any extent and in the days before microphones he had to sing into a horn that in turn relayed the sound to a needle that imbedded it in wax for a master pressing. In order for his voice to be picked up for the pressing, Nick had to sing directly into the horn and he also had to pitch his voice high so that the delicate mechanical devices would record him properly. Therefore, for the first couple of years he recorded for Brunswick, Nick's voice sounded quite high on recordings. As time passed, the recording process advanced and by 1929 his recordings had his voice at a much lower level, although he was still a high baritone or low tenor. Despite selling millions of records during this time, Nick never actually sounded in person the way he did on discs. His natural singing voice was an octave or two lower than was registered on his Brunswick recordings from 1924 through 1929. Decades later, Tiny Tim developed his high singing voice and style by listening to those early Nick Lucas recordings, which in reality were not Nick's natural singing style.

In interviews with James A. Drake done between 1977 and 1979, Gus Haenschen, manager of popular records for Brunswick in the 1920s, stated that he hired Nick to be the company's main crooner since Gene Austin, whom he called "the first crooner," had been having success with Victor Records. In reality, Nick first "crooned" for Brunswick in December 1924, over a month before Austin began making records for Victor. Haenschen, who was later known as bandleader Carl Fenton, also claimed that Nick was a member of the Brunswick studio orchestra and that he mainly played the mandolin. The only orchestra recordings Nick made with Brunswick before going solo were with the Oriole Orchestra and with that aggregation he played guitar and banjo. Haenschen stated that Nick first used the guitar on records with Brunswick. As noted earlier, Nick first recorded with the guitar on records he made with Sam Lanin for Gennett Records.

Regarding Nick's singing on records, Haenschen declared that Nick did not want to be known as a crooner since he came from the *Trovatore* tradition. Haenschen said the two compromised, thus billing Nick Lucas as "The Crooning Troubadour." He claimed Nick did not like making acoustical recordings and stated, "[O]f all the singers I can think of, Nick Lucas was the happiest when electrical recording came in. He could stand in front of a microphone and sing naturally."

The June 23, 1926, *Variety* discussed Nick's Brunswick recordings:

> Nick Lucas, who has been Orpheum-ing the past spring, is recording prolifically again, his latest quartet of releases being "Bundle of Love" coupled with "No Foolin'," the *Palm Beach Girl* song hit. "Bye Bye Blackbird" is on the back of "Adorable." The same precise lyric diction distinguishes "the crooning troubadour"'s guitar-vocalizing. The Brunswick method further enhances every tone and shading of the string instrument which was a problem to "take" on wax under the old process. "Bundle of Love" is unique, in that it is a danceable singing record, being sung in a straightway tempo and very fetching for dance purposes, although not a dance record.

Following his departure from *Sweetheart Time* in early February 1926, Nick resumed his picture house tour. When he appeared at the Palace Theatre in New York City, *Variety* (February 24, 1926) noted, "Lucas is a personable chap with a pleasant baritone voice, [who] also handles his own accompaniment on guitar. The repertoire consists of four pop numbers handled as vocals with a production instrumental spotted between. All of the vocals are handled in the same croony manner which made him a good bet for records and should set him also well for vaudeville." When he appeared again at the Chicago Theatre in March 1926, *The Billboard* (March 13, 1926) stated, "Nick Lucas with his guitar and his crooning proved as popular as ever and he enjoyed encores galore.

He sang one after another of the songs that he has sung to these same people so often before and they seem to never get enough of them. The demand was so great that Lucas stopped the show. His crooning is just as pleasing to listen to as it ever was. Personality is quite an asset for him." Regarding the same stand, *Variety* (March 10, 1926) said he was "called back for four encores." After appearing at the Palace Theatre in Milwaukee, he was at the Orpheum Theatre in St. Louis and *The Billboard* (March 27, 1926) reported, "Nick Lucas, while strumming his guitar, crooningly sang 'Then I'll Be Happy,' 'Always,' 'Sleepy Time Gal,' 'Say It Again,' 'I'm Tired of Everything but You,' 'If You Hadn't Gone Away' and 'A Cup of Coffee, a Sandwich and You.' He has a soft tenor voice and his enunciation is especially good, all of which tended to make him a big hit… [There were] three encores and bows." This was followed by a two-week stand at the Palace Theatre in Cleveland and an early June engagement at the Irvin Theatre in Bloomington, Illinois. In the late summer of 1926, Nick continued to be a vaudeville headliner on the Keith-Orpheum Circuit in Los Angeles, San Francisco, Oakland and Denver. While at L.A.'s New Orpheum Theatre, *The Billboard* (August 21, 1926) stated, "Nick Lucas, 'The Crooning Troubadour,' can well be styled a sensational singing success. He rendered in splendid manner to his own guitar accompaniment ten of the latest ballads and song hits and was recalled again and again, always obliging with an encore." He was held over a week. Its August 28 issue, the same trade paper reported, "Nick Lucas, with a new repertoire of song hits, repeated his success of last week. After doing several encores he gave the Brunswick phonograph some real advertising by singing in unison while two of his records were being played." In the fall of that year Leo Fitzgerald received an offer for Nick to headline the Café de Paris, the top nightspot in London. In England, Nick's records had become best sellers; one of his biggest hits there was "A Cup of Coffee, a Sandwich and You" which Jack Buchanan had introduced earlier on the London stage. Fitzgerald, who Nick later said "had nursed me along to where I got on top and became very big," reckoned tht a London success for Nick would enhance his earnings when he returned

Advertisement for Nick Lucas' recording of "Looking at the World Thru Rose Colored Glasses"/"Let Me Live and Love You Just for Tonight" (September 1926).

to the States. At the time, London was the cultural headquarters of the English-speaking world and good notices there for Nick meant added luster for his already proliferating career. When the London engagement was announced, *Variety* (June 23, 1926) noted, "Lucas' Brunswick recordings are very popular abroad and even more so in Australia…"

Nick returned to the Chicago Theatre in Chicago in the summer of 1926 and was booked for a two-week engagement at the Orpheum Theatre in Los Angeles. He had to leave during the second week due to his father's illness. Regarding his L.A. appearance, *Variety* (July 21, 1926) wrote, "Nick Lucas stopped the show. Lucas uses very few of the vocal tricks of present-day singers. His phonograph style, plain and simple, along with good guitar accompaniment of his own, clicked with local folks.… His numbers included 'Lonesome and Sorry,' 'If I Knew I'd Find You,' 'Bye Bye Blackbird,' 'Talking to the Moon,' 'Say It Again,' and a medley." He returned to the Los Angeles Orpheum in August and *Variety* (August 25, 1926) reported, "Lucas in his easy and sincere manner of selling songs and instrumentation just milked the gang and proved that he was a box office natural." When Nick headlined the Orpheum Theatre in Oakland, California, the same trade journal on September 1, 1926, opined, "Nick Lucas had a position that was just ripe for some vocalizing. This was the second and last week and he used new songs for his act and was forced to make a lot of repeats on his encores. Among the encores Lucas brought out a Brunswick phonograph and synchronized 'Rose Colored Glasses,' 'Let Me Live and Love' and several other selections." Reviewing the same stand, Harry English opined in *The Vaudeville News and New York Star* (September 3, 1926), "Nick Lucas, the guitar manipulator holds them tightly in his l'il old musical fist. You never want him to leave the boards. You can listen to his stuff indefinitely. He virtually stopped the show." This was confirmed by Wood Soanes in the *Oakland Tribune* (September 6, 1926): "Nick Lucas stopped the show.… He genially complied with the encores and drove home his hit by such songs as 'Sleepy Head,' in which his instrument and voice form admirable combination."

When Nick again headlined Chicago's Palace Theatre, *The Billboard* (October 23, 1926) reported that he "played his guitar and sang songs which were received with wholesome applause, and after singing a few of his old favorites he closed with a new one of his own, 'When You're Lonely.' The popular, sweet-voiced boy nearly stopped the show." On the evening of October 30, 1926, Nick was the master of ceremonies at "Clown Night," a fundraiser, in Chicago.

Regarding his Brunswick recordings, Walter D. Hickman wrote in the April 7, 1926, *Indianapolis Times* about "Always/I Don't Believe It But Say It Again":

> I have been informed that Nick Lucas is the best seller of all the individual artists on the Brunswick list. His new record is one of those sure success things—clean, melodious and pretty. …Never has Lucas been better than in the two numbers. There is a glorious something, nearly spiritual, in these two numbers which brings added dignity to the mood. Nick Lucas is glorifying American music as much as a certain stage producer is glorifying the American girl.

In the same newspaper on October 6, 1926, Hickman reviewed "I'm Looking at the World Thru Rose Colored Glasses/Let Me Live and Love You Just for Tonight," saying, "The two records probably show up Nick Lucas at this best." Regarding "How Many Times/Sleepy Head," he called the former "sentimental and sweet" and the latter a "pleasant little sob affair." On December 3, 1926, Hickman reviewed "Precious/I'd Love to Call You My Sweetheart":

Nick certainly puts moonlight and roses and a lot of class into his new Brunswick number. It seems to me that 'Precious' is just the sort of melody that Lucas can tease out of his guitar and his throat with the greatest of ease. This one number has sufficient quality and charm to make it one of the best sellers in this country today. 'Precious' has nifty lyrics and it has a clever little swing.... This one number should carry Nick Lucas to new fame with his public.

Phonograph Monthly Review, in its July 1926 issue, stated of "How Many Times/Sleepy Head," "[Lucas] is good at this sort of thing" and of "Looking at the World Thru Rose Colored Glasses/Let Me Live and Love You Just for Tonight," "The first is sung in an effective characteristic style." In its October 1926 edition, the same journal reviewed "When You're Lonely/Because I Love You," saying, "The voice is smooth and well recorded."

Nick left for London toward the end of October 1926, traveling by luxury liner. Arriving a few days later, he was greeted by Count Anthony de Bosardi, public relations director for Brunswick Records in London. Bosardi immediately had Nick go to a tailor to have a full dress suit made, and to coincide with his opening at the Café de Paris he had Nick autograph 300 copies of his latest records to be given to guests at that performance. The owner of the Café de Paris, Captain Robin Humphries, heavily publicized the November 8, 1926, event and invited a closed audience of the elite, nobility and big-name entertainers. Among the guests were the Prince of Wales, Fred and Adele Astaire (who were appearing in a London revue) and home favorite Jack Buchanan. Also present were Prince and Princess Arthur of Connaught, Lord Ashley, Lord Victor Paget and Nelson Keyes. Not only did his opening night play to a capacity audience, it was broadcast all over England via radio and Nick was the only person on the air in that time period, thus having access to the entire British radio-listening populace. He found his opening night audience to be "great and enthusiastic"; they especially loved the simplicity of his singing and guitar-playing, which was still new to British audiences. Following his one-hour show, Nick received a five-minute standing ovation. He was gratified by his acceptance by the British.

After the show, Captain Humphries asked Nick to present each of the invited guests with a copy of his autographed records as they left. In doing so, Nick asked each one for their comments regarding his performance and their replies were quite complimentary. When the Prince of Wales, a major trend-setter in the English-speaking world, was asked how he liked the show, he smiled at Nick and replied, "It was immensely entertaining and I especially enjoyed your extraordinary rhythm and your guitar-playing."

"With comments like that, I found it hard falling asleep," Nick said of his triumphant London opening. The next day, he was even more gratified by the laudatory comments he received in all the London newspapers. The story of his success was picked up by various wire services and appeared in newspapers across the U.S. *The New York Times* noted in its November 14, 1926, edition,

> Because the Prince of Wales has heard and liked his playing and singing, after the manner of old Provençal Troubadours, Nick Lucas has suddenly become one of the most popular entertainers in London. After hearing Lucas's singing, which he accompanied on his guitar one night last week, the Prince invited him to sing at the ball in honor of the Queen of Spain. Accordingly, Lucas is in great demand, not only in theatres and cabarets, but also at home of the society hostesses.

Variety, in its November 10, 1926, issue, said Nick was "acclaimed one of the biggest receptions ever given any artist in that establishment [the Café de Paris]." The trade journal stated that he "held forth for half an hour while doing 10 songs to insistent applause. His singing was broadcast by radio and while this means instant publicity for his opening it also points to likely popularity."

Following his overnight success, tickets were almost impossible to obtain for Nick's Café de Paris show. He quickly became the biggest sensation in London and was literally the talk of the town. To meet ticket demand, he had to give two performances each night, one at 8 p.m. and the other at 11 p.m., and he received offers to play at other theaters and perform at private parties. At one such party, he played for banking tycoon Otto Kahn at his home, and for one hour's work he got £150 pounds, then the equivalent of about $750. The demand for Nick was so great that besides his two nightly shows at the Café de Paris, Captain Humphries also booked him into the Alhambra Theatre where he did two matinee performances and was "a sensational hit" (*Variety*). On Sundays, when all the London theaters were closed, he performed at the London Palladium; he played there twice to sold-out performances. He also did "standing room only" shows at the posh Kit Kat Club, the Piccadilly Hotel and the Coliseum Theatre, appearing at each daily and nightly, along with a successful week at the Victoria Palace. As a result of being so busy, Nick was unable to appear in a special revue or make recordings. The November 17, 1926, *Variety* stated, "That Lucas is 'over' here is assured, his opening at the Alhambra (vaudeville) being splendid. One of the contributing factors to Lucas' success is his generosity with encores."

The Prince of Wales contacted Captain Humphries and asked if Nick would perform at a private party he was giving for his visiting aunt, the queen of Spain, at the home of Lady Innes Kerr. A special limousine picked up the singer and took him to the manor house several miles outside London. There he found about 40 people, all in formal attire, in a large room, some in chairs and others sitting on the floor. Nick was given a chair and he began to serenade the queen with songs from his act and after a time she asked if he would sing a Spanish song. "I don't know Spanish, your highness," Nick told her. "But I would be happy to sing something for you in Italian." The queen was delighted. He performed the standards "O Sole Mio," "Marie, Ah Marie" and "Sorrento" and she complimented him on his Italian. As Nick was leaving, the esquire (the man in charge) asked if there was any charge for his performance and Nick told him he had appeared with the compliments of the Café de Paris. A few days later, a large story appeared in all the London newspapers about Nick's private recital for the queen; after that, reservations for his engagements became even harder to obtain due to the great demand. The story also appeared in U.S. papers, noting that Nick had become a very popular entertainer with London society.

Frank O'Connell, London correspondent for *The Vaudeville News and New York Star*, chronicled Nick's London success beginning with the December 4, 1926, issue: "Nick Lucas is the latest American artist to achieve an emphatic success in London. He opened at the Café de Paris last Monday, registering big with his songs and guitar accompaniment." After Nick was booked into the Alhambra Theatre by Horace Reeves, O'Connell reported on December 11,

> The debut of Nick Lucas at the Alhambra was the big event of the week, and the moment [he] made his initial bow, he was greeted by a surprisingly warm reception. Strumming his trusty guitar, he crooned "Lonesome and Sorry," revealing a voice of singular sweetness and distinct utterance. Then he gave us "Sleepy Head," followed that with instrumental selections of popular hits, which included "Roses of Picardy," an English number. Nick then crooned "Black

Bird," finishing with one of his records, "Sleepy Time Gal," played on the gramophone. This was a novel idea and registered very strongly. In response to the enthusiastic applause, Nick came in front of the tabs and gave two request numbers, "[A] Cup of Coffee, a Sandwich and You" and "No Foolin'." The success of his act was emphatic, as he was held over a second week after his very first performance at the matinee. Offers have poured in for Australia productions, etc., but Nick says he leaves on January 19 via *Majestic*. He is still working at the Café de Paris since the Prince of Wales' party, is in big demand for society musicales, etc.

Regarding Nick's next stand at the Alhambra, O'Connor stated on December 18, "Nick Lucas in his second week, with only one or two numbers in from the previous week, repeated his former success. In fact, a big reception greeted him on entrance and the usual uproarious demand for encores followed his gramophone bit. He is at the Coliseum next week, doubling this place with the Kit Kat and Piccadilly." When he was at the Kit Kat, O'Connor noted on December 25, "Nick Lucas registered even a bigger hit than he did at the Alhambra and did two encores." On January 8, 1927, *The Vaudeville News and Evening Star* reporter wrote, "Nick Lucas is still continuing his successful way at the Piccadilly and Kit Kat. He goes to Paris and Italy soon and sails for home January 12. Come back again, Nick."

Nick was so busy appearing all over London that Captain Humphries hired a valet to go along with him to assist with his wardrobe and musical instruments. Jack Hylton, the most popular bandleader in Great Britain and that country's equivalent to America's Paul Whiteman, wanted to book Nick to appear in all of his concert tours throughout Great Britain but the offer was declined as plans were being formulated for Nick to appear as a special feature in a revue. Brunswick also wanted Nick to make recordings in London but his busy schedule made that impossible. Nick later recalled of his British popularity, "I was a very big success in London despite the fact I was really a novice and I didn't know too much about show business. I didn't know how to get around. Still I could have stayed in England a couple of years."

Originally he was scheduled to remain in London for six months but after his hectic work schedule of four shows a day, six days a week, plus working on Sundays, for a two-month period, he came down with laryngitis and this marked the end of his engagements at the Café de Paris, Kit Kat Klub and Piccadilly Cafe, as well as canceling a proposed two-week stand in Cannes, France. Still, Nick's stay in London had been vastly rewarding for him both in added popularity and financially, and the Café de Paris management showed their appreciation by giving him a farewell party on the ship (the *Aquitania* or *Homeric*; sources differ) the night before he was to set sail for the U.S. The party included gourmet food and lots of champagne and he celebrated mightily. After the party, he told some friends, including British entertainer Gracie Fields and her husband, that he would see them the next day. During the night, a rough storm hit the ship and when he got up the next day, he was suffering from a severe case of seasickness and was confined to bed for the next two days. On the third day, he was able to get up and walk around the deck as he found the Atlantic Ocean calm and "the sea as smooth as glass." While on deck he ran into Fields and her husband, who invited him to have tea with them. The waiter bringing the tea was cockeyed and his gaze made Nick sick all over again. He immediately returned to his cabin and a diet of only solids and fresh fruits, with no liquids. When the ship docked in New York City the next day, Catherine and Emily were at the dock to meet him. They noticed immediately how frail and thin he looked. The three left for Newark where it took Nick a month to recuperate from the four-day ocean voyage.

The sensation that Nick caused in London was perhaps the apex of his career and it set him on a plateau that few have ever reached in terms of popularity. Of course, all of this came at a time when radio and communications were not as extensive as they are today. Bing Crosby best summed it up years later when he told a group of disc jockeys, "I've been the luckiest guy in the world. If you disc jockeys had been on hand when Nick Lucas hit his stride, he'd be the biggest name in show business."

Another factor that has contributed to the lack of coverage of Nick's popularity in the 1920s has been minimal coverage of cultural history. Until the interest in nostalgia began in the 1960s, events such as Nick's London success was pretty well forgotten. It is interesting that in the 1940s, writers talked about the Frank Sinatra craze and claimed that such a phenomenon had happened once before, to Rudy Vallee in 1929. To an extent they were correct, but in actuality it had happened twice before and the first time was with Nick Lucas in London in 1926. The main difference was Sinatra was the idol of teenagers while Lucas and Vallee appealed to adults.

Nick never again appeared in the British Isles although plans were afoot in both the late 1930s and late 1940s for him to return there. In 1975, a BBC-TV crew came to the Mayfair Music Hall in Santa Monica, California, where Nick was performing, and taped enough footage of him to appear in a trio of television specials that were broadcast in Great Britain. He also was interviewed for the BBC radio program *Star Sound*.

Nick's father, Otto Lucanese, had died in the summer of 1926. He had lived long enough to see his son become a show business success. He was buried at Mt. Olivet Cemetery in Bloomfield, New Jersey. Nick's mother lived until 1940 and was buried with her husband. So are her parents, Antonio Palmieri (1850–1928) and Maria Palmieri (1840–1934), and oldest son, Frank (Lucas) Lucanese (1890–1949).

Leo Fitzgerald booked Nick back on the Keith-Orpheum Vaudeville circuit for 80 weeks at $2000 per week. Fitzgerald also renegotiated Nick's contract with Brunswick Records. By this time, slightly more than two years after recording for the company as a solo artist, Nick had a series of best-selling platters, including four that exceeded sales of a half million copies: "My Best Girl," "Looking at the World Thru Rose Colored Glasses," "Side by Side" and "Bye Bye Blackbird." His other releases sold in excess of 100,000 copies each and his new contract called for him to make enough recordings for release each month and for these he would receive five cents per disc sold in royalties

Nick Lucas pictured with his 1927 recording "Underneath the Stars with You."

plus a flat fee of $3000 for each record he made. In the next four years, Nick became one of the two best-selling vocalists on records (the other was his friend Gene Austin). Even today, only two singers, Bing Crosby and Austin, have sold more 78 rpm records than Nick Lucas. When Nick's contract with Brunswick was re-negotiated early in 1927, the *Scranton* (Pennsylvania) *Republican* (February 7, 1927) reported that it was "one of the biggest contracts that has ever been issued by this company...." Reviewing Nick's latest Brunswick release, *Variety* (January 26, 1927) stated, "Nick Lucas is back from across the briny with a couple of nifties in 'I've Got the Girl,' the Walter Donaldson hit, and 'Hello, Bluebird,' optimistic song."

The May 20, 1927, *Indianapolis* (Indiana) *Times* reviewed another of Nick's platters: "Nick Lucas crashes through with another of those missing gal numbers on his new Brunswick released called 'I'm Looking for a Girl Named Mary.' You recall that Sally disappeared and now it's Mary. On the other side you have 'Underneath the Weeping Willow.' A splendid Lucas record." Another song pairing by Nick was covered by Perth, Australia's *Daily News* (June 29, 1927):

Advertisement for Nick Lucas recording of "I'm Looking Over a Four-Leaf Clover"/"High, High, High Up in the Hills" (1927).

> [Lucas] records "I'm Looking Over a Four-Leaf Clover" and "High, High, High Up in the Air Watching the Clouds Roll By," to an accompaniment of two guitars. The work of this artist is well known and the portamento [sic] effect introduced in his songs has won for him many admirers. His voice is mellow and true, and lovers of a lighter type of music will do well to hear this. The singer was the originator of the "crooning" type of singing, playing his own accompaniment on a banjo.

Of another disc, the same newspaper wrote on October 12, 1927, "[Lucas] is at his best in the melodious 'So Blue.' The first half is given as an ordinary ballad, and the remainder is sung in rhythmic form. There is an accompaniment by guitar, violin and piano. The coupling, 'Moonbeam, Kiss Her for Me,' is equally successful."

For Nick, another form of income that extended for several decades was the Nick Lucas Special guitar manufactured by the Gibson Guitar Company. Nick, who had switched from a Galliano guitar to a Gibson model, had visited the firm's Kalamazoo plant in 1925, and Gibson's general sales manager, Frank Campbell, asked him to help them design a model for his use. He said he would if the company built a guitar to his specifications, one with a wider neck, deeper sides and smaller body, easier to use than the bulky Galliano. Nick was so pleased with the guitar Gibson built for him that he kept it for the rest of his career. In 1926, the Gibson Nick Lucas Special guitar was placed on the market and it remained a good seller into the 1940s. The 1928 Gibson company catalogue declared, "The wizardry of Nick Lucas and his guitar is known to all music lovers. Combining his ideas and knowledge with the skill of Gibson Artist-Craftsmen has given birth to a truly magnificent guitar. Here is an instrument with big, harp-like tone, responsive to the lightest touch, balanced in every register. Crisp, sparkling treble and solid resonant bass that makes your whole being sway to its rhythmic pulsations."

Regarding the Nick Lucas Special, Tom and Mary Anne Gans wrote in *Guitars* (1977), "The guitar has a spruce top, strutted with Martin-type × bracing, rosewood sides and back with white plastic binding, and a sunburst finish. The fingerboard is made of rosewood, with narrow rectangular-section frets, and the neck-to-body junction occurs at the twelfth fret. The headstock is inlaid with 'The Gibson' in mother-of-pearl." They also commented on how it differed from other models: "The body is unusually deep for its size and short for its width. It would seem that the aim of the design was to make a guitar with some added bass resonance for vocal accompaniment, without losing too much of the balance and clarity associated with smaller-bodied instruments." The authors also noted that Nick "had an enormous effect on the sales of acoustic guitars."

In *American Guitars: An Illustrated History* (1990), Tom Wheeler called the Nick Lucas Special

> by far Gibson's nicest flat-top.... It had a spruce top, mahogany body and neck, brown mahogany sunburst finish, rosewood fingerboard, a large rosewood bridge with a carved pyramid at either end, bone saddle, white pins, and white/black ivoroid binding on the bop, back, and neck. The neck joined at fret 12, and the fingerboard featured fancy position markers. In 1933 the neck joined at fret 13...The Nick Lucas was manufactured until 1938. Some of the last models, which did not appear in catalogues, went back to mahogany bodies. The maple-body Lucas guitars are not only superior to the other versions, but they're also certainly among Gibson's very best flat-tops ever.

Eldon Whitford, David Vinopal and Dan Erlewine wrote in *Gibson's Fabulous Flat-Top Guitars: An Illustrated History & Guide* (1994),

> When Gibson chose Nick Lucas to lend his name to their special artist's model in the late '20s, they chose well ... [H]e played a prominent role in the history of the flat-top guitar.... Lucas was a pioneer in using the flat-top guitar as both a rhythm instrument for the big band sound and for accompanying a solo singer. ...[H]e was the first big radio star to play the guitar, preceding by a few years Jimmie Rodgers, country music's first superstar.

The Nick Lucas Special sold for around $90 (some sources say $125). The 1937 Gibson catalogue stated:

> This guitar was designed by Nick Lucas, ...whose popularity is justly revered, as will be enthusiastically verified by anyone who has been fortunate enough to see and hear him play and sing. It has extra depth of tone but with a certain rich brilliancy in its voicing. Nick has inspired many boys and girls to take up the guitar—some of them are well known artists today—and the guitar you hear him play is the Nick Lucas mode, designed for his own personal use and now offered to all guitarists who need this type of instrument.

In *Frets* (April 1979), Nick told Mark Humphrey, "You'd be surprised how this guitar carries. I suggested the depth of the guitar to give it more volume, and it did. This just a supposition—I have no technical knowledge of how to build a guitar."

In the December 1998 *Acoustic Guitar* article "The Nick Lucas Special," Marshall Newman wrote, "The Gibson Nick Lucas Special is a paradox in the history of steel-string guitars: it's both very influential and surprisingly obscure. Elements of its design can be seen in instruments even today." The article quotes Richard Hoover of the Santa Cruz (California) Guitar Company, manufacturer of the Nick Lucas Special-inspired Model H, who stated, "It simply was a guitar ahead of its time. Only now that builders, players, and marketers have an additional fifty years of experience does the beauty of the Nick Lucas Special become obvious." Also quoted in the article is folk singer-songwriter-guitarist Norman Blake: "I've got two of them. They have a loud, punchy sound, real good for old-timey music like I do. They work for both picking and rhythm work, and they record real well. I like them so much that I've had two guitars built in the same style." Another performer who used the Nick Lucas Special early in his career was Bob Dylan.

Over the years, the design of the Nick Lucas Special had several changes. For example, the 1926 model had a rounded shape and a 12-fret neck with scroll shaped inlays, straight bracing and mahogany sides and back. By 1930, the fret neck was 13 and it had an adjustable bridge, tailpiece, X-bracing and rosewood back and sides. Some models were manufactured in curly maple. Some of the later models had mahogany bodies and the fret neck varied from 12 to 14. An extra-deep body shape was the feature of all the Nick Lucas Specials.

The years 1927 to 1931 were top moneymaking ones for Nick and with the big increase in his annual income from vaudeville and recordings, he decided it was time to buy a home for his family, who had mostly resided in apartments in Newark. He purchased 495 Highland Avenue, a home in Forest Hill, a residential section of Newark. The abode had four bedrooms, three bathrooms, a finished attic (Nick used it for a workroom and den) and a full basement with a ten-foot bar designed for entertaining up to 45 people. He found this type of entertaining to be good public relations for him professionally as he had "friends coming out of the woodwork" such as the city's mayor, police chief and other politicians, wanting to bask in the reflected limelight of his show business success. During this period, Nick entertained at home about twice a month when he was not on the road and he realized that domestic help was needed. Two maids were hired at $18 each per week; one did the cooking and the other the cleaning. He also bought a Packard for his wife and a Cadillac for himself. Since Catherine was an avid golfer, he got them a membership in the swank Forest Hill Golf Club. He found it ironic that he should be in the exclusive Bloomfield, New Jersey, golf club since years before, he caddied there in order to make extra money for his family.

Returning to vaudeville, Nick got a terrific reception at New York City's Palace Theatre before the rest of his tour on the Keith-Orpheum Circuit; he played all the major cities in the country with equal success. This was when Nick solidified his success on stage, having learned a great deal working with the entertainers of the medium with whom he shared various bills. He recalled, "Every show, I would stand in the wings and watch the great performers to see how they worked. I learned how to take a bow and all the other tricks of the stage. The performers were very kind to me and made suggestions and were willing to help me. I owe my showmanship to those old vaudeville days when I played with those wonderful and great artists."

During these vaudeville tours, Nick worked with show business legends Sophie Tucker, Pat Rooney, Ole Olsen and Chic Johnson, Bill Robinson and Frank Fay. Although he could "do no wrong" with audiences, occasionally things happened to unnerve him as a performer. He remembered that in one of his first engagements on tour, he was sharing the bill with Ethel Waters and Frank Fay and during his first song a guitar string broke. He managed to fake his way through the rest of his act but came off quite agitated and immediately went out and bought a back-up guitar, an instrument he carried with him for the rest of his career. "I feel I owed it to my audience to be ready at all times," he later said. "Now Eddie Peabody, if he broke a banjo string, would sit on the stage and talk to the audience while he repaired the string and then would go on with his act. I feel the audience has paid to hear me sing and play and not talk to them while I try to repair my guitar string. Therefore if I break a guitar string while I'm on stage, I say to the audience 'just a moment please' and go get my backup guitar and continue with my performance." Over the years Nick saw many changes affecting guitar strings but mainly liked the fact they decreased in price as years went by. Wanting what he termed "a bright tone," he changed guitar strings on a regular basis and used both Gibson and Black Diamond strings. He had no gauge preference.

In his later years, Nick lamented that young entertainers had no training ground such as vaudeville to develop their talents. In the late 1970s, he noted

> Today there is no proving ground in show business for young people and an entertainer has to break in new material cold turkey. Some come up right away and have a hit record and get all the big television shows and yet they have little or no experience and cannot handle the limelight and have nothing to back up their success and soon fade away. I am glad I lived in that era with vaudeville because I learned a lot but today I can't utilize it because there are no more [vaudeville] theatres. If vaudeville did come back, the supply of talent would suffice but today the theatres could not financially operate.

Traveling in vaudeville from week to week, or occasionally doing a split week or playing cut houses where performers did three shows a day, was hectic and tiring but overall Nick greatly enjoyed the experience. All of the travel was by train that in those days provided top-notch service, including the best in cuisine. Travel routes were planned far in advance of the actual tours and few problems ever arose in going from one play date to another. He recalled that the hotels were beautiful and that a suite of rooms could be had for about five dollars a day. "The food was terrific and room service was an art and these hotels had special kitchens. It was a delight and a joy to travel during those days," he said. Nick also noted that the theaters in which he performed all had good house orchestras and the dressing rooms were clean. These theaters also had superb acoustics that made it possible for Nick to project his singing voice to as many as 3000 patrons. He did not use a microphone on stage for several years (although some were located in the footlights) as vaudeville patrons of the time would not accept them.

Traveling from city to city on vaudeville tours involved a lot of preparation, most of which was done by Lucas' secretary Tony Paul. Nick told Dorothy Pisano (*Dallas Evening News*, October 21, 1928), "Sometimes I have such black moods when I'm away [from home], and I get too lonesome, and it's mostly because of this that I keep this secretary, Tony, with me. When I get blue and homesick, he is a good tonic for me, and he cheers me up." The two played golf together regularly on mornings in the various cities

> # NICK LUCAS
> ## "THE CROONING TROUBADOUR"
> Just Concluded a Successful HEADLINE TOUR of the Interstate Circuit.
>
> STATE LAKE, CHICAGO, THIS WEEK (July 17)
>
> Starting a
>
> 40 WEEK TOUR TO HEADLINE THE KEITH and ORPHEUM CIRCUITS
>
> ---
>
> Exclusive Brunswick Artist   Personal Representative—LEO FITZGERALD

Advertisement for Nick Lucas' successful vaudeville tours in 1927.

in which Nick headlined. The writer also noted, "Tony looks after him in many ways. For instance, he clamps down on the purse of his friend and employer when occasion warrants, for Nick Lucas' heart is a big as a cabbage and everybody seems to know it, especially those in the profession. Tony discovered that Mr. Lucas was doing a business in 'touches' on a large scale. So he appointed himself superintendent, took complete charge of affairs and now it is an entirely different manner." A devout Catholic, Nick attended church regularly in the cities where he played.

As noted, upon his return from London early in 1927, Nick took a month to recuperate and then returned to the stage with dates in his hometown where he was proclaimed "Newark's Favorite Son." When he appeared at the Capitol Theatre in Wilkes-Barre, Pennsylvania, the *Wilkes-Barre Times Leader/Evening News* (February 15, 1927) reported, "Nick Lucas has what is without question the greatest number of admirers and followers of any artists who has ever entertained over the air. His original and unique style in singing popular and semi-classic songs have endeared him to literally millions." He followed at Amalgamated Time and Loew's State theaters with full week engagements at New York City's State Theatre and the Metropolitan Theatre in Brooklyn. In March when he was at the New Palace in Chicago, *Billboard* (March 17, 1927) noted, "Nick Lucas, crooning a generous selection of popular tunes, was given generous encores. His medley of guitar numbers hit home strongly." Regarding the same venue, *Variety* (March 16, 1927) reported, "This fellow is a favorite in Chi, and his return was good for plenty of hand music after each of his masterpieces in song. He was spotted fourth, and made more of the position than has been made here for some time. A broken string on his best guitar made him somewhat nervous at the start, but he settled down and proceeded to own the house."

Next came a tour of the southwest. When Nick appeared at the Majestic Theatre in San Antonio, Texas, that city's *San Antonio Light* (May 29, 1927) declared, "He is a past master of extracting every meaning and feeling from his songs, it matters not if they are popular dance hits or ballads, they become masterpieces in Lucas' interpretation. Almost as notable is his remarkable voice renditions of his numbers in his exceptional guitar accompaniment. He uses two guitars and plays all his own accompaniments. His cycle of songs includes a medley of numbers with all his late hits featured." *Variety* (June 1, 1927) reported, "Nick Lucas is breaking box office records on the Interstate Circuit of this State [Texas]. He is receiving $1,500 weekly. Gene Austin is to follow Lucas at $1,000 weekly."

Following his success on the Interstate Circuit, Nick began a 40-week tour of the Keith Orpheum Circuits that July, getting $1750 a week. In a *Variety* advertisement (August 3, 1927), Nick was billed as "The International Star." At his appearance at the Yost Broadway Theatre in Santa Ana, California, the *Santa Ana Register* (September 12, 1927) said he "delighted audiences ... with an extensive repertoire of ballads and special numbers, in which he furnishes his own guitar accompaniment. Included in his offerings are the most popular of present-day songs. During his act, Lucas demonstrates his mastery of the guitar, playing several numbers on the instrument without vocal accompaniment."

Billboard reported in its September 3, 1927, issue on Nick's first week at the New Orpheum Theatre in Los Angeles: "Nick Lucas' appearance was the signal for spontaneous applause. The popular crooning troubadour then sang to his own guitar accompaniments 'Four Leaf Clover,' 'So Blue,' 'Side by Side,' 'Moonbeam, Kiss Her for Me,' 'How Many Times,' 'Broken Hearted' and 'Hello, Bluebird.'" A week later, *Billboard* stated, "Nick Lucas duplicated the hit he made at all of the shows last week. He gave a repertoire of different numbers this week and for encores obliged with numbers requested by the audience." He followed this with an appearance in Oakland, California, where Brunswick advertised, "[Lucas] has the happy faculty of singing to the audience so that each member thinks he is singing directly to him. Most of his songs are about love, because, as he explains, at some time during a lifetime every man or woman has known love." The *Oakland* (California) *Tribune* (September 19, 1927) reported,

> Gathered about Nick Lucas as the headliner, this week is for the best bill the Orpheum has illuminated for many a moon. And the customers at the first show Saturday registered their appreciation by continuous encores given every act.... Especially was the case with Lucas, who has a large following here, for whom the applause swelled to an ovation when his name blazed on the announcers. And the crooning troubadour acknowledged it by several old songs and a couple of new ones to the thrumming accompaniment of masterly-played guitar.

He next appeared at the Golden State Theatre in San Francisco, followed by a two-week run at the Orpheum Theatre in Kansas City, Missouri. Regarding the latter venue, *Variety* (October 26, 1927) wrote, "The vaudeville bill headed by Nick Lucas, with the world of publicity given to him, was a natural... [He] clicked with 'Moonbeam, Kiss Her for Me' and 'Sing Me a Baby Song.' He tried to exit here but was recalled to sing 'Brokenhearted' and 'Side by Side.' Another attempt to escape but it was no use and he favored with an Italian song and could have been singing yet...."

As was often the case, while at the Oakland theater, Nick appeared in person at the phonograph and radio area of a major department store where he autographed his latest Brunswick discs. When he was at the New Palace Theatre in Chicago *Variety* on November 26, 1927, declared tht he "was greatly applauded and was forced to four encores." When he returned at year's end to the Rajah Theatre in Reading, Pennsylvania, the *Reading Times* (December 14, 1927) announced, "Nick Lucas, the famous radio and recording artist with his guitar, has scored a tremendous hit here...." When he was held over for a second week, the same newspaper, on December 23, opined, "The real hit of the program is scored by Nick Lucas...." He finished out the year with engagements at the Rajah Theatre in Grand Rapids, Michigan, and the Riverside Theatre in New York City, where he played through the first week of 1928.

In the January 1928, *Talking Machine World,* it was stated that Nick "is now in the midst of one of the most successful tours of the vaudeville circuit that a recording artist has ever had" and noted that his Kansas City and Des Moines appearances were also "successful for the [Brunswick] dealers from the standpoint of record sales." The next month, the journal announced Nick would make a series of guest appearances on the *Brunswick Hour of Music*, broadcast from WGN in Chicago. He would alternate with other Brunswick recorders, including Marion Harris, Al Jolson, Vincent Lopez, Ben Bernie and Lee Sims. The series debuted on February 8, 1928. In the May 1928, *Talking Machine World*, it was stated, "Personal appearance recently at Keith's, Akron, Ohio, of Nick Lucas ... resulted in a brisk sale of his recordings at all Akron music stores handling the Brunswick line." On February 22, *Variety* reported that Nick, along with Gene Austin, Whispering Jack Smith and the Happiness Boys, was experiencing "terrific sales" in recordings.

Following his appearance at the Riverside Theatre in Gotham early in 1928, Nick headlined the New Garden Theatre in Baltimore and the Palace Theatre in Cleveland. He had a two-week stand at the Temple Theatre in Detroit. When he headlined the State Theatre in Harrisburg, Pennsylvania, that city's *Telegraph* called Nick "most informally entertaining. It appeared that his popularity had preceded him on his first trip to Harrisburg for Lucas was loudly applauded as soon as he emerged from the wings."

The Indianapolis Star (February 27, 1928) wrote of Nick's appearance at that city's Keith's Theatre, "Nick Lucas ... is known in every metropolis and hamlet through his phonograph records. ... He has an unusual manner of putting cross his numbers and it is from this that he gained the title of 'The Crooning Troubadour.' Mr. Lucas first established his name through the medium of phonograph records but his more recent excursion into vaudeville has proved so successful that he divides his time between the studio and the stage. He has a charming tenor voice and a pleasing personality." Regarding the same venue, Walter D. Hickman wrote in the *Indianapolis Times* (February 28),

> Today we are hearing [Lucas] sing songs with a fine regard to the beauty of the English language. He has not lost his natural love to play the guitar, but he has placed the guitar toward the front ranks of musical instruments. In other words he has become the master of his instrument. Lucas has carefully studied his public and he now knows just how to build his program. He often varies his selections because he invites his audience to help him decide what numbers to play. He is sticking to the hits and that is wise because he is speaking the musical language of the hour. But he takes these hits, dresses them up with the melody of his guitar as well as his voice.... He will play 'Brokenhearted' if you want it and he makes a soothing masterpiece of 'A Night in June.' Lucas belongs to the class of men who will never become too big to try and please his audience. He is on top now and he will stay there because he has

those qualities which make for enduring success." Next came stands at the Princess Theatre in Nashville, Tennessee, Keith's Theatres in Louisville and Dayton, the Keith-Albee in Youngstown, Ohio, and the Hennepin-Orpheum in Minneapolis.

While in Nashville, Nick made the first of several appearances on WSM's *Grand Ole Opry*. In those days, the final segment of the nation's longest-running musical radio program was often given over to vaudeville headliners appearing in the city. His appearances were hailed by the show's listeners and his guitar work greatly influenced many future country music performers.

When he headlined at the Main Street Theatre in Kansas City, Missouri, *Variety* (May 16, 1928) reported, "Although third appearance in Kansas City this season, the house was jammed for the Sunday opening, and his followers kept coming all week." After that came a return engagement at the St. Louis Theatre and two-week stands each at the Hippodrome in Toronto and the Stanley Theatre in Philadelphia. In June, Nick signed for another interstate tour of Texas and he also renegotiated his Brunswick contract, turning down a lucrative offer from Victor Records. Following a stand at the Majestic Theatre in Wichita, Kansas, Nick completed his Interstate tour in August with venues in Tulsa, Oklahoma, and the Texas cities of Fort Worth, San Antonio and Galveston. He closed out the year by returning to the Proctor Theatre in Newark.

As the decade of the Roaring Twenties progressed, Nick was not only one of the biggest names in vaudeville, but his popularity on records continued to grow as the two mediums complimented each other. Audiences would come to see and hear Nick perform his latest records and also purchase the discs. By 1928, Brunswick could count on Nick's monthly releases to sell thousands of copies. His best-sellers of the time included "In a Little Spanish Town," "I'm Looking Over a Four Leaf Clover," "Moonbeam! Kiss Her for Me," "(Here Am I) Brokenhearted," "The Song Is Ended," "Together" and "Just Like a Melody Out of the Sky." These songs all became standards closely associated with Nick. Johnnie Ray revived "(Here Am I) Brokenhearted" in the 1950s and Connie Francis did the same with "Together" in the 1960s. The latter song was the theme of the 1944 David O. Selznick feature film *Since You Went Away*.

Regarding Nick's current record releases, the *Knoxville* (Tennessee) *News-Sentinel* (May 8, 1927) wrote, "'So Blue' and 'Moonbeam, Kiss Her for Me' are selections that are selling like the proverbial hot cakes." Regarding the pairing of "Among My Souvenirs" and "(My) Blue Heaven," Walter D. Hickman stated in the *Indianapolis Times* (January 11, 1928), "Lucas on his new Brunswick release makes a classic out of ['Among My Souvenirs'] as well as 'Blue Heaven.' Lucas brings out all the intimate beauty of the two numbers. They suit his style, making this record easily one of the best and sweetest records that he has made for a long time." In its September 12, 1928, issue, *Variety* stated, "Nick Lucas ... is just too bad with a new Brunswick quartet of sentimental ballads. 'When You Say Goodbye' and 'You're a Real Sweetheart' as one couple, and 'Just Like a Melody' and 'For Old Times Sake' another. Lucas' song interpretations are ever distinctive; made more so by intelligent selection of numbers." The next month's release was reviewed by *Variety* on October 31, 1928: "[Lucas] has a couple of pat numbers for his intimately sympathetic vocal delivery in 'Marcheta' and 'Waiting for Ships That Never Come In.' Both are ballad revivals. Violin and guitar accompaniments add further charm to the numbers." The *Emporia* (Kansas) *Gazette* (September 22, 1928) reviewed another of his records, stating, "'Chiquita' is the most effective thing Nick Lucas has done in several months and 'Someday, Somewhere' on the other side, isn't bad." Also a big record for Nick in 1928 was "It

Must Be Love," the official song of that year's Republican National Convention. Regarding that number, which Brunswick paired with "I Can't Do Without You," Noel Houston stated in *The Oklahoma News* (May 26, 1928), "In some respects, the best Lucas has ever done." *Phonograph Monthly Review* wrote of a duo of early 1929 releases, "Nick Lucas has two fine songs in 'I'm Telling You' and 'Some Rainy Day'" and "Nick Lucas couples pleasing versions of 'Coquette' and 'I've Got a Feeling I'm Falling.'" Regarding another of his record releases, Ed in "Jazz Notes" wrote in the *Amarillo* (Texas) *Globe-Times* (April 13, 1928), "Nick Lucas' record of 'Sunshine' is very, very good. A singer like Lucas and a song like 'Sunshine' are a great combination. Guitar accompaniment, of course, and Lucas, I am told, is the greatest player of Spanish guitar in the world."

One of the main reasons for the success of Nick Lucas' Brunswick records was their simplicity. Usually he recorded the discs with just his guitar or occasionally with a violinist (David Rubinoff), pianist (Sammy Stept, William F. Wirges) or organ player (Lew White); for example, Rubinoff provided violin accompaniment on "So Blue" in 1927 and "Marcheta" in 1928. But mostly it was just Nick singing and playing the guitar. He recalled that it was difficult to get a full three minutes out of some of the tunes he was assigned to record and that he often had to improvise in order to stretch a few of them to their full recording time limit. In later years, he was somewhat wryly amused by some of the impromptu guitar solos he did on those records. But the buying public loved them.

In the summer of 1928, Nick placed the following full-page advertisement in *Variety* in the form of a letter dated June 12, 1928:

> I am taking this medium to thank my fellow performers, theatre managers, musicians, stage hands and all concerned in making my tour of the Keith-Albee-Orpheum Circuits which I just completed so successful and pleasant. I am glad to announce that I have re-signed for the above circuits and the Interstate for next season, and also at this time wish to say that I have renewed my contract to record exclusively for the Brunswick Phonograph Company. Many thanks to the entire recording staff and officials, and last but not least my manager, Leo Fitzgerald, for making the above possible. I remain, with my best wishes to all. Sincerely, Nick Lucas.

Announcing his forthcoming appearance at the Majestic Theatre in Dallas, that city's *Dallas Morning News* (September 30, 1928) wrote, "Nick Lucas, accredited with being the originator of the crooning voice in blue songs, whose popularity ranks highest among artists who have played the Majestic Theatre during the last two seasons ... the crooning guitarist on his last appearance here set a record for attendance. Since then he has established high marks for business in most of the bigger vaudeville theaters of the country. Also his popularity as a phonographic recorder has increased...." During his Dallas stand, Nick was interviewed by the same newspaper, in its September 26, 1928, issue, regarding crooning. "Crooning has kept its popularity despite the semi-return of the more blatant 'wah-wah' and 'voo-de-o-do' styles of singing, declares Nick Lucas, who is said to be the originator of the crooning method of song delivery," the newspaper wrote. Lucas said:

> Recently the songsters have gone in for loud forms of syncopated melody and harmony again. However, in my tours of the country, I find crooning still is a favorite of the masses. This I learned through applause in the theater and the continued increases in the sale of my phonograph records. Crooning is a softer form of singing syncopated note arrangements than the robust type of shouting. It's the difference between a bass drum and a violin—you can do more melody with the latter than with the former.

Nick headlined the Majestic Theatre in Fort Worth, Texas, and "was a tremendous box-office success" stated *The Billboard* (October 6, 1928). The writer added, "Lucas is considering offers to enter talking pictures upon the termination of his present Brunswick contract."

In George Spelvin's article "The Gentle Art of Crooning" (*Dallas Morning News*, September 30, 1928), Nick elaborated on popular vocalizing. "Crooning—perhaps the oldest mode of singing, is as popular today as stage entertainment as it ever has been, says Nick Lucas, the man who revived the cradle art.... Lucas is accredited with being the first stage performer to croon.... Not only is Nick's reclame [*sic*] based on his stage success but also on his wax discs." In the article, Lucas stated, "I find that crooning is more popular than when I first started it on the stage. The continued increase in the sale of records and larger crowds in the theaters in which I appear is my way of judging the popularity of crooning. Of course it's the applause of these theater crowds that tell me just exactly how they like every number I do." He added, "Get me right! I don't claim to be the originator of the croon. Crooning is as old as life itself, I guess. The first crooning I ever remembered was that of my mother. I am one of a large family and the mother used to croon the kids to sleep with a lullaby—the lullaby is the original croon. My only claim to the croon is that I was original enough to try it on the stage for the first time." In discussing another aspect of crooning, the article noted,

> Lucas said that recently in looking over music for Negro spirituals he found many arrangements suitable to the crooning method. He said that in between the loud shrieks and moans of the spirituals runs a softer vein of melody and harmony that indicates that the singers of

Nick Lucas and his guitar in the late 1920s.

spirituals also had a hand in giving the croon an outlet. "I found that there were sad songs and happy songs in the spirituals—due to the difference in living conditions of the folk who originated them. In some sections of the South the crooning voice is heard in the saddest melodies and in others happiness gets interpretation in a crooning refrain. These spirituals, particularly those passages that are croonable, express a feeling of sympathizing between words and music that are not always found in the work of acknowledged musicians.

The article also noted that Nick had become "one of vaudeville's highest priced 'single' entertainers."

In another *Dallas Morning News* article (October 1, 1928), it was noted,

A gentleman who is supposed to merely sing and play the guitar does only these things and nothing more at the Majestic this week, and succeeds in making his simple repertoire the most outstanding thing the local vaudeville house has had to offer this season. It is just another case of talent used with taste and well worked skill, stripped of all monkey-business and dedicated to entertainment without motion. Nick Lucas, celebrated performer under discussion, doesn't make a gesture or utter a word that isn't calculated to delight the audience. In no time he has his patrons in a state of ecstasy and works up women to the hysterical point of screaming titles at him as "request" numbers. With a large sector of humanity thus unbalanced, Mr. Lucas makes a final exit, leaving it to the next act to restore order.

Lucas, of course, is known as the Crooning Troubadour and is credited as originator of this style of entertainment. Be this as it may, Lucas is the most popular exemplar of crooning. The croon is a vocal trick that lies midway between a whisper and a falsetto. Lucas has something of an agreeable vocal timbre to go with the method and manages to make it sound always musical, and sometimes tender and caressing. His guitar playing, it may be added, is all that one could ask.

The article also noted, "Lucas' repertoire this year includes 'Blue Grass,' 'Because I Love You,' 'Pickin' the Guitar' (his own composition for instrument only), 'Just Like a Melody Out of the Sky,' 'A Real Sweetheart,' 'Side by Side' and a medley of older favorites." The reviewer concluded by saying, "So insistent are the Majestic audiences that Lucas sing only what they want him to sing that this list probably will be amended before the next show."

In an article in the *Austin Daily Texan* (October 14, 1928), Antoinette Kuehne opined, "Mr. Lucas' greatest charm, perhaps a charm that audiences feel but cannot define, lies in his frankness, his desire not only to entertain and impress the great throngs of theatre-goers, but also to make the mere individual feel the magnetism of his personality." Regarding his work both here and abroad, the writer stated,

Mr. Lucas prefers the American audience. His greatest satisfaction lies in the happiness which he creates and he finds the American audiences more sincere and enthusiastic than the European audiences. "The European conception of a jazz orchestra is just like the American conception of a jazz orchestra playing operatic selections," says Mr. Lucas. His friendship with the Prince of Wales for whom he often sang "Sleepy Head" has endeared England to him, however.... The applause of the people who come to hear him is the main axis of his success, his audiences offer is inspiration.

In her article "Nick Lucas Began as a Street Singer" (*Dallas Morning News,* October 21, 1928), Dorothy Pisano provided a look into Nick's personal life and feelings. He told her that night clubs had lost their attraction for him:

He knows them inside out, and has had enough such nightlife to last a lifetime. He now goes to a night club only occasionally. Sometimes he goes to please a friend who is in the business, and whenever he steps inside one he is always obliged to sing. But when he is up late at night he told me, "[It] upsets my next day, and that affects my performance, and altogether I've learned long ago that I can't do anything to upset my performance. I have to keep regular hours, and get plenty of proper exercise. Why, you would be surprised to know how careful I have to be about all the little things of my daily routine. Every single time that I go out on the stage I want to be at my best, and nothing else will do. My manager makes me rest a great deal between performances, and I cannot do anything to strain my voice, nor talk too much and tire it, before a performance."

Altogether he lives a very quiet and normal life for one who makes his home in hotels most of the time and who is constantly in the limelight. He does not care for liquor or tobacco, and his teeth are pearly white.

Another aspect of Nick's life noted by the article: "[H]e greatly appreciates ... an increased number of friends. 'I have acquaintances everywhere, of course. But it's friendships that count. It's a great joy to me to know that I have friends, real friends, in every city. I was happy to make friends in Europe. That is one of the real gifts of life.'" He also said, "I am looking forward to the time when my work will allow me to be with my family all the time." The previous year, in an article in the *Santa Ana* (California) *Register* (September 13, 1927), the star discussed keeping healthy. The writer stated, "Nick Lucas does not smoke because, he says, it would interfere with the clearness of his voice. 'The only way to maintain my popularity,' he declared, 'is to keep in condition so that I can give my audiences the best there is in me. Smoking would knock out my voice in a very short time. I play golf every day which also aids in my keeping fit.'"

When Lucas appeared in Austin, Texas, in the fall of 1928 at the Hancock Theatre, he was billed as "That red, hot and blue crooner." The *Austin Daily Texan* (October 14) wrote, "Nick Lucas will stop the show at the Hancock.... He has broken all attendance records in the towns in which he plays and indications point to the same in Austin. He's good." Next came Galveston, Texas, where the *Galveston Daily News* (October 28, 1928) stated, "Nick Lucas and his crooning melodies came to the Martini theatre yesterday and easily roped a decidedly worth-while bill. Mr. Lucas needs nothing but his fine voice and a guitar to prove himself the master troubadour he is and with little effort and much charm easily captivates his audiences. Nick Lucas is not a stranger to Galveston audiences, although it is his first personal introduction. Often he has beguiled them through phonograph records, and his ready acquiescence to encores, especially those songs which made him nationally famous, touched a responsive cord."

On January 9, 1929, *The Daily News* of Perth, Australia, reviewed two of Nick's recent Brunswick releases:

> "You're a Real Sweetheart" is familiar to Perth cinema-goers since it has been featured in the program of more than one theater recently. Here Mr. Nick Lucas is heard with accompaniment of organ and guitar—an unexpectedly successful combination. Mr. Lucas is known to his concert admirers as the "Crooning Troubadour." On the other side is "When You Said Good Night" by the same singer. This is the same type as the other, and the "crooning" quality of the voice is remarkably well produced. Another record by the same singer is "For Old Times' Sake," in which the voice is accompanied by a guitar, and in contrast, on the other side is "Just Like a Melody Out of the Sky," in which the voice has an orchestral background. The numerous admirers of this singer will be glad to add these two to their collection.

Nick opened 1929 at the Orpheum Theatre in Des Moines, and then went to the Palace Theatre in Chicago where *Variety* (January 16, 1929) reported, "Nick Lucas, no. 4,

Nick Lucas (right) in Hollywood in the late 1920s, pictured with Tom Murray (left) and Buster Keaton.

could have been just as strong further up. Lucas, a pipe for this house, rang up a score of songs in that familiar crooning of this that had him begging off after a flock of requests." On January 22, he appeared on NBC's *The RKO Hour* with Belle Baker, Mae Murray, Will Fyffe and Henry Santrey and His Band. He broadcast from Milwaukee where he was appearing at the Hennepin-Orpheum for two weeks. Regarding the radio appearance, Abel wrote in *Variety's* "Radio Ramblings" column (January 30, 1929) that Nick was "excellent as behooved an expert Brunswick recording star whose microphonic recording experience gave him a natural advantage for his ether 'bit.' It was Lucas, who when on an Interstate tour last year, boosted himself into a box office sensation through voluntary broadcasts in local stations." When he was at the Orpheum Theatre in Winnipeg, *The Winnipeg Tribune* (February 9, 1929) reported, "Nick Lucas is distinctly individual and different. The mellow tones of his guitar and his soothing melodious voice endear him to his audiences like few others. Lucas has the happy faculty of making one feel that he is singing directly to you alone." This was followed by stands at the Grand Theatre in Calgary and the Orpheum in Vancouver.

By the end of March, Nick was earning $2000 a week in vaudeville. While appearing at the San Francisco Orpheum Theatre with Jack Benny and Ken Murray, he made an April 3 appearance on *The RKO Hour* with Sophie Tucker and Ted Lewis, broadcasting from KFI. A week later, he was back on the same program, crooning three songs. As a result of his being one of the top vote receivers in RKO's All Request Radio Contest, Nick was one of 20 performers who received a gold trophy that was awarded on the radio show. In an article titled "Radio Money Names," *Variety* (April 17, 1929) reported that Lucas "is in the $2000 class as a singing single."

When Nick headlined the Orpheum Theatre in Los Angeles, Harry English wrote in the April 6 *Vaudeville News and New York Star* that Lucas "is the outstanding feature of the RKO bill during the present week, and so great has been his appeal that the quiet fellow has had a hard time begging off, in order to let the rest of the show proceed. We had a chat with Mr. Lucas, and he was refreshing in his marked simplicity of manner." Regarding his rise to fame, the singer told English,

> Some three years ago I entered vaudeville and the three years that I spent in this field have been remarkably happy and successful ones. Everything is lovely. I am a very busy man, have little time to play around, as I am constantly making records, yet although it is very taxing at times, I greatly enjoy it. I get many laughs from inquiries by letter and phone, as to where I get my inspirations. Of course, I try to give encouragement, but many of the questions bring a smile.

The writer declared, "A clean cut, unaffected artist is Nick Lucas, and one who attains his results without fuss or bombast."

Next Nick was at the Orpheum Theatre in Oakland, California. Wood Soanes wrote in the *Oakland Tribune* (April 27, 1929),

> Lucas in an interesting personality. Small, dapper, bird-like in his movements, a smooth guitar player and the possessor of a reed-like tenor, he seems to lack the requisites for thumping success, yet he achieves it without effort. This is due to the fact that he has one important advantage over the majority of vaudeville singers in that he is fully acquainted with the system of getting the most out of his voice. Added to that he has the gift of showmanship which permits him to deliver his goods with an air of gentlemanly attachment that makes for staunch friends on this side of the footlights. He stopped the show with ease.

When Nick did a program on radio station KFI, the *Pasadena* (California) *Post* (May 29, 1929) commented, "You can't keep a popular artist like Nick Lucas out of the limelight, if you chose. Just what the well-imbursed [*sic*] Mr. Lucas will do is of little consequence. Give him his shiny guitar, a bit of moonlight, and he does the rest." The same evening, he did a number and four encores at the N.V.A. Benefit Show in Los Angeles. Next came appearances at the Hillcrest in Los Angeles, the Orpheum theaters in Denver and Omaha (the latter for a two-week run) and the Palace in Chicago. When he headlined in Kansas City, *Variety* (June 12, 1929) stated, "Nick Lucas, stage draw, sure box-office here." The trade journal reported on June 19 of his stand at the Chicago Palace, "Lucas, to a mild reception, did four songs before asking for requests. Lucas may be considered somewhat of a fav in this town, but still didn't take any chances when spotting a plant in the audience to cinch it. He stuck close to his disc song hits." Next came a return engagement at the St. Louis Theatre.

Nick was signed by Broadway producer Florenz Ziegfeld for a leading role in the musical *Show Girl* with Ruby Keeler, the comedy team of Jimmy Durante, Lou Clayton and Eddie Jackson, Eddie Foy, Jr., and the Duke Ellington Orchestra. George Gershwin (with whom Nick had worked in 1920 as part of the Vernon Trio) composed the music for the production, with lyrics by his brother Ira and Gus Kahn. During its Boston tryout, Nick learned that George Gershwin was unhappy with the song "Liza" and suggested to him that he increase the beat of the tune. As a result, "Liza" became the hit of the show, although, ironically, Brunswick Records let Al Jolson, Ruby Keeler's husband, record the song instead of Nick. Jolson had a best-selling record with "Liza" but it did not bother Nick as his Brunswick recordings outsold Jolson's. Like Nick, Jolson had begun recording for Brunswick in 1924 but it was not until his 1928 record "Sonny Boy" that any of his discs for the company made a profit, due to the $5000 advance the company paid him for each record he made.

"Liza" was written for Nick to sing in *Show Girl*, along with "Singin' in the Rain" and "Your Mother and Mine," his current Brunswick record pairing. The production opened on July 2, 1929, at the Ziegfeld Theatre and had a run of 111 performances. "While it is not a smash, [it] is getting good money..." (*Variety*). On opening night, as Nick was starting to perform "Liza," Al Jolson rose from his seat in the theater and took over singing the tune. Most thought this was a publicity gimmick, but it was not, and as a result, Nick and his manager gave the show's management notice and he left the production after seven performances. Jolson continued the serenade from the audience on and off for the rest of the show's run. Nick apparently felt no malice toward Jolson and, when asked about him in later years, would say he was "okay." He enjoyed working with Florenz Ziegfeld and he also liked Ruby Keeler and predicted big stardom for her. When Nick vacated his role in the show, the "Liza" number was given to Jimmy Durante.

Another reason Nick may have left the production early was because MGM demanded he stop singing his latest record coupling, "Singin' in the Rain" and "Your Mother and Mine," in the show. According to *Variety* (July 2, 1929), "M-G-M didn't fancy a Ziegfeld stage musical plugging Metro talkie song hits."

Upon exiting *Show Girl*, Nick was signed to a 40-week booking on the Keith-Albee-Orpheum circuit. One of his first engagements was at the Palace Theatre in New York City. On July 12, 1929, he was scheduled to appear on the *Warner-Whitmark Weekly Hour* broadcast from WABC in New York City but he was delayed by an auto accident and the Williams Sisters substituted for him.

When doing his act in vaudeville, Nick would often use a comedian to help him close the show. He found that interpolating comedy with the final portion of his act brought a much more satisfactory conclusion to the evening's entertainment. While working in New York City, he chose Jack Benny to help him close his shows. The exposure Benny got by appearing with Nick enhanced his career, leading him to headline in vaudeville; he later became radio's top comedy star. Unlike many performers Nick helped along the way, Benny did not forget what Nick had done for his career. Over the years, Benny gave Nick credit for helping him up the ladder of success and in 1951, when Nick was starring in the weekly ABC radio series *Saturday Night at the Shamrock*, broadcast from Houston, Texas, Benny made an appearance on the show as a favor to Nick. (Benny was in Houston to accept an award from the United Jewish Appeal.) After the show, Benny and Nick had dinner together and reminisced about their vaudeville days when Nick was the star of the show and Benny was the rising comedian who helped him close the bill.

In 1928, sound films were coming into vogue. Nick's initial brush with the medium came that year in the Universal production *Lonesome*, directed by Paul Fejos and made in both silent and part-talkie versions. Nick can be heard in the latter singing "Always," a song he recorded in 1926 for Brunswick. In December 1928, he waxed "My Tonia" for Brunswick. The tune was the theme song of the first all-talking Western feature *In Old Arizona*, directed by Raoul Walsh for Fox Pictures. In it, Warner Baxter played the Cisco Kid, a performance that won him an Academy Award. Thus Nick became the first singer to have a best-selling record tie-in with a Western, something most associated with singers like Frankie Laine and Tex Ritter in the 1950s. In addition, he made a three-minute movie singing "My Tonia" for Synchro Song Film. For that company, he also did "Woman Disputed, I Love You" from the feature film *Woman Disputed* (1928).

In March 1929, as Nick was appearing at L.A.'s Orpheum Theatre, *Variety* noted, "That crooner with his guitar and in a frock suit instead of a tux at night makes 'em take it. That Nick greatly resembles Wolfie Gilbert doesn't appear to be a liability in this city." When held over for a second week at the Orpheum, the same trade paper's reviewer complained about "Nick Lucas hogging the stage again, this time for 40 minutes." Nick continued to headline the Orpheum and on May 19, *The Los Angeles Times'* Philip K. Scheuer referred to him as "that crooning troubadour who lulls you into gentle melancholy when you launch the magic needle of your phonograph down the ways...." He continued:

> At the risk of the furious fire of Mr. Lucas' host of admirers, I am moved to remark that he would be better off without his beloved guitar. This twangy, metallic instrument sounds all right when it is lost in the crowd of other instruments that occasionally keep it company, but as an obbligato to the voice of the serenader who has few peers in persuasive balladists, its dissonant flatness can only act as an irritant. Mr. Lucas is not entirely happy in his choice of numbers this week: "I'll Never Ask for More" stands alone in achieving signal nobility. Others are "I'll Get By," "The Song I Love," "How About Me," "A Cup of Coffee" and the Neapolitan street song, "Marie."

On Sunday nights, people from various movie studios, such as producers, directors, stars and talent scouts, would come to see the vaudeville acts at the Orpheum looking for new talent now that "voices" were needed for talking pictures. Following a performance, Nick was approached by a Warner Bros. talent scout who wanted him to talk to the studio's production chief, Darryl F. Zanuck, about appearing in the movie *The Gold Diggers of Broadway* that was already in production. Nick later learned that Zanuck had requested him for the film, a talkie remake of the 1923 silent comedy *The Gold Diggers* from the play by Avery Hopwood.

The next day, Nick auditioned for Zanuck, who said, "Fine, this is just what we want." Zanuck felt that something was lacking in the film's production and he ordered a huge production number developed around Nick while he sang "Painting the Clouds with Sunshine." Zanuck also told the film's writers to beef up Nick's part, one that was not in the original screenplay. Warner Bros. negotiated with Leo Fitzgerald and Nick was to be paid $5000 a week for two weeks work on the feature. Because of production problems, Nick worked for ten weeks at that figure, while still appearing nightly at the Orpheum Theatre. Just prior to his starting the film, Louella O. Parsons wrote in her syndicated newspaper column "Hollywood Happenings" (March 23, 1929), "The radio fans are due for a real thrill. The hero of their favorite indoor sport, Nick Lucas, will sing his best numbers in *The Gold Diggers* for Warner Brothers."

While Nick was working in Los Angeles in March 1929, RKO Radio conducted a contest for its listeners to pick their favorite vaudeville performers, with the winners to appear on an April 2 radio broadcast. The balloting was done at all Keith-Orpheum Theatres. When the first ballots were counted, Nick was among the 15 most popular performers. When the balloting was completed and the final tally was announced on

March 27, Nick was in eighth position with 19,708 votes. Belle Baker and Sophie Tucker tied for first place with 20,326 votes each and they were followed, in order, by Van and Schneck, Rudy Vallee, Waring's Pennsylvanians, Vincent Lopez and Ted Lewis. Coming after Nick in the balloting were the Happiness Boys, Little Jack Little, Leatrice Joy, Cliff Edwards and Ben Bernie. As a result of his high standing in the RKO contest, Nick appeared on the April 2 radio broadcast as he, Sophie Tucker and Ted Lewis performed via remote from Los Angeles station KFI. Also on the NBC show were Rudy Vallee, Belle Baker, Van and Schneck and Ben Bernie. A week later, Nick appeared on another NBC-RKO radio program with Kate Smith, Sophie Tucker, Waring's Pennsylvanians and Ted Lewis; he did the remote broadcast from San Francisco and sang three songs. During Nick's March 1929 run at the Orpheum Theatre, *Variety* mistakenly printed that his salary was $1200 a week but corrected the error in its March 27, 1929, issue by stating it was $2000 per week. On May 11, 1929, Nick was one of the scores of stars appearing at the National Vaudeville Artists Benefit Gala Midnite Show at the Orpheum Theatre in Los Angeles. At the time he was headlining that city's Hillstreet Theatre, supported by Ken Murray.

Nick continued to film his part in *The Gold Diggers of Broadway*. Songwriters Al Dubin and Joe Burke had already composed several tunes for the production, and Zanuck asked them to write another number that could be made into a second big production featuring Nick. On Sunday nights after his Orpheum shows, Nick would get together with Dubin and Burke and exchange ideas for the tune. Out of this collaboration came "Tiptoe Through the Tulips," which Nick "didn't write but I helped it along and gave suggestions on it." Many people have done less on songs and still received co-author status. The two songwriters also wrote a few other tunes, like "In a Kitchenette," for Nick to do

Advertisement for *The Gold Diggers of Broadway* (1929).

in the movie, and they also wrote the dialogue for his part. When Zanuck heard "Tiptoe Through the Tulips," he said, "This is going to be it." He ordered a production number with 36 chorines backing Nick as he performed the song. The sequences took place in a garden and the chorines actually danced through red and yellow tulips, a highlight of the movie's Technicolor process. Technicolor was also used to highlight Nick's "Painting the Clouds with Sunshine" production number.

The reason it took Nick so long to film his scenes in the film was because the production was plagued with numerous problems, most of them resulting from the newness of the sound medium and the use of Technicolor. The latter required lights that were so hot, they caused hairline cracks in Nick's guitar. The heat even put cracks in his patent leather shoes. Because of the excess heat, work had to be curtailed and filming could take place only for short periods, thus dragging out the time it took to shoot the picture. Also, there was no lip synchronization, as there would be in filmed musical productions in just a few years, and there were many retakes on the vocals and production numbers, all having to be done perfectly on the set. A 25-piece band, with its members each being paid $10 an hour, was on the set at all times during shooting. Basically the plot of the film was close to that of the 1923 movie version: A businessman (Conway Tearle) opposes his nephew's (William Bakewell) romance with a chorus girl (Helen Foster). To prove the uncle wrong, her friend (Nancy Welford) vamps him and the two fall in love and get married. When Warner Bros. issued the movie in November 1929, it played up "the crooning of Nick Lucas" in its advertisements and further proclaimed the film as "One hundred per cent Color, an additional feature of the Vitaphone all-talking pictures, doubles the 'life-likeness' of this most vivid and enjoyable talking picture. Look for the thrill of a lifetime the day you see Gold Diggers of Broadway."

To further advertise the movie, Warner Bros. filmed a one-reel trailer hosted by Conway Tearle. Not only did the trailer contain footage from the film but it also had Tearle talking with various member of the cast. In one sequence, Tearle introduced

Publicity picture of Nick Lucas in *The Gold Diggers of Broadway* (1929).

Nick, who briefly discussed his part in the production and then sang abbreviated versions of "Tiptoe Through the Tulips," "Painting the Clouds with Sunshine" and "In a Kitchenette."

The Gold Diggers of Broadway premiered in Atlantic City. Nick was then appearing at the Metropolitan Theatre in Boston, and Warner Bros. had him flown to the premiere as their guest. He was so excited about his film debut that he could not sit through the entire movie and awaited the first night reviews in the theater manager's office. It turned out to be a "terrific picture" and the reviews were very complimentary. Typical was *Photoplay*: "Two things stand out about this gay picture. One is the startling beauty of its all–Technicolor treatment. The other is the fact that it has two catchy tunes." *Variety* opined,

> Lots of color—Technicolor—lots of comedy, girls, songs, music, dancing, production and Winnie Lightner, with Nick Lucas as the main warbler.... That's what's going to send the picture into the money class for the Warners....
>
> And then Nick Lucas. Maybe he's singing a bit too much in *Gold Diggers*, while the original numbers provided by Al Dubin and Joe Burke run too closely in the same key, tempo and general theme, but there's no voice on the discs like Lucas' for the type of number sung by him. He's a paradox, as on the screen, great and can win with his voice, while on the stage Nick must get over on the strength of the canned rep he has piled so high. The two certain songs sung by him along with several other numbers in *The Diggers* are "Tulips" and "Painting the Clouds."

The movie was a huge success. Typical of its earning power was that it stayed for three months at the Winter Garden in New York City. When the film was at that theater, Nick became "the only single act doubling on Broadway" (*Variety*) when he also headlined the RKO Palace Theatre.

Regarding Nick's participation in the movie, *The Brooklyn* (New York) *Citizen* (December 6, 1929) wrote, "Nick Lucas never crooned near as sugary as he does in this picture. His tender love songs, in dulcet tones that says the passion of any heart, were caught by a fascinated audience that lost itself in general applause. He also employs the soft chords of a guitar to enhance the effect." On the other hand, *The Winnipeg* (Winnipeg, Manitoba, Canada) *Tribune* (January 20, 1930) opined, "This crooning troubadour sings in the style in which Nick Lucas' fans have come to admire, but he sings too much and his song numbers all, practically of the same character. 'Tiptoe Through the Tulips' and 'Painting the Clouds with Sunshine' are his principal numbers and they are bound to become a popular in Winnipeg as they are elsewhere but one can get too much even of Nick Lucas." *Exhibitors Herald* (October 5, 1929) noted, "The New York reviewers said there was too much Nick Lucas and not enough of Ann Pennington. Maybe so in New York, but not so in Plainview. As far as we are concerned, Nick could have sung several more. His voice is wonderful." In the same trade journal on November 25, 1929, T.O. Service opined, "To see and hear Nick Lucas sing 'Tiptoe Through the Tulips' is worth the price of admission; he sings several others for good measure." *Film Daily* (September 3, 1929) stated, "Nick Lucas, his banjo [*sic*] and his pleasant voice do considerable for the proceedings, although it does appear he was made to warble more often than necessary." The *Indianapolis* (Indiana) *Times* (October 28, 1929) wrote, "Nick Lucas scores with his mandolin and guitar. He photographs well and we all know that his voice records splendidly. And he knows how to get the crooning melody out of his instrument...." According to Buffalo, New York's *Courier-Express* (November 8, 1929), "Nick sings and sings and sings—much too much, even though his voice is about as fine as the sound machines have recorded in two years."

For Nick, the film was a double success because it not only gave him a role in a major motion picture, it also provided him with the two songs most associated with his career, "Tiptoe Through the Tulips" and "Painting the Clouds with Sunshine." After finishing his scenes for the movie, Nick recorded the tunes for Brunswick Records in Los Angeles and they were issued as a single record at the time of the film's release. Despite the onset of the Depression, the record sold over one million copies in its initial pressing and became the single largest record success in Nick's 70-year recording career. Over the years he re-recorded both songs several times for various companies and his total record sales for "Tiptoe Through the Tulips" went over the three million mark. By the end of 1929, Nick's record of the two tunes was the biggest-selling disc in the country. Sheet music for both songs was issued with Nick and the other stars of the film pictured on the covers; each surpassed the one million mark in sales. *Variety* (November 13, 1929) reported that Nick's recording of "Tiptoe Through the Tulips" was the #1 seller in Los Angeles and #2 in Chicago, while the flip side "Painting the Clouds with Sunshine" was #1 in New York City. In sheet music sales, "Tiptoe Through the Tulips" was #1 in New York City and Los Angeles and ranked fourth in Chicago, while "Painting the Clouds with Sunshine" was #2 in Los Angeles and #4 in New York. A month later, the platter was Brunswick's #1 seller in Chicago, New York and Los Angeles. In 2009, *Billboard* magazine called Nick's Brunswick recording of "Tiptoe Through the Tulips" the #1 song of 1929. In later years, when Nick was asked how much he had sung "Tiptoe Through the Tulips," he estimated at least 10,000 times.

The Gold Diggers of Broadway's success was phenomenal for its time and the movie helped pave the way for many more popular musical extravaganzas since all-talking, all-singing, all-dancing movies were the most popular form of screen entertainment in the early talkie era. No complete prints of the movie are known to exist today. The original negative decomposed long ago, as have all known release prints of the film. Many of the early sound musicals dated badly after only a few years and studios took little care in preserving them since it was thought their reissue value was negligible. In fact, many of the early sound musicals were not even transferred to 16mm film when local TV stations began their voracious demand for almost any sound movies. Although the movie was in release as late as 1939, when it played in Australia, only about ten minutes of its footage is extant, and this contains Nick's garden rendition of "Tiptoe Through the Tulips." At the box office, it was Warners' best moneymaker until *Sergeant York* in 1941.

Darryl F. Zanuck wanted Nick to appear in another Warner Bros.' musical extravaganza, *The Show of Shows*. Leo Fitzgerald negotiated a contract that called for Nick to received $10,000 per week for two weeks work on the film, plus the studio paid for Nick and his wife and daughter's train trip to Hollywood and for their two-week stay at the Ambassador Hotel. Nick was given top billing over Myrna Loy in the "Chinese Fantasy" sequence of the film, a ten-minute production number in which he played a Chinese prince serenading his lady love (Loy) with "Li-Po-Li" while dozens of Oriental chorines dance around them. It took ten days to film this elaborate sequence done in Technicolor and it turned out to be one of the most delightful portions of this $800,000 production. Nick also sang "Lady Luck" and "The Only Song I Know" and traded comedy patter with Frank Fay in a stage show sequence.

In the book *Warner Brothers Presents* (1971), Ted Sennett commented, "For a

Australian sheet music cover for "Tiptoe Through the Tulips" picturing Nick Lucas.

filmgoer of the 'seventies, *Show of Shows* still yields a number of diverting moments.... One of the most elaborate numbers, 'Chinese Fantasy,' is introduced by Rin-Tin-Tin with a series of barks and has Nick Lucas crooning 'Li-Po-Li' to Chinese princess Myrna Loy with girls dressed in what can only be described as Bizarre Oriental prance around them." At the time of the general release early in 1930, *Photoplay* reported, "The Technicolor work is extraordinarily beautiful. But best of all, *Show of Shows* is packed with storms of laughter from start to finish. That alone should send you scurrying in to see the richest and fastest screen revue yet produced."

Seventy-seven stars appeared in the production and Nick was one of the few singled out by the studio for an expensive production number. *The Show of Shows* survives in its complete form and the sequence "The Chinese Fantasy" has lost none of its charm. While the dancing in it may be somewhat dated, Nick's rendering of "Li-Po-Li" is beautifully done and is as entertaining today as when he first sang it. *The Show of Shows* proved to be a box office winner and, along with *The Gold Diggers of Broadway*, it provided Nick with the opportunity of appearing in two of Warner Bros.' top money-making productions. Part of the "Chinese Fantasy" sequence was included in an episode on musical films in the NBC-TV series *Hollywood and the Stars*, aired during the 1963–64 season.

Nick Lucas and Myrna Loy in *The Show of Shows* (Warner Bros., 1929).

Warner Bros. gave Nick a great deal of publicity in their advertising. His picture was prominently displayed on the *Gold Diggers* and *Show of Shows* sheet music, and he got good placement as a "Warner Bros. Star" in *The Witmark Theme Song Dance Folio No. 2*, published in 1930 by M. Witmark and Sons. After *The Show of Shows*, the studio offered Nick a seven-year contract to star in musicals. It called for him to be paid $250 per week with options rising at that amount for each sixth-month renewal. Both Nick and Leo Fitzgerald thought the offer was ridiculously low, in light of how much he had been paid for *Gold Diggers* and *Show of Shows* and how successful they had become. At the time, Nick was offered another 80-weeks booking in vaudeville at $3000 per week and since the movie offer was nowhere near that amount, it was rejected.

When Nick was making his second feature film, an amusing occurrence involving his beloved guitar took place and was reported nationally in newspapers on September 9, 1929:

Nick Lucas makes melody for air, records, movies, et cetera. Nick has a priceless guitar. He'd rather lose his last dime than that guitar. 'Tother day, however, he misplaced it. For hours he hung on the telephone and raided friends' homes. No luck. About 4 a.m. he recollected that he had been in Ray Perkins' office earlier in the day. Mebee he'd left the guitar there. He promptly jingled Mr. Perkins, routing him from sound snores. Lucas refused to wait until later. He was frenzied. He wanted that guitar. So Perkins dressed, went over to the Warner studio, opened his office, and there sat the darn guitar. Ray has issued orders that Mr. Lucas can come to visit him when he has a song on his mind, but he comes with empty hands.

Advertisement for Warner Bros.' *The Show of Shows* (1929).

While making the Warner Bros. movies, Nick became acquainted with various Hollywood notables, including brothers Charles and Sydney Chaplin, Roscoe "Fatty" Arbuckle, Edna Purviance, John Barrymore and Lew Cody. Cody especially liked Nick and gave a big party for him in his Studio City home each time Nick was in Hollywood. Cody, however, would get intoxicated and tell Nick to take over the party so he could retire; Nick would then hand the reins over to his secretary and go home. The party life never appealed to Nick and his usual activity was to make a courtesy call at a party, stay a few minutes and then leave. He always took good care of himself physically and was especially careful of his voice. He kept active with a lifelong love of golf, he never smoked and did not drink alcohol except for a little wine or champagne.

During the time he was at Warner Bros., Nick and his family often went on weekend excursions to Catalina Island, where many of the stars had homes. They made the crossing by boat with a group that usually included Cody, Purviance and Arbuckle and they would stay the weekend before returning to the mainland for work on Monday. Nick was especially fond of Arbuckle, with whom he also worked in vaudeville. Another good friend of his from that medium was Lita Grey Chaplin.

Between his stints in Hollywood in 1929, Nick continued to appear in vaudeville. Regarding his stand at Chicago's New Palace Theatre, *Billboard* (June 15, 1929) said, "Nick Lucas stirred up some real enthusiasm with his crooning melodies to guitar accompaniment. Put his stuff across big and had to respond to insistent demands for an encore." When it was announced that Nick would return to Los Angeles to perform, that city's *Examiner* (July 29, 1929) referred to him as "the boy whose phonograph records continue to have a phenomenal sale." In August 1929, Brunswick announced a second season of recording stars appearing in radio broadcasts, now on the air three nights a week on 29 stations nationwide. Nick was among the regular performers, along with Al Jolson, Belle Baker, Ben Bernie, Mario Chamlee, Hal Kemp, Abe Lyman, Ray Miller and Zelma O'Neill. The series, now called *Brunswick Brevities*, was syndicated by the National Radio Advertising Company. It ran from August 19, 1929, until March 1930. Many of the programs were dubs of Brunswick discs with announcements added to make a 30-minute show. Regarding Nick's record output, Abel in *Variety* reported on March 20, 1929, "Nick Lucas croons 'em wicked with 'Old Timer' and 'Heart O'Mine.' …Latter is a ballad theme and for all its reminiscences, a sympathetic refrain." On September 12, 1929, the same reviewer said of the coupling "When You Said Goodnight/ You're a Real Sweetheart," "Lucas' song interpretations are ever distinctive, made more so by intelligent selection of numbers."

Following an engagement at Boston's Memorial Theatre in late August 1929, Nick returned to the Palace Theatre in New York City. *Billboard* (September 7, 1929) stated that he had an "appealing repertoire of crooning songs, put over to his own guitar accompaniment. Nick sticks to the pop shelves and naturally goes heavy on the ballad stuff. He achieved a decisive show-stop." The same trade journal reported on September 14, "Ken Murray, working here as a wow m.c., gave Nick a big boast before he stepped on, and came on after the show-stopping bows to attract more handclapping for the personable troubadour. But let it be recorded that Lucas clicked on his own. They ate up everything his pipes and fingers served, and would have been happy to take more had he offered it." In regards to his act, the reviewer reported, "His appealing delivery takes to the ballad form nicely and he got rousing receptions with such items as 'Your Mother and Mine,' 'Singing in the Rain,' 'Side by Side,' and one of his old favorites, 'Bye Bye Blackbird.' [Vaudeville] can use Lucas and his phenomenal disc-recording activity makes him a great subject for special exploitation." Regarding the same show, *Variety* (September 4) stated, "The crooning troubadour was recognized, the requests for his Brunswick recordings dating back to the 'Cup of Coffee, Sandwich and You' season. He does a program of his recent disk releases…." *The New York Times* on September 2 reported, "[Lucas] caresses vocally some of Tin Pan Alley's lesser output, including an inevitable mother song, and for doing so he was recalled several times yesterday." That fall, Nick headlined theaters in Tulsa, Fort Worth, Akron, Cincinnati and Buffalo. Regarding the latter engagement, the *Buffalo Courier-Express* (December 1) wrote, "Audiences … are giving Nick Lucas … one of the greatest receptions ever accorded a star in a personal appearance here." This was followed by an engagement at Shea's Hippodrome in Toronto.

The Stock Market collapsed in October 1929 and the country's financial situation was becoming unstable, but things looked very good for Nick. In the five years since he had started recording for Brunswick, his discs had sold in the millions and he was one of the top record sellers in the country. He had appeared in two Broadway productions and in two big-budget Hollywood musicals, along with being one of the best paid performers in vaudeville. The Nick Lucas special, manufactured by Gibson, was a good seller and as he embarked on his 1930 vaudeville tour, he was at the top of his profession. The Depression, however, grew worse and within two years, big-time vaudeville and the record industry were reeling from its effects. The whole course of show business, in which Nick had found so profitable, would be in turmoil that would last well into the beginning of World War II.

In the mid-70s, an episode of the popular CBS-TV series *The Waltons* dealt with a small family inheritance. One of the boys in the family suggested the money be used to buy a phonograph and recordings by Gene Autry and Nick Lucas. Obviously the show's researchers did a proper job for the setting of the program, taking place in the 1930s, for Nick remained one of the top entertainers of the time as well as the leading proponent of the six-string guitar. Although the Depression and the passing time brought many changes in the overall picture of the entertainment industry, Nick continued to be one of its most constant and popular stars.

According to an article in the *Fitchburg* (Massachusetts) *Sentinel* (December 11, 1929)d, "Nick Lucas is one of the most popular entertainers of the day. Translated into dollars, his popularity nets him an income that has been estimated to be from $2,000 to $3,000 a week. That includes his salary as a vaudeville entertainer and royalties from his photograph records." Regarding his demeanor on stage, the article said, "It has been stated that people do not want clean entertainment; that, to succeed, a show must contain a certain amount of obscenity. The career of Nick Lucas is a complete refutation of such notions. In a biographical sketch of the 'crooning troubadour,' the *Kansas City Times* says: 'Nick has one thing ... of which he is mightily proud. That is that he never has sung a song with suggestive or "off-color" lyrics...' 'I can't see that has hurt me," he says. "And it has given me a great deal of peace of mind.'"

On December 19, 1929, an electrical transcription made by Nick was part of a shortwave radio broadcast from Los Angeles station KDKA to the Robert Byrd expedition at the South Pole. Other Brunswick performers appearing on the program: Al Jolson, Belle Baker, Harry Richman, Dick Robertson, Scrappy Lambert and five orchestras.

As the 1930s dawned, Nick was continuing to headline in vaudeville and making $3000 a week, remaining one of the medium's highest paid performers. In February 1930, *The Show of Shows* was given national release and it added to his prestige. The Depression, however, was hurting show business, especially the record industry. Although the sale of platters dropped drastically, Nick continued to record with Brunswick and had best sellers with the combinations "Dancing with Tears in My Eyes/Telling It to the Daisies" and "You're Driving Me Crazy/I Miss a Little Miss" along with the singles "Singing a Song to the Stars" and "Lady, Play Your Mandolin." On some of his records during this period, he worked with an orchestra and was billed as "Nick Lucas and His Crooning Troubadours." Regarding the August 1930, Brunswick release of "Singing a Song to the Stars/My Heart Belongs to the Girl Who Belongs to Somebody Else," *Variety* wrote, "Supreme among those who lull their listeners into pleasurable reverie is this graduate of the early era of symphonic jazz... [The tunes] are characteristic Lucas charmers." With record sales declining in the summer of 1930, Brunswick, Columbia and Victor records all cut their 75-cent records to half price, while a new company, Durium, entered the market with one-sided cardboard discs sold at newsstands weekly at 15 cents each.

Nick began 1930 with appearances at the Minnesota Theatre in Minneapolis and the Michigan Theatre in Detroit. He headlined the *Crooning Along* revue at the Oriental Theatre in Chicago, where he sang five songs, "increasing his applause as he traveled.... Business was excellent" (*Variety*, January 22, 1930). In February, it was announced that he and Ted Lewis and Little Jack Little were each signed for a solid ten weeks by Warner Bros.' vaudeville booking office. These engagements included the Denver Theatre in Denver, two stands at the Branford Theatre in Newark, a return to the Minnesota

Theatre in Minneapolis, the Keith-Orpheum Theatre in Paterson, New Jersey, and the Earle Theatre in Washington, D.C. When Nick appeared at the Ambassador Theatre in St. Louis, the *St. Louis Globe-Democrat* (February 17, 1930) stated, "[E]veryone knows who he is. He lives up to his reputation." According to the February 12, 1930, *Variety*, his recording of "Tiptoe Through the Tulips" was still Brunswick's #1 seller in New York City, #2 in Chicago and #5 in Los Angeles, while "Painting the Clouds with Sunshine" was #4 in both Chicago and New York City. A month earlier, the platter had been #1 in both New York City and Los Angeles and #2 in Chicago. Its staying power kept it at #6 in Chicago in March 1930. Nick's double platter of "Telling It to the Daisies/Dancing with Tears in My Eyes" charted at #6 in New York City in July 1930, followed by "Singing a Song to the Stars/My Heart Belongs to the Girl," which was #5 in that city in August and #6 there the following month.

When Nick appeared at the Stanley Theatre in Philadelphia, *Variety* (March 5, 1930) reported, "Lucas was the big b.o. [box office] magnet with lobby lines shortly after noon. Worked independent of regular unit, refusing to appear in front of stage band, and whammed with his crooning." After playing the Mastbaum Theatre in Philadelphia and a third stand at the Banford in Newark, he was on stage in Reading, Pennsylvania, where he gave away autographed copies of his Brunswick records supplied by local dealers to 100 women at matinees. Free coffee was also supplied. *Variety* (April 30, 1930) noted, "The stunt brought capacity nightly and all but one matinee." This was followed by a stand at the Keith-Orpheum Theatre in Paterson, New Jersey.

The June 25, 1930, *Variety* carried an advertisement by Nick thanking Louis Katzman, Jimmy O'Keefe and Jack Kapp for assisting his signing a new one-year contract to record with Brunswick Records. Despite falling record sales, at the end of 1930 Brunswick listed Nick as one of its disc leaders along with Al Jolson, Harry Richman, Libby Holman, Marion Harris, Belle Baker, Red Nichols and the bands of Ben Bernie, Phil Spitalny, Ozzie Nelson, Abe Lyman, Earl Burtnell and Isham Jones.

When Nick appeared at the Astor Theatre in Reading, Pennsylvania, the *Reading Times* (April 23, 1930) reported he "continues to take his audience by storm with his crooning melodies, his strumming guitar and the personality that served him so splendidly in *Gold Diggers*, *Show of Shows* and Ziegfeld's *Show Girl*. Lucas sings all the numbers he made popular in his screen hits, including 'Painting the Clouds with Sunshine,' 'Tiptoe Through the Tulips,' 'In a Kitchenette,' 'Lady Luck' and other Brunswick record hits." During a matinee he gave away ten of his Brunswick platters to ladies in the audience, and at a later seminar he told "some interesting things about his wild sidekick, Winnie Lightner, in *The Gold Diggers*." The day before, the same newspaper stated,

> [Lucas] received a tremendous ovation yesterday at the Astor Theatre, where he is appearing in person three times daily, singing and playing his popular Brunswick record hits. Lucas has the personality and the crooning art that has placed him foremost of all songsters today.... His work ... was applauded to the echo last evening, and the theatergoers were not satisfied until Nick came back with a bit of a curtain speech, that took them back to the good old days when performers stepped before the footlights at the close of the big third act and acknowledged the enthusiasm of the patrons. The more applause the more Lucas sings and everyone was surely delighted with his work last night.

Nick also continued to get rave reviews in vaudeville as exemplified by his appearance at the RKO Palace Theatre in New York City in early December 1930. The *New York Sun* (December 8, 1930) said, "Mr. Lucas, whose virtuosity with the guitar surpasses even his crooning, stopped the show until he had dished up many of his old favorites." The *New York Evening Graphic* (December 8, 1930) noted, "Lucas sings without effort, and the result is so pleasant that one wishes that there could be more crooners like him. His style is certainly distinctive." The *New York Herald Tribune* (December 8, 1930) stated, "Nick Lucas can still pick the guitar to perfection and his singing is above reproach," while the *New York Daily News* (December 8, 1930) called him "[t]he daddy of all crooners." *Billboard* (December 13, 1930) reported that he "clicked easily ... with his crooning and guitaristics. Lucas drew big applause in three numbers before taking the bows and almost wearing out his welcome with encores.... Lucas was in good voice, and the regulars sensed it." The *New York World* (December 8, 1930) reported, "Mr. Lucas was received with tremendous enthusiasm...." When he was at the Brooklyn's RKO Albee late in 1930, the *Brooklyn Citizen* (December 28, 1930), stated, "Lucas' method of 'putting over' a song is without equal in his line." On December 27, 1930, Nick appeared on *The RKO Hour* with Lita Grey Chaplin, Ken Murray and Harry Richman in the program's anniversary party, held aboard the S.S. *Leviathan*.

During this period, Nick was very active on network radio. Included were regular appearances on NBC's *RKO Theatre of the Air* and *The Ludwig Baumann Hour*. When he sang on the former, David Bratton wrote in Brooklyn's *The Times Union* (December 26, 1930), "Lucas was splendid with his appealing radio voice."

The year 1930 brought Nick two more lucrative sources of income. The previous year, he had joined forces with Eddie Lang, Carson Robison and Andy Sannella to edit *The Mastertone Guitar Method,* published by Robbins Music Corporation. In 1930, he signed with the Nicomede Music Company in Altoona, Pennsylvania, to compile *The Nick Lucas Guitar Method for Pick Playing*. Nicomede was owned by Joseph W. (Joe) Nicomede, a music teacher, and Nick's guitar instruction book was the first of many he compiled for the company. Next came *The Nick Lucas Guitar Method for Pick Playing, Volume 2* for advance players; Nick went on to do three volumes of *The Nick Lucas Plectrum Guitar Method* and many more (see "Song Folios" in the appendices). In addition to compiling these guitar instruction books and song folios, Nick composed scores of songs included in them. Not only were the guitar instruction books intended to teach students how to play the guitar or advance their playing knowledge, they were often used by music schools and individual instructors. Many editions had a back page with a "Students Daily Report" for listing dates and times of lessons, practice times and parents' initials. At the bottom of the report was space for satisfactory completion by the student and a grade, signed by the teacher. These instruction books sold for around a dollar each.

Music Trade Journal (July 30, 1930) stated, "The Nicomede Music Company publishers ... report that the *Nick Lucas Guitar Method* and *Premier Folio for Guitar Solos* for pick style playing, written by Nick Lucas, celebrated soloist, were exhibited at both conventions of teachers and dealers recently in Providence, Rhode Island, and New York City, respectively. The books have been favorably accepted and highly recommended by many of the leading teachers and dealers."

Most editions of Nick's guitar books contain the following introduction by the publisher: "No greater exponent of this spectacular style of guitar playing has ever lived than Nick Lucas. The ensuing pages are the result of painstaking labor to present, in a simple manner, the artistry of this guitarist. This method is therefore, presented with the greatest confidence in its popularity and usefulness." The popularity of Nick's guitar books continues to this day and thousands of people since 1930 have used his method to learn and advance their skills on the six-string guitar. In 1946, Mills Music of New York City bought the catalogue of Nicomede Music, which had been in operation for 28 years. Mills Music continued the publication of Nick's guitar instruction books, renewing the copyrights in 1968. In addition to his guitar books and folios, Robbins Music Corporation published *Nick Lucas Collection of Neapolitan Love Songs* in 1935 containing 26 Italian romantic ballads, including "O Sole Mio," "Celeste Aida," "Come Back to Sorrento," "Oh Marie" and "Vesti la Giubba."

There was a drawback to Nick's reputation as a master of the guitar as reported in *The Knoxville* (Tennessee) *News-Sentinel* (February 27, 1932): "Rarely a week goes by that Nick Lucas ... isn't approached by someone eager to finance a correspondence school of guitar playing with Nick's name on it. But Lucas promises there'll never be any Nick Lucas guitar school, the only hope or virtue of which would be the fame of the entertainer's name."

Following the success of his initial guitar instruction books, Nick entered into another profitable business venture: Joe Nicomede agreed to pay him a royalty to sell a line of guitar picks with his name on them. The guitar pick Nicomede manufactured was first designed by Luigi D'Andrea in 1928; he and Nick chose this model, known as Number 351, for their line of guitar picks. Will Hoover wrote in *Picks!* (1995), "The finished product featured a stylized impression of the artist's name, the first guitar pick to bear an imprint. Unlike any pick before it, this unique design was exclusively associated with the guitarist. Thus, it became forever linked with the guitar. The No. 351 was, and still is, THE guitar pick. Like most D'Andrea shapes, the No. 351 was never patented—meaning anyone was free to use it. Nevertheless, for many years even competing pick marketers referred to it as the 'Nick Lucas shape.'" The Nick Lucas guitar picks, available in soft, medium and hard designs in a variety of colors, sold for a dime each or three for twenty-five cents and came in display cards containing two dozen picks. From the 1930s through the 1950s, the Nick Lucas brand was billed as "the pick with the crooning tone" and was advertised for both the guitar and banjo. This brand of guitar pick flourished for decades and is still used today.

In the late 1920s and early 1930s, Rudy Vallee caused a sensation appearing with his band, the Connecticut Yankees, in person and on radio. Rudy was billed as a crooner and publicity people at Victor Records, for whom Vallee recorded, and Brunswick decided it would result in good box office for both Nick and Rudy if a "feud" was created between them over who was the first crooner. Despite some newspaper copy to the contrary, neither performer wanted any part of this, and the matter was soon dropped. Over the years, the two remained friends. Through the years, Nick and Rudy only had kind words for each other. Nick said, "Rudy Vallee is a very nice man"; for his part, Vallee stated, "Nick Lucas ... is a dear, kind artist and human being." Nick found Rudy to be amusing and liked to relate a story about running into him in a Hollywood bank in 1975 and commenting on the fur coat he was wearing. Rudy said he bought the coat while at Yale University in 1926. Nick laughingly said, "Here is a guy with all the money in the world and he is still wearing a coat he bought 50 years ago."

Nick had his share of imitators and those who claimed to be his protégés. A singer-guitarist who performed in Nick's style was Charlie Palloy (*née* Charles Costello), who recorded for Crown Records in 1932 and '33. Crown parlayed his similarity to Nick in advertising Palloy's records, but actually he sounded more like Russ Columbo. An even more overt attempt to imitate Nick came in the 1936 transcribed five-minute radio series *Melody Lane* in which the star, simply billed as "The Troubadour," sounded so much like Nick that many thought they *were* listening to him. (The singer was Larry Burke.) Many performers, like Don Bova, who appeared on radio in Cincinnati, admitted they were influenced by Lucas and performed in his style, singing to their own guitar accompaniment. There were also women imitating Nick, including Lea Warwick, who in 1933 billed herself as "The Female Nick Lucas."

Still there was only one Nick Lucas and his appeal was exemplified in *The Optimist* (January 8, 1931), the student newspaper of Abilene (Texas) Christian College: "When it comes to soft, sweet selections. Nick Lucas ... takes the crown. His music generally fits all occasions. His following among the weaker sex is not to be overlooked."

In the spring of 1930, Brunswick Records was purchased by Warner Bros. and by the end of the year, a budget label, Melotone Records, had been created. This business shift did not particularly affect Nick at the time although the company did begin to experiment somewhat with his records, sometimes giving him a backup and billing him as "Nick Lucas and His Crooning Troubadours." Also, his final recordings for Brunswick, done four years later, were released on Melotone and related labels.

As Nick continued to headline in vaudeville, he noticed that more and more theaters began subjugating vaudeville acts to movies. "Motion pictures were putting vaudeville out of business, making it obsolete," he later recalled. Still Nick continued to have success in the medium and he opened 1931 with a stand at Gotham's 86th Street Theatre where *Variety* (January 7, 1931) said he "walked off after slamming across a pair of songs, making the next two look like encores. Ended with his stooge playing up the laughs for the comedy touch." Regarding the same stand, the *Brooklyn Daily Eagle* (January 11, 1931) reported, "With each successive appearance, Lucas seems to bring his legion of admirers closer to him than ever before.... [He and his guitar] make a rare entertainment duo, Lucas with his intimate crooning voice and the guitar with its plaintive accompaniment." Next he appeared in the "Auto Show Frolic" at the Minnesota Theatre in Minneapolis, resulting in the venue seeing a big reversal after a financial slump. In the January 21, 1931, *Variety*, Nick's Brunswick recording of "You're Driving Me Crazy/I Miss a Little Miss" was listed as the #1 seller in Chicago, #2 in New York City and #5 in Los Angeles. The next week, the record was #2 in Los Angeles and #6 in Chicago. The next month, Nick had three charted records: "Walking My Baby Back Home" was #5 in New York City, "Hello Beautiful" was #6 in Gotham and "Lady, Play Your Mandolin" was #3 in Los Angeles and #4 in Chicago. In June, Nick's recording of "Let's Get Friendly" charted at #3 in Chicago.

In March 1931, Nick was at the Buffalo Theatre in Buffalo, New York, sharing the bill with the Ruth Chatterton film *Unfaithful*. *Variety* (March 18, 1931) reported that with Nick on stage, "[t]his show should get $30,000 this week despite unfavorable notices on the picture." The March 25, 1931, *Variety*, reported, "Nick Lucas on stage excellent at $29,000." In April, Nick began a vaudeville tour for Paramount Publix that included Boston's Metropolitan Theatre. The *Rocky Mountain News* (May 8, 1931) reported of his appearance in Denver: "And the melody—such melody!—flows in bountiful quantities from the ingratiating vocal chords and deft fingers of that prince of entertainers—Nick Lucas. A packed house yesterday gave the world to know that it regards Nick Lucas as one of the most popular persons who ever smiled across Denver footlights." When he headlined the Paramount Theatre in New Haven, Connecticut, the *New York Sun* reported, "Mr. Lucas, whose virtuosity with guitar surpasses even his crooning, stopped the show until he had dished up many of his old favorites." The next week he was in Boston: "First time in Boston's history S.R.O. business on 'Good Friday' at the Metropolitan, Boston" (Paramount-Publix). *The Omaha* (Nebraska) *Bee-News* (April 22, 1931) raved, "Nick Lucas' crooning rates high, but the combination of his crooning and guitar accompaniment is irresistible." When he was at the Denver Theatre in Denver in May 1931, the *New York Graphic* reported, "Nick Lucas crooned to hitdom with half dozen numbers, accompanying himself on guitar. Lucas sings without effort, and the result is so pleasant one wishes there could be more crooners like him." Of his engagement at the Lyric Theatre in Indianapolis, the *Indianapolis Star* (July 13, 1931) wrote,

> The silvery tones of the immaculate troubadour, Nick Lucas, were soothing to at least one untroubled breast and pleasing to the patrons in general when he took his bow and sang away.... The willingness of the audience to hear exceeded that of the artist to perform and the result was such satisfaction as escapes us when a good thing is overdone.... Nick Lucas has an easy, soft voiced method of delivery that slips him into the liking of his listeners in short order and keeps him there... [He] favors those present with several of the musical numbers he helped to make popular.... Upon request, he renders "Tiptoe Through the Tulips" and "Side by Side," which were appreciated. His act is not long, but it is good.

Of the same stand, Walter D. Hickman opined in the *Indianapolis Times* (July 14, 1931),

> Songs that Nick Lucas sang in the movies and some that he crooned a year or two ago are the ones in demand at the Lyric this week. When Lucas invites his audience to name what they want to hear, it is the old tunes which are requested the most. And the interesting thing about the affair is that those crying out for certain melodies keep on insisting until Nick strikes up the melody on his guitar. He is a much more polished performer than he has been. When he was first getting famous, Nick did not use makeup. Now his makeup is faultless. He is wise in leaving the major part of the program up to his audience. I am glad to see that Lucas does not attempt any stories and jokes. He sings and he plays and while he is doing that, he is failure-proof. The people want soothing and pleasant melody these days and Lucas has that satisfying brand. He is sincere in his curtain talk when he thanks the audience for his fine reception.

During his Indianapolis engagement, Nick awarded prizes to the best local guitar players who took part in a contest held at the Lyric where he was headlining.

Upon his return to Chicago's Palace Theatre, *Variety* (July 28, 1931) opined, "Nick Lucas, doing his single, closed the show for the headline position. Started right in under the reception and using a comedy stooge bit on one song he worked it up nicely." When he appeared in Ohio that August, Archie Bell wrote in the *Cleveland News*, "[Lucas is] the sort of fellow you'd like to drop in any time, day or night, and entertain you with a song, the best modern representative of the ancient troubadour." The same month he was in Washington, D.C., and that city's *Evening Star* (August 16, 1931) reported, "Nick Lucas, who heads the stage program at the Earle, would have stopped the show if the management had permitted. Furnishing his own instrumental music, he offers a few songs and is compelled to give several repeat numbers as a result of demands from the audience." When he appeared in Buffalo, *The Angola Record* (October 8, 1931) stated, "In perfect form and fine voice, laden with a large repertoire of new popular song numbers and with a guitar under his arm, Nick Lucas seems to bring his legion of admirers closer to him with each successive appearance. He is distinctly individual and different. The mellow tone of his guitar and his soothing melodious voice endear him to his audiences like few others." Reviewing the same venue, Buffalo's *Courier-Express* stated, "Nick Lucas in two years has become one of the nation's leading recording and radio artists. His return to the stage finds him one of the highest salaried single acts in the country." This stand was followed with a week at Shea's Hippodrome in Toronto. In October, Nick was back at the Palace in Gotham and *Variety* (October 27, 1931) reported, "After two numbers he asked for requests and sang what he wanted to. A plant on the shelf helped a lot." In November 1931, Nick and Helen Morgan headlined a benefit at the New Amsterdam Theatre for the *New York American and Evening Journal*'s Christmas and Relief Fund.

Nick also continued to record. The *Winnipeg* (Manitoba) *Tribune* (March 7, 1931) wrote, "A welcome return to records is Nick Lucas, the same old crooning troubadour who put 'Bye Bye Blackbird' across in the days when the world was younger. Nick has a couple of pathetic ones in 'You Didn't Have to Tell Me' and 'When You Were the Blossom of Buttercup Lane.' It's the same old Nick and the same old croon with an orchestra that carries out the spirit of his offerings. Good items these."

In August 1931, Nick had a best-selling Brunswick disc with the coupling of "When the Moon Comes Over the Mountain/That's My Desire," but he halted his association with the company after making "Goodnight Sweetheart" with Victor Young and His Orchestra in October. "When the Moon Comes Over the Mountain" will be forever remembered as Kate Smith's theme song (she co-wrote it) and "That's My Desire" launched Frankie Laine to stardom in 1947. Nick was the first to record both numbers. He recalled liking Kate Smith, who he worked with on several of her radio and TV programs, and her manager Ted Collins.

A national poll taken in the fall of 1931 noted that 64 percent of those questioned were aware of Nick, the same percentage for Ted Lewis and Albert Einstein. Around this time, Nick stepped up his radio appearances. The September 15, 1931, *Variety* noted, "NBC has already passed the word out to radio circles that it wouldn't be at all surprised if Lucas emerged to steal the lime-light from both [Bing] Crosby and [Russ] Columbo, despite the current fuss over the latter two." The October 31, 1931, *Variety* carried the headline, "Lucas on Commercial" and reported, "Six weeks of sustaining broadcasts five nights weekly, have sold Nick Lucas as a commercial at $2,000. The vaudeville and disc singer will croon for soup on the *Campbell Program* over NBC starting around November 1." Despite the fact he had not recorded for Brunswick in nearly three months, at the end of 1931 the company listed Nick as one of its four best record sellers, along with Bing Crosby, the Boswell Sisters and the Mills Brothers.

Nick was very popular in the south and southwest and during his tours in those areas, he became friends with Louisiana governor (and later Senator) Huey Long. Nick recalled, "Any time I appeared in the Louisiana area Huey Long would come to see me. He was a big fan of mine." Historians have painted Long in an unfavorable manner; *The Columbia-Viking Desk Encyclopedia* (1953) states, "[H]e promoted a 'Share-the-Wealth' program by ruthless and demagogic means." But Nick remembered Long as a very nice and gregarious individual and had only kind things to say about him. While Nick was pretty much apolitical, he did openly endorse the re-election of President Herbert Hoover in 1932; other celebs in Hoover's corner included Lew Cody, Wallace Beery, Conrad Nagel, Bebe Daniels, Buster Keaton, Mae Murray, Al Jolson, Mary Brian, Ethel Barrymore, Ann Harding, Paul Muni, Ginger Rogers, Lewis Stone and Ernest Truex.

On March 27, 1931, Leona Lucas, wife of Nick's brother Frank, was arrested in Springfield, Missouri. She was charged with slashing construction worker Bentley West, a former sweetheart. She posted a $1000 bond pending trial on the charge.

Nick's NBC radio series was on the air from August 31, 1931, to January 31, 1932. Fifteen minutes long, it was broadcast three times a week in prime time. Following the program's debut, David Bratton wrote in his *Brooklyn* (New York) *Times Union* (September 3, 1931) column,

> Nick Lucas ... came on the air last evening as a steady feature ... [I]t doesn't matter what he sings, for he makes all songs sound great ... [I]t is the guitar playing as well as his singing that goes to make him the featured attraction that he is. Nick could give most other entertainers in this particular field all sorts of handicaps and win in a walk. ...[O]n the stage, in the movies or over the air, there is but one Nick Lucas and there is no crooner nor modern troubadour who can compare with him. He'll undoubtedly be a commercial in quick order, notwithstanding the high salaries that he has been commanding.

Regarding one of the series' final broadcasts, the columnist opined on January 4, 1931, "Lucas is splendid at any time and he was in fine voice last evening."

The January 19, 1932, *Billboard* announced, "Nick Lucas has been placed under contract to record for Durium, the fifteen cent Hit-of-the-Week record. Lucas is the fourth artist to be secured by Durium. Previous three are Rudy Vallee, Phil Spitalny and Erno Rapee. Vallee and Spitalny are under exclusive Durium contract, while Lucas and Rapee are not." Nick made two records for Durium, "An Evening in Caroline" and "All of Me/Goodnight Ladies" and his picture was on the back of the cardboard discs. Hit-of-the-Week claimed sales of 300,000 copies per record and Nick's two discs for the company sold in that range. By the end of the year, however, Nick and Brunswick had settled their differences and he returned to the label for another two years.

Regarding Nick's career, *Who's Who on the Air 1932*, published by the Ludwig Baumann Company in New York City, stated, "Traveled over three thousand miles to fame. That is he left his home in Newark for Hollywood where he sang his way into talking pictures. Oh! yes, while in London he taught the Prince of Wales to play the guitar." The publication noted that he was a "Ludwig Baumann Guest Artist" and, beginning in 1930, he made several appearances on the program over the next two years.

When Nick's NBC radio series ended early in 1932 in part thanks to heavy competition from Bing Crosby, he returned to vaudeville. *Variety* (January 5, 1932) reported on his stand at Brooklyn's Fox Theatre: "Nick Lucas in person is better than anything in a long time." It was announced that Nick was going to appear in a new Irving Berlin musical but the engagement never came about. Of his appearance at the Roxy Theatre in New York City, *Variety* (January 12, 1932) reported, "Lucas' voice was carried well enough by the house amplification system, but he missed the intimacy of the smaller houses. And Lucas is a polite singer whose effectiveness diminishes with distance." On January 28, 1932, Jo Ranson in the *Brooklyn Daily Eagle* column "Radio Dial-Log" reported, "Nick Lucas and N.B.C. have parted company, Nick planning to go into vaude until summer because no sponsor wanted to pay his price." In the same column on January 11, 1932, Ranson revealed, "Nick Lucas and Fred Waring, in a huddle backstage at the Roxy, suspected of composing a new song." On February 11, 1932, Lucas headlined the opening of the RKO-Orpheum Theatre in Denver that seated 2800 patrons. *Variety* reported, "Thousands stood in line and many were turned away the first day." Next he appeared in

Nebraska and at the Main Street Theatre in Kansas City, Missouri, the week of February 27. In her *Brooklyn Daily Eagle* column (March 19, 1932), Ranson noted, "Nick Lucas is mighty proud these days, having received a mere 13,000 letters after his last broadcast." On April 13, 1932, she wrote "[H]is vaudeville tour has been such a success that Nick Lucas has been booked solid in vaudeville until August 11, but he'll continue to broadcast while on the road...." When he appeared in Rochester, New York, in April, Nick was reunited with an old friend, Ken Whitmer, with whom he had once worked with in an orchestra. Whitmer had urged him to become a professional singer.

As the spring progressed, Nick kept busy on stage in Cleveland, New York, Rochester, Syracuse, Minneapolis, St. Paul, St. Louis, Seattle and Tacoma.

Money was a factor in Nick not returning to network radio, as noted in the February 18, 1932, *Radio Guide*:

> Nick Lucas ... waited just so long and no longer for a sponsor to come across with his prices and then bowed off the air-waves until the hot Summer breezes start blowing, when he might go back and become one of the pieces of goods on the NBC shelves.... But Nick is off to start an extended vaudeville tour.... Nick's price for microphoning was a little high and he almost dot-lined a commercial, but the sponsor balked at Lucas getting more money for a week than the president of the client gets for a month....

Murray Rosenberg in his *Brooklyn Daily Citizen* column "Radio Rays" (March 17, 1932) reported, "Nick Lucas will be featured on a program to start in September and he's touring in vaudeville now. At present he is ducking invitations from friends and radio

Nick Lucas in Los Angeles in 1933 with Tom Mix.

stars who want him to preside over a spaghetti pot because in an unguarded moment he gave out his favorite recipe for spaghetti and a woman's page editor printed it!"

In May, he returned to New York City to audition for two radio series, one of which would have teamed him with dialect comedian Henry Burbig. The next month he was back in Seattle for a two-week Orpheum Theatre run followed by a stand in Portland, Oregon. He was offered a role in MGM's Marion Davies film *Good Time Girl* (released as *Blondie of the Follies*) but had to turn it down due to his stage schedule. Regarding his stand at the Orpheum Theatre in Oakland, California, Wood Soames wrote in the *Oakland Tribune* (July 2, 1932), "Nick Lucas, who has to answer for the flood of crooners that people the radio and stage because he led the way, remains after a long absence one of the most engaging of entertainers and his virtuosity on the guitar is as brilliant as ever. The pity is that he doesn't use more guitar, but his public wants songs and he gave it six yesterday, old and new, all popular."

When he played the Orpheum Theatre in Los Angeles, *Variety* (July 12, 1932) noted, "Lucas always okay around here, was welcomed, not overstaying or reaching in his repertoire as he has done in the past." Next came a series of engagements that included the Keith-Orpheum Theatre in New Orleans, the Rialto in Louisville, the Palace Theatre in Chicago, the Earle Theatre in Washington, D.C., and the Hippodrome in Baltimore. Regarding his appearance at Fay's Theatre in Providence, Rhode Island, *Variety* (October 18, 1932) stated, "Nick Lucas ... doing all the pulling which is plenty. House has built up Lucas strong, especially with Italian theatergoers. Looks like a home run...." Next came a two-week stand at Keith's in Boston followed by the Albee Theatre in Brooklyn. Regarding this venue, Brooklyn's *Times Union* (November 7, 1932), reported that Nick "offers some vastly entertaining diversion with a snappy repertoire of old and new hits...."

While working on the RKO Circuit, Nick returned to the Palace Theatre in New York City on November 16, 1932; he was the last act to headline there before it was converted into a movie house. After that, the theater had four live shows a day and a motion picture. On July 22, 1932, a greyhound named Nick Lucas won the day race at the Mineola, Long Island, Fair Grounds track before 8000 people. Nick appeared in Indianapolis in the spring of 1933 in the "Carnival of Fun" program. After his last performance at the Indiana Theatre, he was the guest of honor of the race drivers in that city's annual 500 Mile Race. His Indianapolis stand was reviewed by Walter D. Hickman in the *Indianapolis Times* (May 15, 1933):

> Have told you about Nick Lucas and his guitar many times. Years of experience have ripened the artistry of his fingers. His voice is suitable to his style of crooning. The big thing about Nick is what he can do with his guitar. He really has made a grand piano out of that instrument. He has dignified the guitar until it has become the most honorable instrument. Watch the way this man develops "A Farewell to Arms." Watch his fingering and the tone he gets out of his instrument. Am beginning to think that it is Lucas' quick method of delivery, this determination to keep away from comedy attempts and his clear interpretation of the theme of a song that has kept him a favorite before his audiences all these years.

In 1933, Lucas made two one-reel short subjects for Master Art Products, both of which re-teamed him with organist Lew White, with whom he had worked at Brunswick. The titles were *Organloguing the Hits with Nick Lucas, the Crooning Troubadour* and *Home Again*. In the summer of 1933, Universal signed Nick to star in the first of its Menotone musical short subject series, *Vaudeville on Film*. He headlined *On the Air and*

Off, a musical comedy about a board of directors persuaded to advertise its soap on the air. Nick was the star of the radio program and sang the romantic ballad "Lonely Moonlight Troubadour." Filming took place at Brooklyn's Universal studio.

Nick opened 1933 with stands in Newark at both Keith's and Proctor's theaters and at the Ritz Theatre in Elizabeth, New Jersey. After headlining the Palace Theatre in Albany, he took part in the 17th Annual St. Patrick's Day Evening Benefit Show in Chicago in March. Also on the bill: Paul Ash and His Orchestra. Also appearing at the Palace was Bob Hope; it was there that the two began a lifelong friendship. During his Chicago stand, Nick was a special guest of the Illinois State Legislature. *The Decatur* (Illinois) *Herald* (April 14, 1933) reported, "So dull was the legislative program Thursday the statesmen willingly and joyously interrupted their work to hail the visit of Nick Lucas, …who was led to the speaker's high desk from which he sang with guitar accompaniment the classic ballad 'Gold Diggers of Broadway' [sic]. Lucas received a great hand and smilingly dedicated his number to Representative Benjamin Adamowski."

Following appearances in Milwaukee, Cedar Rapids, Memphis and Buffalo in the spring and early summer of 1933, Lucas worked at Toronto's Hippodrome Theatre, followed by a stand at the Earle Theatre in Washington, D.C., in August and the Metropolitan Theatre in Boston in September. On August 26, Nick and George Murphy were among the headliners at a benefit for Fitkin Hospital at the Monmouth Hotel in Spring Lake, New Jersey. When he returned to the Palace Theatre in New York City, *Variety* (September 5, 1933) stated, "Middle-of-the-bill attraction is Nick Lucas, a truly finished performer. With his guitar and songs he has material that hits home easily. And can he play that guitar!" This was followed by appearances at the Century Theatre in Baltimore and the Fox Theatre in Philadelphia.

Regarding his stand at the Brooklyn Paramount Theatre, the *Brooklyn Times Union* (October 7, 1933) wrote that he "is always worth the spontaneous applause he receives." When he appeared in Scranton, Pennsylvania, a big gala was held November 16, 1933, at which he was the guest of honor. On November 18, Nick appeared in Wilkes-Barre in vaudeville and did a radio benefit program on WBAX for the city's fire department's efforts to obtain old and broken toys to be repaired and distributed to the poor and needy at Christmas time. Late in 1933, he teamed with bandleader Ray Teal and His Floridians for a successful tour of the south, where they played for two months at mostly capacity business before ending with a month's stay in Miami at Gene Geiger's Tropical Jungle Club and the Paramount Theatre. Nick and Teal became lifelong friends; Teal left music to become a character actor in films and television. He was probably best known for his role as Sheriff Roy Coffee on the TV series *Bonanza*. The Lucas-Teal show also included dancers Marie and Antoinette, comedy acrobats The Kelso Brothers, and torch singer Beatrice Howell. When it appeared in Winston-Salem, North Carolina, in November 1933, they shared the bill with cowboy film great Tom Mix. Earlier in the month, the unit was at the Paramount Theatre in Nashville and the *Nashville Banner* (November 3, 1933) opined, "Mr. Lucas offers many lilting, narrative melodies that brought down the house at every show." When Nick played in Knoxville, Tennessee, Jo Ruth Perry of the *Knoxville News-Sentinel* (November 30, 1933) stated, "Nick Lucas, on stage at the Tennessee last half, really 'picks.' His guitar playing and his high tenor voice brought him volumes of applause at last night's show. He played his program numbers and request numbers with a smile that showed many a dazzling tooth and he won many a smile in return."

At an engagement at the Tivoli theater in Chattanooga, Tennessee, that city's *Daily Times* (December 7, 1933) referred to him as the "velvet-voiced Nick Lucas" and noted, "The mellow renditions of Lucas ... are the outstanding feature of the program.... Lucas does not have a tremendous voice, but it has a sweetness and smoothness that is striking. ...[T]o hear him in person is to understand his success. He offers several popular numbers ... 'The Last Round-Up,' with special lighting effect, the best of the group."

The Alexandria City, Alabama, *Outlook* writer Duke Merritt commented in his December 14, 1933, column "What They Say," regarding Nick's appearance at the Paramount Theatre in Montgomery where he was asked to sing "The Last Roundup": "A most effective campfire light of some sort was thrown on the singer as he sang this number, in his silvery tones. The weird light and the spell of this song held the audience spellbound, in one of the most enchanting renditions this writer heard. Needless to say, Lucas sang to a packed house." When Nick appeared in Selma, Alabama, that city's *Times-Journal* (December 10, 1933) wrote a biographical article about him, noting his mother's support:

> Mrs. Lucas is her son's proudest and most enthusiastic admirer, as well she should be, for he learned many of his enchanting songs at her knee, and the music that wells from his soul was bottled up in her own heart for years. Not long ago Nick sang "Go Home and Tell Your Mother" on the NBC network, and Mrs. Lucas listening in, jumped to her feet with smiling face and danced joyously about the loud speaker. "He's singing about me!" she cried, with tears running down her cheeks. "My boy is singing about me."

Also during 1933, there was a concerted effort to get Nick back on radio on a sustaining basis. While appearing in Chicago in March, he auditioned for NBC and the next month Maybelline officials announced that they wanted

Publicity photographs of Nick Lucas in the mid–1930s.

to sponsor Nick on the air. Nellie Revell in *Variety*'s July 17, 1933, "Air Line News" column stated, "Nick Lucas signed for new commercial for three 15-minute periods a week. This time Nick will have a special background and plenty of build up." In September, it was announced he and several other stars (including James Melton and Xavier Cugat) were candidates to advertise Pepsodent's Junis facial cream on radio. On September 26, 1933, *Variety* told readers, "Nick Lucas and the Casa Loma Orchestra appear to be all set for that Pepsodent face powder program."

Around this time, Nick's younger brother Libby had a brief singing career. One of his engagements was at the Star of the Sea benefit show in Long Branch, New Jersey, in March 1933; the headliner was Baby Rose Marie. Libby billed himself as Lib Lucas.

In 1934, Nick was back with Warner Bros. starring in the short subject *What This Country Needs*. It told of a theatrical firm setting up a musical bank; Nick sang several songs including a reprise of "Tiptoe Through the Tulips." In March 1934, Nick returned to network radio headlining a series for the Columbia (CBS) network. The show had Nick singing and strumming the guitar, backed by Freddie Rich's orchestra. It was broadcast each Wednesday at 11 p.m. and Friday at 6:30 p.m. Publicity for the program noted that Nick played three banjos at one time during his song recitals on the show, which ran for over a year. Another handout for the 15-minute series declared that Nick was "probably the only crooner on the air who doesn't mind being called one." The program originated from the Columbia studios in New York City and on it the network dubbed him the "CBS Troubadour." *Variety* (March 27, 1934) wrote "[CBS has] excellent radio star timber in Lucas. Essentially a mike performer, …Lucas knows his audible delivery and evidences that handsomely on his quarter hour…. He manifests canny choice of numbers, warbling his pops in tip-top manner to self–guitar accompaniment. The solo strings comes through effectively on the breaks and interludes…. Essentially a seasoned variety trouper, Lucas should benefit handily from a couple of months of ether builder-upper." The June 1934 issue of *Radio Stars* declared, "Hats off to Nick Lucas. He is the only man in history who, knowing darn well he is a crooner, is willing to wear the label." *Radio Dial* (December 1934) gave some personal observations about Nick, saying he was 5'7½", weighed 150 pounds, had gray eyes and dark brown hair, liked spaghetti and ravioli, and drove a Maybach Zeppelin automobile. In the story "Pet Peeves," the *Brooklyn*

1934 publicity picture of Nick Lucas.

Times Union (May 12, 1934) reported, "Nick Lucas would rather not entertain at private parties or talk about his work." In August 1934, Nick did several remote broadcasts of his radio show from the Dante Lodge on Long Island. At the same time, *Radio Guide* (August 18, 1934) reported that Nick "has an odd method which he employs for several hours each day. Nick is a great mandolin [sic] player, and in order to keep his fingers as supple as possible he squeezes a rubber ball, first in one hand and then in the other."

About a month after Nick started his CBS radio show, an amusing incident occurred:

> Nick Lucas ... was accosted by a somewhat tipsy gentleman as he was entering the Columbia building the other evening for his broadcast, carrying four banjos under his arms. The stranger's eyes opened banjo-like when he saw the four instruments. He averred that he had always wanted a banjo and would give 50 cents for one. Nick refused to sell, but his would-be customer was persistent. He grabbed the singer by the shoulder. With the burden of four banjos, Nick was at a disadvantage. Seconds passed quickly, and it was close to air time. The passerby seized an instrument and matters began to look bad for the crooning troubadour. Just then a musician with a big bass violin walked out of the building. Nick's assailant spied the colossal fiddle, and made for it, probably on the theory of more instrument for his money. Lucas dashed into the elevator, shot up to the twenty-second floor, and made the broadcast—in the nick of time.

Regarding broadcasting styles, the *Brooklyn Times Union* (June 7, 1934) stated, "Rosa Ponselle and Nick Lucas represent two extremes in microphone positions. While the 'crooning troubadour' finds it advantageous to 'almost bite the microphone,' as he phrases it, the opera star stands nearly six feet away from it when broadcasting." Earlier in the "Outside Listening In" column in the *Brooklyn Times Union* (May 16, 1934), Nick was quoted as saying, "I don't see why some of those soft-voiced radio singers object to being called 'crooners.' By any other name, they'd still be that. I've been a 'crooner' for years, ever since I started recording before radio came into its own, and I'd put up a pretty stiff fight if anyone tried to take that label from me."

While doing the CBS radio show, Nick continued making personal appearances as noted by his participation in the May 29, 1934, Philadelphia Municipal Works fund benefit for locally unemployed musicians. Also on the program were George Raft, Leopold Stokowski, Bill Robinson and bandleader Jimmy Joyce. In June 1934, he headlined at the Valencia Theatre in

Nick Lucas on his CBS radio series, heard in 1934 and 1935.

Brooklyn with Jacques Renard and His Orchestra. He also made an appearance at the International Spectacular in Bakersfield, California, in the fall of 1934. *The Bakersfield Californian* (September 19, 1934) opined that Nick "is as big as ever in the entertainment world.... Judging by current successes he has found a new audience.... Year in and year out, Nick Lucas remains a headline attraction and fairgoers can have a terrific time wandering down memory lane with him and his guitar...." In November 1934, Nick headlined the Capitol Theatre (replacing ailing Donald Novis) and then the State Theatre, both in New York City. He closed out the year at the Buffalo Theatre in Buffalo, New York.

When he made a return appearance at the Astor Theatre in Reading, Pennsylvania, the *Reading Times* (January 28, 1935) stated, "The large crowds that visited the Astor Theatre Saturday extended an enthusiastic welcome to Nick Lucas... [He] offers a pleasing array of songs that have placed him in a class with the foremost songsters of today." In April, Nick was in Minnesota, first appearing at the State Theatre in Minneapolis, followed by a run at the Paramount Theatre in St. Paul. Regarding the latter, *Variety* (April 24, 1935), said, "Nick Lucas in next-to-shut. In good voice, but somehow didn't wow 'em when caught." For his appearance at the Stanley Theatre in Pittsburgh, along with Barney Rapp and his Orchestra, *Variety* (May 1, 1935) noted, "Starts slowly but doesn't take him long to warm up and a stooge in the balcony, who keeps yelling 'Side by Side,' gets him some laughs." In the spring of 1935, Nick headlined the *Havana Casino Revue* at the Hershey, Pennsylvania, Community Theatre. The *Harrisburg* (Pennsylvania) *Telegram* (May 10, 1935) reported, "Nick Lucas scored his usual success with the capacity audience, left them yelling for more. Good old 'Tiptoe Through the Tulips' and other favorites

A 1933 Nick Lucas Special, manufactured by the Gibson Guitar Company.

clinched his claim to the title of head man in his line. How all of us would like to bear down on a guitar as he does too." Of this performance, the *Harrisburg Evening News* said, "Nick Lucas, a real troubadour, with a bubbling personality, presents seven songs with his own inimitable syncopation and how the faithful went for his 'Tiptoe Through the Tulips.' He was generous indeed with all the stage presence of the trooper that he is." Next came a stand at Shea's Hippodrome in Toronto, Canada, for the rest of May. Early in July, he starred at the Baltimore Century Theatre and the next month he was at Dorney's in Stroudsburg, Pennsylvania, returning there for a second run in September. Regarding his stand at the Century Theatre in Baltimore, *Variety* reported on July 3, 1935, "Nick Lucas ... walking on to swell greeting and tightening hold on 'em with each succeeding clef. Chiefly pops delivered, with a novelty piece sung for variety. Is using a plant who shouts down several times from balcony early in act, with Lucas supplying the denouement to business and getting a couple of cackles through it. Over punchily." Also in July, he was at the Earle Theatre in Philadelphia on the bill with the film *College Scandal*. The July 17, 1935, *Variety* reported, "Nick Lucas helped it to be $14,000, about two grand above recent average."

On August 13, 1935, Nick was the guest headliner at Hoffman Night at the Monmouth Country Club in New Jersey at a celebration in honor of Governor Harold G. Hoffman. Nick appeared at the behest of his friend, State Senator Frank Durand. The Red Branch, New Jersey, *Daily Standard* (August 22, 1935) reported, "The finale was carried out by the well-known star of stage and radio, Nick Lucas, whose melodious voice and original manner of playing the guitar has gained him an enviable reputation throughout the nation. He sang popular selections and was obliged to give an encore during which he sang those songs requested by the audience." In October it was reported that Nick was asked to take charge of the Café Continental, formerly the Carlton, in his hometown of Newark.

In the July 1935 issue of the British monthly magazine *B.M.G.* (Banjo, Mandolin, Guitar), Geoff Sisley presented an in-depth look at Nick's guitar-playing and singing in the article "A Gallery of Guitarists: Nick Lucas." He wrote, "It would appear that [Lucas] can safely claim to be the first player to use the guitar in a dance band. But vocalist-guitarist is his forte, and his radio and recording work consists of the singing of popular tunes to his own guitar accompaniment, with an occasional guitar solo chorus."

The writer went on to assess Nick's guitar work:

> Let us first examine his style, or styles, of guitar accompaniment. As an example I am taking the Rex No. 8219a "Love Thy Neighbor." Now, many musicians seem to think that, because the accompaniment Nick Lucas mostly uses consists of the bass note and chord style, he is not a rhythmic player. The first hearing of this disc, however, will prove otherwise, for, if one listens carefully, it soon becomes apparent that an enormous amount of rhythm is really there. Note how the chords on the off-beats are clean-cut and staccato. Incidentally, in some of his accompaniments, Nick Lucas makes great use of six-note positions, the very fact of the strings being stopped, enabling him to "damp" the chords after playing them. It is very interesting to endeavor to analyze one of the Lucas accompaniments, such as that to the verse of "Let Me Live and Love You Just for Tonight." Some of the left hand positions used are quite unique. Later in this record is a solo chorus in Lucas' own neat style. Note the quaint breaks played between the phrases, particularly the one occurring about half way through the chorus and terminating with two grace notes. This, so far as I can gather, is played in the key of C, commencing on G (fifth string), and finishing with the open first string, an E-flat (played on the second string) being the grace note. Another typical Lucas solo guitar chorus is to be found

on Brunswick 2931b entitled "Brown Eyes, Why Are You Blue?" The general technique displayed by Nick Lucas in this number is truly remarkable: runs, full chord effects, glissandos, etc., apparently presenting no difficulty whatsoever. I earnestly request our leading recording companies to consider to the re-issue of some of the Lucas discs, or, better still, approach Nick with a view to making more. Nick is also a master of the tenths. This is very apparent in "How About Me" (Brunswick No. 3194b). Tenths occur in the introduction and many of the later passages in this record, which is also noteworthy for the really sweet tone that pervades throughout. Such tone is one of Lucas' strong points. Seldom, if ever does the tone sound forced. This is a sure sign of real musicianship.... Although most of the Lucas discs are in four-four time, we find one in waltz time. This record is entitled "Underneath the Stars with You" (Brunswick No. 3518b). In the introduction Nick Lucas hums the melody, with his usual self-accompaniment on the guitar. This effect is most attractive and is again produced later in the record. Ascending sevenths are used occasionally with great effect in the accompaniment in various parts of the record. This is rather unique, for while one often encounters descending sevenths in popular songs, rarely are they met with in ascending order.

Regarding Nick's singing style, the author noted,

I am told that Nick Lucas claims to be the original "crooner," and, if the number of years he has been recording are any criterion, I do not doubt this for one moment. But while the labels on most of his records describe him as the "Crooning Troubadour," I consider that his vocal efforts are something more than what is considered crooning today, especially when I hear his crescendos on some of the sustained notes in "A Thousand Goodnights." ...These notes suggest a power and volume in his voice that is not the work of the sound engineer in the recording studio. I am still further convinced of his possessing a really powerful voice when I recollect his singing, unaided by a microphone, on the occasion of his last visit to England. I sincerely hope that we will again hear him in this country on the near future.

In the mid–1930s, Leo Fitzgerald suggested to Lucas that he should form a band as this type of entertainment was becoming popular and he thought Nick would make a successful bandleader, especially with his early experience as a sideman. Following the end of his CBS radio show in the spring of 1934, Nick set about putting together a band. Nick Lucas and His Troubadours, as the unit was called, toured for the next year and a half. The group played dates mostly in the Eastern states and was financially successful, mainly because of Nick's name. But he did not like the experience of fronting a band. He considered the affair a "big headache." "Musicians are prima donnas, every two weeks they want a raise," he recalled. "Every time they had to go out of town they reneged. They would complain they had to pay two rents because they had to leave their families behind and they always needed excess dollars." Nick said that "it was not in the cards" for him to lead a band and that the musicians ended up getting the money from the venture. Also, there was rivalry with several other bands, especially the Dorsey Brothers. There was also the expense of hiring a bus for the band's tours and employing a special driver. "I just didn't like it, there was too much responsibility," he recalled. "Leo Fitzgerald thought I would strike it big with the band, but he was wrong," Nick stated. Advertising for the unit said it had 14 artists and came directly from New York City's Hollywood Café. During that time, Nick and his band were responsible for the success of several popular songs, including "Robins and Roses," "One Rainy Afternoon" and "Secret Rendezvous." By the summer of 1936, the unit was advertised as Nick Lucas and His Orchestra. Murray Rosenberg in his "Radio Rays" column in *The Brooklyn Citizen* (October 12, 1935) stated, "Nick Lucas will play one-night stands at the head of his own program to break it in and then will play a fortnight in Pittsburgh to build up the band for a network series." The band made an appearance at the Detroit Federation of Musicians Thanksgiving Ball on November 28, 1935. The 13-piece unit was one of 26 orchestras playing at the event, broadcast via station WJBK in Detroit.

Nick had resumed recording with Brunswick at the end of 1932, making the third recordings of his self-penned guitar solos "Picking the Guitar" and "Teasin' the Frets." On December 21, 1932, he waxed a quartet of tunes ("I'm Sure of Everything But You," "More Beautiful Than Ever," "Till Tomorrow" and "I Called to Say Goodnight") for Brunswick and then did four more ("Love Thy Neighbor," "A Thousand Goodnights," "Carry Me Back to the Lone Prairie" and "Goin' Home") in the spring of 1934 with Victor Young and His Orchestra. These were released on the American Recording Company's (ARC) budget labels. On August 3, 1934, Nick recorded the songs "Moon Glow" and "For All We Know" with Victor Young and again they were placed on ARC's low-price labels. This session marked the end of Nick's decade-long association with Brunswick.

Although Nick did not record with his band, he did make a short subject with the unit, *Nick Lucas and His Troubadours*, released by Warner Bros. in 1936. In it, he and the band did several songs, including another rendition of "Tiptoe Through the Tulips." Also for Warners he appeared solo in a clown costume singing "Broken Hearted Troubadour" in the one-reel musical short *Vitaphone Headliners*; this scene was also included in Warner Bros.' 1947 short *Big Time Revue*.

Nick and his band also did a CBS radio series in 1936, *Nick Lucas and His Orchestra*. The 15-minute program originated from New York City's WABC and also featured vocalist Mimi Rollins.

Nick Lucas and His Troubadours opened the year 1936 playing the Mosque Theatre-Ballroom in Newark, followed by a stand at Fay's Theatre in Philadelphia. Next the aggregation began a stand at the Hollywood Restaurant in Gotham. It was there that Nick and his band appeared in a new edition of *Hollywood Revels* that summer. On March 29, he was master of ceremonies at the second annual dinner dance and entertainment of the Paul Doyle Association in Brooklyn, to benefit boxers. Regarding the band's stay at the Hollywood Restaurant, *Billboard* (May 23, 1936) wrote,

> The Lucas band is a pleasant surprise. Lucas is proving he can be a first-rate bandleader as well as a star singer. He has organized a strong combo of thirteen men which avoids the extremes of swing styles and superdignity [sic]. Band instead dishes out sweet and lively rhythms—but can get hot when the customers seem to like it that way. Lucas himself leads, crooning an occasional number (including his famous "Tiptoe Through the Tulips") and strumming an electric guitar. Vic Merlin leads the boys during the show in which Lucas is spotted as a solo vocalist. Lucas did "When April Comes Again," socking that number over in his usual masterly style.

After several months at the Hollywood Restaurant, the band went on tour. *Billboard* (August 8, 1936) noted that it was "playing Eastern Ohio park spots to swell business. At Chippewa, Lake Park, near Medina, Ohio, July 25 [the] band played to 3,300 paid admissions to the biggest week's gross for the last five years. Dixie Lee is the songstress and Nick croons several recent hits and revivals. Lucas's band is heading westward." Nick turned down an Australian tour to remain with the Troubadours. In August, Nick appeared with his orchestra at the Orpheum Theatre in Madison, Wisconsin. That city's *Capitol Times* (August 14, 1936) reported, "Nick sang 'Tiptoe Through the Tulips' and a group of other melodious songs ... and won a good hand for his work.... Melody was the keynote of the tunes furnished by the Lucas orchestra. As a happy relief, the orchestra omitted all 'swing' tunes from the program." On September 24, 1936, the unit performed at Joplin, Missouri's, Memorial Hall and a month later the Showmen's League Benefit in Cleveland. When Nick and his group headlined *Broadway Hit Parade* at the Hershey, Pennsylvania, Community Theatre, the *Harrisburg* (Pennsylvania) *Telegraph* (November 20, 1936) stated, "Nick Lucas in full voice and expert on the guitar led a great array of stage talent as well as his orchestra. Nick is generous with selections." In December, the unit played the RKO Theatre in Troy, New York.

By the beginning of 1937, the band experience was beginning to wear thin as noted by *Billboard* (January 8, 1937) when the aggregation appeared at Fay's Theatre in Philadelphia:

> Nick Lucas, who was always a single sock around these parts, and still is, makes a serious mistake in trying to pass off as a bandleader.... Lucas has a dozen tooters behind him who benefit the house band only.... With a guitar in hand Lucas is much at home. But waving a wand in mechanical one-two-three-four fashion, and ill at ease while going through his exercises, only goes to prove that Lucas didn't know when he was well off. Taking the spot on his own, Lucas sells his songs worth a million. Rest should be passed off as an unfortunate experience.

As noted, Nick Lucs kept physically fit by golfing. The July 1936 issue of *Radio Mirror* reported that he shot in the 80s, along with Paul Whiteman, George Olsen, Ben Bernie, Little Jack Little and Abe Lyman. He and bandleader Freddie Rich, who conducted the orchestras for Nick's NBC and CBS radio shows, were often golf partners. Announcer Andre Baruch was another regular partner. *Radio Stars* (March 1938) carried a story about how Baruch almost lost his prized mustache as the result of a bet with Nick over a golf game.

The *Brooklyn* (New York) *Times Union* (September 22, 1934) reported, "Nick Lucas showed the other CBS artists that he can handle a golf club as well as a guitar when he walked off with first honors in the network golf tournament."

Following the disbanding of his orchestra in 1937, Nick did a series of transcription records that were sold directly to radio stations. He waxed them for the C.P. MacGregor Transcription Company in Hollywood and he was paid per song. The recordings made up weekday 15-minute radio programs syndicated throughout the country. Nick also continued making guest appearances on various network radio programs and in February 1937, he became the regular vocalist on CBS's *Watch the Fun Go By* starring Al Pearce. *Billboard* (February 27, 1937) reported, "Nick Lucas's tenor crooning, to become a steady fixture on the program, is all right." Nick remained with the program into early 1939 but by this time it was on NBC and was called *Al Pearce and His Gang*.

Regarding his appearing on Pearce's program, Mary O'Neil wrote in the Albany, New York, *Knickerbocker News* (August 7, 1937), "What keeps Nick Lucas from being a big name in radio? He has one of the smoothest voices ever recorded.... I caught him on that Tuesday Al Pearce show ... and a very likable manner helps him contribute a sparkling bit to an hour that is packed to the brim with refreshing uproarious humor and excellent music. *Watch the Fun Go By* is my choice as one of the first five hits of the air...." *Radio Daily* (February 16, 1937) opined, "Nick Lucas ... adds decided value to the nice platter of variety served by Al Pearce on Ford's CBS program Tuesday nights. Pearce has built up a very entertaining show in general, with an array of lively talent, good tempo and neatly weaved-in commercial spot comments."

Nick not only appeared with Al Pearce and his troupe on radio but he also toured with them in the latter part of 1937. An amusing incident was recounted by *The Oklahoma News* (September 14, 1937) when the unit played a date in Oklahoma City. At the hotel where he was staying, Nick was introduced to a young employee, Dorothy Kengle, who asked him to sing her favorite song, "My Melancholy Baby." He told her, "'Melancholy Baby' should be sung with the lights lowered and perhaps a moon in the background." The article continued, "As a concession, however, the troubadour turned on the personality and gave the, by this time sizeable, audience of bellhops, clerks, traveling salesman and hotel patrons 'Tiptoe Through the Tulips.' Miss Kengle thanked Mr. Lucas prettily…." A guest later stated that after that, "he could hear under Dorothy's breath the lilting air of 'Tiptoe Through the Tulips,' her new favorite." The article also noted, "Last night at the Shrine Auditorium Mr. Lucas entertained an audience of more than two thousand…." When Nick appeared with the Pearce unit before 4000 Ford car dealers at Constitution Hall in Washington, D.C., on September 27, 1937, that city's *Evening Star* (October 3, 1937) declared it "splendid entertainment."

Nick continued to appear in what was left of vaudeville, mostly playing between features at movie houses. He recalled that it was rough work as he often performed three or four shows a day at theaters. In 1939 when the movie *Jesse James* was shown at the Roxy Theatre in New York City. he did six shows a day with the movie. *Variety* (January 18, 1939) noted, "Lucas scores nicely with his voice and guitar, opens with a hit from a recent picture, following with a pop and coming into the stretch with 'Great American Home,' a novelty number." He also did several benefit shows, such as Scranton's annual one on February 25, 1937, and he was master of ceremonies for a show to benefit crippled children on April 24, 1937, in Hartford, Connecticut. That month Nick was away from performing briefly doing jury duty in Newark but was soon back playing in theaters. When he headlined L.A.'s Pantages Theatre, *Variety* (August 25, 1937) reported that the venue's profitable week was "helped by Nick Lucas on stage." The week prior he was at the same city's Orpheum Theatre and the trade paper on August 18 declared, "With Nick Lucas, oldtime Orph. circuit fav. headlining the vaude show, house looks headed for very good $7,800." On November 19, 1937, he opened at the Oriental Theatre in Chicago and the next week he headlined the Fox Theatre in Detroit where *Billboard* (November 27, 1937) opined, "Nick Lucas closed and scored with several troubadour styled songs. Makes a clean-cut appearance and delivers with far more appeal than many of his competitors. Did 'You Can't Stop Me from Dreaming,' 'Harbor Lights,' 'That Great American Home' and an audience request time." When Nick was at the Fox Theatre in Detroit, *Variety* (December 1, 1937) stated, "Nick Lucas' warbling gets sock reception…." Next he appeared at the RKO Theatre in Boston where he was supported by comic newcomer Red Skelton. When he closed out the year at the Roxy Theatre in New York City, the same trade journal on December 29 declared, "[T]he vet of years of 'troubadour' trouping has them nibbling out of his palm for the first guitar plunk and lift of a note. He might sing a bit more leisurely, since he impresses as helter-skeltering through his four pieces. For a windup, he has precisely the doctor's prescription for the audience—'Bei Mir Bist du Schoen,' picked up the mob so completely at show caught, that the whole house was joining in the choruses."

In May 1937, Nick found himself in federal court in Pittsburgh as the defendant in a lawsuit filed in 1933 by songwriters Frank Stasio and Ralph Anthony, who claimed that Lucas promised to publish their song "When Your Road Leads My Way" in return for permission to use it on radio. Their suit stated he used the song but never published it.

The agreement called for a fifty-fifty royalty split between Lucas and the two composers. *Variety* (May 12, 1937) reported, "Lucas said he tried to interest a flock of publishers in the tune, but without avail." He said he plugged the song in 1931 and 1933 "but that didn't awaken sufficient interest for any publisher to chance it." In its May 18 issue, *Radio Daily* reported, "Nick Lucas ... recently won a Federal court battle over a song written by two Pennsylvania youngsters without having to put up a defense. He celebrated his victory by rendering, without benefit of guitar, 'Tiptoe Through the Tulips,' in a marble corridor of the courthouse at the request of six women jurors who sat on the case." The same publication stated that he left the cast of the Al Pearce show on September 27, 1937, but returned on January 11, 1938.

Nick headlined the Gala New Year's Eve Celebration at Burlew's Restaurant in Keyport, New Jersey, and then was at Shea's Buffalo Theatre in Buffalo starring in the stage show *Hits of 1937* with *Variety* (January 12, 1938) noting, "Nick Lucas, in person, eight nights, extra midnight show, skyrocketed takings to swell $22,700." On the same date, the trade paper reported that he was going to appear at Ciro's Club in London, but the engagement never happened. *Variety* followed him to the Fox Theatre in Kansas City, Missouri, where it detailed on January 19, 1938, "Smooth Nick Lucas ... is a nice and badly needed change of pace. He clicks with his guitar and romantic tunes, 'Rosalie' being particularly effective. He gets added support of the line for curtain." A week later he was at the Strand Theatre in Brooklyn; *Variety* (January 26, 1938) reported: "Nick Lucas adds his very familiar informal singing and stringing. 'Bei Mir Bist du Schoen' and 'Ah, Marie,' highlight as auditors join in choruses." Regarding the same engagement, Herbert Cohen in the *Brooklyn Daily Eagle* (January 24, 1938) wrote, "Nick Lucas headlined this week's stage show and headed it well, with a program of romantic and novelty songs done in the unique Lucas manner." *The Brooklyn Citizen* (January 22, 1938), stated,

> In perfect form and fine voice, laden with a large repertoire of new popular song numbers and with a guitar under his arm, [Lucas] appears on the local theatrical horizon this weekend.... With each successive appearance Lucas seems to bring his legion of admirers closer to him than ever before if that is possible. He is distinctly individual and different. The mellow tones of his guitar and his soothing melodious voice endear him to his audiences like few others. Lucas has the happy facility of making one feel that he is singing directly to you and you alone.

When Lucas appeared in Manitoba, Canada, the *Winnipeg Tribune* (March 1, 1938) noted, "Nick Lucas ... was called back time and time again last night at the Playhouse as he headlined a good vaudeville show that is playing all week. With a splendid repertoire of popular songs, he delivers them in a manner that is altogether pleasing and a packed house greeted in the best Winnipeg manner." On March 23, Nick was at the second annual Kentucky Night at the Cuvier Press Club, along with tenor John Steel, magician Paul Rosini and Texas Tommy and his Wonder Horse "Baby Doll." Also in attendance was Kentucky Governor A.B. "Happy" Chandler. Sometime before, Nick had been made a Kentucky Colonel by Chandler. In April, he appeared for two weeks at the Miami Club in Milwaukee.

Billboard (April 27, 1938) noted, "Nick Lucas and Phil Harris and band headed the vaude(ville) bill at the Lyric, Indianapolis, two weeks ago and broke Eddy Duchin's former top record for that house." The article announced that Nick would then appear in theaters in Chicago, Dayton and Kansas City. Regarding another Indianapolis playdate,

The Indianapolis Star (August 6, 1938) reported, "Mr. Lucas has lost not a sliver of the large chuck of popularity he inspires in Indianapolis audiences. His voice and his guitar aroused so many encores yesterday that he might well have called for a small shuttle train to carry him from wings to microphone and back again. He 'obliged' with many old and new favorites...." When he appeared at the Fox Theatre in St. Louis, the Union, Missouri's *Franklin County Tribune* (May 6, 1938) called the 60-minute variety revue "fast-moving." In June 1938, Nick was back at the Roxy Theatre in Gotham with *Variety* (June 27, 1938) reporting, "Vaude's vet troubadour Nick Lucas, in the closer. Delivers pop song requests, plus his own familiar repertoire, and is rung in for the only large scale production number of the show." Also appearing with Nick in the "Fanchon and Marco Revue" was Paul Ash and His Orchestra. After a brief holiday in Atlantic City, and becoming godfather to heavyweight boxer Tony Galento's son in a ceremony in Orange, New Jersey, Nick headlined Atlantic City's Dollar Pier. In July, Nick was at Chicago's Bon Air Club and was offered a second week but had to turn it down to perform a two-week stand at that city's Chez Paree. On August 20, he made a one-night appearance at the Orpheum Theatre in Omaha, followed by another week at the Chez Paree there. In September, he was at the RKO Colonial Theatre in Dayton, Ohio. The same month, he also headlined the State Theatre in Chicago, with *Variety* (September 7, 1938) reporting, "Closing is Nick Lucas, who has added a couple of new songs but who basically continues with his standard warbling, including the comedy plant who keeps requesting 'Side by Side.' Old stuff but still solid." Of the same stand, *Billboard* (September 2, 1938) wrote, "Show doesn't reach the clicking stage until the closing spot when reliable Nick Lucas and his guitar furnish fifteen minutes of genuine entertainment; offers a generous number of old and new tunes, buttressed with a pleasing voice, easygoing mannerisms and a disarming delivery. Winds up with an old favorite, the house girls augmenting the scene for an eye-filling background."

In the fall of 1938, Nick, Connee Boswell, Joe Cook and Jimmie Greer and His Orchestra appeared in the musical revue *Jubilesta* in the Midwest. When the show ran for nine days in Kansas City, Missouri, it drew a two-day opening crowd of 11,000 and a gross in excess of $100,000. *Variety* (September 21, 1938) stated that he "registered strongly although his appearance midway in the show forced him to decline strong encore calls." After stands at the Miami Club in Milwaukee and the Ohio Villa in Cleveland, Nick appeared at Brooklyn's Strand Theatre. *Variety* (December 28, 1938) noted, "Nick Lucas, back again after about a year, is kept down. Usual requests dropped while troubadour with guitar gives off with his own three selections, one a new novelty. Also asked to judge for a second jitterbug contest."

Also in 1938, Nick began to appear in night clubs, a venue that would provide him with lucrative income for the next three decades. At the time he went into this field, night clubs were beginning to come out of an era where they were considered low-grade entertainment. While appearing at the Beverly Hills Club in Cincinnati in March 1938, Nick told newspaper interviewer Norine Freeman, "Night clubs used to be bad because the audiences were inattentive, but that is not true here. Of course, I have to accustom myself to having my audience where I can see it. On the stage the spotlight is in your eyes, prevents your seeing anyone in front of you. But I am enjoying it and I think I'll do more night club work." He later recalled that he did not like the majority of the night clubs he played in that period because "people smoked and the public address system never worked well and they did not pay as well as vaudeville." Still, at the time, work in show business was hard to get due to the still lingering Depression and he followed the night club circuit on and off for three decades.

While appearing in Cincinnati in 1938, Nick told a newspaper interviewer what he did *not* like about the life of the show person. According to the writer:

> Every time [Nick] appears in public, the crowd flocks around him and begs him to sing for them. Even if he is just another paying customer like themselves, the public insists that Lucas become a part of the show. "It is the only thing about show business that I don't like," he says ruefully. "Your time is not your own. You belong to the public. You can't go out and have a big night of it once in a while even if you want to, because it will not only ruin your singing but possibly your reputation and you probably won't have a good time anyway because of the public." Lucas says he is looking forward to the day when he will have retired, although he says that is still a long way off. Then, he says, he will be able to tell the public to ask somebody else to sing and leave him alone when he wants to have a good time. Although singing in night clubs is a new experience for Lucas, he thinks that the night club business is the only show business now. That does not mean, he said, that vaudeville is out. Far from it. But the night clubs are carrying on the tradition and after all, he believes that the acts in night clubs and vaudeville are interchangeable. Even so, while he was being interviewed, he received a telephone call from someone who had seen him then (when he first appeared in Cincinnati in the 1920s) and had remembered him and wanted to visit him. "See," he said. "That's just the way it is all the time."

Nick's income for 1938 was $108,000 with income tax liabilities of $8800.

During this time, Nick reported that he received as many fans letters from men and children as from women. He was especially proud of photographs and letters sent to him by children. His daughter Emily was enrolled in Georgian Court College in Lakewood, New Jersey, and for a time studied art and singing. She spent the summer of 1938 in stock school before graduating in 1940. After graduation, Emily married Leonard Bissell, who she had met in college. Following the wedding, Nick and Catherine decided to sell their Newark home and move to the West Coast where they felt he could better advance his career.

Following an appearance at the Top Hat in Utica, New Jersey, Nick opened 1939 at Loew's Theatre in Montreal, Canada, followed by engagements at the Schubert Theatre in Newark and the Roxy Theatre in New York City. In the Newark stand, he appeared with Ann Sothern and her bandleader husband Roger Pryor. *Variety* reported on February 15, 1939, of his appearance at the Roxy Theatre in Atlanta, Georgia: "Troubadour warbles 'Jeepers Creepers' and 'Umbrella Man,' strumming his own guitar accompaniment. Also sings 'Tiptoe Through the Tulips' and 'Mexicali Rose,' encoring with 'Great American Home,' which he introduced on Al Pearce's radio show. Lucas had difficulty getting off, finally bringing on Roxyettes for closing number...." On February 22, 1939, Nick appeared at the NVA Annual Benefit Show in New York City along with Sophie Tucker, Rudy Vallee, Vincent Lopez, Ben Bernie, Theda Bara, Betty Hutton, Henny Youngman and Beatrice Kay. Next he was at the Lyric Theatre in Indianapolis; according to *Variety* (March 15, 1939), "[Lucas] sang 'Jeepers Creepers,' 'Penny Serenade,' 'This Can't Be Love' and medley of tunes suggested by audience, closing with special parody of 'Side by Side.' Voice, as always, very much okay, as is twanging guitar. Nicely received." At the end of March, he appeared for one week at Shea's Theatre in Toronto.

In the spring of 1939, Nick headlined *The Platinum Blonde Revue* at the Mishler Theatre in Altoona, Pennsylvania. *The Altoona Tribune* (April 12, 1939) reported, "Lucas, who strums a mean guitar in accompaniment to his light airy voice, renders several modern songs and includes some of the earlier hits from his screen and radio days. An ingratiating performer he wins the approval of his audience in short order… [He] puts over his songs smoothly and simply, the kind of fellow you like to hear again and again." He continued to tour with the show in various East Coast cities and at the end of May he did a sold-out stand at Shea's Hippodrome in Toronto.

During this time, Nick entered into a new realm of show business: television. He began appearing on experimental programs, debuting May 31, 1939, on New York City's station W2XBS, an NBC affiliate. Also on the show was Judy Canova with her siblings Annie and Zeke. Nick told the *Sydney* (Australia) *Morning Herald* (August 8, 1939), "I nearly passed out when I saw my yellow green face and blue lips in the looking glass before I was televised for the first time in New York City. They then covered my guitar with putty to take the shine off of it to televise. I wore the lightest of blue suits. In other words I was covered in panchromatic color. But the experience was interesting. Television is improving all the time in New York."

In the late 1930s, Nick made a temporary home in California while scouting around for a permanent West Coast house for himself and his wife. He kept active by working in night clubs and in the remnants of vaudeville. He also appeared in a Columbia two-reeler, *Yankee Doodle Home,* singing "The Great American Home." In the summer of 1939, he took part in a convention touting string instruments in Niagara Falls. By this time, Nick's manager Leo Fitzgerald had retired and Nick had signed with the Fanchon and Marco agency located in New York City's Rockefeller Plaza. In 1939, booking agent Frank Neill offered him a lucrative contract for a two-year world tour to commence with an engagement in Australia, where vaudeville was still popular. He signed to appear on the Tivoli Theatre circuit there with stands in Melbourne, Sydney and Brisbane. He was very popular Down Under due to his phonograph records and the fact that *The Gold Diggers of Broadway* was still being screened there. According to the *Sydney Morning Herald* (June 7, 1939), the Australian Broadcasting Commission had secured exclusive recording rights "to overseas artists soon to appear in Australia," including Lucas, the Mills Brothers and George Robey. The newspaper stated, "Nick Lucas will broadcast twice weekly during the time he remains in Australia."

With his impending two-year tour, Nick and Catherine decided to delay the sale of their Newark home. On June 7, 1939, Nick and his manager Tony Paul left Los Angeles by passenger ship, the *Maraposa* (some sources claim the *Monterey*), for the three-week journey to Australia. Nick's sea legs had not improved since his return voyage from London in 1927 and he was seasick most of the time. When the ship docked at Pago Pago in the American Samoas for about eight hours to take on passengers and supplies, a group of about a dozen natives were waiting at the dock to greet Nick, whose name they had seen on the vessel's manifest. These natives all had Nick Lucas guitars, his instruction books and picks. After giving him a big welcome, the group took Nick to a nearby saloon that was crowded with many of his fans and they asked him to sing and play for them. Since the islanders were so adamant, he serenaded them until it was time for his boat to leave. In the Fiji Islands, the same thing happened: Again he was asked to entertain an enthusiastic crowd. Nick said the islands were among "the most beautiful places I have ever been and if I had had my way I would have stayed there"—but he had the commitment in Australia. Nick had no idea he had such a fan following in that part of the world.

After docking in Australia at Melbourne on July 7, 1939, Nick took a couple of days to "get rid of my sea legs" and then opened at the Tivoli Theatre, headlining a ten-act vaudeville program that also included Hoosier humorist Herb Shriner, dancer Sunnie O'Dea and character comedian Scott Sanders. Nick was very successful in this presentation in which he did a half-hour act and then took part in the finale with the rest of the cast. *The* (Melbourne) *Argus* wrote, "Nick Lucas … walks away with the proceedings.… Lucas is a very capable 'tunesmith.' Possessor of a smooth, suave voice, that is constantly fading into the languorous pianissimi of lovelorn ballads, Nick, with his flashing smile and tuneful playing on the guitar, creates a longing, and still more longing for his songs. He is a bright and melodious contribution." On September 2, 1939, Adelaide's *The Mail* reported,

> Just as Larry Adler is credited with the return to popularity of the mouth organ, so to Nick Lucas goes much of the credit for the existing vogue of the guitar. This instrument had fallen into neglect when Nick adopted it as the ideal accompaniment to crooning. He has launched scores of melodies that have been successes, and is always on the lookout for more. He has brought out some new numbers to Australia, and is introducing them, both on stage and on the air. One which he considers will catch on here is "The Man with the Mandolin." He is keen to hear what Australian composers can do, and hopes to find material while he is here to take back to America with him.

When in Australia, Nick had many invitations to "go to stations," the Aussie expression for a weekend in the country. He "had a wonderful time" during his Melbourne stay but then Great Britain declared war on Germany and Japan; when Australia followed suit, things changed very quickly in the country. Nick found it difficult to call his wife in the United States and during one conversation his mother began speaking to him in Italian and they were immediately cut off. His mail was also censored and in order to send money out of the country to his agent or pay insurance premiums, both the agent and the insurance company would have to write to him saying the money was due them since that was the only way he could get money out of the country. "I was trapped there," he recalled.

While appearing in vaudeville in Melbourne, Nick also starred in a radio show on the 3AW Broadcasting Station weekdays at 6 a.m. His theme song for the show was "Good Morning," which he recorded with a trio for the Regal Zonophone label that billed him as "Nick Lucas—The Singing Guitarist." He waxed six sides for the label in November 1939, including "Over the Rainbow." On Nick's 42nd birthday, *The Age* (August 22, 1939), a Melbourne newspaper, wrote, "Nick Lucas is very popular. He sings a song in perfect tempo, and with a lightness which accentuates with touches of pathos. 'Wishing,' 'Tiptoe Through the Tulips' (with the ballet in delightful background), 'My Blue Heaven,' 'Singin' in the Rain,' 'Side by Side' and 'Hello' are his repertoire, and his 'request' numbers are pleasantly unexpected." Regarding his radio show, *Variety* (September 20, 1939) reported, "[He] has no trouble in hitting popular favor, looks like a good bet for the A.B.C.… Lucas can be classed as a major air hit in Australia." On radio he gave numerous solo performances along with appearing opposite bandsmen Jim Davidson and Harry Bloom. He was also heard on the *After Dinner, All Star Variety* and *When Day Is Done* programs.

After nearly three months in Melbourne, Nick played an engagement in Sydney at the Tivoli Theatre. *The Sydney Morning Herald* (October 6, 1939) stated, "[Lucas'] main asset was a clear cut sense of rhythm, which gave a new and adventurous quality to well-known popular songs." Eight days later, the same source reported, "No less than six and seven additional songs are called for by the crowds at the Tivoli from Nick Lucas." On October 21, the newspaper wrote,

In the United States he does a lot of radio work. Nothing but popular songs figure in his repertoire, because he is not interested in anything else. He complains that, although songs come pouring forth in their hundreds every year, very few really good ones are written. As each new success comes along, hosts of imitators follow. Then the life of a popular number is only six weeks now, thanks to the "plugging" that goes on by means of radio and dance bands. The precise thing that makes one dance tune a success, another a flop? Mr. Lucas cannot tell. Songwriters like Irving Berlin, he says, have "a gift from above," and more precise examination is fruitless.

In the same edition, the newspaper stated, "Now in his third week of success, Nick Lucas continues to delight the Tivoli crowds with his singing and his expert manipulation of the guitar." The article also reported that Nick's stay in Sydney would end on November 15. While in Sydney, Nick headed the Tivoli cast that provided entertainment for the Remembrance Day Celebration by the Jewish Returned Sailors and Soldiers Association on November 11.

Nick then traveled to Brisbane where he opened at the Regent Theatre on November 24. While he was there, that city's *Courier-Mail* (November 24, 1939) stated, "He came to Australia, he said, because his records sold well in this country and he wanted to find out why. He discovered that it was because he sang songs that were plain and melodious and not too highly arranged. Intricately arranged music, which was popular in America, failed in Australia." The article also reported that Nick purchased golf clubs in Sydney "because he wanted something useful to take back from Australia." After four months in the country, he left Australia on the last boat to sail from Down Under to the U.S. until the end of the war. He remembered the voyage home as "three weeks of torture" since all the windows had to be painted black, everything was camouflaged and the boat traveled in a zigzag pattern for fear of being attacked by Japanese planes. The war unfortunately ended Nick's plans for a world tour.

Back home, Nick returned to the night club and vaudeville worlds, as well as the movies. When he headlined the Orpheum Theatre in Los Angeles early in 1940, the *Los Angeles Examiner* (January 4, 1940) reported,

> Not all the good things in entertainment are brand new. There is Nick Lucas, headline performer for over a decade, who retains today all his show-stopping popularity ... [T]he crooning guitarist was enthusiastically applauded and could have remained indefinitely playing request numbers. Lucas has not varied his style in the least since his first successes. He sings in an odd, high-pitched voice, with a half smile on his face. He never tells a joke or changes his position at the microphone as he plunks away. He enunciates excellently, and this may be the secret to his hold on audiences. You always understand what Lucas is singing about.

In April, Nick did a week at Baltimore's Hippodrome, followed by the Banker's Convention in Kansas City, Missouri. This was followed by two weeks a Kaliner's Little Rathskeller, marking his Philadelphia nitery debut. Next he headlined the Chez Paree in Denver, and then starred in the *Three Cheers* musical revue that proved so popular when it played in Emporia, Kansas, on May 8, 1940, for three shows instead of the originally scheduled two in order to meet ticket demand. On May 31, 1940, Nick starred at the formal opening of the Cosgriff Hotel in Craig, Colorado. The city's *Craig Empire Courier* (June 5, 1940) reported that he "delighted a capacity crowd of diners.... Many heard him for the first time but not a few recalled hearing him at some former occasion, on the Orpheum stage or merely recalled that they had recordings of his songs. He was liberal with his encores and seemed to enjoy entertaining for the Craig people." During the summer of 1940, Nick was held over for two weeks at New York City's Roxy Theatre. He headlined the Commercial Hotel in Elko, Nevada, in August. He was at the Golden Gate in San Francisco in September and then returned to Hollywood to make the Universal short subject *Congamania*. Nick was back at the Earle Theatre in Washington, D.C., where *Variety* (October 16, 1940), noted that youngsters in the audience "couldn't quite see what all the excitement was about, but agreed he was an O.K. warbler. Those who remembered when he sang 'Tiptoe Through the Tulips' gave him strong applause.... Lucas discards guitar and returns to do 'Apple Blossom and Chapel Bell' as line appears with flower horseshoes for formation stuff as perfume oozes out of the vents all over the house."

In the fall of 1940, Nick headlined *The All American Revue* in Oakland, California. It had a cast of twenty performers. Then he made a coast-to-coast tour. Reviewing his Oakland appearance, the *Oakland Tribune* (September 1, 1940) reported, "Nick Lucas again finds favor with Oakland audiences with his original song stylings and playing and singing both old and new favorites." In October, he was at Curley's Night Club in Minneapolis. From October 10 to 20, he was at the San Francisco Fair where he "wound up the season playing to the biggest audience of the year," according to *Billboard*. This was followed by an appearance at a Minneapolis-St. Paul night club. While there, he and bandleader Freddie Fisher visited the Mayflower Novelty Company in St. Paul. In November, Nick did two weeks at the Tic Toc Club in Montreal and then did another two-week stanza at Covington, Kentucky's Lookout House. Of this engagement,

Nick Lucas (second from right) pictured with Babe Zaharias (middle) and her wrestler husband George Zaharias (right) in the early 1940s. The men on the left are unidentified.

Billboard (November 19, 1940) wrote, "Nick Lucas, long a fave in these parts, rang the bell with his solid warbling and guitar work. Starting with 'Ferryboat Serenade,' he follows with 'Trade Winds,' 'Tiptoe Through the Tulips' and 'Maybe.' Called back, he offered 'Singin' in the Rain,' 'That Great American Home,' a patriotic ditty without the corn, and wound up with 'Thanks for the Memories.' Lucas worked his usual showmanly [*sic*] fashion despite the slim off-night crowd."

Nick opened 1941 appearing in the *New Year's Revue* at the Lyric Theatre in Indianapolis. *Variety* (January 1, 1941) groused, "Acts are all standard and okay, but the best name they could find for the show is Nick Lucas, who isn't strong enough with the present generation to keep the wicket turning out front." But the writer added, "This is no reflection on Lucas' ability as an entertainer, as he fills the next-to-closing spot neatly with a mixture of current pops and old favorites.... His turn won a hearty round of mitt slaps at show caught." At his Tower Theatre appearance in Kansas City, Missouri, *Variety* (January 22, 1941) stated, "Lucas is something of an old fave hereabouts and clicks well as ever with his pop-song verses and guitar self-accompaniment. The closing spot is his assignment and he rings in a goodly share of current choruses, including 'Down Argentine Way' and 'We Three' as well as digging deeper into the book for such tunes as 'My Melancholy Baby,' 'Painting the Clouds with Sunshine,' 'Tiptoe Through the Tulips' which by this time have achieved a nostalgic worth for his followers." The next month, Nick was at the Olympia in Miami; *Billboard* (February 15, 1941) reported, "Miami audiences apparently eat up the nostalgia stuff, and Lucas had little trouble establishing a hold. Though he is very reserved, his crooning is every bit as good as ever and his educated fingers pluck a very nice accompaniment." Next came the Colonial Theatre in Dayton, Ohio, where *Variety* (February 26, 1941) caught his act and wrote, "Returning here after several years' absence, Lucas and his guitar have no trouble wowing the customers with a string of time-tried tunes ... ending with 'That Great American Home' for a patriotic finale." This was followed by a stand at the Villa Madrid in Pittsburgh where he broke an eight-month record but had to turn down a second week due to laryngitis. In March, he headlined the Continental Nite Club in Portsmouth, Ohio, followed by three weeks at the Continental Club in Chesapeake, Ohio. April had Nick doing a nine-day stand at the Chez Ami in Buffalo, followed to a return to Chicago at the State Lake Theatre with Charles "Buddy" Rogers. *Billboard* (April 11, 1941) stated, "Nick Lucas is still the dependable song salesman he's been for years. Looks well and sings with ease and assurance."

Variety reviewed Nick's initial week at the Golden Gate Theatre in San Francisco (May 21, 1941): "Gets right into 'You Walked By' and 'Amapola,' swinging the last chorus of the latter, then introduces his next, 'Painting the Clouds with Sunshine.' Trots to the wings but bounces right back with 'Singing in the Rain' and 'That Great American Home.' At show caught, his reception was hearty. Answered the palm pounding with 'Thanks for the Memory' and bowed off." Regarding his second week at the Golden Gate, the trade paper wrote (May 28, 1941), "Nick Lucas, held over from last week, is on ... with 'Wise Old Owl' and 'My Sister and I.' Discards last week's aloofness to ask for requests and audience warms up immediately. Does 'Tiptoe Through the Tulips,' 'My Blue Heaven,' while stooge keeps shouting for 'Side by Side,' which is good for some laughs. Finally does the number...." Nick remained is San Francisco to replace Jimmy Durante at the Stairway to the Stars cabaret. When he appeared in Kansas City, Missouri, in late June, the *Ames* (Iowa) *Daily Tribune* (June 23, 1941)

Nick Lucas (left) pictured with Robert Taylor (center) and bandleader Al Donahue during World War II.

reported, "Nick Lucas … heads a lively performance at the Tower." In July, he was at Holberg's in Santa Rosa, California, and at the end the month he had an engagement at the Steel Pier in Atlantic City. During August, he did a San Francisco radio show sponsored by Regal Beer. The next month, he was back at the Orpheum Theatre in Los Angeles for three weeks.

In the fall of 1941, Nick was signed to appear in *The Silver Screen*, a musical-comedy production recounting the history of the movies. Produced by John Murray Anderson, it was staged at the Wiltshire Bowl in Los Angeles with Nick performing several songs from the early days of the talkies. The rest of the cast was made up of film veterans (Bryant Washburn, Betty Compson, Clara Kimball Young, Snub Pollard, Chester Conklin, Hank Mann, Clyde Cook) and contemporary performers (Cynda Glenn, Gitta Alper, Grace Pozzi and Igor, the Mangeans, Jack Holland, Darryl Harp's Orchestra). A lavish, costly production, it failed to generate sufficient box office to keep it afloat; it debuted on September 10 and closed October 6. Leaving this production, Nick headlined the Golden Gate in San Francisco and in October he was at the Show Box in Seattle. Next he did two weeks at the Cave Cabaret in Vancouver. *The Salt Lake City* (Utah) *Tribune* (November 23, 1941) reported, "As a special attraction, Nick Lucas, said to be the highest salaried cabaret star ever brought to Salt Lake City, has been signed by Harry Miles for a week's engagement at El Rancho club." This engagement was followed by a stand at the Bannock Hotel in Pocatello, Idaho.

Nick's management contract with Fanchon and Marco expired in February and for a time he worked freelance. Then in the summer, he signed with General Amusement Corporation. He headlined the Green Hills Club in Kansas City, Missouri, and the Villa Madrid in Pittsburgh in January and the next month he was at Salt Lake City's El Rancho and Helsing's Vodvil Lounge in Chicago where he played two weeks at $600 per week doing four shows a night. In March, he was at the Club Lido in South Bend, Indiana, where he was held over a second week. *Billboard* (March 14, 1942) reported, "The two-week date of Nick Lucas broke records and the management reports that the $1,200 paid him for that engagement was a good investment." At the end of March, Nick opened at the Ka-Cee Club in Toledo and in the spring he toured with Joe Venuti and His Orchestra and vocalist Kay Starr. When he appeared in Warren, Pennsylvania, at the Marconi Outing Club, that city's *Times Mirror* (February 4, 1942) reported "a large crowd on hand to welcome him. ...[H]e thrilled those who heard him with his singing and electric [*sic*] guitar." During May, he was at the Club Trocadero in Henderson, Kentucky, for a two-week stand, followed by another two weeks at Montreal's Esquire Club. In June, he appeared at the Club Top Hat in Montreal and while there he signed to make a series of commercial radio transcriptions for Masons United Advertising Agency in Toronto. By the end of June, he was back at Pittsburgh's Club Madrid and a month later he appeared at the Steel Pier in Atlantic City, followed by the Continental Grove in Akron and the Casanova Club in Detroit. When he was at the Music Hall at the Steel Pier, *Variety* (August 5, 1942) stated, "Lucas ... sings 'One Dozen Roses' and 'Johnny Doughboy' and 'Painting the Clouds.' Encores with 'Tiptoe Through the Tulips,' which is good for much applause, and is followed by 'Side by Side,' brought up to date with appropriate war theme. Received big hand at show caught...." Of his stand at the Continental Grove, *Billboard* (August 29, 1942) reported, "Nick Lucas broke all attendance records ... according to Lew Platt, owner of the spot."

Nick Lucas (right) pictured with Gene Autry in Kansas City, Missouri, circa 1942.

At the Club Casanova, the same trade said he "broke the club's Sunday record, August 23." In October, he headlined Fay's in Philadelphia and The Pier in Dunkirk, New York, and in November he was back at Akron's Continental Grove. December had Nick working for two weeks at the Miami Club in Staten Island, New York, with a three-week run back at Helsing's Vodvil Lounge in Chicago.

In the fall of 1942, Nick had a 15-minute weekday radio show, *Nick Lucas, the Singing Troubadour,* broadcast over 47 stations in Canada. The transcribed program was sponsored by Brylcreem and MacLean's Toothpaste. On station CJRC in Winnipeg, it was called *Nick Lucas, Voice of Memory.* It was on the air from September 1942 until 1945 and was made up of the commercial transcription recordings he did for Masons United Advertising Agency.

Nick began 1943 with his engagement at Helsing's Vodvil Lounge in Chicago. *Billboard* (January 2, 1943) reported, "Lucas was one of the more profitable attractions to play here and he should repeat the record with little trouble. The man is a performer and a thoroughly pleasing, guitar-strumming crooner. He keeps the act up to date by using new tunes and at the same time retains old and builds new friends with his nostalgic set." *Billboard* also reported that he was being paid between $500 and $750 a week for his club work. In January, when he did eight days at the Bama Club in Phenix City, Alabama, *Billboard* (January 30, 1943) noted, "Al H. Mulligan, manager of the Bama Club, says Nick Lucas did the best business in the club's history, surpassing by 60 percent such names as Mildred Bailey and Wingy Mammone, and by 40 percent Alice Dawn; and others by even a larger percentage." Next he played for two weeks at Palumbo's Cabaret Café in Philadelphia. *Billboard* (February 20, 1943) wrote,

> Palumbo's is enjoying a new cycle of excitement with Nick Lucas, the first time that Lucas has held forth on a local nitery floor. Nitery ops here have been missing a good bet for a long time in not snagging the singing troubadour. Apart from being an effective hypo in filling the many tables in this large room, Lucas still packs plenty of lyrical appeal in his pipes. Strumming his own guitar accomps and with plenty of rhythmic and romantic urge in his song selling,

Advertisement for the national tour of the stage show starring Joe Venuti, Nick Lucas and Kay Starr in the spring of 1942.

he adds plenty of sugar to the nostalgic note in giving out on the old favorites, peppered with pop hits. There was no getting enough of his song session here.

Next Nick was held over in a return to St. Louis' Club Hi-Hit in February. That city's *Globe-Democrat* (March 7, 1943) noted, "Nick Lucas ... is remaining a second week at the Club Hi-Hat, where he continues to sing sentimental songs...." In March, he was at the Roosevelt Hotel in New Orleans and then was back in Indianapolis for a stand at Keith's Theatre where *Variety* (March 24, 1943) opined, "Nick Lucas pleases his fans as neatly as ever in his current appearance.... They go for his memory gem, 'Tiptoe Through the Tulips,' as well as 'I've Heard That Song Before, 'I Had the Craziest Dream' and other recent hits which he sings in this high-pitched tenor. Got two encores when caught." Regarding the same venue, Corbin Patrick wrote in *The Indianapolis Star* (March 19, 1943),

> Nick Lucas ... whose high-pitched tenor has been drawing crowds here many years, is the bright, particular star of the new show at Keith's. Time has dealt kindly with Nick and his stuff is as good as it ever was. That horrid word "crooning," we note, is used in his billing, but even if it applies, Nick is one crooner who can sing above a whisper. With his sweet, clear voice he sticks to the romantic style and favors those present with such agreeable themes as 'For Me and My Gal,' 'I Had the Craziest Dream,' 'Tiptoeing Through the Tulips' and 'I've Heard That Song Before.' His program is generous and yesterdays audience enjoyed it, as of old.

Nick was on the cover of the April 3, 1943, *Billboard* with the statement, "Lucas has steadfastly maintained his well-earned reputation as one of the most talented guitar-playing songsters, and it keeps him busy with bookings the year round." Nick's club appearances were being booked by the Coast-to-Coast Agency.

During April, Nick was at the Palomar Club in Vancouver, and in May he was back at the El Rancho in Salt Lake City. Then he headlined a stage show at the Warfield Theatre in San Francisco with Milt Britton and His Orchestra. After that came Las Vegas' El Cortez Hotel in May and the Florentine Gardens in Hollywood. He closed out the month appearing at Loew's Warfield Theatre in San Francisco. In June, he headlined Paul's Music Hall in Portland and the Palomar Club in Seattle. When Nick appeared at the Orpheum Theatre in the *Gay Nineties Idea* stage show, the *Oakland* (California) *Tribune* (July 2, 1943) reported that he found an appreciative audience awaiting him at the matinee "and he responded with an excellent budget of old and new tunes. He began rather quietly with 'Hello Bluebird' and 'Coming in on a Wing and a Prayer,' and then moved into some of the familiar songs.... He could have held the stage indefinitely...." Of the same venue, *Billboard* (July 24, 1943) stated, "Nick Lucas ... had little trouble getting a show-stop with his guitar strumming and smooth vocals. 'Mr. Bluebird,' 'Comin' In on a Wing and a Prayer,' 'Painting the Clouds with Sunshine,' 'Tiptoe Through the Tulips' and 'Side by Side,' the last name with timely lyrics, bringing down the house." In July, he returned to Salt Lake City for a stand at the Lyric Theatre, to Vancouver where he did one week each at the Beacon Theatre and Palomar Supper Club, and to Madison, Wisconsin, where he headlined at the Orpheum Theatre. When Nick was at the Orpheum Theatre in Omaha in September, *Billboard* (October 9, 1943) noted, "Lucas appears in the closing spot with five numbers. The troubadour had a hard time breaking away from the plaudits. Numbers were 'Put Your Arms Around Me,' his trademark 'Tiptoe Through the Tulips,' 'Side by Side,' the currently popular 'In My Arms' and 'I Heard You Cried Last Night.'" In the same issue, the trade journal reported, "Nick Lucas' rendition of 'Side by

Side' was instrumental in having that tune adopted by the Atlanta District of the Treasury Department as the official song of the Third War Loan drive." Next came an October stand at the Club Casanova in Detroit, followed by appearances in Toledo, Ohio, and in Albany, New York. For the Detroit date, that city's *Evening Times* (October 20, 1943) reported, "Nick Lucas, ... an object of much feminine adoration, is playing an eagerly awaited return engagement as star of Lowell Bernhardt's Club Casanova's floor show." According to the article, "Nick acquired the 'singing troubadour' label from his continental rovings." He did five weeks at the Hotel Roosevelt's Blue Room in New Orleans where *Variety* (November 24, 1943) opined, "Audiences go in a big way for his memory gems and he had to beg off. He drew bravos for several recent hits, but it was tunes like 'Tiptoe Through the Tulips,' 'My Blue Heaven,' 'Side by Side,' 'Singing in the Rain,' and other old faves that audience liked best." This was followed by two weeks at Tony's Subway Club in Peoria. He closed the year appearing in Shamokin, Pennsylvania.

In 1944, Nick was signed by the RCM Company to appear in four short musicals for Soundies Corporation of America, a company co-founded by songwriter Sam Coslow and James Roosevelt, son of President Franklin D. Roosevelt. The Soundies were presented in juke box–like machines, with the customer paying ten cents to see and hear performers doing popular songs. Nick's Soundies were *Tiptoe Through the Tulips*, *Side by Side*, *Good Night Wherever You Are* and *An Hour Never Passes*. Soundies were very popular during the World War II years. After they ran their course, they were purchased by Official Films for the 16mm home market and later television.

Nick Lucas in *Goodnight, Wherever You Are* (Soundies Corporation of America, 1944).

Nick began 1944 at the 885 Club in Chicago where he was booked for two weeks and held over for two more. Regarding this venue, *Billboard* (January 22, 1944) wrote,

> Nick Lucas provides pleasant entertainment for diners at this Rush Street spot. Nick has long been a favorite of Chi café-goers since the days when he started out at The Tent back in the 20s and he fits perfectly with the intimate atmosphere of the 885... [H]e strums his guitar and sings the newer ballads and a flock of oldies that revive pleasant memories. He has lost none of his charm and his mellow, restful renditions of such numbers as, "Oh, What a Beautiful Morning," "My Heart Tells Me" [while] old favorites "Tiptoe Through the Tulips" and "My Blue Heaven" also win the audience acclaim. He injects a bit of comedy with a modernized version of "Side by Side."

Next came two weeks at the Continental Club in Decatur, Illinois, where he appeared with Stepin Fetchit. This was followed by another holdover at the Kentucky Club in Toledo. He was held over again at the Hotel Raddison's Flame Room in Minneapolis in March. He did two weeks at the Jewell Box in Tampa and a week at Miami's Olympic Theatre in April. Next came two weeks each in June at Philadelphia's Latin Casino and Atlanta's Henry Grady Hotel. Regarding his appearance at the Tower Theatre in Kansas City, Missouri, *Variety* (July 5, 1944) stated, "With Nick Lucas heading a fast moving 40-minute bill, The Tower is reaping its heftiest gross in several months. Walking on casually with his guitar, Lucas was greeted with a big hand before he sung a word at the opening show. He tees off with 'San Fernando Valley,' and then follows with 'I'll Be Seeing You.' After several bows, he revives earlier hits.... Begs off with stockholders clamoring for more." Next he headlined Park Plaza's Crystal Terrace in St. Louis, Missouri, in August. When he appeared at the Downtown Theatre in Chicago in the fall, *Variety* again took note (September 27, 1944): "Nick Lucas does 'Swinging on a Star' and 'Time Waits for No One' and then turns back the years with a couple of tunes associated with him in the past. Latter are 'Tiptoe Through the Tulips' and 'Side by Side,' sending him off with a big hand." This was followed by a stand at the Stork Club in Council Bluffs, Iowa, for a month. From October 30 to November 11, he was at the Stork Club in Denver.

While in Chicago, Nick recorded a series of spot radio announcements for Holsum Bread. In November 1944, it was announced that he was one of 68 stars donating time to perform at USO-Camp Shows' hospital units. During World War II, Nick did extensive work entertaining for the USO (United Service Organizations).

Nick opened 1945 at the Town Barn in Buffalo, followed by stands at Palumbo's Cabaret Café in Philadelphia and the Terrace Room in Newark. In February, he was at Dailey's Terrace Room in Newark and in March he headlined the Kitty Davis Airliner Club in Miami. He returned to Buffalo's Stork Club in the spring. During June, he held sway at the Bowery Theatre in Detroit where he drew 10,000 customers the first week and 11,000 the next. When he was at the Vine Gardens in Chicago, opening there July 2 for a month, *Billboard* (August 11, 1945) reported, "Headliner in Nick Lucas, who has the crowd with him all the way, while he sings his old songs.... Lucas is still one of the top song sellers in the business and knows how to put over a song. With his voice and his guitar playing he would be a natural for radio." In the fall of 1945, he was at the Club 400 in St. Louis, followed by a stand at the Shore Acres Country Club in Henry, Illinois. Regarding the Club 400 engagement, *Billboard* (October 6, 1945) called him "a pleasant relief from the over-abundance of swooning baritones of the modern school. He offers his songs in a straightforward tenor style.... Opens with 'Rosemary,' then goes to the tunes he made popular.... Wins plenty of applause with each number and finally has to make a speed to beg off." From October 19 to November 7, Nick was at the Sky-Vu Gardens in Dallas. At year's end he recorded five songs for the radio show *Program Themes*, which was syndicated to 400 stations. The tunes were used to open local programs. He spent most of December headlining at D'Jais in Secaucus, New Jersey.

In January 1946, Nick appeared for two weeks at the Panda Club in Newark. In March and April, he was the headliner at the opening of Fort Worth's Skyline Supper Club. Next he headlined Frank Palumbo's Cabaret Café in Philadelphia, followed by a two-week stand (April 22 to May 5) at the Miami Club in Toledo. In June and July, he was at the Top Hat Club in Detroit where he drew over 4000 customers in mid–July. Now exclusively booked for theaters by Jack Kalcheim, Nick was back in New York City at Loew's State Theatre, doing "solid business" (*Variety*, August 7, 1946) in a show with Grace McDonald. The trade paper reported, "[Lucas] is still identified with some of the song hits of two decades ago which he helped introduce on the screen. ...[He] rated two encores at show caught." Regarding the same stand, *Billboard* (August 10, 1946) wrote, "Nick Lucas with his black guitar is still a top seller of nostalgic melodrama without trick arrangements. Tenor opened with 'Seems Like Old Times'; using tune for a medley of oldies that the audience ate up...." He was booked for two weeks at the Blue Mirror club in Newark but left after the first week due to lack of publicity and advertising and then played at the Capitol Theatre in Washington, D.C. In September, he appeared in Yonkers, New York, at the Lowe's Theatre. When he returned Washington, D.C.'s Capitol Theatre later in the month, *Variety* (September 23, 1946) stated, "Top billing goes to Nick Lucas, who, like most veterans, makes his stance on the basis of 'Auld Lang Syne.' Lucas and his guitar can still register even with the younger members of the audience. Does best with his old standbys.... Opener, 'Seems Like Old Times,' straight and parodied, plus a guitar number, completes the act. His pleasant voice plus his simple manner garner nice response." In October, he was at Cleveland's Hollenden Hotel and at the end of the month he started a two-week stand at the Stork Club in Omaha. At the time, his Diamond Records recording "What Ya Gonna Do?" was listed in the "BMI Pin Up Sheet Hit Tunes for October." From November 25 to December 7, Lucas headlined the Plamor Club in Cheyenne, Wyoming; then he played Salt Lake City's Lyric Theatre where he was billed as "America's Singing Troubadour." This was followed by a stand at Ogden, Utah's Last Frontier Club.

After World War II, Nick and Catherine Lucas sold their Newark home and in 1947 they moved to Hollywood. The housing situation at the time was very crowded and had to settle for a one-room apartment that was so small they had to cook in the bathroom. They considered buying a small ranch in Colorado Springs, Colorado, since it was where their daughter and her family lived, but the altitude proved too high for both of them, especially Catherine, who suffered from emphysema. In 1948, they purchased a home in Encino, California, where Nick took part in various civic activities that brought him into contact with a resident who became a good friend, John Wayne. Nick considered the Duke one of the nicest people he knew in show business.

Among his continuous appearances in 1947 was a two-week stand at the El Rancho Hotel in Las Vegas followed by headlining the Hawaiian Gardens in San Pedro, California, in February. The next month, he signed with Frederick Brothers for exclusive management and starred in a musical revue in Knoxville, Tennessee, in April. During the summer of 1947, he was at Denver's Colonial Manor followed by two weeks at the Lake

Shore Lounge in Oakland, California. In September, he was at Sandra's in Hayward, California, and this was followed by a two-week stand at the Matteonis Club in Stockton, California. On October 22, 1947, Nick entertained at a testimonial dinner for flier Paul Mantz at the Lake Side Country Club in North Hollywood. Among the 300 attendees were John Wayne, Bob Hope, Dennis Morgan, Charles Coburn, John Carroll and pianist Eddie Dunstedter. On November 21, 1947, he headlined a six-act vaudeville show at the Elk's Lodge annual homecoming event in San Bernardino, California. That month he signed a recording contract with Hucksters Records; Henny Youngman and Lillian Lane were also on that label.

After settling in Encino, Nick gave serious thought to retiring since he was financially comfortable. But he met an agent who offered him a lucrative tour of the Hawaiian Islands that included two weeks at the Waikiki Lau Yee Chais in Honolulu. It turned into a seven-week run. On January 24, 1948, he was guest artist at the Hawaiian Magician's Society Show with proceeds going to Honolulu's polio fund. From March 11 to 14, Nick headlined the National Orange Show in San Bernardino, California; *Billboard* (March 27, 1948) reported, "Nick Lucas ... opens with 'Beg Your Pardon' and goes into 'Golden Earrings.' Capitalizing on the current popularity of 'Four-Leaf Clover,' Lucas, an outstanding showman, uses it for transition into the oldies. He really scores solidly with 'Tiptoe Through the Tulips' and encores with 'Side by Side.'" Next he appeared at the Olympia in Miami and Club La Jolla in Tucson.

Back in California, he was strolling down Hollywood Boulevard and bumped into Ken Murray, an old friend with whom he had worked in vaudeville and radio. Murray was enjoying great success with his *Ken Murray's Blackouts* at Hollywood's El Capital Theatre. The most popular production on the West Coast, it featured guest performers appearing for a short time in addition to Murray, co-star Marie Wilson and a large cast. Murray asked Nick to appear in the show for two weeks and he agreed to the engagement, then extended for another month. When this run was up, Murray requested that Nick remain with the show indefinitely; he was in the production for the next two years. *Billboard* reported, "If you happen to be one of the fortunate public to get seats to *Ken Murray's Blackouts* and you hear the scream of 'teenagers' you will know that Nick Lucas is center stage. He is better than ever." In another review, the trade paper stated on July 17, 1947, "Troubadour Nick Lucas proves that time hasn't diminished his voice, song styling or his selections...." Fred Bloomfield wrote in the North Hollywood *Valley Times* (June 28, 1948), "Nick Lucas, who has been identified with first class entertainment since his schooldays, represents one of the outstanding acts of the new show." During its West Coast run, *Ken Murray's Blackouts* did big business due to the number of G.I.s stationed in Southern California; they and their dates flocked to it, especially on weekends. Nick noted, "You couldn't get near the theatre for the crowds." When Nick celebrated his 25th year in show business, Murray gave him a celebration dinner on June 9, 1948. On the cover of the July 2, 1949, *Billboard* was a picture with Nick, Murray and Marie Wilson celebrating Nick's second anniversary with the show, Wilson's seventh anniversary with it and the production's eighth anniversary.

After more than a decade away from commercial recording in the U.S., Nick redid "Tiptoe Through the Tulips" and "Always" for Premier Records late in 1945. The next year, he signed with Diamond Records; the four platters he waxed for the label sold well. The March 6, 1946, *Radio Daily* stated that Melrose Records planned to release four records by Nick but this probably refers to the Diamond discs that came out that

Nick Lucas in *Ken Murray's Blackouts* at the El Capitan Theatre in Hollywood in 1948 (photo courtesy Ken Murray).

summer. Around 1946, Nick also did another batch of transcription recordings for the C.P. MacGregor Company that were later released in Canada by United Transcribed System. In 1948, he did several songs for Huckster Records with the masters later being sold to Capitol, which released "Tiptoe Through the Tulips/Side by Side" to good sales. As a result, Nick signed a one-year contract with Capitol and had two sessions with the label, the second being with Frank De Vol and his orchestra on a popular redo of "Bye Bye Blackbird." Regarding the initial platter, "Tiptoe Through the Tulips/Side by Side," *The Indianapolis* (Indiana) *Star* (October 15, 1948) reported that it "proves he still has a way with a song." Dewey Dunn in his "On the Records" column in the Madison, Wisconsin, *Capital Times* (December 6, 1948) opined, "If you remember this artist and these tunes, you're getting older. ...Still apt, likeable stuff." In the *Terre Haute* (Indiana) *Tribune* (December 12, 1948), J.J. Brassie wrote, "[Having] won fame with 'Tiptoe Through the Tulips,' old timer Nick Lucas revives the song for competition of the hit parade. It may well find its former niche." According to *Cashbox* (October 23, 1948), "A pair of sides that scored heavily ages ago by a performer who made them hits is offered here in pleasant manner. ...The wax and the songs should have heavy sentimental appeal." Reviewing the same platter in the *San Bernardino* (California) *Sun* (October 17, 1948), Leo H. Cross declared, "If the ladies remember this one they won't admit it because it will give away their age—but they'll enjoy it just as much now as they did in days gone by. The current crop of revivals is nicely enriched with this Capital release of the great Nick Lucas's work on two of our most clinging tunes."

From late November 1948 into February 1949, "Side by Side" appeared in the *Cashbox* charts as one of the top ten songs on various U.S. radio stations. On November 27, 1948, it was #9 at KFAM in St. Louis, on December 11, 1948, #4 at WPIK in Alexandria, Virginia, and it was #6 at that station on February 12, 1949. On January 1, 1949, it was #5 in Wheeling, West Virginia, on January 8, the song was #5 in Reno.

The January 19, 1949, *Cashbox* listed Nick's Capitol recording of "Tea Time on the Thames" as #5 on station KFWB in Los Angeles. The "In the Groove" column in the *Amarillo* (Texas) *Daily News* (January 21, 1949) stated, "'Don't Gamble with Romance' [features] the ageless vocal artistry of Nick Lucas, who is backed on this slow moving romantic tune by a Hammond organ. Linked is 'Tea Time on the Thames,' an English styled melody again featuring Nick vocalizing with a Hammond at slow tempo in a soft mood." In his "On the Record" column, Dewey Dunn wrote in Madison, Wisconsin's *Capital Times* (June 25, 1949) about the coupling of "Bye Bye Blackbird" and "Don't Call Me Sweetheart Anymore": "The 'Crooning Troubadour' has lost none of his luster or appeal. His song-selling is first rate as of old." Regarding his re-recording of "Tiptoe Through the Tulips," *The Valley Times* (North Hollywood) reported on October 16, 1948, "Singing a duet with himself. That is the 'Ripley' Nick Lucas has completed for a new record.... To accomplish the duet he first recorded the lyrics and then sang some harmony notes and interludes that have also been dubbed onto the platter." The February 5, 1949, *Cashbox* reviewed "Don't Gamble with Romance": "Old-time vaude singer ambles through this sleeper tune without special force or sympathy. Organ backing." *Cashbox* said of "Tea Time on the Thames," "Dull, feelingless performance, a complicated, no-appeal tune." On April 6, 1949, the same trade journal covered another Lucas-Capitol single: "Don't Call Me Sweetheart Anymore": "The old-time troubadour tries a 'You Call Everybody Darling' follow-up here, complete with shuffle chorus. Pleasant enough stuff, but nothing to get excited about." Of "Bye Bye Blackbird": "Another oldie from the 'Four-Leaf Clover' era but the guitarist-warbler does it straight. Some group whistling in the extreme of the production." *Billboard* (July 2, 1949) said of Nick's recording "Bye Blackbird/Don't Call Me Sweetheart Anymore," "In the opinion of Capital executives, one of the best pieces of work the veteran troubadour has ever done."

During this period, Nick made guest appearances on radio shows, including *All-Star Western Theatre* with his friend Foy Willing of the Riders of the Purple Sage. Willing was one of a number of country-western music performers influenced by Nick and his guitar playing. Among them were Gene Autry, Merle Travis, Eddie Dean, Jimmy Wakely and Johnny Bond. Regarding Nick's longtime friendship with Willing, Jimmy Pusateri wrote in a syndicated newspaper story (November 3, 1953), "While attending high school in Waco, Foy at 16 was playing popular music. It was at this time that the famous guitarist, Nick Lucas, traveling through the Lone Star state, met and changed young Willing's life. Lucas met Foy in a Dallas music store, took a liking to the young Texan and presented him with a guitar and began teaching him how to play it. Lucas changed young Foy's style of playing and predicted his protégé would become of the country's best guitarists."

Prior to joining the cast of *Ken Murray's Blackouts*, Nick headlined the San Bernardino Air depot civilian employee Valentine's party on February 13, 1948. On March 29, he portrayed show business legend Gus Edwards at the Hollywood Comedy Club's vaudeville show, with Mrs. Edwards in attendance. Others in the cast were Arthur

Treacher, Jim Burk, Billy Curtis, Raymond Largay, Jed Dooley and Lynn Cowan. He then starred at the Lakewood Country Club in Wilmington, California, on May 4, 1948.

Early in 1949, Nick's personal manager, Jack Beekman, attempted to negotiate a deal for Nick to return to the London Palladium but it never happened. This coincided with a year's option renewal on his Capitol Records contract along with signing for a second year with *Ken Murray's Blackouts*. At the same time, Nick signed with Teleways Radio Productions to make a series of radio transcriptions. *Billboard* reported, "Teleway E.T. [electric transcriptions] show emphasizes Lucas' past experience in entertaining European royalty and world celebs, with gimmick used to intro songs that were favored by yesteryear greats." Regarding Nick's appearance in *Ken Murray's Blackouts*, *Billboard* (July 16, 1949) opined, "Troubadour Nick Lucas is in his second year with *Blackouts* and is better than ever. Applause is spontaneous for his yesteryear offerings which are enjoying a comeback. Patrons get a kick out of the faves sung by the man who first made them famous. Lucas displays fine command of his guitar in addition to his fine vocal work."

On July 25, Nick was guest at a tribute to Eddy Arnold held at Hollywood's Knickerbocker Hotel, along with Gene Autry, Hank Thompson, Carolina Cotton, Pat Buttram and Julien Aberbach. Robert Mitchum served as master of ceremonies.

Ken Murray asked Nick to continue in *Blackouts*, which was to be transferred to Broadway (Billy Rose's Ziegfeld Theatre) following its August 27, 1949, closing in Hollywood. Marie Wilson was not able to continue with the show due to West Coast movie and radio commitments. The production had run on the West Coast for over seven years with 3844 performances, an audience of over four million patrons and a gross in excess of $5.5 million. When *The Blackouts of 1949* opened on Broadway that fall, it got mediocre reviews and ran for only six weeks. Typical was Brooks Atkinson's September 7 *New York Times* review: "[This] is a routine music-hall show put on in an informal manner.... Until Nick Lucas came on in the last end of the show, with some lucid songs, the only tunes your reviewer could sort out from the general pandemonium were 'Silver Threads Among the Gold' and 'Put on Your Old Grey Bonnet.'"

After *The Blackouts of 1949* shuttered, Nick remained in New York City for six months, working at various nightspots, including Lowe's Melba Theatre in Brooklyn in October, and visiting relatives in New Jersey. That year his brother Frank died at age 59. Although Frank never reached the heights attained by his younger sibling, he was an accomplished musician, especially on the piano and accordion, and he had performed in London, Glasgow, Paris, Hamburg and Berlin. Frank was known to have mob connections and for many years Nick was reluctant to work with biographers since he said that many of them only wanted to discuss Frank's underworld activities. Frank was the author of the songbook *The Frank Lucas Chord-Rhythm and Fill-In Book for Accordion*, published by Nicomede Music Company in 1934.

In New York City, Nick made his national television debut on the premiere of *The Ken Murray Show* on January 7, 1950. Through the years, Nick and Ken remained good friends and Murray said of him, "[H]e's a solid citizen, and our relationship, while not sprinkled with humorous happenings to relate, has been one of mutual respect and admiration." Shortly after appearing on Murray's program, Ed Sullivan asked Nick to appear on his CBS-TV series *The Toast of the Town*. Sullivan told Nick the show was barely managing to keep its head above water and could only offer him a small sum for his appearance. Nick agreed to do the show since Sullivan promised he would return the favor by having him back for several more appearances at a much higher fee. After doing the program, Nick said he never heard from Sullivan again. He also related a similar experience about Red Skelton.

Nick returned to California by working in various night spots across the country. Of his stand at the Fox Theatre in St. Louis, Missouri, Herbert L. Monk wrote in the *St. Louis Globe-Democrat* (January 15, 1950), "All in all, Lucas ... proved it takes a trouper of the old school to get really close to an audience. Singing from the orchestra platform, Nick had yesterday's first audience eating out of his hand and responding with applause that sounded like it came from the heart and not out of politeness." Regarding the same venue, *Variety* (January 18, 1950) reported, "The 'Strolling Troubadour' strumming his guitar with nonchalance whams over 'Seems Like Old Times,' 'Dear Hearts and Gentle People,' 'Tiptoe Through the Tulips' and encores with 'I'm Looking at the World Thru Rose Colored Glasses' and 'Bye Bye Blackbird." When he returned to L.A.'s Orpheum Theatre, the same trade paper noted on March 1, 1950: "Nick Lucas ... pleases with 'Dear Hearts,' the single concession to modern tunes but the customers came to hear 'Tiptoe Through the Tulips,' 'Bye Bye Blackbird,' 'Side by Side' and sundry other oldies in the Lucas catalog." Regarding the same engagement, *Billboard* (March 4, 1950) wrote, "Nick Lucas tops a strong bill to bring down the house with his nostalgic troubadouring. A fine showman, he makes 'em beg for more." In April 1950, he was back in L.A. at the Biltmore Bowl and *Variety* (April 12, 1950) wrote that Nick's vocalizing stint "is geared to elicit greatest response for nostalgia and he makes it pay off nicely. Opening night audience included a sizable coterie of his fans who greeted with relish his reprise of some of his disclicks." *Billboard* (April 22, 1950) also covered the show: "Nick Lucas rates hefty hands all the way. Displays the sales savvy and ability which have served him in good stand through the years. He's at home with pop tunes and novelties, but his oldies ... found the most favor with ringsiders."

It was during this time that Nick was sometimes billed as "The Strolling Troubadour."

When Nick returned to Dallas in the summer of 1950, Fairfax Nisbet in the column "Dining and Dancing" in the *Dallas Morning News* (August 11, 1950) noted, "It has been far too long since Nick Lucas played Dallas, but now that he's back, and appearing at the Mural Room, it's nice to report that the Crooning Troubadour and his guitar still deal out the grand old tunes that have become popular classics in the manner that has kept him on top of the heap for more than two decades." In August and September, he had an extended run at the El Casbah in Kansas City, Missouri.

During a stopover in Las Vegas, Nick saw performers making very good money in cocktail lounges, an avenue that would prove very lucrative for him during the next decade. When he headlined the Happytime Revue and Night Club at the Oklahoma State Fair in October 1950, it was noted he "has enjoyed sustained success thru two decades of revolutionary change in show business." This was followed by October dates at the Oklahoma Free State Fair in Muskogee and a stand in Lubbock, Texas, with the Denny Beckner Revue. He closed out the year at Chi Chi's Starlite Room in Palm Springs, with *Variety* (December 6, 1950), reporting, "Nick Lucas currently packing 'em in there."

Back in Hollywood in 1951, Nick signed with producer Duke Goldstone to make seven Snader Telescriptions, three-minute musicals for TV syndication. They were very similar to the Soundies he did seven years earlier. He appeared in *Bela Bimba*, *The Sunshine of Your Smile*, *Get Out Those Old Records*, *Looking at the World Thru Rose Colored*

Glasses, Marie Ah Marie, Mexicali Rose and *Walking My Baby Back Home*. Most of the Snaders featured a trio of female singers. That year, Nick recorded still another version of "Tiptoe Through the Tulips," backed by "My Blue Heaven," for Boney Records.

In 1951, Nick returned to network radio via the ABC series *Saturday Night at the Shamrock,* broadcast from the Shamrock Hotel in Houston. The series, which presented a variety of acts each week, ran for one season. By now Nick had starred on radio programs for all three major networks and did several syndicated transcription shows. Throughout the 1950s, he continued to make radio appearances, usually on variety shows. He was often a guest with his friend Jimmy Wakely on the latter's CBS series in the mid–1950s. The year 1951 also marked Nick's return to feature films with a guest star role in the Allied Artists release *Disc Jockey*. He portrayed himself in the production singing "Let's Meander Through the Meadow" in a sequence that was a tribute to the early days of radio. Besides having a number of big-name guest stars, the movie also featured many of the nation's top disc jockeys. Since the record industry was recovering from the setbacks of the Depression and the material shortages due to World War II, this musical movie proved popular. As a result of his success in *Disc Jockey*, *The Valley Times* (North Hollywood) reported on December 1, 1951, that Nick "is being considered for another flicker deal at Monogram."

In the spring of 1951, Nick got national attention thanks to a May 10, 1951, story by Virginia MacPherson, United Press Hollywood Correspondent. She wrote:

> Nick Lucas, who's been singing "Tiptoe Through the Tulips" since grandpa was a wolf, confessed today he's a hoarder—of guitars. "I've got almost every guitar I ever owned," the veteran entertainer said. "I can't throw them away. Every single one has some little incident of show business connected with it." Nick, who still has the longest eyelashes of anybody in the business even if he is a grandpa, tucks his worn-out guitars away in the hall closet ... in the basement ... under his bed ... anywhere there's room. The house may look like a pawn shop for musicians, but it's nobody's business but Nick's and the missus and they don't mind a bit. Lucas tells how one of his guitars got a big gash in the side the night he worked with the rowdy comedy team of Ole Olsen and Chic Johnson. "Another one got a big dent in it when I dropped it during my first headliner run. Wouldn't part with that one for anything," he stated, adding, "They may look like a collection of junk to you but they add up to a lot of mighty happy memories for me."

Nick also told the writer that a shiny guitar is a must for his stage act:

A Nick Lucas publicity photograph from the early 1950s.

It's like a tuxedo. It's part of your costume.... So, if I show up with a seedy-looking instrument, people begin to nudge each other and say, "Aha—he's slipping. Can't even afford a high-class guitar any more." You have to impress night club owners, too. If you got a beat-up guitar they figure they can get you for less dough.

The writer noted, "It'll be some time before they can pull that on Lucas. Not only are the old-timers coming back to hear the songs they courted grandma with—they're bringing their grandchildren with 'em." Regarding his popularity with younger fans, Nick said, "It's a big kick to have a new generation in the audience. But I got a shock the other night. A guy came up and said: 'I've been wanting to meet you for a long time. Twenty years ago I went to hear you sing and your romantic songs got me so excited I eloped. And brother—I've hated you ever since!" Hedda Hopper, in her June 12, 1951, syndicated newspaper column, reported on another of Nick's hobbies: "Nick Lucas, who collects hit musical arrangements, has papered the walls of his den with them. Imagine one room with $50,000 worth of wallpaper."

In July 1951, Nick purchased a 250-acre ranch in Black Forest, near Colorado Springs. He retained the property for the rest of his life and visited it on several occasions but never lived there due to the high altitude.

As the 1950s progressed, Nick continued to make guest appearances on national TV series, including those of Art Linkletter, Liberace and Kate Smith. Some of the top night spots in which he played were the Mark Hopkins in San Francisco, the Capitol Theatre in Washington, D.C., the Monteleo and the Roosevelt in New Orleans, the Biltmore Bowl in Los Angeles, the Olympia in Miami, the Peacock Club in Jacksonville, the Oriental and Palace in Chicago, Adolph's Hotel in Dallas, the Broadmore Hotel in Colorado Springs, the Beverly-Hilton Hotel in Beverly Hills, Park Lane Hotel and Embers in Denver, Muehlebach Hotel in Kansas City, and the Colony Club in Omaha. While Nick was appearing at Bimbo's Club in San Francisco, agent Sam Rosen offered him a deal to headline the Holiday Hotel in Reno at $2500 per week. He agreed to give the offer a trial run of four weeks, for this meant performing in cocktail lounges, an area of show business that was alien to him. He put together a group with a piano player, bass and drums and they opened to very good business. The act, however, required the group to perform four sets a night with each running between 40 and 45 minutes, and Nick singing most of the time. He found it "really hard work" and "I didn't like it too well." At the end of the month's engagement, Nick wanted to quit but the hotel's management offered him $3000 a week with a solid 12 weeks booking each year. The offer was too lucrative to turn down and he would remain on the cocktail lounge circuit for the next decade, not only appearing at the Holiday Hotel but also at Reno's Mapes and Golden hotels, and at the Last Frontier and El Rancho hotels in Las Vegas.

When Nick and Dick Contino headlined the bill at the Orpheum Theatre in Los Angeles early in 1951, Thomas Reddy reported in the *Los Angeles Examiner* (January 19, 1951), "Nick Lucas, whose name has long adorned marquees with such 'greats' as Sophie Tucker and Blossom Seeley, has the audience in the palm of his hand from the word go. With his plinking guitar he 'Tiptoes Through the Tulips,' and awakens memories of a more peaceful world with 'Four Leaf Clover,' 'Side by Side' and score of others like them." After a stand at the Last Frontier in Las Vegas, he appeared at the Shamrock Hotel's Emerald Room in Houston; *Variety* (February 21, 1951) opined, "Nick Lucas, the indestructible, opened a two-week engagement ... and proved that old-timers have that certain spark to set off enthusiastic applause. Once he started crooning the old faves, they wouldn't let him off. The new tunes in his routine were well received, but he got best return from 'My Melancholy Baby,' 'Side by Side' and his trademark, 'Tiptoe Through the Tulips.'" When he appeared at Larry Potter's Supper Club in Studio City, California, *Billboard* (May 5, 1951) noted, "Nick Lucas ... shows that he has lost none of this charm and ability to sell a tune. He got enthusiastic returns.... His opener, 'Get Out Those Old Records,' led into excerpts of three former disk hits, 'Four-Leaf Clover,' 'My Melancholy Baby' and 'Bye Bye Blackbird.' He begged off after several encores with all piping on 'My Blue Heaven' and 'Singing in the Rain.'" When Nick returned to the Palace Theatre in New York City, the same trade journal reported on May 26, 1951, "Nick Lucas sold nostalgia for big returns. He gave the house exactly the tunes it expected in okay voice. Good special lyrics for 'Seems Like Old Times' and 'Side by Side' sold well too." In the fall, Nick starred at the San Joaquin County Fair in Stockton, California, for five days and in October he did two weeks at Reno's Mapes Hotel. In December, he returned to the National Orange Show in San Bernardino, California, and ended the year headlining the Los Angeles Pacific Coast Showmen's Association annual banquet ball; he contributed $50 to their charity and asked for a membership application. He closed out 1951 at Greeley, Colorado's, Rosedale Inn.

During this period, singer-songwriter-guitarist Paddy Labato, a Cleveland resident, billed himself as "Nick Lucas' Protégé." Labato composed the theme song of the Cleveland Indians' baseball team, "There's No Place Like First Place," and later wrote the tune "A Nick Lucas Serenade."

In February 1952, Nick headlined the Olympic Hotel's Georgian Room in Spokane, Washington, and the next month he was at George Amato's Supper Club in Portland. Then he flew to Chicago to tend to a throat infection. On May 7, 1952, *Variety* reported, "Nick Lucas, Danny Martin, Cooper Sisters and Burns Twins and Evelyn are putting on a socko bill at the 1952 Home Show" in Portland. The event, running from April 18 to 27, drew 75,152 attendees at 24 performances, 20 percent over the previous year's show. Banjoist Eddie Peabody was also in Portland at the time with the Shrine Circus and he and Nick exchanged engagements at each other's shows. At the Pittsburgh Home Show the same month, Lucas set a "Record Breaking Engagement" attendance record. When he headlined the Crystal Inn in Bakersfield, California, the *Bakersfield Californian* (May 19, 1952) declared, "He was once the Frankie Laine and Frank Sinatra of the crooning world [and] still attracts crowds wherever he appears." In June 1952, he returned to Dallas for a two-week stand at the Baker Hotel's Mural Room, and then headlined the San Diego County Fair in Del Mar, California, from June 29 to July 6, in *Fiestacades of 1952* with the Bell Sisters and Bob Williams. In August 1952, he was in Houston at the Shamrock Hotel. He was back at Dallas' Baker Hotel for another engagement before taking a three-week vacation in Colorado Springs. In the fall, he signed for new management with Bill Loeb in Hollywood. On September 24, Nick was one of over two dozen stars entertaining at the Masquers Club's charity show celebrating the 200th anniversary of show business in the United States. When Nick appeared at the Crystal Inn in Bakersfield, California, in the fall of 1952, he performed ten songs, including "Get Out Those Old Records," "I'm Looking Over a Four Leaf Clover," "Walking My Baby Back Home," "I'm Looking at the World Thru Rose Colored Glasses" and "I Love the Sunshine of Your Smile." In late September, he was at the Italian Village in San Francisco; he played a return engagement there the next month. When he headlined the Jung Hotel's Cotillion Room in New Orleans, *Variety* (September 13, 1952) reported, "Lucas shuns gags, novelty numbers and elaborate arrangement to put across his songology." Regarding his second stand of the year in San Francisco, Don Steele wrote in the *Oakland* (California) *Tribune* (October 4, 1952), "Nick Lucas is proving that old showmen always draw crowds at the Italian Village."

As 1952 ended, Mozelle Britton Dinehart opined in the North Hollywood *Valley Times* (December 22, 1952), "[Lucas] will be adding much to the Christmas holiday season by playing appropriate numbers on his famed guitar at many benefits to be held in the Valley and elsewhere. Nick Lucas is always one of the most willing to contribute talent to the worthy causes from show business!"

On April 5, 1952, an article by Ted Kovach appeared the *Valley Times* which declared that Nick, "who won the young hearts of the nation's college crowd during the raccoon days of the roaring '20s, is being readied for a blistering comeback trail. An artist who can woo two successive generations is rare indeed. But Encino's Nick Lucas, a three-time winner in the grandfather circle, is returning by public demand to satisfy the 'straight' singing craves of modern youths." Kovach stated that from 1929 to 1932, Nick was "the undisputed 'King of the Crooners'" and quoted him as saying, "The youngsters weren't quite so riotous over their idols in those days as they are today…. They were more reserved, more polite. They'd send us mail, phone us if possible and worship from afar. Today they tear off coat buttons and worship the buttons! …The music business certainly changed. In those days, a song would remain a hit for one or two years. Today, three months and—pfsst—the song's dead—played to death!" The article concluded, "As the little troubador … once a giant of song … prepares for the big comeback, his wife, lovely Catherine, will be standing by his side … needle in hand … ready to sew on coat buttons torn loose by hungry bobby-soxers."

The year 1953 began with Nick signing a managerial contract with the Milt Deutsch Agency and then embarking on a night club tour to promote his new Cavalier recordings, appearing at the Tehran Shrine Temple's Rainbow Room in Fresno, California, beginning January 12, 1953. Next came an engagement at the Golden Hotel in Reno; the *Reno Evening Gazette* (January 31, 1953) reported, "Crowds happily follow [Lucas] down memory lane…. Few present-day 'star attractions' can match this singing Troubadour's record. After more than 25 years in the limelight of show business, Nick Lucas is as popular as ever in the entertainment field. Generous with his songs and music he happily responds to encore calls and special requests of Terrace Room Crowds." The next month he was the singing star of Ern Westmore's Beauty Show at the Jefferson Hotel in Birmingham, Alabama, and on February 22, 1953, he starred in the City of Hope's (California) benefit show at the Sartu Theatre.

In April 1953, Nick headlined the charity ball at the Ambassador Athletic Club in Salt Lake City and the Texas Light and Power Show at the State Fair Auditorium in Dallas. That month also saw him returning to San Francisco for a recording session with Cavalier Records. On May 30, the *Valley Times* reported, "Nick Lucas to appear in first untitled production in the Wigmar TV series *The Narcotics Pushers* to be filmed at Goldwyn Studios with George Carillon as producer." In June, he appeared at Harrah's Reno Show Lounge, and on July 29, 1953, he headlined a vaudeville show in Yuba City, California. In August, he was at the Italian Village in San Francisco for an extended run as well as headlining the annual fair variety show at Ukiah, California. The *Oakland* (California) *Tribune* (September 10, 1953) reported, "Nick Lucas doing capacity biz at the Italian Village." Regarding the Ukiah date, the *Ukiah News* (August 27, 1953) stated, "Nick

Lucas and his guitar took many a listener back to the beginning radio years of the late 20s with his fine medley of old hit tunes."

From August 21 to 30, Nick appeared with Hank Penny at the Farmers Fair of Riverside County in San Bernardino, California, followed by a stand at the Mirador Club in Denver and another trip to San Francisco to record for Cavalier. In October, Nick worked at Stan Y's Club in Medford, Oregon, had a return engagement at Reno's Golden Hotel, and appeared at Club Marina in San Diego and the Palm-Olive Tavern in Fresno. He closed out the year with stands at Piluso's in Eugene, Oregon, in November, and headlined the Sun Carnival in El Paso in December.

On October 12, Nick was a guest at groundbreaking ceremonies and an invitational party at the Circle J Golf Club (which he was a member) in Newhall, California. Also attending were William Boyd, J. Carrol Naish, Maria Costi and Helen Westcott. The next month it was announced that Nick was under the management of the Crown Theatrical Agency.

Jimmie Fidler, in his "In Hollywood" column (May 10, 1953), wrote that Nick wanted to establish night clubs for youth in order to keep them away from taverns and other places that bred juvenile delinquency. He wrote, "Such clubs, Nick tells me, would sell only soft drinks, and would provide meeting places, properly controlled and conducted, for boys and girls in the teen-age bracket. I believe Nick has something here, and more power to him for advertising this idea."

The *Greeley* (Colorado) *Daily Tribune* (January 13, 1954) stated that Nick bought the Ouray Inn in Woodland Park, Colorado, in a sheriff's sale, paying $589 for the property.

After Nick opened 1954 with an engagement at the Kennewick Hotel in Kennewick, Washington, he headlined a show at the Veterans Memorial Building in Eureka, California; Margaret Delaney wrote in that city's *Times Standard* (February 9, 1954),

> [Lucas] carried his audience back into the carefree days of the late 'twenties, on the wings of his crooning voice and the notes of the ballads, which he himself in yesteryear made famous as a part of America's popular folk music. His performance highlighted the entertainment program.... For more than a half hour Lucas conducted his listeners along musical memory lanes ... [songs] which have survived the passing whims and fancies of the years, concluding with a special arrangement of 'My Blue Heaven,' sung in response to a special request by Mabel Mix, widow of the famous western film star and circus operator [Tom Mix] who chanced to be in the audience. Lucas' presentation, as one enthralled listener put it, was "strictly for dreamin'!"

Lucas next appeared at the El Cortez in Las Vegas and the Italian Village in San Francisco and then headlined the Cheyenne, Wyoming, Auto Show in April. In May, he was at the Calaveras County Fair and Jumping Frog Jubilee in Angels Camp, California, with the Hoosier Hot Shots. In June, with Jimmy Joy and His Orchestra and the Cell Block Seven, he starred in a musical revue at the Fort Worth, Texas, Casino, followed by headlining the "Fun Unlimited" stage show at the Alameda County Fair in Pleasanton, California, from June 28 to July 4. He then appeared at the San Mateo (California) Fair, where on opening night he brought along Nancy Welford, who was with him a quarter of a century before in *The Gold Diggers of Broadway*. *The San Mateo Times* reported that his rendition of old-time favorites "drew many a nostalgic sigh from the audience." In July 1954, he starred in the Variety Show at the Humboldt County Fair at Ferndale, California, along with the Hoosier Hot Shots, Laraine Stephens and Phil Arden. The same month he played an engagement at Angelo's in Omaha, and in the fall he appeared at the

Golden Hotel in Reno; the *Reno Evening Gazette* (September 18, 1954) stated, "[Lucas] is thrilling capacity crowds nightly." In his syndicated newspaper column (October 7, 1954), E.V. Durling reported, "[Lucas] continues to be a top night club attraction." Nick closed out the year with his fourth return engagement at San Francisco's Italian Village. In November 1954, it was reported that Hunt-McCafferty Productions of Hollywood was providing package shows for state fairs in 1955 including the Nick Lucas Revue, which would have a supporting cast and chorus line.

In his syndicated newspaper column "Inside Hollywood" (March 27, 1953), Jimmy Fidler talked about consulting Nick regarding memorable music, calling him an "eminent authority." Fidler wrote,

> Music that is tuneful, wrapped around words that have meaning—melodies that are lilting, lending themselves to beautiful harmony—are the type of compositions that live on and on in the memory and in fact. I have this analysis from none other than Nick Lucas who has for 30 years helped make history in the show business with a wonderful singing voice and a wonderfully trained—and tuned—guitar.
>
> …Nick Lucas tabs "Tiptoe Through the Tulips" as his greatest song hit, and next is "Side by Side." …Then there was "Painting the Clouds with Sunshine," and more recently "Coquette" and "Tear Drops." Once upon a time, Nick recalls, the song plugger was the fellow who started songs on the road to popularity and success, but today the plugger has been supplanted by the disc jockey. A good disc jockey can take a tuneful melody and make a hit of it, says Nick. I guess he's about right there.
>
> But what impressed me most is that all of Nick's successes have been of beauty, wholesome sentiment and full of ringing, sweet melody. He says that lovers of music are today just as critical as in a generation ago, and that the hit tunes that last out the years are the same quality now as in the roaring twenties, or the Gay Nineties.

Over the years, Nick had some unsatisfactory dealings with record producers. One example was when Hucksters Records sold his masters to Capitol. "I made these recordings for Hucksters was paid the usual amount for such work. Then the masters were sold to Capitol for a profit. Of course my contract went with the sale and I was then under contract to Capitol. Before I could make any real money off the arrangement, the records had to sell big, as I would only get royalties. They released a few of them and they did all right, but it was Hucksters and Capitol who got most of the money. There are some real promoters in this business."

For Tony Spinosa's San Francisco–based company Cavalier Records, Nick cut eight sides that became his first long-playing album, a ten-inch disc titled *Tiptoe Through the Tulips with Nick Lucas*. The individual songs from the album were also released on four singles. He recalled that the recordings were made under somewhat primitive conditions and that he was also offered a chance to invest in the company but declined. The North Hollywood *Valley Times* (March 5, 1953) reported that Lucas "has again become a best seller in the record field, through four transcriptions made for Cavalier Records."

Billboard magazine reviewed two of Nick's Cavalier single recordings as well as the album. In its December 27, 1952, issue the trade magazine covered the two singles: "'Lady Be Good'—The evergreen by the Gershwin Freres gets a lively, pleasant vocal by Lucas, whose guitar and quintet are backing. The arrangement, a straight, melodic one, shows off the piano backing nicely." Regarding "Til the End of Forever: "Troubadour Lucas here delivers himself of a routine ballad. Much schmaltz and corny sentiment on this side." Regarding the second coupling, the reviewer wrote: "'Coquette'—Lucas …

sounds pretty much like he did a couple of decades ago. Good nostalgia here as he chants the familiar old ballad for a listenable side. 'Tear-Drops'—Ditto."

On May 2, 1953, *Billboard* ran a second review of "Tear Drops/Coquette." Regarding the first song, it opined, "A pleasant effort receiving nice performance from the troubadour, who accompanies himself on guitar over a so-so arrangement." Of the latter it said, "Nick Lucas hands the oldie a smooth warble backed in routine fashion by a combo." The ten-inch Cavalier album *Tiptoe Through the Tulips with Nick Lucas* was covered by *Billboard* (September 25, 1954): "On this, [Lucas'] first record for the label, he does a first-rate job with a collection of songs that have long been part of his act. And he does them with the same contagious feeling that has always marked his work. ...The older set will be interested in this release."

Late in 1954, Nick signed with the Los Angeles–based firm Crown Records and did a single for them, "Looking at the World Thru Rose Colored Glasses/Did You Ever See a Dream Walking?" It was announced that Nick would also do an album for Crown but this fell through because he said he was not paid for the single. In reviewing Nick's Crown disk, the *Dallas* (Texas) *Morning News* wrote, "[I]f you like good banjo, get a copy of Nick Lucas' Crown recording of 'I'm Looking at the World Thru Rose Colored Glasses.' It's his first banjo effort in twenty-five years." *Cashbox* (April 9, 1955) called the single "a couple of good o'd standards."

In the fall of 1953, Nick was guest columnist for Jimmie Fidler's "Inside Hollywood" newspaper column. In his September 27, 1953, article "Class Entertainment," he wrote,

> From where I sit, the amusement-seeking portion of the American public definitely demands wholesomeness in its motion pictures and other forms of entertainment, now as never before. What approximated an era of sophistication, perhaps synthetic, has passed into oblivion, as far as I can see. Now the customers want clean, family-style entertainment—not the kind that's geared for the risqué and hoodlum type of mind and appetite.
>
> ...I make it my regular policy to question the public regarding their tastes in songs which I sing, as well as in other phases of entertainment. I find that most people want the song numbers which have lasted many, many years in popularity because of a wholesome and nostalgic quality. They want the kind of lyrics they can sing with their children, without offending their tastes and giving them a wrong conception of how people behave. They want songs which truly reflect America—not the phony concoctions which mirror the thinking of a small, sophisticated group of people. This, in my opinion, is a positive symptom of American tastes—and Hollywood will do well to watch it closely.

On February 22, 1954, York, Pennsylvania's *Gazette and Daily* carried John Lester's column "Radio and Television" stating, "CBS-TV has signed the veteran guitarist-singer Nick Lucas for a summer series titles *Birth of a Song*." In his column "Dallas After Dark" in the *Dallas Morning News* (June 18, 1954), Tony Zoppi reported that the previous week, Nick had appeared "before a cheering audience of 2,000 in Fort Worth" and called him "one of the great headliners in show business." He quoted Lucas as saying, "There's some great new talent in show business today. You didn't have to travel any further than the Jack Benny show here in Dallas to see a kid named Sammy Davis, who in my opinion will become an immortal." He also commented on the failure of some crooners to sustain their popularity: "Perhaps the biggest single reason is their lack of ability to sell themselves. They have the equipment to sing a song beautifully, but they're lost when they get before an audience. That's why so many of them do terrific business the first time on the circuit. After that, they start to fade. The people come to see them out of curiosity and often times, they are let down." Asked to define showmanship, Lucas ventured, "I guess you could say it's Ted Lewis' high hat, or Harry Richman's cane, Durante's nose, Cantor's eyes, or—my black guitar." Zoppi also noted that when Nick appeared on a telethon sponsored by Bing Crosby and Bob Hope to raise funds to send the nation's Olympic team to Europe, Crosby "wrapped an arm around Nick's shoulder and told the vast TV audience, 'I've learned more from this guy than anybody in the business.'"

Nick headlined the six-act vaudeville *Fair Follies* show in Santa Rosa, California, in June 1954, followed by appearing at the Alameda County Fair in Pleasanton, California, and the Lake Worth Casino in Fort Worth. In July 1954, he appeared at the Napa County Fair in Calistoga, California, and then starred in the *Fun Unlimited* stage show at the Court of Four Seasons in Oakland, California, followed by headlining at the Humboldt County Fair at Ferndale, California, where he was billed as "The Cavalier Troubadour." When Nick headlined San Mateo, California's Fiesta Jubilee, the *San Mateo Times* (August 9, 1954) wrote, "The reminiscent tunes of Nick Lucas ... drew spontaneous applause from the audience ... that would not let him leave the stage." In the fall of 1954, Nick, bandleader Horace Heidt and singer Sunny Gale starred in a Reno stage show. He closed out the year at the Italian Village in San Francisco. Also during 1954, a song Lucas composed, "I Tip My Heart to You," was waxed by Madalane on Musica Records. In August Nick recorded the song "Sadie Thompson" for Cavalier Records.

In 1955, Nick headlined at the Westward-Ho Hotel in Phoenix, Charlie Foy's nitery in North Hollywood (with Maxie Rosenbloom), the Colony Club in Omaha and the Showboat in Las Vegas. Regarding his Omaha appearance, *Variety* (June 1, 1955) reported that he was "packing them [in]": "The troubadour stays apace with the times

Nick Lucas performing in a nightclub in the 1950s.

(i.e., a novel 'Davy Crockett' piece) and keeps the payees happy...." He also had stands in Dallas, the Beverly Hilton Hotel in Hollywood, the Sun Valley Lodge in Sun Valley, Idaho, and the Wort Hotel in Jackson Hole, Wyoming. He played a return engagement at Las Vegas' Showboat in the summer and also appeared in Frontier Days at the Plains Hotel, Cheyenne. The September 5, 1955, *Valley Times* (North Hollywood) stated that actor Stanley Adams had been engaged by Nick to write material for his night club engagements. In October, Nick headlined the Kern County Fair in Bakersfield, California, along with actor-ventriloquist Max Terhune. On December 29, the *Valley Times* reported, "Friends of Nick Lucas ... gave him a dinner party at the Circle J Guest Ranch, Newhall, prior to his leaving for El Paso, Texas, on a supper club tour." He closed out the year in El Paso at the Café Charmant.

Nineteen fifty-five was also the year that Nick began recording with Accent Records; he stayed with the label on a non-exclusive basis for the rest of his life. Accent was owned by musician-composer Scott Seely, whose music abilities Nick greatly admired. Nick's initial sessions with Accent produced three singles: "Bella Nonna/Paper Roses," "Soldier's Guitar/Kind and Considerate" and "Pasta Cheech/Not Guilty." "Pasta Cheech" was composed and published by Harry Warren, who told Nick it was his favorite of the recordings of his songs. *Billboard* (November 26, 1955) wrote of "Kind and Considerate," "[Lucas] hasn't been on wax for a long time, and his old-time fans will welcome this sweetly sung and strummed moralizer." *Billboard* on "Soldier's Guitar": "Lucas sounds as good as he ever did on this side, but he has stronger material on the flip side." On December 10, the same trade journal reported of "Soldier's Guitar," "The record has been steadily building since it was released and is now stirring up noises in Chicago, Cleveland and Boston as well as Los Angeles." The article also quoted Nick as saying, "It's been a long time between hits, but this one was worth waiting for."

Late in 1956, Nick returned to Cavalier Records and cut five more songs. They were combined with most of the songs from his 1952 ten-inch album to make his initial 12-inch LP, *Tiptoe Through the Tulips with Nick Lucas*. A single from the album, "Francine/Get Out Those Old Records," was issued to good reception. *Billboard* (April 20, 1957) reviewed "Get Out Those Old Records": "[Lucas] returns to disks with the popular Lombardo oldie. Good, if modestly produced side, that will get a few curiosity spins." *Billboard*'s take on "Francine": "Lucas' smooth tenor handles this romantic beguine-rhythm opus with old-fashioned chorus. Not much here for the kids."

In August 1957, Nick was signed by Decca Records to record 13 songs reprising some of his best-sellers from the Brunswick years. The sessions were produced by former bandleader Sonny Burke. A dozen tunes were put on the album *Painting the Clouds with Sunshine*. The LP proved to be a steady seller for Decca and it remained in the company's catalogue for over 15 years. It was released in March 1958, as part of the company's "Star Time" package of 16 albums, including ones by Burl Ives, the Mills Brothers, Toni Arden, Sammy Davis, Jr., the Four Aces, Al Hibbler, Earl Grant, Lenny Dee, Carmen McRae and a Bing Crosby vintage compilation. In the "Listening Post" column in the *Dallas Morning News* (March 2, 1958), a reviewer stated,

> All the warmth of a poignant, sometimes sad-faced singer on the scene a quarter-of-a-century is captured by Decca in a radiant, superb album by Nick Lucas. There is somehow a feeling of optimism conveyed in about everything Lucas sings. The album is appropriately entitled "Painting the Clouds with Sunshine." The little man sings the same songs that kept Hotel

Adolphus Century Room patrons—even the younger set who had never heard of the Singing Troubadour as he was known years ago—applauding, almost pleading for more.

The Redlands (California) *Daily Fact* (April 7, 1958) noted in its "Record Review" column, "Now Decca has recorded a dozen numbers by [Nick] Lucas on an LP that will cement his old friendships and should win him new ones." Earlier in the year, Stanton Dann wrote in the *Mobile* (Alabama) *Journal* (January 24, 1958) that, "according to the disc jockeys and the ratings ... Gene Austin and Nick Lucas are panicking the teen-agers of this day just as they did when you were young."

When Nick headlined the Statler Ballroom in Dallas early in 1956, the *Dallas Morning News* (February 7, 1956) reported he had three encores for his first show. Eddie Greene, vice-president of Music Corporation of America, attended the performance and told a reporter,

> Twenty years ago Nick and Catherine invited my wife and I to a big dinner party at their home in New Jersey. There were a lot of show people there, close friends he'd made in the business through the years. When we had finished with dessert, he stood up and said he had a few words to say. Then he told us his annuities were coming due and he was quitting show business. That was twenty years ago. Since then he has bought a lovely home out in California and has tried to settle down. But the job offers continued to come in and the money is too good to turn down, so Nick just keeps tip-toeing through the tulips.

In response, Nick said, "I tried to quit, but it's no use. When they start waving that money at you." He added that he gets "tired of playing golf every day, [and] it feels good to hit the road and get out in front of an audience. I stay in good shape and my voice is as good today as it was when I was playing the Palace, so I keep singing. Someday I guess I'll toss in the towel." Then he added, "Never quit when you're ahead."

The Valley News (Van Nuys, California) stated in its April 28, 1956, issue, "Nick Lucas of Van Nuys vacationing at Alex Springborg's Glen Ivy Hot Springs between major club singing engagements. Nick leaves soon on a Southwest tour."

One day in 1956, Nick received a telephone call from Colonel Tom Parker, Elvis Presley's manager, who asked him to come to the Metro-Goldwyn-Mayer lot to meet Elvis, who was there filming a movie. Nick had known Parker since the 1930s when Parker was road manager for Gene Austin; Nick and Parker kept in touch as Parker managed Eddy Arnold, Hank Snow and Nick's friend Eddie Dean. At MGM, Parker introduced Nick to Elvis, saying, "Elvis, I want you to meet Nick Lucas. He's the best guitar player in the world." Nick found Presley to be a nice and unassuming young man and they got along well. Parker suggested that Elvis take guitar lessons from Nick, who was amenable. But due to their conflicting schedules, this never came about.

In an article on the then-controversial new music genre of rock'n'roll, the *Dallas Morning News* (July 30, 1957) called Nick "the man who first popularized the guitar and thus is indirectly responsible for the phenomenon of Elvis...." The piece had Nick stating, "Rock'n'roll is all right. It is an outlet for youngsters to express their inner feelings." Also quoted was his business manager, Cliff Walbon: "I think rock'n'roll is a great outlet. In the opinion of some school officials in California, it is a great deterrent to juvenile delinquency. There was more violence in the Charleston than in rock'n'roll dancing."

Nick headlined venues in Jackson Hole, Denver, Seattle, Anchorage, Dallas, San Francisco and more. When he appeared in Kansas City, Missouri, *Variety* (May 23, 1956) reported,

Rep build up over the years singing in vaude, cafes, film, radio and TV register solidly for Nick Lucas, back in town after a five-year lapse, and this time at a different stand, the deluxe Terrace Grill at Hotel Muehlebach.... As it has been for over 30 years, Lucas' contribution is good singing backed by his guitar plucking. His 30 minutes is pretty much a rundown of the numbers linked to him over the years.... To these are added a current pop or two, a newcomer, "Pasta Cheech," and "Come Back to Sorrento," especially done well. It's the nostalgia that the customers go for, being generous with response to the old faves and begging Lucas for more. It's all on a chummy level and builds to a virtual beg off for the vet singer.

The Nick Lucas Revue played venues such as the Sonoma County Fair in Santa Rosa, California, in July 1956 and the Mother Lode Fair in Santa Rosa, California, in August. The September 8, 1956, *Billboard* reported that Nick was signed to play the lead in a pilot, "Tangiers," for the new television series *Ticket to Adventure* for Thor Brooks Productions. When Nick and Beatrice Kay headlined the Italian Village in San Francisco at the end of the year, *Variety* (December 19, 1956) took note of the fact that both entertainers offered nostalgic fare: "Beatrice Kay and Nick Lucas both can sell a song, as they proved again here (for the ninth time)." The reviewer added that Nick was "surprisingly engaging. ...The voice isn't so sure as it once may have been, but he still has appeal and when he lets fly 'Tiptoe Through the Tulips' the whole crowd's with him."

When he appeared at Lenzi's Supper Club in Eureka, California, Nick told a *Times Standard* (April 10, 1956) reporter, "I think that we entertainers are like race horses. We have good and bad days but the moral is always the same. And the moral is that an entertainer has to keep in condition all the time." The writer said that Nick proved his point by spurning a second Scotch and soda and disdaining a cigarette. Regarding the Lenzi's show, the *Times Standard* (April 7, 1956) wrote, "Nick Lucas and his famed guitar have appeared all over the world and has never failed to thrill everyone in the audience. A Must See!" In the summer of 1956, he headlined the Sonoma County Fair in Santa Rosa, California. Around that time, Erskine Johnson reported in his nationally syndicated newspaper column "In Hollywood" (June 18, 1956), "There's a 'Singing Troubadour' TV idea cooking for singer Nick Lucas with Howard Estabrook at the writing reins." Estabrook was an Academy Award–winning screenwriter.

In the spring of 1957, Nick was elected to the Board of Straight Men at the Comedy Club in Hollywood. That year's headline venues for Nick included stands in Tulsa; the Citrus Fair in Cloverdale, California; the Moongate in North Hollywood; the Green Triangle in Pocatello, Idaho; the California State Fair in Sacramento, and the Town and Country Club in Seattle. *Variety* (July 31, 1957) reported on his appearance at the Adolphus Hotel in Dallas:

The old pros still know their way around the bistro belt. Veteran Nick Lucas stepped on the Century Room floor ... and confidently took charge of the near-capacity audience—and kept the crowd with a nostalgic rundown. ... Strumming guitar, Lucas doesn't offer a single new lyric, he doesn't have to for his hefty score. Aside from "Around the World in 80 Days" he runs through a batch of evergreens ("Tiptoe Through the Tulips" with an inserted "Sounds like Hound Dog" and "My Blue Heaven" are clinchers), but added fillips bring tablers to life. Lucas pipes "Sorrento" in Italian, tosses between comedy lines and, à la Tony Martin, gets off easily by taking the bandstand and singing while the terping begins.

When he appeared in Wausau, Wisconsin, in August, Ernie Farrow's Wallace Brothers circus shows gave him a surprise birthday party. Following an appearance in Pasadena, the *Pasadena Independent* (December 7, 1957) reported, "Long before Elvis

Presley was born, Nick Lucas was thrilling America with his guitar and happy songs. Long after the pelvis kid is forgotten Nick will be strumming and humming the songs America loves best. The 'Tip Toe' Troubadour thrilled a big dinner crowd with songs he's made famous and a few 1957 hits. As was expected, Nick evoked thunderous cheers and applause." When he appeared at the Hesperia Inn in Pasadena, the *Pasadena Independent* (December 19, 1957) carried the story: "Lucas and his one instrument orchestra currently has a TV show titled *Nick Lucas and His Guitar* heard in more than 100 cities across the nation."

In the summer of 1957, it was announced that actor Slick Slavin (aka Trustin Howard) would portray Nick Lucas in a film about the singer-guitarist's life called *Tiptoe Through the Tulips*. Nick and Slavin formed the Troubadour Production Company to make the film with Hollywood producer Howard Chevie showing interest in the project. Negotiations were underway with several Hollywood companies to release it. The film never came about although plans for a movie based on Nick's life continued to be bandied about well into the 1970s. In the spring of 1959, it was announced that Nick was signed to appear in the motion picture *Even Steven*, an independent outing from producers Patric Knowles and George Kellner, but it too was never made.

The year 1958 proved to another busy one for Nick with personal appearances at the Raddison Hotel's Flame Room in Minneapolis for two different stands; lengthy separate engagements at the Holiday Hotel in Reno with his group, the Townaires; and at the Bal Taberin in Lake Tahoe, Nevada. It was announced in the spring of that year that he would join Betty Grable, June Havoc, Lou Bellson, April Stevens, Leif Erickson, Dale Robertson, Muzzy Marcellino and Patti Lewis as a guest vocalist on the RCA Victor recording *The Ted Fio Rito Alumni Album*. When he appeared at the Holiday Theatre Lounge in Reno, the *Nevada State Journal* (May 24, 1958) reported tht Nick

Nick Lucas publicity photograph from January 1957.

> can be classified as the all-time great singing troubadour.... Lucas is without doubt the epitome of singing troubadours, bringing nostalgia with his music as well as refreshing and timely arrangements to both old and young alike.... His old favorites ... bring back memories to the older music lovers, and at the same time he gives the younger set a deeper appreciation of the finest in theatre lounge entertainment not only with his songs but his warmth and personality as well. Here is an entertainer whose old favorites bring to young and old alike the

type of music not found elsewhere. Nightly standing room only attests to his popularity. The demands made on him for requests prove that Nick Lucas will remain in the hearts of all as one of America's favorites.

In the fall of 1958, when Nick headlined the Holiday Hotel in Reno, the same newspaper wrote on September 6, 1958, "Loved by all, Nick Lucas proves himself to be popular not only with the audience but with each individual in the audience; an honor bestowed on only a few entertainers today. …[His] voice is just as rich in tone quality today as it was in the days [when his] songs were new, and the warmth of his personality has increased with added years." He ended the year in Calexico, California, sharing the stage with Frankie Laine and Lucille Norman in the C.P. MacGregor–promoted "Shrine Family Show" on December 17, 1958.

Nick kicked off 1959 with a two-week stand in St. Louis; *Variety* (January 21, 1959) opined,

> Although it has been many a year since the ageless troubadour, Nick Lucas, has played St. Louis, Father Time seemed to be up to some trickery as far as first-nighters were concerned at his Sheraton-Jefferson Blue Room opening. The old vocal magic is still there, hardly changed an iota from the old days and the passing years have been so gentle with him he still looks a youngster, senior grade. …Aside for a brief nod or two to the current hit parade, Lucas sticks to the evergreens, strolling ringside now and then with his guitar, and has no trouble at all keeping all hands in a responsive mood all the way.

Regarding the engagement, the *St. Louis Globe-Democrat* (January 15, 1959) noted "a covey of Kansas City fans of Nick Lucas making a special trip here to catch Nick's opening at the Boulevard Room." He followed with an appearance at the Bal Taberin in Las Vegas. During the year he played a total of fourteen weeks at the Holiday Hotel in Reno. At one of his stands there, *Variety* (March 11, 1959) reported,

> Nick Lucas' nitery appeal is evident: it's his styling and choice of titles and he can do no wrong with either. [Audience] reaction for his playback in this room indicates the veteran minstrel will undoubtedly become a semi-annual returnee…. Lucas makes no attempt to latch onto the updated titles, but wisely offers those associated with his name. …Lucas' most ardent fans are in the older set (with more money to drop at the tables) but he's also winning admirers from the younger salooners.

Lucas headlined the Second Annual Santa Monica (California) Home show at that city's Civic Auditorium on May 6–10, 1959. The North Hollywood *Valley Times* reported (August 25, 1959), "Leon Charles is dickering with Nick Lucas to play an important role in *Count Your Blessings* by Dorothy Collingwood, which he will produce and direct in Los Angeles this coming season." Earlier, on April 23, Nick and Catherine Lucas were honored at a dinner commemorating their 42nd wedding anniversary at the Sands Hotel in Las Vegas. In the fall of 1959, it was announced that Richard Blalock had written a new song for Nick for his upcoming supper club tour.

While Nick was appearing in St. Louis, he was interviewed by Joan Foster of the *St. Louis Globe-Democrat* (January 15, 1959), who called him "the man responsible for the wave of nostalgia sweeping the city these days." In the article, Nick discussed his long career:

> My clientele has gotten older too, because we all grew up together. People come up to me and say they remember me when they were in school, or that they had all my records when they were courting and I sure bring back memories. Gee, they say, you must be 70. Well, I'm 60, going on 61, and I don't mind admitting it. I don't overwork, don't smoke and don't drink so that I can keep in shape. I rest and take care of myself. I figure you owe it to the people who

come to hear you.... I stuck in this business and when they see me they say they're amazed to see I'm still going. It's because I like the business. I give it all my attention.

He also told Foster this poignant story: "One woman must have been 70 or so and when she came up to see me after the show, she was crying because I brought back memories of her husband when they were courting. I've got lots of friends and admirers all over the country that I don't know."

Continuing night club work, Nick had several successful seasons at the Holiday Hotel in Reno. *The Frederick* (Maryland) *News Post* (March 26, 1960) reported, "Nick Lucas, and with his talented Troubadours, continues his record breaking appearances at the Holiday Hotel. Nick is the rare and talented performer who not only continues to build an ever increasing new audience but maintains a hold on those who have heard him time and time again." When he appeared at the hotel's Theatre Lounge, the *Reno Evening Gazette* (March 18, 1960) noted, "Nick Lucas is still one of the nation's top attractions. He's still a star attraction at the nation's biggest hotels and night spots and makes frequent television appearances." In the early 1960s, Nick moved to Harrah's Club in the same city where he was guaranteed 16 weeks booking each year, both there and at Harrah's other establishment in Lake Tahoe. At the latter venue, early in 1960, he headlined the *Winter Olympic Revue* in the Nevada Room at the Nevada Lodge in conjunction with the Winter Olympic Games being held in that area.

Often at these engagements, from the late 1950s well into the 1960s, Nick was assisted by a trio of musicians. The act was billed as "Nick Lucas and His Troubadours." On November 18, 1959, *The Nevada State Journal* stated, "'Tiptoe' Nick Lucas and his talented Troubadours close their last week at the holiday with an enviable record. With each appearance at the Holiday, Nick has set a new attendance record and this, his fourth appearance, has topped them all." The February 5, 1960, *Reno Evening Gazette* reported that Nick was headlining the Winter Olympics Revue in the Nevada Room of the Nevada Lodge-Casino in Lake Tahoe, adding, "Nick Lucas' reviews describe him as an able and polished showman that is one of the strongest attractions to appear on the stages of the nation's top night spots." Around this time, singer Janice Jones was added to Nick's act. When they appeared at the Nevada Lodge at Lake Tahoe, *The Nevada State Journal* (February 27, 1960) declared, "Nick Lucas, his Troubadours and pretty Janice Jones were a smash success in the first week of their engagement." The same newspaper on April 1, 1960, opined, "Lovable Nick Lucas, 'the Elvis Presley of the Stone Age,' continues to prove his popularity nightly in the Theatre Lounge of the Holiday Hotel.... Nick's warm marvelous personality ranks him as a peer in current today lounge presentations (and he) is still one of the nation's top attractions." The story also said that Allie Lorraine, "a small beauty of about four feet ten inches," had joined Nick's act. "She voices the same mellow music that made Nick famous to blend a favorable combination," the reviewer concluded. The April 8, 1960, *Nevada State Journal* called Nick's stand at the Wagon Wheel in Lake Tahoe "an informal type show that features friendly Nick playing his beautiful guitar.... Lucas and His Troubadours [take] audiences down memory lane ... with a liberal sprinkling of up-to-date numbers thrown in for added pleasure. Year in and year out Lucas remains a solid headline attraction with his soothing voice and guitar playing."

In September 1960, Nick headlined with Woody Herman and His Orchestra at the Dollar Music Hall in Dallas. When Nick and the Troubadours appeared at the

California Spring Festival in Sacramento from April 15 to 23, 1961, it was announced, "Lucas has played the top night clubs of the nation and judging by his current successes, Nick has found a new audience field in which he appears to be a tailor-made attraction— the annual county and State fairs." In August 1960, Nick was a candidate for the office of third vice-president of the American Guild of Variety Artists (AGVA).

During this time, Nick was making $3000 a week but found the work to be very tiring. He was also losing money gambling, later reckoning that he lost approximately $75,000 playing craps over the years; he gave up gambling in 1962. He worried about his wife's deteriorating health. Her doctors had warned her not to go out at night or be around people who smoked, but like Nick, she enjoyed gambling. He became more concerned about her health while he was appearing in cocktail lounges. Nick's doctor told him that if he kept up the pace of the cocktail lounges, he would eventually lose his voice. In 1965, Nick bade farewell to the cocktail lounge circuit and he and Catherine returned to their apartment at the Fontenoy Towers in Hollywood. Nick had had this apartment for business purposes and as a base of operations since the late 1940s and they decided to remain there. Also residing in the apartment building, where James Cagney once had a penthouse, was Nick's friend, actor Jack Mulhall, who appeared in movies from 1910 to 1959. He and Nick first met when they were in *The Show of Shows* and later they both did the Hollywood and Broadway runs of *Ken Murray's Blackouts*. Mulhall retired in 1977 and died in 1979; Nick was an honorary pallbearer at his funeral.

In the summer of 1962, Nick headlined the Masonic Youth Benefit show and dance in San Bernardino, California, an event booked by C.P. MacGregor. Nationally syndicated newspaper columnist Earl Wilson reported on June 12, 1962, that Nick "was among those applauding beautiful Arlene Dahl when she opened at the Latin Quarter" in New York City. In his "Bright Lights" column in the (San Mateo, California) *Times* (December 7, 1962), Lloyd Johnson noted that Nick "is still one of the best entertainment draws in the business… [H]is song-selling voice never fails to keep audiences in a nostalgic frame of mind until he 'Tip-Toes' off the stage. Nick's last-night opening at Bimbo's 365 Theatre-Restaurant received one of the greatest ovations these ears have heard in years." Also reporting on that San Francisco appearance, Perry Phillips wrote in his "Night Sounds" column in the *Oakland Tribune* (December 14, 1962), "Well, time has passed on, but it hasn't left Nick Lucas behind. …[I]f you think some of today's singers enjoy immense popularity then you'd be amazed at the following Lucas had during a period when there was no record distribution such as that enjoyed by today's artists. If it were possible, he could go on singing forever and to me that's not a bad idea." In 1964, Nick was signed as a semi-regular on ABC-TV's *The Lawrence Welk Show* and his half-dozen appearances on the program brought much viewer response and critical acclaim. When the contract expired, he expected to be signed to the show permanently but Welk told him he was "becoming too popular" and his contract was not renewed. He also made several appearances on Gene Autry's *Melody Ranch* TV series with host Johnny Bond on Channel 5 in Hollywood.

Between his engagements with his trio in Reno and Lake Tahoe, Nick would also play single dates. He was especially popular in Dallas. In the fall of 1963, he was booked for a two-week run at the Cabana Club there. His friend Tony Zoppi, entertainment editor of the *Dallas News*, gave his show a good review and the club was packed every night. Zoppi later became vice-president in charge of publicity, advertising and entertainment at Las Vegas' Riviera Hotel.

Zoppi called Nick and told him that their friend Bob Hope was to be in Dallas to attend the SMU-Air Force football game at the Cotton Bowl and entertain at the SMU Coliseum; Zoppi promised to bring Hope to Nick's Cabana Club show. After his October 7, 1963, performance, Nick joined Hope and Zoppi at their table and while they were talking, a man came over, congratulated him on his performance and told him, "Nick, you are great and I have been a fan of yours for years." The man gave the three of them passes to a strip joint he owned in Dallas, the Carousel Club. After the John F. Kennedy assassination a month later, no matter where Bob Hope saw Nick, the comedian reminded him, and anyone else in earshot, that it was Nick Lucas who introduced him to Jack Ruby.

Regarding Nick's stand at the Cabana's Bon Vivant Room, the *Dallas Morning Mail* (October 1, 1963) noted, "[A] huge crowd greeted Lucas ... many of them fans since the days he set vaudeville records here." The article stated that "Tiptoe Through the Tulips" "still stops the show. There are several other nostalgic favorites.... But Lucas also put his unique vocal stamp on such contemporary hits as 'San Francisco,' 'Painted, Tainted Rose' and 'Days of Wine and Roses.' ...A gifted entertainer who knows what is required to please any audience."

During this period, Nick sometimes shared star billing at Harrah's Reno Show Lounge with entertainers such as bandleader Les Brown in March, Jerry Colonna in June and Big Tiny Little in October. In June, he was co-billed with the King Sisters at Harrah's Stateline Lounge in Lake Tahoe. When he appeared at the National Orange Show in San Bernardino in the spring of 1964, he was dubbed "the indestructible guitar-strumming crooner." Back at Lake Tahoe's Stateline Lounge in the spring of 1964, Nick shared the bill with the De Castro Sisters. That fall, he headlined with Billy Eckstine and Woody Herman's Herd in the Show Lounge at Harrah's Club in Reno, after having been with Herman the previous month at Lake Tahoe's Stateline Lounge. Early in 1965, he alternated with Louis Prima, Gia Malone and Sam Butera and the Witnesses at Harrah's Show Lounge in Reno. Regarding this outing, Perry Phillips wrote in "Night Rounds" (*Oakland Tribune*, January 15, 1965), "[Lucas] shares the bill with the Louis Prima Show. He 'Tiptoes Through the Tulips' nightly to the delight of the big following he's built up over the years. They still love him." In February 1965, Nick co-starred with bandleader Harry James and the singing duo of (Tony) Sandler and (Ralph) Young at Harrah's Stateline Lounge. In the fall, he was back at Harrah's in Reno with Della Reese and Judy Lynn.

In mid–1965, after returning to Hollywood, Nick decided to semi-retire after being active for a half-century. Not wanting to completely give up work, he began to appear in what he called "casual dates," still doing some night club work along with state and county fairs. Due to the slower pace, he succeeded in saving his voice. He particularly liked working the fair circuit, not only because he did only one show a night but also because the response he got from promoters and audiences was very good and he found this type of work to be very lucrative. He appeared at the San Joaquin County Fair, Fresno District Fair, Oregon State Fair, San Mateo Flower Festival, Sacramento County Fair, Pleasanton Fair, Orange Show in San Bernardino, Pittsburgh Home Show, Portland Home Show and the Colorado Springs Show of Progress.

When he headlined the 31st Annual San Mateo County Fair, that city's *Times* (August 10, 1965) reported, "Singing the old hits that made him famous when movies first discovered sound, Lucas thrilled his audience with [his standards] and current hits 'I Left My Heart in San Francisco' and 'I Could Have Danced All Night.'"

On February 16, 17, 23 and 24, 1966, Nick starred at the Fire Station Night Club and Inn in Garden Grove, California. When he appeared in the Fleur de Lis room in the Hotel Adolphus in Dallas in 1966, Francis Raffetto reported in the *Dallas Morning News* (March 9, 1966) that his act "was vibrant, vigorous, packed with nostalgic tunes...." Besides the old favorites, Raffetto said Lucas interspersed his program with newer numbers like "I'm Getting Married in the Morning" and "The Shadow of Your Smile." Following the performance, Lucas told Raffetto, "There's no show business anymore. No more Keith vaudeville circuit, Orpheum circuit, Interstate circuit. I used to come down here and be sure of 10 or 12 weeks every year. Now you play a date in Dallas one night and in Seattle, Washington, the next." He said he wanted his three grandsons "to be lawyers or doctors" but added, "I love people, to try to make them happy. I enjoy my work."

Nick's other 1966 playdates included an appearance before the Long Beach United School Districts Adult Teacher Association in Long Beach, California, in April; guest starring in a preview performance of *Don Marlowe's Vanities* in October at the Institute of Lifetime Learning in Long Beach; and a December engagement at the Hotel Aladdin in Las Vegas. When he was back in Long Beach for a Mother's Day program, he told Sherm Williams of the city's *Press-Telegram* (May 7, 1966), "I'm old enough to collect Social Security"; the writer reported that Nick "didn't look a day older" than when he had first interviewed him two decades earlier. Lucas told Williams, "I have never overworked. I believe in vacations and I book shows that permit it. I don't diet and I don't believe in strict exercise."

The mid–1960s found Nick back with Accent Records and its owner, Scott Seely, whom he considered one of the finest arrangers he ever worked with. In 1964, Nick re-recorded "Tiptoe Through the Tulips" backed by "Hello, Dolly" for Accent. *Billboard* (April 11, 1964) gave the platter a "good" rating. Two years later, Nick waxed a song he composed and used to close his act, "It's Been a Good Life." For business reasons, the tune was credited to David Garvin, Accent Records' one-time assistant A&R chief. Regarding this platter, seer Criswell wrote in his October 23, 1966, syndicated newspaper column "Criswell Predicts," "I predict the new Nick Lucas recording of 'It's Been a Good Life' and 'Darling, I Love You' will hit the top 40 just as 'Tiptoe Through the Tulips' did a few years ago."

In the summer of 1966, Nick headlined the stage revue *The Blackouts of 1966* at the Cal-Neva Lodge at Lake Tahoe; appearing in the club's lounge was his friend Gene Austin. The show also was staged in Las Vegas and other locales. A session with Accent in 1967 resulted in a quartet of the finest records Nick ever made: a redoing of "Brown Eyes, Why Are You Blue?," "Worryin'," "Our San Diego" and "I'm Blue for You." In its "Best Bets" record column, *Billboard* (April 24, 1968) wrote of Nick's revival of "Brown Eyes, Why Are You Blue?," "Old fashioned song styling features a light orchestral backing and the vocal talent of Nick Lucas. Coin operators delight."

The year 1967 had Nick at the Exposition in Las Vegas in March; the International Exposition of Flight at the Convention Center in Las Vegas in April; the Police Academy Show in Pasadena and the Santa Teresita Hospital's Pediatrics Wing dedication in May; the Hubbard Kearney Testimonial Dinner at the Los Angeles Ambassador Hotel in June. There was an August engagements at the Farmers Fair of Riverside County in San Bernardino with Pat Buttram. Nick also participated in Senior Citizens Day in Victorville and San Bernardino; appeared in September at the Al Malaikatl Temple's Family Show at the Shrine Auditorium in Los Angeles with Rosemary Clooney. In October, he headlined the Woman's Club at Leisure World in Long Beach and appeared on the TV special *Mr. Blackwell's Hollywood* with Yvonne De Carlo, Kim Hunter, Peter Palmer, June Foray and Paul Gilbert. Late in 1967, Nick had his fifth return engagement at Diamond Jim's Supper Club in St. Paul. During this period, he was represented by Premier Artists.

The March 6, 1967, *San Mateo* (California) *Times* reported that the Hollywood Overseas Committee announced that Nick would be one of several stars scheduled to go on a forthcoming tour of Vietnam. On April 21, Nick and Catherine Lucas celebrated their fiftieth wedding anniversary in Colorado Springs where they were honored with a dinner at Antlers Plaza. Attending were members of their immediate family, including their daughter Emily and her husband Leonard, who resided in nearby Black Forest, and their three grandsons, Leonard A. Bissell, Jr., who was in the Navy; Nicholas W. Bissell, a student at Trinidad Junior College; and Mark Lucas Bissell. A week later, Nick, Arthur Godfrey, Herb Shriner, Bill Dana and hostess Susan Oliver performed at the International Exposition of Flight in L.A.

In 1968, Nick, Freddie Morgan, Kenny Vernon, Harold Morrison and Don Poltha, were pictured in a full page magazine advertisement for the Fender banjo that hyped "Top Stars Play Fender Banjo!"

In February 1968, Nick appeared for two weekends at the Fire Station Night Club and Inn in Garden Grove, California. On July 25, he was one of the stars appearing in the production *The Great Old Days of Radio* at the Hollywood Bowl, presented by orchestra leader Frank De Vol. Also in the production (broadcast over L.A. radio station KABC)

Nick Lucas (second from left) with Ronald Reagan (second from right) in the late 1960s. Others are unidentified.

were Hal (Harold) Peary, Jack Leonard, the Merry Macs, Ezra Stone, Ginny Simms, Jack Smith, Forrest Lewis, Walter Tetley, Les Tremayne, Janet Waldo, Ned Weaver, Jay Jostyn, Barbara Luddy, Karl Swenson, Bill Thompson and announcer Ken Carpenter. The Van Nuys, California, *Valley News* (August 21, 1968) reported that Nick "received a rousing ovation proving that people still like old favorites." In October 1968, he was at Burbank's Parents and Friends of Mentally Ill Children's benefit and in December he headlined the Rose Queen Coronation at the Civic Auditorium in Pasadena.

One day in 1968, as Nick was walking along Hollywood Boulevard, he ran into an old friend who asked him, "Who is this guy Tiny Tim? He's trying to steal your stuff." Nick had never heard of Tiny Tim, but he was soon to find out that this tall, longhaired ukulele-strumming singer was to have a profound effect on his career.

NBC-TV's *Laugh-In*, a series of comedy blackouts hosted by Dan Rowan and Dick Martin, debuted as a mid-season replacement in January 1968 and quickly became TV's top-rated show, holding that distinction for a short time during its five-year run before finally being gunned down by its time slot rival *Gunsmoke*. Nick never appeared on the show but it greatly affected his career. Featured on the program was the frizzle-haired, hook-nosed, multi-talented singer Tiny Tim, who sometimes performed the male and female portions of vintage duets like "On the Old Front Porch." Tiny Tim (real name: Hubert Khaury) accompanied himself on the ukulele and had a penchant for the songs of yesteryear; he often prefaced his number by telling the audience who originally introduced it. Since his mainstay was "Tiptoe Through the Tulips," he often spoke of Nick Lucas, thus giving Nick a great deal of free publicity before the program's millions of viewers. Not long after hearing about Tiny Tim, Nick saw him on the show and realized that the young man was emulating the sound of his early Brunswick records.

As a result of the publicity Tiny Tim was giving him on national television, Nick began to receive offers of work from all over the country. Not long after Nick learned that Tiny Tim was living not far from him in Hollywood, he gave the singer a call. Tiny Tim was very flattered to hear from Nick and told him, "Mr. Lucas, I want to meet you. I have all your recordings and you have been my inspiration through the years." The next day, Nick took his guitar to Tim's apartment where he met members of the singer's large entourage and sang a few songs for Tim. The singer was so happy with Nick's visit that he asked him to appear with him on Johnny Carson's *Tonight Show*. Arrangements were made for NBC to pay Nick's way to New York City where he appeared on the Carson show on September 18, 1969.

On that episode, which got a good buildup by the network, Tim announced his engagement to 17-year-old Victoria Budinger of Haddonfield, New Jersey. In an off-hand way, Johnny Carson suggested having the wedding on the air and Tim accepted the invitation. In his first appearance on *The Tonight Show*, Nick Lucas sang a medley of "Margie," "Maria Elena" and "Somebody Stole My Gal," and he and Tiny Tim did a duet on "Tiptoe Through the Tulips." Nick talked to Carson at some length about his career and he surprised the studio audience when he said he had been married for 52 years and that he wed at age 20. The audience was again astounded to learn Nick was 72 years old, as he looked much younger. Following this appearance, Nick guest starred on Richard Lamparski's radio program *Whatever Became of...?* and he was featured in one of Lamparski's *Whatever Became of...?* books in 1973.

Prior to Nick's *Tonight Show* appearance, he recorded *The Nick Lucas Souvenir Album* for Accent Records. It included a number of songs associated with him, like

"Tiptoe Through the Tulips," and newer ones such as "Those Were the Days." The album was done in the style of Nick's Brunswick recordings with his playing the guitar and singing, accompanied by a piano or bass. The LP sold well and was reissued in 1975 and 1978. In Great Britain, it appeared on Beacon Records as *Those Were the Days*. The February 22, 1969, *Billboard* gave the album a four-star rating. In the fall of 1969, Nick recorded a second album for Accent Records, *Rose Colored Glasses*, that also featured a dozen songs associated with Nick; like the first LP, it was made in the simplistic style of his Brunswick records. This album also had respectable sales with requests for it coming from as far away as South America and Australia. Forrest Duke wrote in the *San Bernardino* (California) *County Sun* (July 3, 1969), "Nick Lucas in to see pal Dean Martin in Hotel Riviera reveals that he signed to do three albums in five years on the Accent label."

Thanks to his *Tonight Show* appearance and the publicity from Tiny Tim, Nick received far more work offers than he could handle and was forced to turn down many jobs because of his wife's precarious health. Fortunately, he was very comfortable financially, not only from his various incomes from investments and insurance but also from Social Security.

On December 17, 1969, Nick Lucas made a second *Tonight Show* appearance for the wedding of Tiny Tim and Victoria Budinger. On the program, Nick talked with Carson about his long career and marriage and said that he and his wife had actually spent about one-half of their married lives apart due to his show business travels. He told Carson how he had been in Australia for six months, adding, "But I wrote and sent flowers once in awhile," getting a big audience laugh. On the program, Nick sang "Looking at the World Thru Rose Colored Glasses" and "Tiptoe Through the Tulips." It turned out to be the most viewed segment in the series' history up to that time, seen in 21.4 million homes. On the show, Carson asked Nick if he had any advice for Tiny Tim; Nick said he wanted to give it to Tiny Tim in private. What Nick told Tim was to save his money because show business was precarious and he could be on top one day and down the next. Tim, however, informed Nick that all he wanted was stardom and he was not interested in money. Within a few years, Tim's marriage, which produced a daughter named Tulip, collapsed and he was bankrupt.

As 1970 arrived, Nick appeared with Tiny Tim as his guest at Don Weston's Troubadour, a Los Angeles night club. Kathy Orloff wrote in the *Chicago Sun Times* (February 19), "Perhaps the highlight of the show was [Tim's] introduction of Nick Lucas, who came out of the audience, to duet with Tim on 'Tiptoe Through the Tulips.'"

Nick's wife Catherine died suddenly on April 15, 1970. "Her death was a big shock to me and it was hard to believe that after being married for 53 years she was no longer with me," he said. Following his wife's death, he was so brokenhearted he decided to stop performing. Both his daughter and doctor tried to persuade him to continue to work as they thought it would be good therapy for him and would take his mind off his grief. But he remained inactive in show business. But, being a lifelong boxing fan, he did entertain at the Golden State Boxing Association Show in Wilmington, California, on August 15, 1970, along with Mantan Moreland.

Finally, as nothing seemed to help him forget his loss, Nick decided to resume performing. He began to appear for various organizations like Shriners, Elks, Eagles, Rotary, Kiwanis and other charity clubs, along with senior citizens centers and veterans' hospitals. He found working for fraternal organizations to be most profitable and enjoyable in that he only did one show a night, and was given good dressing rooms and backup bands in addition to handsome monetary compensation. In June 1971, he headlined the Ladies Night San Francisco Trade Club Show and on August 26, he appeared at *A Night at the Orpheum* at Los Angeles' Alexandria Hotel. Produced by Will Ahern and hosted by Charles "Buddy" Rogers, the nostalgic program also featured Benny Rubin. In the fall, he was at the Gala Room in Twin Falls, Idaho, and in December he headlined the new Last Frontier Club in Power County, Idaho. He closed out the year at the Gala Holiday Revue at the Milwaukee Performing Arts Center.

One of Nick's agents, Walter Trask, asked him to do a benefit show at the Santa Teresita Hospital in Duante, California, a voluntary, non-profit hospice provided by the Carmelite Sisters of the Sacred Heart. He did a show for the medical staff and met the hospital's administrator and one of its three founders, Mother Margarita Maria. "I am very happy to say that this was the beginning of a great friendship, for she is a wonderful person and I have never refused her requests when she asked me to entertain," Nick later said of his continuing charity work for the hospital.

In his syndicated newspaper column "Little Old New York," Ed Sullivan, on August 19, 1971, discussed a conversation he had with Col. Tom Parker following an Elvis Presley concert at the Hilton International in Las Vegas: "[Parker] told of his old days with singing star Nick Lucas, who is still downcast over the death of Ted Fio Rito." Fio Rito, Nick's boyhood friend and later co-worker, died July 22, 1971, in Scottsdale, Arizona.

In the summer of 1972, Nick was a guest on an episode of TV's *The Merv Griffin Show* that paid tribute to the music of the various decades of the 20th century. He led off the program with a tribute to the 1920s, singing "Tiptoe Through the Tulips" and talking with Griffin about his career and the era of the '20s when he had his greatest success. Rudy Vallee, the Andrews Sisters, Pat Boone and Chubby Checker represented other decades on the program, but it was Nick who got the biggest ovation from the studio audience and was the hit of the show. He liked working with Griffin as he said the host helped him prepare for his portion of the event by aiding in rehearsals and taking an interest in his contribution to the program. From July 26 to 29, 1972, Nick and Jimmy Durante headlined the Grand Aerie Convention of the Fraternal Order of Eagles in Atlanta. Part of the program included several noted boxers, including Nick's

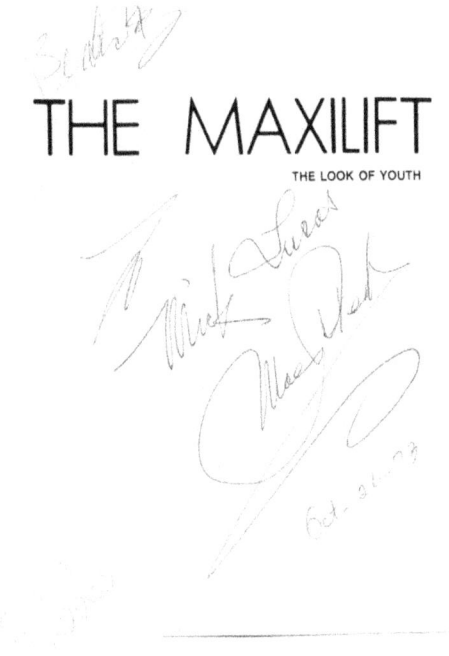

Nick Lucas meets Mae West at the Mayfair Music Hall in Santa Monica, California, October 26, 1973. The program is also signed by Beatrice Kay and Bubbles of Buck & Bubbles.

friend, former heavyweight contender Tony Galento. Early in 1973, Nick and Rudy Vallee starred in a nostalgia production staged at McCormick Center in Chicago. Nick was the headliner of *This Is Show Business* on May 5, 1973, at L.A.'s Sheraton West Hotel. The Film Welfare League's 42nd benefit show, it was hosted by Vivian Duncan and Charles "Buddy" Rogers.

On March 31, 1974, Nick was the master of ceremonies and chairman of the day for the Opera Reading Club of Hollywood's show at the Los Angeles Palladium. When Nick starred at the Kern County Fair's International Spectacular, the *Bakersfield Californian* (August 19, 1974) wrote, "Nick Lucas, the Italian Troubadour, after years in the limelight of show business, is as big as ever in the entertainment world.... Judging by current success, he has found a new audience.... Year in and year out Nick Lucas remains a headline attraction...." In his December 29, 1974, nationally syndicated newspaper column "Criswell Predicts," the noted seer declared, "I predict Ginger Rogers will revive her Charleston dancing days in a nostalgic blaze of glory with Nick Lucas in *Not So Long Ago*, a TV spectacular. The demand has been for entertainment on TV and I predict that these two stars will give it to you very soon."

Nick Lucas at a Senior Citizens Day show at Disneyland in October 1973.

In the next few years, Nick began to make more West Coast appearances as well as being on various local radio and TV programs and telethons. Sam Yorty, a musician and the former mayor of Los Angeles, became the host of a popular radio show after leaving office in 1973. He and Nick had been friends for many years and so Nick started appearing regularly on the show. (Nick was also a friend of the show's producer, Wally George; he had often made appearances on George's radio show in the 1960s when George was a disc jockey.) In 1975, *The Sam Yorty Show* came to KCOP-TV where it remained for three years, becoming the most popular and controversial variety talk program on the West Coast. Nick often appeared on the show to good audience

Nick Lucas (left) with Zumba and George Liberace in Sacramento, California, in December 1973.

response. On one episode, he serenaded Gene Autry on his birthday with "That Silver Haired Daddy of Mine."

Early in 1974, Nick received a telephone call from composer-arranger Nelson Riddle, whom he had known for several years, asking if he would be interested in singing the vocal on a song in Paramount's remake of *The Great Gatsby*. Taking place in the 1920s, this opulent production was a visual recreation of the Jazz Age and its soundtrack boomed with authentic music of the period. Riddle, its musical director, had just returned from Great Britain where he had unsuccessfully searched for someone to sing "When You and I Were Seventeen," a song that plays a very important part in the picture. Then Riddle remembered Nick and called him. Agreeing to the financial terms for the job, Nick met Riddle at Paramount where he sang the song over the already recorded soundtrack. "When You and I Were Seventeen" is first heard in a scene where Jay Gatsby (Robert Redford) and his lady love Daisy (Mia Farrow) are enjoying a moment of romantic bliss; later in the film, Gatsby listens to a phonograph recording of the song just before he is murdered. Nick's vocal added authenticity to the film and Riddle and the movie's producers were so impressed that they asked him to also record the vocals to "I'm Gonna Charleston Back to Charleston" and "Five Foot Two, Eyes of Blue" for inclusion on the film's soundtrack album. Riddle also wanted Nick to sing the movie's theme song, "What'll I Do?," but the producers had already signed actor William Atherton.

Thanks to Nick's three vocals and Riddle's fine arrangements, the soundtrack album became a best-seller in the U.S. and Great Britain. Although the film took a critical lambasting, it scored at the box office and its music score received an Academy Award. Regarding the film's soundtrack recording released by Paramount Records, Criswell wrote in his "Criswell Predicts" column (June 23, 1974): "I predict that you will experience nostalgia supreme when you hear Nick Lucas ... sing in *The Great Gatsby*.... The soundtrack of *The Great Gatsby* will be the number one Christmas gift of the year. The past is captured by Nick Lucas." *The Naugatuck* (Connecticut) *Daily News* (April 25, 1974) opined, "[O]ne of the highlights [of the album] is 'Five Foot Two, Eyes of Blue' which is sung by Nick Lucas...."

Nick's contribution to *The Great Gatsby* was the last item of production on the movie. Since the film's credits had been printed before he sang the vocals, Nick received no screen billing although he is credited on the soundtrack album. As a result of his receiving no screen credit for the film, Nick got more publicity than he would have if he had been credited and this led to coverage in show business trade publications. Nick also got a lot of attention because he had allowed his hair to become its natural white color. "I got more response about my white hair than on anything else," he said at the time. Even with snow-white hair, Nick remained a youthful looking seventy-ish crooner.

Following *The Great Gatsby*'s success, Nick did a TV commercial for Datsun cars that was seen all over the U.S.; in it, he sang a few Gatsby-era songs to advertise the automobile. He also began headlining at the Mayfair Music Hall in Santa Monica. His appearance in the spring of 1974 resulted in sellout crowds and laudatory reviews. *The Los Angeles Times* (May 23, 1974) wrote, "[T]he silver throated (and haired) Nick Lucas suits the Mayfair beautifully. ...[H]e sings the old songs with appropriate sentiment—but not a trace of camp. A glowing star for a very pleasant show." Bill Pollock wrote the *Los Angeles Herald-Examiner* (April 26, 1974), "[H]is act is not a faded bit of memorabilia. It's solid entertainment done in a way that is destined never to go out of style." *The Hollywood Reporter* (April 25, 1974) declared Nick "a sensational addition to the room as he succeeds in turning the clock back to a more simple time with his mellifluous treatment of songs he made famous… [He] is still a vital and warm performer, with the music hall atmosphere lending a perfect setting as he trips down memory lane...." *Variety* (April 25, 1974) stated,

> Veteran Nick Lucas may have a new career beginning for him. With a shot in the arm from the Great Gatsby soundtrack, ...Lucas has assembled a very good club act, full of nostalgia that's well done and presented with experienced showmanship. ...[He] establishes a close rapport with the audience as he belts them [songs] with surprising vim.

Nick made a return appearance at the Mayfair the following spring and afterward headlined the theater about three times each year, always to SRO crowds and enthusiastic reviews. The Mayfair was one of the few theaters in the country with live entertainment each week of the year and it had a permanent cast in addition to guest performers. Nick felt that the Mayfair was a "very good showcase in that lots of Hollywood producers and directors catch the show."

In the fall of 1974, Paramount again contacted Nick about singing in a movie, this time *The Day of the Locust*. In this story about the mental destruction of a Hollywood hopeful (Karen Black), Nick can be heard singing "I Wished on the Moon" via a radio program. The soundtrack to the album was issued by London Records. The day Nick recorded the song at Paramount, the film's director John Schlesinger was in the recording studio. After the session, he told Nick, "Mr. Lucas, you have a beautiful voice."

That December, Nick trekked to New York City for the first time in five years to star in two concerts at Town Hall where he was well-received by both audiences and

Nick Lucas performing in the mid-1970s.

critics. He enjoyed the trip to the Big Apple, not only due to the success of the shows, but because it gave him the opportunity to go to New Jersey and visit relatives. He also re-recorded "Tiptoe Through the Tulips," as Jack O'Brian noted in his nationally syndicated newspaper column on February 5, 1975: "Nick Lucas recorded his famed 'Tiptoe Through the Tulips' 46 years ago and now he's sung it again on Accent Records; 'Silver Sails' on the flip; the original Brunswick hotcake sold 5,000,000..."

Nick kicked off 1975 with two appearances on the popular syndicated TV series *Vaudeville*: He appeared in the initial episode with Milton Berle and the Wiere Brothers. The show was hosted by Eddie Foy, Jr., his co-star in the 1929 Broadway production *Show Girl*. Regarding his appearance on the program, *Daily Variety* (January 17, 1975) reported, "Nick Lucas, sounding as he did almost a half century ago, demonstrates how to sing authentic 'Tiptoe Through the Tulips,' 'Painting the Clouds with Sunshine' and 'Has Anybody Seen My Gal' and audience reaction is solid as ever." Later in the year, he appeared again at the Mayfair Music Hall in Santa Monica, headlining a vaudeville revue. A crew from the BBC of London shot enough footage of Nick Lucas for inclusion in a trio of British TV specials. At the same time, he was interviewed for the BBC radio series *Star Sound*.

In the summer of 1975, Nick was hired by MGM to sing six songs in the film *Hearts of the West* starring Jeff Bridges, Andy Griffith and Blythe Danner. It was a comedy about the making of vintage Saturday matinee cowboy movies in the 1930s and Nick's vocals were used to recreate the era, just as he had done in *The Great Gatsby* and *The Day of the Locust*. It was director Howard Zieff who wanted Nick for its vocals, having been a fan of the singer since he was a boy and his parents took him to see Nick on stage in Southern California. On the movie's soundtrack, Nick sang "Happy Days Are Here

Again," "Ja Da," "We'll Make Hay While the Sun Shines," "Wang Wang Blues," "My Blue Heaven" and "I'll See You in My Dreams." The latter song was heard over the film's closing credits. "I recorded them all in just three hours—no rehearsals," Nick recalled.

Hearts of the West met with a good reception but seemed to get lost in the shuffle as MGM put more effort into advertising *The Sunshine Boys*, which it hoped would win an Academy Award. The studio failed to properly promote the movie and in doing so it robbed this pleasant comedy of the success it deserved. MGM did not issue a soundtrack album. When the film premiered in October 1975 at the San Francisco Film Festival, Nick attended the publicity party. MGM also released quite a bit of publicity about Nick and his contribution to the movie.

Regarding his longevity in show business, Nick told *Los Angeles Times* (August 5, 1975) writer Lynn Simross,

Nick Lucas at the premiere of *Day of the Locust* (Paramount, 1974) in San Francisco.

> If you sing properly you can sing a long time and your voice doesn't get tired. The most important part is resonance. It's all in the diaphragm. It's the breathing, you see. Of course it depends on what food you eat, too. No pie, no ice cream and no milk for me for three days before I have to do any singing. That is hard, too, because I like all those things.... I've stayed in good shape. I do a lot of walking. I go down the [Hollywood] Boulevard every day and talk to my friends, storekeepers, all the people I know. I play a little golf, too.

Regarding the remnants of his New Jersey accent, he declared, "Sometimes people ask me how I still have it, and I say, 'Once you have it, you never lose it.'"

Californians, like everyone else, found it boring standing in long lines to receive vehicle license plates. A friend of Nick's, Phil Lee, manager of the Department of Motor Vehicles license branch in Glendale, asked him to relieve the tedium by serenading his customers one warm day in February. The next day, a wire service picture of Nick singing to the patrons appeared in newspapers all over the country and there was film of him singing on news programs throughout the Los Angeles area. While he was not paid for serenading the customers, he received many times his usual fee in free publicity for this favor that was not designed as a publicity stunt.

Regarding Nick's DMV performance, Kathy Burke wrote in *The Los Angeles Times* (February 4, 1976), "Although some waiting drivers refused to be wooed by the entertainment (or at least refused to show they were), others plainly enjoyed the diversion and there were bursts of applause after each song.... To Lucas, still singing in a clear, youthful voice at 78, the appearance was 'a good idea. It gets me close to my public.... It lets me know what they like and don't like.'" The writer noted that one 20-year-old waiting in line was an old-song buff familiar with Lucas' numbers and he felt, "It took away a little bit of the hatred for the DMV."

During this time, Tiny Tim sought to return to record stardom with the single "Tiptoe to the Gas Pump with Me," spoofing the gasoline shortage crisis of the day.

Paramount called Nick a third time in 1976 with a request for him to do the vocals on two songs for its upcoming release *Won Ton Ton, the Dog Who Saved Hollywood*. He recorded "To Be Loved by You" and "They're Playing Our Song (The Won Ton Rag)" for the film. A few days later, studio executives screened the finished product, declared it was a "dog" and opted not to spend the $10,000 necessary to incorporate Nick's vocals onto the soundtrack. This is a pity since these were two of the finest vocals Nick sang in the latter years of his career and they could have resulted in a hit record had the studio had the foresight to issue the songs as a single.

That summer, Nick celebrated his seventy-ninth birthday and again gave serious thought to retirement. He mentioned this to Mother Margarita Maria at the Santa Teresita Hospital and she told him to forget the notion. She said, "Mr. Lucas, you do not

Marquee for Nick Lucas' appearance at the Mayfair Music Hall in Santa Monica, California, in 1975.

want to do that. Everyone enjoys sharing in your remarkable gifts that God has given you so bountifully. Not just that but of a voice that seems to become richer and a heart that is ever warm, reflecting [a] love of mankind." With that in mind, Nick changed his mind about retiring. Mother Margarita Maria and the Sisters at Santa Teresita hosted a party for him on August 21, 1977, to celebrate his upcoming eightieth birthday. Scores of Nick's friends and family came from all over the country to join him in the celebration. Clips from several of Nick's movies were shown and he entertained his audience with a half-dozen songs, including "Marie, Ah Marie," a special favorite of Mother Margarita Maria. The Sisters baked him a huge birthday cake, emblazoned with yellow tulips. Mother Margarita Maria later wrote, "We Sisters are truly Mr. Lucas' loyal fans. For so many years ... he has entertained, without fee, at Santa Teresita for parties and special events. He is a superb entertainer with a rare talent for making those in his audience forget their troubles. No wonder he is loved by a number of generations." Nick felt his birthday celebration was "one of the most beautiful days of my life" and added that Mother Margarita Maria's support "made me feel that I still had something to offer" in life.

When Nick returned to the Mayfair Music Hall in the summer of 1977, Connie Challenger wrote in *Casting Call* (July 28–August 3, 1977),

> Like rare wine, Mr. Lucas improves with age. He is both a delight to watch and to listen to.... Mr. Lucas' voice is better than ever, very clear, and every word is perfectly enunciated. I understand the younger generation has "rediscovered" Mr. Lucas and by the audience response at the Mayfair, I would agree to that fact. They loved the nattily attired Nick! ...Mr. Lucas' career truly does seem to be hitting new heights. But he's a performer who definitely deserves the best. After seeing him in action, you would have to agree with "The Chairman" of the Music Hall, Bernard Fox, when he says, "That's what show business is all about."

In September 1977, Nick appeared on the TV special *Murphy's Hollywood* both in an interview and performing, filmed for Irish television. That month the King Features Syndicate column "Ripley's Believe It or Not" noted that he had been making records for 54 years and was still an active performer at age 80. The column appeared in hundreds of newspapers around the world. In November, he was the first artist to headline Los Angeles' Variety Arts Theatre, a venue designed to continue the field of vaudeville. Of his opening, Connie Challenger reported in *Casting Call Weekly*, "Mr. Lucas presents all the old favorite songs in a new, fresh, appealing style. That is what artistry is all about. This ability to sell a song as if it were being introduced for the first time. Also, the ability to project a warm, engaging personality across the footlights to your audience. ...Impeccably attired, Mr. Lucas cuts a commanding figure with his shock of white hair and charming manner." Reporting on the same show, Noble "Kid" Chissell, whose columns appeared in several West Coast papers including the *Hollywood Independent* (December 1, 1977), wrote, "Nick Lucas added more devotees from the young crowd to we nostalgists, who never tire of 'Tiptoe Through the Tulips' and the great melodies of our era. He had seven standing ovations." At the beginning of 1978, it was announced that Nick was one of the headliners who would take part in the "Vaudeville Lives" series at the Variety Arts Theatre. Others chosen were Edgar Bergen, Buddy Ebsen, George Jessel, Dick Martin, Ken Murray, Donald O'Connor, Martha Raye, Rose Marie, Benny Rubin, Phil Silvers and Rudy Vallee. The program was sponsored by the College of Continuing Education at the University of Southern California. In February 1978, braving cold temperatures, Nick came to Indianapolis to headline the Murat-Shrine's annual variety show.

He gave four performances to enthusiastic crowds who loved his melodies of yesteryear. He made a return appearance at the same venue in June 1980.

In a story in the Riverside, California, *Enterprise* (May 14, 1978), Joyce Smith noted of Nick, "[I]n no way does he live in the past. He's aware of current phases of entertainment and likes to work with young performers.... One thing he does not like is the electric amplification of the guitar. 'I detest it,' he says. 'It made the standard guitar obsolete for bands.'" On October 14, 1978, Nick starred at the Los Angeles Street Scene, a two-day celebration of renaissance of the Los Angeles central city. As he sang, Lawrence Christon of the *Los Angeles Times* observed "old people applauding, young women with romantic expressions over the songs their grandmother knew, and behind the stage a derelict singing shyly along." As the year ended, there were more personal appearances.

The year 1979 was the fiftieth anniversary of Nick Lucas introducing and making famous "Tiptoe Through the Tulips." (There was talk he would perform it at the White House but it did not happen.) Still he could look back on a long and prosperous career, having been in show business for more than 60 years—and during most of that time, he had been a headliner. He was definitely one of the greatest names in vaudeville and recordings, along with everything else. When he appeared as a part of National Music Week at Los Angeles' City Hall Mall, Jack Smith wrote in the *Los Angeles Times* (May 9, 1979), "Maybe [his] voice was brassier than in 1929, but it was strong, resonant and compelling.... When he started to sing 'Tiptoe Through the Tulips' there was applause and whistling the way there used to be when Judy Garland started to sing 'Over the Rainbow' ... They loved him."

Since the 1940s, Nick's base of operations was in Hollywood, where he resided in an apartment-office. In the mid–1970s, he bought a home in Hemet, a desert community east of Los Angeles, near Palm Springs. He divided his time between these two domiciles as most of his work was in Southern California, despite still receiving offers from all over the country. He said in 1980, "I traveled for more than fifty years and now I like to take it easy." Occasionally he went to Colorado Springs, where he still owned a ranch, to visit his daughter and her husband.

Nick Lucas celebrating Christmas in 1978, in front of his Hemet, California, home.

His three grandsons were grown and working at various occupations. His younger brothers, Librato and Anthony, still lived in Newark and were retired. His sister Tessie died in 1979; she had ten children and six of her sons were in the music business.

In Hollywood, Nick saw many of his old friends and counted most of the people he knew in show business over the years as friends. He often lunched at the Friars Club or the Roosevelt Hotel, he played golf (although not as much as in the past) and he liked to attend boxing matches at the Los Angeles Olympic Auditorium. Boxing was Nick's favorite sport and he counted former heavyweight boxing champion Jack Dempsey and onetime heavyweight contender Tony Galento as close friends. Noble "Kid" Chissell wrote in the *Hollywood Independent* (October 3, 1979), "Nick is a great fight fan and has attended or bought tickets for all of our dinners honoring boxers and wrestlers. He jetted back to New Jersey to help raise funds for ailing ex–World Middleweight Boxing Champ Mickey Walker."

Life for Nick Lucas in his later years was basically free of worries. He was active in his profession and in his eighties continued to be a star headliner. Personal appearances were no longer work as they were when he was earning a living by them; he found it fun to entertain and make people happy. "I like all my fans from long ago but it's nice to have people come up to me and say, 'You know, I never heard of you until my mother and dad told me about you and they were right, you are great!'" he proudly said. Nick was not one to live in the past; he lived for today and looked forward

Nick Lucas publicity photograph, mid–1970s.

A 1978 publicity photograph for Nick Lucas' appearances.

to tomorrow where there might be a new show business summit to conquer.

Unlike some of his contemporaries, who seemed to have saved every scrap of paper on which their name appeared, Nick had little memorabilia. What he did save was mostly donated to the Society for the Preservation of Variety Arts in Los Angeles. His family accumulated some items from his long career, mostly phonograph records and transcription discs.

Nick sometimes wondered why he never invested in property at the various locales where he performed. "When I started, America was still growing but I didn't realize it at the time. There were many places where I worked where I could have bought property and held on to it and today I'd be a multi-millionaire but I didn't give it a thought...." He remembered working in vaudeville on the Interstate Circuit that included a ten-week tour of Tulsa, Oklahoma City, Fort Worth, Dallas, Houston, San Antonio, Beaumont and New Orleans.

Advertisement for Nick Lucas' appearance at the Mayfair Music Hall in 1974.

On one occasion in 1930, a land speculator in Texas took him to see some property and "I got my shoes full of black dirt, which happened to be oil." One reason he did not invest in property, although he had a chance to do so in diverse spots such as the Honolulu beach front, Los Angeles and Hollywood, was because in 1929 he lost over $400,000 in the Stock Market Crash, along with another quarter of a million dollars in real estate investments. From that point on, Nick "stuck to what I know best, singing and playing my guitar."

Religion, too, played a very important part in Nick's life. A devout Roman Catholic, he always put his trust in God and not secular things. Loyal to his friends, he maintained a standard for himself that earned him the respect of those who came to know and work with him. While the milk of human kindness has not always been found among the denizens of show business, Nick was one of those rare individuals who was beloved by his colleagues, as well and his family and friends and a legion of fans.

Front: May Hoffman, Nick Lucas, Claire Jolley, Milton Berle, Michael Grayson, Holly Harris, Doodles Weaver, Dave Smith; Back: William Campbell, Peter Eastman, Ken Babal, Jack Berle, Al De Crescent, Mel Steinberg. From the Motion Picture Home Show "Nostalgia 1976" (March 28, 1976).

The 1980s opened with Nick appearing before an estimated audience of 40,000,000 people worldwide on television when he was in the Tournament of Roses Parade in Pasadena. With the parade theme of "Music of America," he rode on a float appropriately titled "Tiptoe Through the Tulips" and serenaded the crowd along the parade route. The program was televised live nationally and filmed for world distribution and Lucas called it "the greatest thrill of my life." He remained active with personal appearances and often appeared on Wally George's TV shown on KCOP-TV.

Late in 1980, he made a single record, "Are You Lonesome Tonight?/How Did You Have the Heart to Break My Heart" at Accent's new recording studio in Palm Springs. In 1981, he returned for his final record session, performing "The Magic Waltz," which he co-wrote.

Early in 1981, he headlined the National Date Festival in Indio, California, where he was billed as the "Senior Citizens" Favorite Singer. Around the same time, he took part in the dedication of a bust of his friend Jimmy Durante at the Villa Scalabrini Retirement Center in Sun Valley. United Press International carried Vernon Scott's lengthy story on Nick, which appeared in newspapers on April 22, 1981. He told Scott, "They won't hold any benefits for me. I still love to work and I've memorized about one hundred of the great old songs. As long as people want to hear me sing, I'm more than happy to oblige." Scott wrote,

Nick was the Sinatra and Presley of his day and can honestly lay claim to being the progenitor of every minstrel and troubadour in this country who accompanies himself on the guitar.... Today Nick is a charming geezer in fine fettle, excellent voice and still an unabashed romantic. He has a young lady friend of sixty-three who shares many a chilly evening with him at his desert home in Hemet, California. Nick is an inspiration to other old people and the kind of guy who doesn't like the palliative "senior citizen" euphemism.... Nick is a slender, vital man. He exercises every day, watches his diet and has a drink now and then. He credits his longevity and good health to moderation.

Regarding his audience appeal, Nick told Scott,

It was more than nostalgia. Ten out of 10 old folks remember me when they were young. They were brought up on my music. Almost everybody in the crowds were fans of mine. But my music appeals to this generation, too. I did a Merv Griffin show a couple of months ago and the young people loved my songs because they've got a beat, they're melodic and they can understand the lyrics. Those old songs have a meaning and a story. And that's how I've always sung them. So they appeal to all age groups. In my concerts around the country, people come up to say their grandfather or grandmother told them about me. That's very touching and satisfying to hear.

Early in May 1981, Nick was one of the stars of National Music Week at the Los Angeles Triforium, as he had been since that event began two years before. He also headlined the Gala Variety Show Benefit for the City of Hope on May 16. The previous month, he was in Las Vegas to negotiate doing a stage show with Dolly Parton that never came to fruition. While there, he guest starred on *The Merv Griffin Show* and sang "Tiptoe Through the Tulips." Not long afterward, he appeared on PBS-TV's "The Nelson Riddle Show" singing "What'll I Do" and "Five Foot Two, Eyes of Blue" from *The Great Gatsby*. On August 21, 1981, the day before his 84th birthday, he headlined the "Nick Lucas Strolls Down Memory Lane" commemorative program at Glendale's Los Feliz Plaza and followed it with an appearance at the Oregon State Fair. He ended the month working at Barnsdall Park in Hollywood and continued to remain active throughout the remainder of 1981, negotiating a new record album and making personal appearances. An article in the *Italian Tribune* (December 4, 1981) closed by saying, "For sheer musical expertise, and durability, the likes of Nick Lucas, the kid from the streets of Newark, has never been equaled."

Early in 1982, Nick began to have health problems, mainly with his back. The situation did not improve and in June he suffered a stroke and was hospitalized in Santa Monica. He was in a coma for several weeks but emerged from it in July and appeared to be on the road to recovery. He was moved to a Colorado Springs nursing home where he died from complications from double pneumonia on July 28, 1982, at St. John's Hospital. He was buried with his wife Catherine at Shrine of Remembrance in Colorado Springs. In addition to his daughter, son-in-law and three grandsons, he was survived by his two younger brothers: Librato, who died August 27, 1989, and Anthony, who died January 15, 1992. Nick's daughter Emily Bissell died January 13, 2013, in Colorado Springs.

Nick Lucas' passing brought an end to a show business era. He was one of the last surviving stars of the golden age of vaudeville and recordings. His passing left a void that could not be filled.

Back in the fall of 1981, Lucas had been elected to the Gibson Guitar Hall of Fame in Nashville, Tennessee, and he said he considered it "a great honor at my age eighty four." His memory lives on not only through his guitar and the influence he had on it in popular culture but also upon the many entertainers who considered him their inspiration in the field. Chet Atkins, Merle Travis, Barney Kassell, Gene Autry, Eddie Dean and Glen Campbell are among the many guitarists who said that Nick influenced them to take up the instrument. He also survives through his recordings and appearances in movies, radio and TV. One of the true legends of the entertainment world, Nick Lucas brought enjoyment and happiness to many generations for over seven decades.

Perhaps Nick Lucas himself best summed up his long career when he said, toward the end of his life, "Show business has been very kind to me and I have met some wonderful people in my travels all around the world. If I had my life to live over again, I would do the same thing. It's been a great life." In reflecting on what his parents might have wanted for him, Dorothy Pisano in the *Dallas Morning News* (October 21, 1928) wrote,

> [C]ertainly neither of them ever had the most remote dream that their boy would some day lift the burdens from the souls of millions of people and make their hearts throb with joy and beauty. They could not guess that their son's name would be a byword throughout the whole country, almost as well known as the country's President, nor that his fame would spread to every continent on the globe.

Discography

Listed are Nick Lucas' single recordings and their various issuances. The date in bold refers to each recording session.
This sample entry is provided with explanations:

May 1929

    Brunswick Records, Los Angeles, California
    Nick Lucas (vocal, guitar)
    Painting the Clouds with Sunshine (LAE-497)
    10"-78 Brunswick 4418
    10"-78 Brunswick 4418 (Australia)
    10"-78 Brunswick 4418 (British)
    10"-78 Brunswick A8322 (Germany)
    12"-LP ASV AJA-5022 (British)
    CASSETTE ASV ZC-AJA-5022 (British)
    CASSETTE "Sounds of a Century" 1875-A
    CD ASV CD-AJA-5329 (British)
    CD "Sounds of a Century" 1875-A
    MP3 Emerald Echoes
    MP3 Hallmark
    MP3 Vintage Music

    Provided is the recording date, record company and location, accompaniment if known, song title, matrix number, record size and speed, and record label and number. The issued take, if known, is listed after the matrix number. Record sizes listed in the discography are 10-inch-78 rpm, 10-inch long playing album (LP), 12-inch long playing album (LP), seven-inch 45 rpm, 16-inch ET (Electric Transcriptions at 33⅓ rpm),

    CD (Compact Disc) and MP3. Issuances for audiotapes are Cassette, 8-Track and Reel-to-Reel. All recordings are United States issuances unless otherwise noted after the record number (i.e., [Australia]).

    Following the record session listings are Lucas' albums (LPs and CDs) and commercial tape recordings. This listing provides title, company and number, record size, issue date, reissue source and song titles. Information on other format releases (i.e., cassettes or 8-Track tapes) is given following the song titles. Another section lists the above information for Compilation Albums (LP and CD) on which Lucas appears and the song or songs he performs are listed.

1912

Edison Records, West Orange, New Jersey
Nick Lucanese [Lucas] (instrumentals)
Cylinder Test Records; titles unknown

June 4, 1917

Victor Records, New York City
Earl Fuller's Famous Jazz Band (Earl Fuller, piano; Walter Kahn, coronet; Ted Lewis, clarinet; Nick Lucas, banjo, mandolin; Harry Raderman, trombone; John Lucas, drums)
   Slippery Hank
   10"-78 Victor 18321
   Yah-De-Dah
   10"-78 Victor 18321

August 13, 1917

Victor Records, New York City
Earl Fuller's Famous Jazz Band (same personnel as above)
   Beale Street Blues
   10"-78 Victor 18369
   Old Grey Mare
   10"-78 Victor 18369

September 10, 1917

Victor Records, New York City
Earl Fuller's Famous Jazz Band (same personnel as above)
   Lil Liza Jane
   10"-78 Victor 18394
   Coon Band Contest
   10"-78 Victor 18394

Note: Lucas is confirmed by OCLC as a member of the above sessions and he told the author he recorded with Earl Fuller's Famous Jazz Band.

July 1920

Brunswick Records, New York City
The Vernon Trio (Bert Ralston, alto saxophone, supreme saxophone, oboe; Nick Lucas, banjo; George Gershwin, piano)
   Whispering [4199]
   10"-78 Brunswick 2049
   My Midnight Frolic Girl [4257]
   10"-78 Brunswick 2049

February 1, 1921

Columbia Records, New York City
The Vernon Country Club Orchestra (including Nick Lucas, banjo)
   I Never Knew (I Could Love Anybody Like I'm Loving You) [79705]
   10"-78 Columbia A-3378
   10"-78 Regal G-7657 (as Regal Novelty Orchestra)
   Look for the Silver Lining [79706]
   10"-78 Columbia A-3378
   10"-78 Regal 3054 (as Regal Novelty Orchestra)

September 1921

Pathe Freres Phonograph Company, New York City
The Vernon Country Club Orchestra (including Nick Lucas, banjo)
   It's You [69400]
   10"-78 Pathe Actuelle 020653
   10"-78 Pathe Actuelle 10253 (as Casino Dance Orchestra)
   Roses and You [69401]
   10"-78 Pathe Actuelle 020652
   10"-78 Pathe Actuelle 10233 (as Casino Dance Orchestra)
   Hugs and Kisses [69402]
   10"-78 Pathe Actuelle 10267 (as Casino Dance Orchestra)

October 15, 1921; New York City

Gennett Records, New York City
Bailey's Lucky Seven (Sam Lanin; leader; Doc Behrendson, coronet; Benny Bloom, trumpet; Jimmy Durante, piano; Moe Gappell, trombone; Benny Krueger, Loring McMurray, alto saxophone; Nick Lucas, banjo; Jack Roth, drums)
   How Many Times? [7668]
   10"-78 Connorized 3034

10"-78 Gennett 4795
10"-78 Rich-Tone 7014 (as The Jazz Harmonizers)
Wimmin (I Gotta Have Em, That's All) [7669]
10"-78 Connorized 3035
10"-78 Edison Bell Winner 3697 (British)
10"-78 Gennett 4795
10"-78 Westport 468

December 1921

Gennett Records, New York City
Bailey's Lucky Seven (Sam Lanin, leader; Doc Behrendson, coronet; Jimmy Durante, piano; Benny Krueger, Loring McMurray, alto saxophones; Nick Lucas, banjo; Phil Napoleon, trumpet; Charlie Panelli, trombone; Jack Roth, drums)
I've Got My Habits On [7711]
10"-78 Connorized 3045
10"-78 Gennett 4815
In My Heart, on My Mind All Day Long [7712]
10"-78 Connorized 3045
10"-78 Gennett 4815
10"-78 Rich-Tone 7022 (as The Jazz Harmonizers)

February 1922

Gennett Records, New York City
Bailey's Lucky Seven (Sam Lanin, leader; including Nick Lucas, banjo)
My Mammy Knows [7751]
10"-78 Apex 489
10"-78 Connorized 3058
10"-78 Gennett 4831
10"-78 Starr 9210 (Canada)
On the 'Gin 'Gin 'Ginny Shore [7752]
10"-78 Apex 489
10"-78 Cardinal 523 (as The Cardinal Dance Orchestra)
10"-78 Connorized 3058
10"-78 Edison Bell Winner 3734 (British)
10"-78 Gennett 4831
10"-78 Starr 9210 (Canada)

February 1922

Pathe Freres Phonograph Company, New York City
The Don Parker Trio (Don Parker, alto saxophone; Nick Lucas, banjo; Frank Banta, piano)
Silver Stars [69779]
10"-78 Pathe Actuelle 020809
10"-78 Perfect 14040
Who'll Take My Place? [69780]
10"-78 Pathe Actuelle 020809
10"-78 Perfect 14040

March 1922

Pathe Freres Phonograph Company, New York City
Lucas Novelty Quartet (including Nick Lucas [banjo] and Frank Lucas [accordion])
Love Dreams
10"-78 Pathe Actuelle 020747

March 1922

Pathe Freres Phonograph Company, New York City
Lucas Ukulele Trio (Nick Lucas and Frank Lucas [ukuleles] and violin)
Ji Ji Boo
10"-78 Pathe Actuelle 020817
10"-78 Pathe Actuelle 30517
10"-78 Perfect 11047 (as Nick Lucas' Ukulele Trio)
Down Old Virginia Way
10"-78 Pathe Actuelle 020817
10"-78 Pathe Actuelle 30517
10"-78 Perfect 11047 (as Nick Lucas' Ukulele Trio)

March 1922

Gennett Records, New York City
Bailey's Lucky Seven (Sam Lanin, leader; Phil Napoleon, Jules Levy, Jr., trumpets; Loring McMurray, Benny Krueger, alto saxophone, tenor saxophone; Nick Lucas, banjo)

Label to "Down Old Virginia Way" with Nick Lucas' Ukulele Trio (1922).

I Wonder Blues (I've Got the Wonder Blues) [7808]
10"-78 Connorized 3065
10"-78 Gennett 4855
10"-78 Starr 9232 (Canada)
10"-78 Velvet Face 1049 (as Joe Richardson's Orchestra)

Pick Me Up and Lay Me Down in Dear Old Dixieland [7809]
10"-78 Connorized 3065
10"-78 Gennett 4855
10"-78 Starr 9232 (Canada)
10"-78 Velvet Face 1053 (as Joe Richardson's Orchestra)

March 1922

Edison Records, New York City
The Don Parker Trio (Don Parker, alto saxophone; Nick Lucas, banjo; Frank Banta, piano)

Pick Me Up and Lay Me Down in Dear Old Dixieland [8398]
10"-78 Edison Blue Amberol 4557
10"-78 Edison Diamond Disc 50963

Georgia [8399]
10"-78 Edison Blue Amberol 4571
10"-78 Edison Diamond Disc 50961

April 1922

Gennett Records, New York City
Bailey's Lucky Seven (Sam Lanin, leader; Phil Napoleon, Jules Levy, Jr., trumpets; Loring McMurray, Benny Krueger, alto saxophone, tenor saxophone; Nick Lucas, banjo)

Poor Little Me [7825]
10"-78 Apex 477
10"-78 Connorized 3074
10"-78 Gennett 4857

Don't Leave Me, Mammy [7826]
10"-78 Apex 481
10"-78 Connorized 3074
10"-78 Gennett 4857
10"-78 Starr 9235 (Canada)

April 1922

Pathe Freres Phonograph Company, New York City
The Don Parker Trio (Don Parker, alto saxophone; Nick Lucas, banjo; Frank Banta, piano)
  Every Day [69653]
  10"-78 Pathe Actuelle 020745
  10"-78 Pathe Actuelle 10469
  10"-78 Pathe 1672
  10"-78 Perfect 14016 (as The Will Carroll Trio)
  Georgia [69654]
  10"-78 Pathe Actuelle 020738
  10"-78 Pathe Actuelle 10328
  10"-78 Pathe 1583
  10"-78 Perfect 14002 (as The Will Carroll Trio)

April 1922

Gennett Records, New York City
Bailey's Lucky Seven (Sam Lanin, leader; Nick Lucas, banjo, guitar; Vincent Grande trombone; Phil Napoleon, trumpet; Gus Sharp, clarinet, alto saxophone; Loring McMurray, alto saxophone, piano, drums)
  Hortense [7846]
  10"-78 Apex 481
  10"-78 Gennett 4874
  10"-78 Starr 9235 (Canada)
  10"-78 Velvet Face 1048 (as Joe Richardson's Orchestra)
  Carolina Rolling Stone [7847]
  10"-78 Connorized 3075
  10"-78 Gennett 4868
  10"-78 Rich-Tone 7037 (as The Jazz Harmonizers)
  10–78 Starr 9245 (Canada)
  California [7848]
  10"-78 Apex 480
  10"-78 Connorized 3075
  10"-78 Gennett 4868
  10"-78 Starr 9242 (Canada)

April 1922

Gennett Records, New York City
Bailey's Lucky Seven (Sam Lanin, leader; Nick Lucas, banjo, guitar; Phil Napoleon, trumpet; Vincent Grande, trombone; Gus Sharp, clarinet, alto saxophone; Loring McMurray, alto saxophone, piano, drums)
  Do It Again [7856]
  10"-78 Apex 478
  10"-78 Gennett 4872
  10"-78 Starr 9244 (Canada)
  10"-78 Velvet Face 1050 (as Joe Richardson's Orchestra)
  Some Sunny Day [7857]
  10"-78 Apex 480
  10"-78 Connorized 3078
  10"-78 Gennett 4872
  10"-78 Rich-Tone 7037 (as The Jazz Harmonizers)
  10"-78 Velvet Face 1054 (as The Pavilion Players)

May 1922

Pathe Freres Phonograph Company, New York City
The Don Parker Trio (Don Parker, alto saxophone; Nick Lucas, banjo; Frank Banta, piano)
  I Love Her—She Loves Me [69706]
  10"-78 Pathe Actuelle 020769
  10"-78 Pathe Actulle 10328
  10"-78 Pathe 1583
  10"-78 Perfect 14021 (as The Will Carroll Trio)
  Nola [69707]
  10"-78 Pathe Actuelle 020769
  10"-78 Pathe Actuelle 10395
  10"-78 Pathe 1631
  10"-78 Perfect 14021 (as The Will Carroll Trio)

May 1922

Gennett Records, New York City
Bailey's Lucky Seven (Sam Lanin, leader; Nick Lucas, banjo, guitar; Phil Napoleon, trumpet, Vincent Grande, trombone; Gus Sharp, clarinet, alto saxophone; Loring McMurray, alto saxophone, piano, drums)

Kicky-Koo (You for Me—Me for You) [7871]
10"-78 Apex 473
10"-78 Gennett 4887
10"-78 Starr 9256 (Canada)
10"-78 Velvet Face 1054 (as The Pavilion Players)
Those Longing for You Blues [7872]
10"-78 Gennett 4887

May 1922

Gennett Records, New York City
Bailey's Lucky Seven
Rock Me in My Swanee Cradle [7889]
10"-78 Gennett 4903

June 1922

Gennett Records, New York City
Bailey's Lucky Seven
A Dancing Fool [7917]
10"-78 Apex 467
10"-78 Cardinal 531
10"-78 Gennett 4908
10"-78 Starr 9272 (Canada)
Those Longing for You Blues [7918]
10"-78 Gennett 4887
Kicky-Koo (You for Me—Me for You) [7919]
10"-78 Gennett 4887

June 1922

Gennett Records, New York City
Bailey's Lucky Seven (add Cliff Edwards, vocal, ukulele, kazoo*)
Sweet Indiana Home [7936]
10"-78 Apex 471
10"-78 Edison Bell Winner 3811 (as The Pavilion Players) (British)
10"-78 Gennett 4910
10"-78 Starr 9267 (Canada)
Nobody Lied* [7937]
10"-78 Apex 471
10"-78 Edison Bell Winner 3796 (as The Pavilion Players) (British)
10"-78 Gennett 4909
10"-78 Starr 9267 (Canada)

10"-78 Westport 3018 (as The Pavilion Players)
12"-78 Queen-Disc Q059 (Italy)

July 1922

Gennett Records, New York City
Bailey's Lucky Seven
Mary Dear [7969]
10"-78 Apex 465
10"-78 Cardinal 529
10"-78 Gennett 4969
10"-78 Starr 9280 (Canada)
Who'll Take My Place (When I'm Gone)? [7970]
10"-78 Apex 465
10"-78 Gennett 4929
'Neath the South Sea Moon [7971]
10"-78 Gennett 4922

July 1922

Pathe Freres Phonograph Company, New York City
Nick Lucas [Lucanese] (guitar) with Phil Boutelje (piano)
Picking the Guitar [020794]
10"-78 Pathe Actuelle 020794
10"-78 Pathe Actuelle 10392
10"-78 Perfect 11041 (as Nick Lucanese)
10"-78 Silvertone 1207
Teasin' the Frets [020794B]
10"-78 Pathe Actuelle 020794
10"-78 Pathe Actuelle 10392
10"-78 Perfect 11041 [as Nick Lucanese]
10"-78 Silvertone 1207

August 1922

Gennett Records, New York City
Bailey's Lucky Seven
Truly (I Love You) [7992]
10"-78 Apex 464
10"-78 Gennett 4934
Hot Lips [7993]
10"-78 Cardinal 531 (as The Cardinal Dance Orchestra)
10"-78 Edison Bell Winner 3797 (as The Pavilion Players) (British)

10"-78 Gennett 4935
10"-78 Starr 9285 (Canada)
Chicago [7994]
10"-78 Gennett 4933
10"-78 Starr 9283 (Canada)

September 1922

Gennett Records, New York City
Bailey's Lucky Seven (add Cliff Edwards, vocal, ukulele* and Lillian Robbins, slide whistle**)
No Wonder I'm Lonesome** [8032]
10"-78 Apex 461
10"-78 Edison Bell Winner 3868 (as The Regent Orchestra) (British)
10"-78 Gennett 4975
10"-78 Starr 9298 (Canada)
10"-78 Westport 2044 (as The Regent Orchestra)
Tomorrow (I'll Be in My Dixie Home Again) [8033]
10"-78 Apex 461
10"-78 Edison Bell Winner 3812 (as The Diplomat Orchestra) (British)
10"-78 Gennett 4975
10"-78 Starr 9298 (Canada)
10"-78 Westport 2117 (as The Diplomat Orchestra)
Homesick* [80343]
10"-78 Apex 459
10"-78 Edison Bell Winner 3869 (as The Regent Orchestra) (British)
10"-78 Gennett 4979
10"-78 Starr 9299 (Canada)

September 1922

Pathe Freres Phonograph Company, New York City
The Don Parker Trio (Don Parker, alto saxophone; Nick Lucas, banjo; Frank Banta, piano)
It's Getting Dark on Old Broadway [69871]
10"-78 Pathe Actuelle 020844
10"-78 Pathe Actuelle 10395
10"-78 Pathe 1631
10"-78 Perfect 14063 (as The Will Carroll Trio)
Vamp Me (and I'll Vamp You) [69872]
10"-78 Pathe Actuelle 020844
10"-78 Perfect 14063 (as The Will Carroll Trio)

October 1922

Gennett Records, New York City
Bailey's Lucky Seven
Stuttering [8059]
10"-78 Apex 459
10"-78 Edison Bell Winner 3798 (as The Diplomat Orchestra) (British)
10"-78 Gennett 4980
Toot-Toot-Tootsie [8060]
10"-78 Apex 457
10"-78 Edison Bell Winner 3977 (as The Diplomat Novelty Orchestra) (British)
10"-78 Gennett 4980
10"-78 Starr 9306 (Canada)
10"-78 Westport 3100 (as The Diplomat Novelty Orchestra)
Carolina in the Morning [8061]
10"-78 Edison Bell Winner 3797 (as The Pavilion Players) (British)
10"-78 Gennett 4979
10"-78 Starr 9309 (Canada)

November 1922

Gennett Records, New York City
Bailey's Lucky Seven (Sam Lanin, leader; Nick Lucas, banjo, guitar; Phil Napoleon, trumpet; Charlie Panelli, trombone; Jimmy Lytell, clarinet, alto saxophone; Benny Krueger, alto saxophone; Jack Roth, drums)
Carolina Home [8099]
10"-78 Edison Bell Winner 3862 (as The Pavilion Players) (British)
10"-78 Gennett 5002
10"-78 Portland 9003 (as The Pavilion Players)
10"-78 Starr 9319 (Canada)
Gee, But I Hate to Go Home Alone [8100]
10"-78 Edison Bell Winner 3861 (as The Diplomat Orchestra) (British)

10"-78 Gennett 5001
10"-78 Starr 9317 (Canada)
10"-78 Westport 3072 (as The Diplomat Orchestra)
Tomorrow Morning [8101]
10"-78 Apex 453
10"-78 Edison Bell Winner 3861 (as The Diplomat Orchestra) (British)
10"-78 Gennett 5001
10"-78 Starr 9317
10"-78 Westport 3142 (as The Diplomat Orchestra)

November 17, 1922

Gennett Records, New York City
Bailey's Lucky Seven
Bees Knees [8109]
10"-78 Apex 451
10"-78 Gennett 5004
10"-78 Starr 9321 (Canada)
Lost (a Wonderful Girl) [8110]
10"-78 Apex 451
10"-78 Edison Bell Winner 3862 (as The Pavilion Players) (British)
10"-78 Gennett 5005
10"-78 Portland 9003 (as The Pavilion Players)
10"-78 Starr 9320 (Canada)
Where the Bamboo Babies Grow [8111]
10"-78 Apex 586
10"-78 Edison Bell Winner 3816 (as The Diplomat Orchestra) (British)
10"-78 Gennett 5004
10"-78 Starr 9321 (Canada)

December 1922

Gennett Records, New York City
Bailey's Lucky Seven
'Way Down Yonder in New Orleans [8141]
10"-78 Edison Bell Winner 3864 (as The Pavilion Players) (British)
10"-78 Gennett 5016
10"-78 Starr 9328
10"-78 Westport 2070 (as The Pavilion Players)
Open Your Arms, My Alabamy [8142]
10"-78 Edison Bell Winner 3865 (as The Pavilion Players) (British)
10"-78 Gennett 5017
10"-78 Starr 9328 (Canada)
Baby Blue Eyes [8143]
10"-78 Gennett 5012
10"-78 Starr 9330 (Canada)

January 1923

Gennett Records, New York City
Bailey's Lucky Seven
You Know You Belong to Somebody Else [8175]
10"-78 Gennett 5030
10"-78 Starr 9345 (Canada)
Apple Sauce [8176]
10"-78 Gennett 5030
10"-78 Starr 9345 (Canada)

February 1923

Gennett Records, New York City
Bailey's Lucky Seven
Sweet One [8196]
10"-78 Apex 431
10"-78 Gennett 5049
10"-78 Starr 9351 (Canada)

March 1923

Gennett Records, New York City
Bailey's Lucky Seven
My Blue and Gold Girl/Sigma Chi Dream Girl [8252]
10"-78 Gennett Special Record
Gypsy Lady [8253]
10"-78 Apex 430
10"-78 Gennett 5057
10"-78 Starr 9369 (Canada)
Pay Day Blues [8254]
10"-78 Gennett 5057
10"-78 Starr 9369 (Canada)

March 1923

Gennett Records, New York City
Bailey's Lucky Seven (Sam Lanin, leader; Nick Lucas, banjo, guitar; Phil

Napoleon, trumpet; Miff Mole, trombone; Jimmy Lytell, clarinet, alto saxophone; Benny Krueger, alto saxophone; Jack Roth, drums; Ernest Hare, vocal*)

    Wet Yo' Thumb [8271]
    10"-78 Gennett 5076
    10"-78 Starr 9380
    Everything Is O.K. In K.Y.* [8272]
    10"-78 Gennett 5078
    10"-78 Starr/Operaphone 9379 (Canada)
    Carolina Mammy* [8273]
    10"-78 Gennett 5078
    10"-78 Starr/Operaphone 9379 (Canada)

March 1923

Gennett Records, New York City
Bailey's Lucky Seven
    Snakes Hips [8285]
    10"-78 Apex 431
    10"-78 Edison Bell Winner 3950 (as The Regent Orchestra) (British)
    10"-78 Gennett 5110
    10"-78 Starr 9377 (Canada)
    Down Among the Sleepy Hills of Ten-Ten-Tennessee [8286]
    10"-78 Apex 430
    10"-78 Gennett 5110
    10"-78 Starr 9377 (Canada)

April 1923

Gennett Records, New York City
Bailey's Lucky Seven (with Irving Kaufman, vocal*)
    Down by the River [8342]
    10"-78 Apex 425
    10"-78 Cardinal 517 (as The Cardinal Dance Orchestra)
    10"-78 Gennett 5153
    10"-78 Starr 9397 (Canada)
    That Sweet Somebody O' Mine [8343]
    10"-78 Apex 425
    10"-78 Gennett 5145
    10"-78 Starr 9392 (Canada)
    My Old Ramshackle Shack* [8344]
    10"-78 Apex 424
    10"-78 Gennett 5145
    10"-78 Starr 9392 (Canada)

May 1923

Gennett Records, New York City
Bailey's Lucky Seven (with Irving Kaufman, vocal*)
    March of the Mannikins [8362]
    10"-78 Apex 428
    10"-78 Gennett 5153
    10"-78 Starr 9382 (Canada)
    Bebe [8364]
    10"-78 Gennett 5154
    10"-78 Starr 9395 (Canada)
    Yes! We Have No Bananas* [8365]
    10"-78 Gennett 5154
    10"-78 Starr 9395 (Canada)

June 1923

Gennett Records, New York City
Bailey's Lucky Seven
    When June Comes Along with a Song [8404]
    10"-78 Apex 421
    10"-78 Gennett 5193
    First, Last and Always [8405]
    10"-78 Apex 388
    10"-78 Gennett 5183
    10"-78 Starr 9425 (Canada)
    Pickles [8406]
    10"-78 Gennett 5197

June 1923

Gennett Records, New York City
Bailey's Lucky Seven (Sam Lanin, leader; Nick Lucas, banjo, guitar; Phil Napoleon, trumpet; Miff Mole, trombone; Jimmy Lytell, clarinet, alto saxophone; Benny Krueger, alto saxophone; Jack Roth, drums; Frank Signorelli, piano; Billy Jones, vocal*)
    Oh! Gee, Oh Gosh, Oh Golly, I'm in Love* [8417]
    10"-78 Apex 420
    10"-78 Gennett 5186
    10"-78 Starr 9417 (Canada)
    Dirty Hands! Dirty Face! [8418]
    10"-78 Apex 420
    10"-78 Edison Bell Winner 3964 (as The Regent Orchestra) (British)

10"-78 Gennett 5186
10"-78 Starr 9417 (Canada)

July 23, 1923

Victor Records, New York City
Tennessee Ten [Phil Napoleon, Jules Levy, Jr., trumpet; Nick Lucas, banjo; Rudy Weidoeft, Loring McMurray, alto saxophones; Frank Signorelli, piano; Charlie Panelli, trombone; Jimmy Lytell, clarinet; John Hellenberg, brass bass; Jack Roth, drums]
Tin Roof Blues [28305–1-2-3-4]
10"-78 Unissued
That Big Blonde Mama [28306–2]
10"-78 Victor 19130

August 1923

Gennett Records, New York City
Bailey's Lucky Seven (Sam Lanin, leader; Nick Lucas, banjo, guitar; Henry Gluck, trumpet; Miff Mole, trombone; Jimmy Lytell, clarinet, alto saxophone; Benny Krueger, alto saxophone; Jack Roth, drums, Frank Signorelli, piano; Lewis James, vocal*; Irving Kaufman, vocal**)
I've Got the Yes We Have No Banana Blues** [8464]
10"-78 Apex 418
10"-78 Edison Bell Winner 3948 (as The Diplomat Orchestra) (British)
10"-78 Gennett 5241
10"-78 Starr 9433 (Canada)
No, No Nora** [8465]
10"-78 Apex 418
10"-78 Edison Bell Winner 3976 (as The Regent Orchestra) (British)
10"-78 Gennett 5232
10"-78 Westport 3183 (as The Regent Orchestra)
Foolish Child* [8466]
10"-78 Apex 413
10"-78 Gennett 5232
10"-78 Starr 9438 (Canada)

August 1923

Gennett Records, New York City
Bailey's Lucky Seven

Home [8482]
10"-78 Apex 411
10"-78 Gennett 5243
10"-78 Starr 9436 (Canada)
Oh! Min [8483]
10"-78 Gennett 5249
10"-78 Starr 9435 (Canada)
That Big Blonde Mama [8484]
10"-78 Gennett 5243
10"-78 Starr 9437 (Canada)

September 1923

Gennett Records, New York City
Bailey's Lucky Seven (with Billy Jones, vocal*)
Oh! You Little Sun-uv-er-Gun* [8514]
10"-78 Apex 409
10"-78 Edison Bell Winner 4207 (as The Regent Orchestra) (British)
10"-78 Gennett 5258
10"-78 Starr 9444 (Canada)
Tell All the Folks in Kentucky [8515]
10"-78 Gennett 5264
10"-78 Starr 9450 (Canada)
Stealing to Virginia [8516]
10"-78 Edison Bell Winner 3996 (as The Pavilion Players) (British)
10"-78 Gennett 5258
10"-78 Starr 9450 (Canada)

October 1923

Gennett Records, New York City
Bailey's Lucky Seven (with Lewis James, vocal*)
Covered Wagon Days [8566]
10"-78 Gennett 5290
10"-78 Starr 9471 (Canada)
That Bran' New Gal of Mine [8567]
10"-78 Gennett 5300
10"-78 Starr 9465 (Canada)
Easy Melody* [8586]
10"-78 Edison Bell Winner 3996 (as The Pavilion Players) (British)
10"-78 Gennett 5290
10"-78 Starr 9464 (Canada)

October 20, 1923

Brunswick Records, New York City
Nick Lucas (guitar) with Ted Fio Rito (piano)
Pickin' the Guitar [11674]
10"-78 Brunswick 2536
10"-78 Brunswick 2536 (British)
CASSETTE "Sounds of a Century" 1875-B
CD ASV CD-AJA-5329 (British)
CD "Sounds of a Century" 1875-B
MP3 Emerald Echoes
Teasing the Frets [11676]
10"-78 Brunswick 2536
10"-78 Brunswick 2536 (British)
CASSETTE "Sounds of a Century" 1875-C
CD "Sounds of a Century" 1875-C

November 1923

Gennett Records, New York City
Bailey's Lucky Seven
"Linger Awhile" [8594]
10"-78 Edison Bell Winner 3977 (as The Pavilion Players) (British)
10"-78 Gennett 5300
10"-78 Starr 9468 (Canada)
Roamin' to Wyomin' [8595]
10"-78 Gennett 5301
Not Here—Not There [8596]
10"-78 Gennett 5301

November 1923

Gennett Records, New York City
Bailey's Lucky Seven
Take, Oh Take Those Lips Away [8620]
10"-78 Gennett 5308
10"-78 Starr 9468 (Canada)
Arcady [8621]
10"-78 Gennett 5325
Blue Rose [8622]
10"-78 Gennett 5308

December 1923

Gennett Records, New York City
Bailey's Lucky Seven
I'm Goin' South [8648]
10"-78 Gennett 5324
10"-78 Starr 9485 (Canada)
A Smile Will Go a Long, Long Way [8649]
10"-78 Gennett 5324
10"-78 Starr 9485 (Canada)
You're in Kentucky as Sure as You're Born [8650]
10"-78 Edison Bell Winner 4071 (as The Regent Orchestra) (British)
10"-78 Gennett 5325

December 1923

Gennett Records, New York City
Bailey's Lucky Seven
Steppin' Out [8677]
10"-78 Edison Bell Winner 4056 (as The Diplomat Novelty Orchestra) (British)
10"-78 Gennett 5349
I Love the Girl Who Kisses (I Hate the Girl Who Don't) [8678]
10"-78 Edison Bell Winner 4057 (as The Regent Orchestra) (British)
10"-78 Gennett 5344
Are You Lonely? [8679]
10"-78 Edison Bell Winner 4072 (as The Regent Orchestra) (British)
10"-78 Gennett 5344
10"-78 Portland 9009 (as The Regent Orchestra)
10"-78 Starr 9053 (Canada)

December 1923

Gennett Records, New York City
Bailey's Lucky Seven
I Wonder Who's Dancing with You Tonight? [8684]
10"-78 Gennett 5350
Eileen [8685]
10"-78 Gennett 5350
Maybe (She'll Write Me, She'll Phone Me) [8686]
10"-78 Apex 400
10"-78 Edison Bell Winner 4012 (as The Diplomat Novelty Orchestra) (British)
10"-78 Gennett 5349
10"-78 Starr 9503 (Canada)

January 1924

Gennett Records, New York City
Bailey's Lucky Seven
The One I Love Belongs to Somebody Else [8705]
10"-78 Apex 400
10"-78 Gennett 5357
10"-78 Starr 9502 (Canada)
Lovey Came Back [8706]
10"-78 Gennett 5363
Where the Lazy Daisies Grow [8707]
10"-78 Edison Bell Winner 4071 (as The Regent Orchestra) (British)
10"-78 Gennett 5357
10"-78 Starr 9507 (Canada)

January 1924

Gennett Records, New York City
Bailey's Lucky Seven
Mindin' My Business [8720]
10"-78 Gennett 5364
10"-78 Starr 9512 (Canada)
Hula Lou [8721]
10"-78 Gennett 5363
Soothing Lullaby [8722]
10"-78 Unissued
If You'll Come Back [8723]
10"-78 Gennett 5364
10"-78 Starr 9519 (Canada)

May 28, 1924

Brunswick Records, Chicago, Illinois
The Oriole Orchestra (Ted Fio Rito, leader, piano; Danny Russo, violin; Nick Lucas, banjo, guitar; Freddy Hulme, George Jernberg, trumpet; Hal Matthews, trombone; Don Mangano, Mutt Mayes, clarinet, soprano saxophone, alto saxophone; Clayton Naset, clarinet; Jack Wuerl, violin; Frank Papile, piano, accordion; Ralph Walker, brass bass; Charlie Puchta, drums)
Step, Henrietta! [A-122-3-4]
10"-78 Brunswick 2633
10"-78 Brunswick 2633 (British)
You'll Never Get to Heaven with Those Eyes [A-125-6-7]
10"-78 Brunswick 2633
10"-78 Brunswick 2633 (British)
The Little Old Clock on the Mantel [A-128]
10"-78 Brunswick 2637
10"-78 Brunswick 2637 (Australia)
10"-78 Brunswick 2637 (British)
I Need Some Pettin' [A-132-3-4]
10"-78 Brunswick 2637
10"-78 Brunswick 2637 (Australia)
10"-78 Brunswick 2637 (British)

October 16, 1924

Brunswick Records, Chicago, Illinois
The Oriole Orchestra
Eliza [14001]
10"-78 Brunswick 2741
10"-78 Brunswick 2741 (British)
10"-78 Silvertone 3028 (as Lake Shore Dance Orchestra)
Mandy, Make Up Your Mind [1400-5/8]
10"-78 Brunswick 2741
10"-78 Brunswick 2741 (British)

October 18, 1924

Brunswick Records, Chicago, Illinois
The Oriole Orchestra
Cophenhagen [14015/17]
10"-78 Brunswick 2752
10"-78 Brunswick 2752 (British)
10"-78 Silvertone 3028 (as Lake Shore Dance Orchestra)
CD Transatlantic Radio TR-002
My Rose Marie [14018/90]
10"-78 Brunswick 2752
10"-78 Brunswick 2752 (British)
10"-78 Silvertone 3028 (as Lake Shore Dance Orchestra)

October 20, 1924

Brunswick Records, St. Louis, Missouri
The Dixie Stars (Al Bernard, Russel Robinson) with Nick Lucas (guitar)
Keep On Going [14037]
10"-78 Brunswick 2762
10"-78 Brunswick 2762 (Australia)

Let My Home Be Your Home (When You're Down in Dixieland) [14040]
10"-78 Brunswick 2813
10"-78 Brunswick 2813 (Australia)

October 21, 1924

Brunswick Records, St. Louis, Missouri
The Dixie Stars (Al Bernard, Russel Robinson) with Nick Lucas (banjo)
Birmingham Papa (Your Memphis Mamma's Comin' to Town)
[14047]
10"-78 Brunswick 2813
10"-78 Brunswick 2813 (Australia)

October 27, 1924

Brunswick Records, St. Louis, Missouri
The Dixie Stars (Al Bernard, Russel Robinson) with Nick Lucas (banjo)
My Poodle-Oodle Dog [14079]
10"-78 Brunswick 2762
10"-78 Brunswick 2762 (Australia)

November 21, 1924

Brunswick Records, Chicago, Illinois
Nick Lucas (vocal, guitar)
Dreamer of Dreams [14336-7-8]
10"-78 Brunswick 2768
10"-78 Brunswick 2768 (Australia)
CASSETTE "Sounds of a Century" 1875-C
CD "Sounds of a Century" 1875-C
My Best Girl [14339]
10"-78 Brunswick 2768
10"-78 Brunswick 2768 (Australia)
CASSETTE "Sounds of a Century" 1875-B
CD ASV AJA-CD 5329 (British)
CD "Sounds of a Century" 1875-B
MP3 Emerald Echoes

November 22, 1924

Brunswick Records, Chicago, Illinois
The Oriole Orchestra (with Nick Lucas, vocal*)
I Can't Stop Babying You [14341-2-3]
10"-78 Brunswick 2797
Back Where the Daffodils Grow [14344-5-6]
10"-78 Brunswick 2769
10"-78 Brunswick 2769 (British)
Oh! Mabel* [14347-8-9]
10"-78 Brunswick 2769
10"-78 Brunswick 2769 (Australia)
12"-LP ASV AJA-5022 (British)
CASSETTE ASV ZC-AJA-5022 (British)
MP3 Hallmark

December 23, 1924

Brunswick Records, New York City
Marion Harris (vocal) with Nick Lucas (guitar), Bennie Krueger (saxophone), Phil Ohman (piano)
I'll See You in My Dreams [14537-8-9]
10"-78 Brunswick 2784
MP3 Emerald Echoes

December 23, 1924

Brunswick Records, New York City
Nick Lucas (vocal, guitar)
Because They All Love You [E-14543-4-5]
10"-78 Brunswick 2803
10"-78 Brunswick 2803 (Australia)
CD "M.C. Productions Vintage Recording No. 2"
CD "Vocalist's Showcase 1"
"Somebody Like You" [E-14540-1-2]
10"-78 Brunswick 2803
10"-78 Brunswick 2803 (Australia)
CD "M.C. Productions Vintage Recording No. 2"
CD "Vocalist's Showcase 1"

January 17, 1925

Brunswick Records, Chicago, Illinois
Nick Lucas (vocal, guitar) with Fred Rose (piano)
If I Can't Have You [14702]
10"-78 Brunswick 2827
10"-78 Brunswick 2827 (Australia)
10"-78 Brunswick 2827 (British)

My Baby [14706]
10"-78 Unissued

February 18, 1925

Brunswick Records, Chicago, Illinois
Nick Lucas (vocal, guitar)
I've Named My Pillow After You [E-14989]
  10"-78 Brunswick 2827
  10"-78 Brunswick 2827 (Australia)
  10"-78 Brunswick 2827 (British)
When I Think of You [E-14994]
  10"-78 Brunswick 2846
  10"-78 Brunswick 2846 (Australia)
The Only, Only One [14991]
  10"-78 Brunswick 2846
  10"-78 Brunswick 2846 (Australia)

May 29, 1925

Brunswick Records, New York City
Nick Lucas (vocal, guitar)
Isn't She the Sweetest Thing? (interpolating My Best Girl) [E-15919–0-21]
  10"-78 Brunswick 2906
  10"-78 Brunswick 2906 (Australia)
  10"-78 Brunswick 2906 (British)
  CASSETTE "Sounds of a Century" 1875-B
  CD "Sounds of a Century" 1875-B
  CD "Vocalist's Showcase 1"

June 3, 1925

Brunswick Records, New York City
Nick Lucas (vocal, guitar)
By the Light of the Stars [E-15929-0-1-32]
  10"-78 Brunswick 2906
  10"-78 Brunswick 2906 (Australia)
  10"-78 Brunswick 2906 (British)
  CASSETTE "Sounds of a Century" 1875-C
  CD "Sounds of a Century" 1875-C
  CD "Vocalist's Showcase 1"

June 18, 1925

Brunswick Records, New York City
Nick Lucas (vocal, guitar) with Frank Paris (piano)
I Might Have Known [E-15996–97–8]
  10"-78 Brunswick 2940
  10"-78 Brunswick 2940 (Australia)
  10"-78 Brunswick 2940 (British)
  12"-LP ASV AJA-5022 (British)
  CASSETTE ASV ZC-AJA-5022 (British)
  CASSETTE "Sounds of a Century" 1875-C
  CD "Sounds of a Century" 1875-C
  CD "M.C. Productions Vintage Recording No. 1"
  CD "Vocalist's Showcase 1"
  MP3 Hallmark

June 22, 1925

Brunswick Records, New York City
Nick Lucas (guitar, vocal) with Frank Paris (piano)
I'm Tired of Everything But You [E-16025–6-7]
  10"-78 Brunswick 2940
  10"-78 Brunswick 2940 (Australia)
  10"-78 Brunswick 2940 (British)
  CASSETTE "Sounds of a Century" 1875-B
  CD "M.C. Productions Vintage Recording No. 1"
  CD "Sounds of a Century" 1875-B
  CD "Vocalist's Showcase 1"

September 4, 1925

Brunswick Records, New York City
Nick Lucas (vocal, guitar)
I Found Somebody to Love [E-16345–6-47]
  10"-78 Brunswick 2990
  10"-78 Brunswick 2990 (Australia)
  10"-78 Brunswick 2990 (British)
If You Hadn't Gone Away [E-163742–3-44]
  10"-78 Brunswick 2961
  10"-78 Brunswick 2961 (Australia)
  10"-78 Brunswick 2961 (British)
  CD "M.C. Productions Vintage Recording No. 1"
  CD "Vocalist's Showcase 1"

Discography

Label for Nick Lucas' 1925 Brunswick record "I'm Tired of Everything But You."

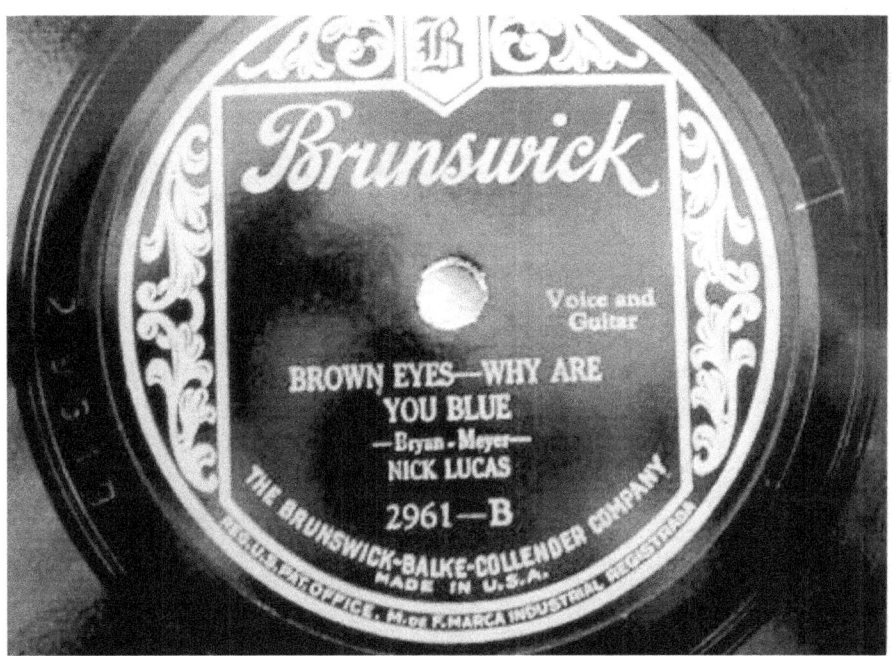

Label for Nick Lucas' 1925 Brunswick record "Brown Eyes, Why Are You Blue."

September 29, 1925

Brunswick Records, New York City
Nick Lucas (guitar, piano)
Brown Eyes, Why Are You Blue? [E-16556]

10"-78 Brunswick 2961
10"-78 Brunswick 2961 (Australia)
10"-78 Brunswick 2961 (British)
CD ASV CD-AJA-5329 (British)
CD ASV CD-AJA-5525 (British)

CD "M.C. Productions Vintage Recording No. 1"
CD "Vocalist's Showcase 1"
MP3 Hallmark
MP3 Ingrooves
MP3 K-Tel

November 23, 1925

Brunswick Records, New York City
Nick Lucas (vocal, guitar) with Gus Haenschen (piano)*, Lucien Schmidt (cello)*
Sleepy Time Gal* [E-16943–4-5]
10"-78 Unissued
Somebody Won a Wonderful Pal (When Somebody Won My Gal) [16946–7-8–9]
10"-78 Unissued

December 14, 1925

Brunswick Records, New York City
Nick Lucas (vocal, guitar)
Smile a Little Bit [E-17077–8-9]
10"-78 Brunswick 3021
10"-78 Brunswick 3021 (Australia)
10"-78 Brunswick 3021 (British)
CASSETTE "Sounds of a Century" 1875-B
CD "Sounds of a Century" 1875-B
CD "Vocalist's Showcase 1"
Sleepy Time Gal [E-17080–1-82]
10"-78 Brunswick 2990
10"-78 Brunswick 2990 (Australia)
10"-78 Brunswick 2990 (British)
CD ASV CD-AJA-5329 (British)
MP3 Emerald Echoes
MP3 Ingfooves
MP3 K-Tel ALL

December 18, 1925

Brunswick Records, New York City
Nick Lucas (vocal, guitar) with piano
Whose Who Are You? [E-17136–7-8]
10"-78 Brunswick 3052
10"-78 Brunswick 3052 (Australia)
10"-78 Brunswick 3052 (British)
CD "M.C. Productions Vintage Recording No. 1"
Forever and Ever with You [E-17139–0-1]
10"-78 Brunswick 3021
10"-78 Brunswick 3021 (Australia)
10"-78 Brunswick 3021 (British)
CASSETTE "Sounds of a Century" 1875-C
CD "Sounds of a Century" 1875-C
CD "Vocalist's Showcase 1"

January 29, 1926

Brunswick Records, New York City
Nick Lucas (vocal, guitar) with Sid Reinherz (piano)
A Cup of Coffee, a Sandwich and You [E-17742–3-4]
10"-78 Brunswick 3052
10"-78 Brunswick 3052 (Australia)
10"-78 Brunswick 3052 (British)
12"-LP ASV AJA-5022 (British)
CASSETTE ASV ZC-AJA-5022 (British)
CD ASV CD-AJA-5329
CD "M.C. Productions Vintage Recording No. 1"
MP3 Emerald Echoes
MP3 Hallmark

February 5, 1926

Brunswick Records, New York City
Nick Lucas (vocal, guitar) with violin and cello
Always [E-17946–7-8-9]
10"-78 Unissued
I Don't Believe It—But Say It Again [E-17850–1-2]
10"-78 Unissued

February 14, 1926

Brunswick Records, New York City
Nick Lucas (vocal, guitar) with cello and violin*
Always* [1798–9-0–1]
10"-78 Brunswick 3088
10"-78 Brunswick 3088 (Australia)
10"-78 Brunswick 3088 (British)
CD ASV CD-AJA-5329 (British)
CD "M.C. Productions Vintage Recording 1"

CD Sony Music Special Products A26545
CD "Sounds of a Century" 1875-A
CD "Vocalist's Showcase 1"
MP# Emerald Echoes
MP3 Ingrooves
MP3 K-Tel
I Don't Believe It—But Say It Again [17982-3-4]
10"-78 Brunswick 3088
10"-78 Brunswick 3088 (Australia)
10"-78 Brunswick 3088 (British)
CASSETTE "Sounds of a Century" 1875-C
CD "Sounds of a Century" 1875-C
CD "M.C. Productions Vintage Recording 1"
CD "Vocalist's Showcase 1"

March 12, 1926

Brunswick Records, Chicago, Illinois
Nick Lucas (vocal, guitar)
My Bundle of Love [18451]
10"-78 Unissued

April 23, 1926

Brunswick Records, Chicago, Illinois
Nick Lucas (vocal, guitar) with piano
Adorable [E-18876]
10"-78 Brunswick 3184
10"-78 Brunswick 3184 (Australia)
10"-78 Brunswick 3184 (British)
CASSETTE "Sounds of a Century" 1875-C
CD "Sounds of a Century" 1875-C
No Foolin' [E-18877]
10"-78 Brunswick 3141
10"-78 Brunswick 3141 (Australia)
10"-78 Brunswick 3141 (British)
CD "Vocalist's Showcase 1"
I Wish I Had My Old Girl Back Again [E-18881]
10"-78 Unissued
Bye Bye Blackbird [E-18896]
10"-78 Brunswick 3184
10"-78 Brunswick 3184 (Australia)
10"-78 Brunswick 3184 (British)
12"-LP ASV AJA-5022 (British)
CD "Sounds of a Century" 1875-A
CASSETTE ASV ZC-AJA-5022 (British)
MP3 Emerald Echoes
MP3 Hallmark
My Bundle of Love [E-18899]
10"-78 Brunswick 3141
10"-78 Brunswick 3141 (Australia)
10"-78 Brunswick 3141 (British)
LP ASV AJA-5022 (British)
CASSETTE ASV ZC-AJA-5022 (British)
CD ASV CD-AJA-5329 (British)
CD "Vocalist's Showcase 1"
MP3 Emerald Echoes
MP3 Hallmark
I'm Glad I Found a Girl Like You [E-18900-1-2]
10"-78 Brunswick 3185 [single sided disc]

June 16, 1926

Brunswick Records, New York City
Nick Lucas (vocal, guitar) with Sammy Stept (piano)*
Let Me Live and Love You Just for Tonight* [E-19596-7-8]
10"-78 Brunswick 3283
10"-78 Brunswick 3283 (Australia)
10"-78 Brunswick 3283 (British)
How Many Times? [E-19593-4-95]
10"-78 Brunswick 3229
10"-78 Brunswick 3229 (Australia)
10"-78 Brunswick 3229 (British)
LP ASV AJA-5017 (British)

June 17, 1926

Brunswick Records, New York City
Nick Lucas (vocal, guitar)
Sleepy Head [E-19605-6-7]
10"-78 Brunswick 3229
10"-78 Brunswick 3229 (Australia)
10"-78 Brunswick 3229 (British)
CASSETTE "Sounds of a Century" 1875-C
CD "Sounds of a Century" 1875-C
CD "Vocalist's Showcase 1"

July 26, 1926

Brunswick Records, New York City
Nick Lucas (vocal, guitar)
Looking at the World Thru Rose Colored Glasses [E-19930–1-2]
   10"-78 Brunswick 3283
   10"-78 Brunswick 3283 (Australia)
   10"-78 Brunswick 3283 (British)
   12"-LP ASV AJA-5022 (British)
   CASSETTE ASV ZC-5022 (British)
   CD ASV CD-AJA-5329
   CD "M.C. Productions Vintage Recording 1"
   CD "Sounds of a Century" 1875-A
   CD "Vocalist's Showcase 1"
   MP3 Emerald Echoes
   MP3 Hallmark
   MP3 Vintage Music

October 26, 1926

Brunswick Records, New York City
Nick Lucas (vocal, guitar) with Sammy Stept (piano)
When You're Lonely [E-20524–25]
   10"-78 Brunswick 3367
   10"-78 Brunswick 3367 (Australia)
   10"-78 Brunswick 3367 (British)
   CASSETTE "Sounds of a Century" 1875-B
   CD "Sounds of a Century" 1875-B
Precious [E-20526–277]
   10"-78 Brunswick 3369
   10"-78 Brunswick 3369 (Australia)
   10"-78 Brunswick 3369 (British)
   CASSETTE "Sounds of a Century" 1875-C
   CD "Sounds of a Century" 1875-C
   CD "Vocalist's Showcase 1"

October 28, 1926

Brunswick Records, New York City
Nick Lucas (vocal, guitar) with Sammy Stept* (piano)
Hello, Bluebird* [E-20662–63]
   10"-78 Brunswick 3370
   10"-78 Brunswick 3370 (Australia)
   10"-78 Brunswick 3370 (British)
   CD "Sounds of a Century" 1875-A
   CD "Vocalist's Showcase 2"
I'd Love to Call You My Sweetheart* [E-20564–5]
   10"-78 Brunswick 3369
   10"-78 Brunswick 3369 (Australia)
   10"-78 Brunswick 3369 (British)
   CASSETTE "Sounds of a Century" 1875-B
   CD "Sounds of a Century" 1875-B
   CD "Take Two" TT-CD
   CD "Vocalist's Showcase 1"
   MP3 "Stardust"
   MP3 "Tunecore"
Because I Love You [E-20566–67]
   10"-78 Brunswick 3367
   10"-78 Brunswick 3367 (Australia)
   10"-78 Brunswick 3367 (British)
   CASSETTE "Sounds of a Century" 1875-C
   CD "Sounds of a Century" 1875-C
I've Got the Girl* [E-20568/70]
   10"-78 Brunswick 3370
   10"-78 Brunswick 3370 (Australia)
   10"-78 Brunswick 3370 (British)
   12"-LP ASV AJA-5022 (British)
   CASSETTE ASV ZC-AJA-5022 (British)
   CASSETTE "Sounds of a Century" 1875-C
   CD "Sounds of a Century" 1875-C
   CD "Vocalist's Showcase 2"
   MP3 Hallmark

January 18, 1927

Brunswick Records, New York
Nick Lucas (vocal, guitar) with second guitar*
Put Your Arms Where They Belong [E-21223–24–25]
   10"-78 Brunswick 3433
   10"-78 Brunswick 3433 (Australia)
   10"-78 Brunswick 3433 (British)
   10"-78 Brunswick A432 (Germany)
   CD "Vocalist's Showcase 2"
In a Little Spanish Town* [E-21226–7-8]
   10"-78 Unissued

January 18, 1927

Brunswick Records, New York City
Nick Lucas (vocal, guitar) with Orchestra and Frank Paris (piano)
In a Little Spanish Town [E-21275–77]
10"-78 Brunswick 3433
10"-78 Brunswick 3433 (Australia)
10"-78 Brunswick 3433 (British)
10"-78 Brunswick A432 (Germany)
CD "Vocalist's Showcase 2"

January 25, 1927

Brunswick Records, New York City
Nick Lucas (vocal, guitar) with second guitar*
I'm Looking Over a Four Leaf Clover* [E-21304–05–06]
10"-78 Brunswick 3439
10"-78 Brunswick 3439 (Australia)
10"-78 Brunswick 3439 (British)
CD ASV CD-AJA-5329
CD "M.C. Productions Vintage Recording 1"
CD "Sounds of a Century" 1875-A
CD "Vocalist's Showcase 2"

MP3 Emerald Echoes
High, High, High Up in the Hills [E-21307–08–9]
10"-78 Brunswick 3439
10"-78 Brunswick 3439 (Australia)
10"-78 Brunswick 3439 (British)
CASSETTE "Sounds of a Century" 1875-C
CD "Sounds of a Century" 1875-C
CD "M.C. Productions Vintage Recording 1"
CD "Vocalist's Showcase 2"

February 10, 1927

Brunswick Records, New York City
Nick Lucas (vocal, guitar) with piano*
I'm Looking for a Girl Named Mary [E-21480–81–2]
10"-78 Brunswick 3466
10"-78 Brunswick 3466 (Australia)
CASSETTE "Sounds of a Century" 1875-B
CD "Sounds of a Century" 1875-B
Underneath the Weeping Willow* [E-21483–4–5]
10"-78 Brunswick 3466

Label for Nick Lucas' 1927 Brunswick record "In a Little Spanish Town."

10"-78 Brunswick 3466 (Australia)
CASSETTE "Sounds of a Century" 1875-C
CD "Sounds of a Century" 1875-C

March 10, 1927

Brunswick Records, New York City
Nick Lucas (vocal, guitar) with David Rubinoff* (violin) and piano**
   Moonbeam! Kiss Her for Me** [E-21825–6-7]
   10"-78 Brunswick 3492
   10"-78 Brunswick 3492 (Australia)
   10"-78 Brunswick 3492 (British)
   10"-78 Brunswick A7501 (Germany)
   CASSETTE "Sounds of a Century" 1875-B
   CD "Sounds of a Century" 1875-B
   CD "M.C. Productions Vintage Recording No. 1"
   CD "Vocalist's Showcase 2"
   So Blue* [E-21828–29–0]
   10"-78 Brunswick 3492
   10"-78 Brunswick 3492 (Australia)
   10"-78 Brunswick 3492 (British)
   10"-78 Brunswick A7501 (Germany)
   CASSETTE "Sounds of a Century" 1875-C
   CD ASV CD-AJA-5329
   CD "Sounds of a Century" 1875-C
   CD "M.C. Productions Vintage Recording 1"
   CD "Vocalist's Showcase 2"
   MP3 Emerald Echoes

March 24, 1927

Brunswick Records, New York City
Nick Lucas (vocal, guitar) with Sammy Stept* (piano)
   Side by Side [E-22106–7-8]
   10"-78 Brunswick 3512
   10"-78 Brunswick 3512 (Australia)
   10"-78 Brunswick 3512 (British)
   10"-78 Brunswick A7505 (Germany)
   CD ASV CD-AJA-5329
   CD "M.C. Productions Vintage Recording No. 1"

Label for Nick Lucas' 1927 Brunswick record "Side by Side."

   CD "Sounds of a Century" 1875-A
   CD "Vocalist's Showcase 2"
   MP3 Emerald Echoes
   MP3 Vintage Music
   Why Should I Say That I'm Sorry (When Nobody's Sorry for Me)*
   [E-22109–0-1]
   10"-78 Brunswick 3512
   10"-78 Brunswick 3512 (Australia)
   10"-78 Brunswick 3512 (British)
   10"-78 Brunswick A7505 (Germany)
   CASSETTE "Sounds of a Century" 1875-B
   CD "Sounds of a Century" 1875-B
   CD "M.C. Productions Vintage Recording No. 1"
   CD "Vocalist's Showcase 2"

March 29, 1927

Brunswick Records, New York City
Nick Lucas (vocal, guitar) with Sammy Stept* (piano)

Discography

Label for Nick Lucas' 1927 Brunswick record "Why Should I Say That I'm Sorry."

Rosy Cheeks* [E-22144–5-46]
10"-78 Brunswick 3518
10"-78 Brunswick 3518 (Australia)
10"-78 Brunswick 3518 (British)
10"-78 Brunswick A446 (Australia)
CASSETTE "Sounds of a Century" 1875-C
CD "Sounds of a Century" 1875-C
CD "Vocalist's Showcase 2"
Underneath the Stars with You [E-22147–48-9]
10"-78 Brunswick 3518
10"-78 Brunswick 3518 (Australia)
10"-78 Brunswick 3518 (British)
10"-78 Brunswick A446 (Germany)
CASSETTE "Sounds of a Century" 1875-C
CD "Sounds of a Century" 1875-C
CD "Vocalist's Showcase 2"

July 6, 1927

Brunswick Records: New York City
Nick Lucas (vocal, guitar) with William Wirges* (piano)

Sing Me a Baby Song [E-23857–8-59]
10"-78 Brunswick 3602
10"-78 Brunswick 3602 (Australia)
10"-78 Brunswick A492 (Germany)
CASSETTE "Sounds of a Century" 1875-C
CD "Sounds of a Century" 1875-C
CD "M.C. Productions Vintage Recording 1"
(Here Am I) Broken Hearted* [E-23860–1-2]
10"-78 Brunswick 3602
10"-78 Brunswick 3602 (Australia)
10"-78 Brunswick A492 (Germany)
CASSETTE "Sounds of a Century" 1875-C
CD "Sounds of a Century" 1875-C
CD "M.C. Productions Vintage Recording 1"

July 26, 1927

Brunswick Records, Chicago, Illinois

Advertisement for Nick Lucas' 1927 Brunswick record "Underneath the Stars with You"/"Rosy Cheeks."

Nick Lucas (vocal, guitar) with accordion*
Sweet Someone* [E-24118–19]
10"-78 Brunswick 3614
10"-78 Brunswick 3614 (Australia)
10"-78 Brunswick A429 (Germany)
CASSETTE "Sounds of a Century" 1875-C
CD "Sounds of a Century" 1875-C
CD "M.C. Productions Vintage Recording 1"
CD "Vocalist's Showcase 2"
I Can't Believe That You're in Love with Me [E-24121–2]
10"-78 Brunswick 3614
10"-78 Brunswick 3614 (Australia)
10"-78 Brunswick A492 (Germany)
CASSETTE "Sounds of a Century" 1875-B
CD "Sounds of a Century" 1875-B
CD "M.C. Productions Vintage Recording No. 1"
CD "Vocalist's Showcase 2"

October 13, 1927

Brunswick Records, Chicago, Illinois
Nick Lucas (vocal, guitar) with William F. Wirges (piano)
Among My Souvenirs [27418–9-20–1]
10"-78 Brunswick 3684
10"-78 Brunswick 3684 (Australia)
10"-78 Brunswick A7572 (Germany)
CD "M.C. Productions Vintage Recording No. 1"
CD "Sounds of a Century" 1875-A
CD "Vocalist's Showcase 2"
MP3 Vintage Music
(My) Blue Heaven [27422–3-24]

Label for Nick Lucas' 1927 Brunswick record "I Can't Believe That You're in Love with Me."

10"-78 Brunswick 3684
10"-78 Brunswick 3684 (Australia)
10"-78 Brunswick A7572 (Germany)
CD ASV CD-AJA-5329
CD "M.C. Productions Vintage Recording No. 1"
CD "Vocalist's Showcase 2"
MP3 Emerald Echoes
MP3 Van-Up Records

November 22, 1927

Brunswick Records, Chicago, Illinois
Nick Lucas (vocal, guitar) with piano* and string trio**
 The Song Is Ended** [C-1364–65]
 10"-78 Brunswick 3736
 10"-78 Brunswick 3706 (British)
 10"-78 Brunswick A7558 (Germany)
 CD "M.C. Productions Vintage Recording No. 1"
 CD "Vocalist's Showcase 2"
 Kiss and Make Up* [C-1368–69]
 10"-78 Brunswick 3736
 10"-78 Brunswick 3706 (British)
 10"-78 Brunswick A7558 (Germany)
 CD "M.C. Productions Vintage Recording No. 1"
 CD "Vocalist's Showcase 2"
 I Can't Believe That You're in Love with Me [C-370–1]
 10"-78 Unissued

December 10, 1927

Brunswick Records, New York City
Nick Lucas (vocal, guitar) with William Wirges* (piano)
 Keep Sweeping the Cobwebs Off the Moon* [E-25513–14]
 10"-78 Brunswick 3749
 10"-78 Brunswick 3749 (Australia)
 10"-78 Brunswick 3719 (British)
 CD "Vocalist's Showcase 2"
 Together [E-25515–16]
 10"-78 Brunswick 3749
 10"-78 Brunswick 3749 (Australia)
 10"-78 Brunswick 3719 (British)

CD "Vocalist's Showcase 2"
MP3 Vintage Music

January 12, 1928

Brunswick Records, New York City
Nick Lucas (vocal, guitar) with William F. Wirges (piano) and two violins
 Without You, Sweetheart [25978–9]
 10"-78 Brunswick 3773
 10"-78 Brunswick 3773 (Australia)
 10"-78 Brunswick 3736 (British)
 CASSETTE "Sounds of a Century" 1875-D
 CD ASV CD-AJA-5329
 CD "Sounds of a Century" 1875-D
 MP3 Emerald Echoes
 My Ohio Home [25975–76–7]
 10"-78 Brunswick 3773
 10"-78 Brunswick 3773 (Australia)
 10"-78 Brunswick 3736 (British)
 CASSETTE "Sounds of a Century" 1875-D
 CD "Sounds of a Century" 1875-D

February 24, 1928

Brunswick Records, New York City
Nick Lucas (vocal, guitar) with William F. Wirges* (piano); David Rubinoff (violin) and Mikiel Hanapi (steel guitar)**
 Sunshine* [E-26657–8]
 10"-78 Brunswick 3850
 10"-78 Brunswick 3850 (Australia)
 CASSETTE "Sounds of a Century" 1875-D
 CD "Sounds of a Century" 1875-D
 Marcheta** [E-266950–0]
 10"-78 Brunswick 3853 [cancelled]

February 25, 1928

Brunswick Records, New York City
Nick Lucas (vocal, guitar) with David Rubinoff* (violin) and second guitar**
 I'm Waiting for Ships That Never Come In** [E-26691]
 10"-78 Brunswick 3853 [cancelled]
 10"-78 Brunswick 3968

10"-78 Brunswick 3968 (Australia)
CASSETTE "Sounds of a Century" 1875-D
CD "Sounds of a Century" 1875-D
Marcheta* [E-26670]
10"-78 Unissued
I Still Love You [E-26671–2]
10"-78 Brunswick 3850
10"-78 Brunswick 3850 (Australia)
CASSETTE "Sounds of a Century" 1875-D
CD "Sounds of a Century" 1875-D

April 23, 1928

Brunswick Records, New York City
Nick Lucas (vocal, guitar) with William F. Wirges (piano)*
It Must Be Love [27393-A-B]
10"-78 Brunswick 3925
10"-78 Brunswick 3925 (Australia)
10"-78 Brunswick A7736 (Germany)
CD "Vocalist's Showcase 3"
I Can't Do Without You* [27392-A-B]
10"-78 Brunswick 3925
10"-78 Brunswick 3925 (Australia)
10"-78 Brunswick A7736 (Germany)
CD "Vocalist's Showcase 3"

June 11, 1928

Brunswick Records, New York City
Nick Lucas (vocal, guitar) with David Rubinoff (violin)*
Marcheta* [E-27690-A-B]
10"-78 Brunswick 3968
10"-78 Brunswick 3968 (Australia)
CASSETTE "Sounds of a Century" 1875-B
CD "Sounds of a Century" 1875-B
Just Like a Melody Out of the Sky [E-27691-A-B]
10"-78 Brunswick 3965
10"-78 Brunswick 3965 (Australia)
CASSETTE "Sounds of a Century" 1875-A
CD "Sounds of a Century" 1875-A
MP3 Vintage Music

For Old Times' Sake [E-27692-A-B]
10"-78 Unissued

June 15, 1928

Brunswick Records, New York City
Nick Lucas (vocal, guitar)
When You Said "Goodnight" (Did You Really Mean "Goodbye"?) [E-27721-A-B]
10"-78 Brunswick 3966
10"-78 Brunswick 3966 (Australia)
CASSETTE "Sounds of a Century" 1875-C
CD "Sounds of a Century" 1875-C
CD "Vocalist's Showcase 3"
You're a Real Sweetheart [E-27722-A-B]
10"-78 Brunswick 3966
10"-78 Brunswick 3966 (Australia)
CASSETTE "Sounds of a Century" 1875-B
CD "Sounds of a Century" 1875-B

July 6, 1928

Brunswick Records, New York City
Nick Lucas (vocal, guitar)
For Old Times' Sake [E-27837-A-B]
10"-78 Brunswick 3965
10"-78 Brunswick 3965 (Australia)
CASSETTE "Sounds of a Century" 1875-B
CD "Sounds of a Century" 1875-B

August 2, 1928

Brunswick Records, New York City [Lew White Organ Studios]
Nick Lucas (vocal, guitar) with Lew White (organ)
Someday, Somewhere (We'll Meet Again) [E-27955-A-B-C]
10"-78 Brunswick 4016
10"-78 Brunswick 4016 (Australia)
10"-78 Brunswick A8130 (Germany)
CASSETTE "Sounds of a Century" 1875-B
CD "Sounds of a Century" 1875-B
Chiquita [E-27956-A-B-C]

10"-78 Brunswick 4016
10"-78 Brunswick 4016 (Australia)
10"-78 Brunswick A8130 (Germany)
CASSETTE "Sounds of a Century" 1875-D
CD "Sounds of a Century" 1875-D

December 7, 1928

Brunswick Records, New York City
Nick Lucas (vocal, guitar) with orchestra
My Tonia [E-28882-A-B-C]
10"-78 Brunswick 4141
10"-78 Brunswick 4141 (Australia)
10"-78 Brunswick A8067 (Germany)
CASSETTE "Sounds of a Century" 1875-B
CD "Sounds of a Century" 1875-B
The Song I Love [E-28883-A-B-C]
10"-78 Brunswick 3926 (British)
10"-78 Brunswick 4141
10"-78 Brunswick 4141 (Australia)
10"-78 Brunswick A8067 (Germany)
CD "Sounds of a Century" 1875-A
CD "Take Two" TT-411CD

December 19, 1929

Brunswick Records, New York City
Nick Lucas (vocal, guitar)
I'll Get By [E-29000-A-B]
10"-78 Unissued
How About Me? [E-29001]
10"-78 Unissued

December 28, 1928

Brunswick Records, New York City
Nick Lucas (vocal, guitar) with William Wirges (piano)
When the World Is at Rest [E-29012-A-B]
10"-78 Brunswick 4171
10"-78 Brunswick 4171 (Australia)
CASSETTE "Sounds of a Century" 1875-B
CD "Sounds of a Century" 1875-B
I'll Never Ask for More [E-29013-A-B]
10"-78 Brunswick 4171
10"-78 Brunswick 4171 (Australia)

CASSETTE "Sounds of a Century" 1875-D
CD "Sounds of a Century" 1875-D

circa January 1929

Synchro Sound Films, New York City
Nick Lucas (vocal, guitar)
My Tonia
10"-78 Unissued
Woman Disputed, I Love You
10"-78 Unissued
Note: The recordings made for Synchro Sound Films were designed only for theatrical release.

January 17, 1929

Brunswick Records, Chicago, Illinois
Nick Lucas (vocal, guitar) with Jules Stein (piano) and Frank Quantrell (trumpet)*
I'll Get By [C-2817]
10"-78 Brunswick 3194 (British)
10"-78 Brunswick 4156
10"-78 Brunswick 4156 (Australia)
CASSETTE "Sounds of a Century" 1875-D
CD ASV CD-AJA-5329 (British)
CD "Sounds of a Century" 1875-D
MP3 Emerald Echoes
(You're Not Asking Me) I'm Telling You* [C-2818]
10"-78 Brunswick 4214
10"-78 Brunswick 4218 (Australia)
10"-78 Brunswick 5007 (British)
CASSETTE "Sounds of a Century" 1875-B
CD "Sounds of a Century" 1875-B
Some Rainy Day* [C-2819]
10"-78 Brunswick 3949 (British)
10"-78 Brunswick 4214
10"-78 Brunswick 4214 (British)
CASSETTE "Sounds of a Century" 1875-D
CD "Sounds of a Century" 1875-D

January 18, 1929

Brunswick Records, Chicago, Illinois
Nick Lucas (vocal, guitar) with orchestra

How About Me? [C-2833]
10"-78 Brunswick 3914 (British)
10"-78 Brunswick 4156
10"-78 Brunswick 4156 (Australia)
CASSETTE "Sounds of a Century" 1875-D
CD "Sounds of a Century" 1875-D

January 19, 1929

Brunswick Records, Chicago, Illinois
Nick Lucas (vocal, guitar) with cello, flute and two violins
Old Timer [C-2831]
10"-78 Brunswick 3949 (British)
10"-78 Brunswick 4215
10"-78 Brunswick 4215 (Australia)
CASSETTE "Sounds of a Century" 1875-D
CD "Sounds of a Century" 1875-D
Heart O' Mine [C-2832]
10"-78 Brunswick 4215
10"-78 Brunswick 4215 (Australia)
10"-78 Brunswick 5007 (British)
CASSETTE "Sounds of a Century" 1875-D
CD "Sounds of a Century" 1875-D

March 26, 1929

Brunswick Records, Los Angeles, California
Nick Lucas (vocal, guitar) with piano* and orchestra**
I've Got a Feeling I'm Falling* [LAE-434]
10"-78 Brunswick 3998 (British)
10"-78 Brunswick 4302
10"-78 Brunswick 4302 (Australia)
10"-78 Brunswick A8300 (Germany)
Coquette [LAE-435]
10"-78 Unissued

March 29, 1929

Brunswick Records, Los Angeles, California
Nick Lucas (vocal, guitar) with piano and trumpet
Coquette [LAE-438]
10"-78 Brunswick 3998 (British)

Label for Nick Lucas' 1929 Brunswick record "Old Timer."

10"-78 Brunswick 4302
10"-78 Brunswick 4302 (Australia)
10"-78 Brunswick A8300 (Germany)

April 1929

Brunswick Records, Los Angeles, California
Nick Lucas (vocal, guitar)
Sing a Little Love Song
10"-78 Unissued
Hittin' the Ceiling
10"-78 Unissued

May 1929

Warner Bros. Studios; Burbank, California
Nick Lucas (vocal, guitar) with The Vitaphone Orchestra
  Painting the Clouds with Sunshine
16"-78 Vitaphone Disc VA-3442-1-1
CD Soundies SCD-4134
  Tiptoe Through the Tulips
16"-78 Vitaphone Disc VA-3443-1-1
12"-LP Sandy Hook SH-2076
12"-LP "Take Two" TT-104
CD Soundies SCD-4134
  In a Kitchenette
16"-78 Vitaphone Disc VA-3443-1
  Go to Bed
16"-78 Vitaphone Disc VA-3444-1-1
  What Will I Do Without You?
16"-78 Vitaphone Disc VA-3446-1-1

Note: The Vitaphone Disc recordings were done for the soundtrack of the motion picture *The Gold Diggers of Broadway* (Warner Bros., 1929) and were not intended for commercial release.

May 1929

Warner Bros. Studios, Burbank, California
Nick Lucas (vocal, guitar) with the Vitaphone Orchestra
  Painting the Clouds with Sunshine
16"-78 Vitaphone Disc VD-3060-1-5
  Tiptoe Through the Tulips
16"-78 Vitaphone Disc VD-3060-1-5
12"-LP "Take Two" TT-110
  In a Kitchenette
16"-78 Vitaphone Disc VD-3060-1-5
12"-LP "Take Two" TT-110

Note: The Vitaphone Disc recordings were done for the soundtrack of the theatrical trailer for the motion picture *The Gold Diggers of Broadway* (Warner Bros., 1929) and were not intended for commercial release.

May 9, 1929

Brunswick Records, Los Angeles, California
Nick Lucas (vocal, guitar) with Orchestra
  Just Another Kiss [LAE-496]
10"-78 Brunswick 4390
10"-78 Brunswick 4390 (Australia)
10"-78 Brunswick A8319 (Germany)
  Painting the Clouds with Sunshine (LAE-497)
10"-78 Brunswick 4418
10"-78 Brunswick 4418 (Australia)
10"-78 Brunswick 5048 (British)
10"-78 Brunswick A8322 (Germany)
12:-LP ASV AJA-5022 (British)
CASSETTE ASV ZC-AJA-5022 (British)
CASSETTE "Sounds of a Century" 1875-A
CD ASV CD-AJA-5329 (British)
CD "Sounds of a Century" 1875-A
MP3 Emerald Echoes
MP3 Hallmark
MP3 Vintage Music
  Tiptoe Through the Tulips [LAE-498]
10"-78 Brunswick 4418
10"-78 Brunswick 4418 (Australia)
10"-78 Brunswick 5048 (British)
10"-78 Brunswick A8322 (Germany)
12"-LP Decca DEA-7-1
CASSETTE "Sounds of a Century" 1875-A
CD ASV CD-AJA-5329 (British)
CD AAO Music
CD Music & Memories 131772/RCA Special Products BMG Direct Marketing DMC-2-1111-1

CD Pro Jazz
CD "Sounds of a Century" 1875-A
CD "Take Two" TT-502-CD
MP3 Compendia
MP3 Emerald Echoes
MP3 Leverage
MP3 Oldies But Goodies

May 13, 1929

Brunswick Records, Los Angeles, California

Nick Lucas (vocal, guitar) with Roy Fox (whispering trumpet)*; with cornet, piano and trombone**; with orchestra***

Your Mother and Mine* [LAE-503]
10"-78 Brunswick 4378
10"-78 Brunswick 4378 (Australia)
10"-78 Brunswick A8289 (Germany)
12"-LP ASV AJA-5022 (British)
CASSETTE ASV ZC-AJA-5022 (British)
CASSETTE "Sounds of a Century" 1875-D
CD "Sounds of a Century" 1875-D
MP3 Hallmark
Singin' in the Rain** [LAE-504]
10"-78 Brunswick 4378
10"-78 Brunswick 4378 (Australia)
10"-78 Brunswick 4378 (Canada; alternate take)
10"-78 Brunswick A8289 (Germany)
12"-LP ASV AJA-5022 (British)
CASSETTE ASV ZC-AJA-5022 (British)
CASSETTE "Sounds of a Century" 1875-A
CD ASV CD-AJA-5329 (British)
CD "Sounds of a Century" 1875-A
MP3 Emerald Echoes
MP3 Hallmark
When My Dreams Come True*** [LAE-505]
10"-78 Brunswick 4390
10"-78 Brunswick 4390 (Australia)
10"-78 Brunswick A8319 (Germany)

July 22, 1929

Brunswick Records, New York City
Nick Lucas (vocal, guitar)
Ich Liebe Dich (I Love You) [E-30365-A-B]
10"-78 Brunswick 4464
10"-78 Brunswick 4464 (Australia)
CD "Vocalist's Showcase 3"
Until the End [E-30366-A-B]
10"-78 Brunswick 4547
10"-78 Brunswick 4547 (Australia)
Where Are You Dream Girl? [E-30367-A-B]
10"-78 Unissued
Sweethearts' Holiday [E-30368-A-B]
10"-78 Brunswick 4468
10"-78 Brunswick 4468 (Australia)

July 26, 1929

Brunswick Records, New York City
Nick Lucas (vocal, guitar)
My Song of the Nile [E-30394]
10"-78 Brunswick 4464
10"-78 Brunswick 4464 (Australia)
CD "Vocalist's Showcase 3"
Unknown Title [E-30395-A-B]

August 7, 1929

Brunswick Records, Los Angeles, California
Nick Lucas (vocal, guitar)
I Don't Want Your Kisses (If I Can't Have Your Love) [LAE-594]
10"-78 Brunswick 4547
10"-78 Brunswick 4547 (Australia)

September 6, 1929

Brunswick Records, New York City
Nick Lucas (vocal, guitar)
Where Are You Dream Girl? [E-30535-A-B]
10"-78 Brunswick 4468
10"-78 Brunswick 4468 (Australia)

November 1929

Warner Bros. Studios; Burbank, California
Nick Lucas (vocal, guitar) with The Vitaphone Orchestra

Li-po-li
16"-78 Vitaphone Disc
Lady Luck
16"-78 Vitaphone Disc
The Only Song I Know
16"-78 Vitaphone Disc

Note: The Vitaphone Disc recordings were done for the soundtrack of the motion picture *The Show of Shows* (Warner Bros., 1929) and were not intended for commercial release. Lucas can also be heard on the soundtrack to the trailer to the film. The trailer number is 3060-1-5.

June 7, 1930

Brunswick Records, New York City
Nick Lucas (vocal, guitar) with celesta, piano and violin*
Dancing with Tears in My Eyes* [E-33039-A-B]
10"-78 Brunswick 4834
10"-78 Brunswick 4834 (Australia)
10"-78 Brunswick 01012 (British)
10"-78 Brunswick A8799 (Germany)
CD "Vocalist's Showcase 3"
MP3 Vintage Music
Telling It to the Daisies [E-33040-A-B]
10"-78 Brunswick 4834
10"-78 Brunswick 4834 (Australia)
10"-78 Brunswick 01012 (British)
10"-78 Brunswick A8799 (Germany)
CD "Vocalist's Showcase 3"

June 28, 1930

Brunswick Records, New York City
Nick Lucas (vocal, guitar)
My Heart Belongs to the Girl Who Belongs to Somebody Else
    [E-33292-A-B]
10"-78 Brunswick 4847 [cancelled]
Singing a Song to the Stars [E-33293-A-B]
10"-78 Brunswick 4847 [cancelled]

July 15, 1930

Brunswick Records, New York City
Nick Lucas (vocal, guitar)
Singing a Song to the Stars [E-33430]
10"-78 Brunswick 4860
10"-78 Brunswick 4860 (Australia)
10"-78 Brunswick A8818 (Germany)
CASSETTE "Sounds of a Century" 1875-D
CD "Sounds of a Century" 1875-D
CD "Vocalist's Showcase 3"
My Heart Belongs to the Girl Who Belongs to Somebody Else
    [E-33431]
10"-78 Brunswick 4860
10"-78 Brunswick 4860 (Australia)
10"-78 Brunswick A8818 (Germany)
CASSETTE "Sounds of a Century" 1875-D
CD "Sounds of a Century" 1875-D

August 20, 1930

Brunswick Records, New York City
Nick Lucas (vocal, guitar)
Don't Tell Her What's Happened to Me [E-33974]
10"-78 Unissued
Just a Little Closer [E-34075]
10"-78 Brunswick 4896
10"-78 Brunswick 4896X (Australia)
10"-78 Brunswick 01030 (British)

August 27, 1930

Brunswick Records, New York City
Nick Lucas (vocal, guitar)
Don't Tell Her What's Happened to Me [E-34106]
10"-78 Brunswick 4896
10"-78 Brunswick 4900X (Australia)
10"-78 Brunswick 01030 (British)
Unknown Title [E-34107]
Unknown Title [E-34108]

September 4, 1930

Brunswick Records, New York City
Nick Lucas (vocal, guitar)
The Kiss Waltz [E-34197]
10"-78 Brunswick 4900

10"-78 Brunswick 4960X (Australia)
10"-78 Brunswick 01026 (British)
CD "Vocalist's Showcase 3"
Go Home and Tell Your Mother [E-34198]
10"-78 Brunswick 4900
10"-78 Brunswick 4900X (Australia)
10"-78 Brunswick 01026 (British)
CD "Vocalist's Showcase 3"

September 25, 1930

Brunswick Records, New York City
Nick Lucas (vocal, guitar) with The Anglo-Persians (Louis Katzman, director)
Siboney [E-34632]
10"-78 Brunswick 4954
10"-78 Brunswick 4954X (Australia)
10"-78 Brunswick 01047 (British)
10"-78 Brunswick A8902 (Germany)
12"-LP ASV AJA-5022 (British)
CASSETTE ASV ZC-AJA-5022 (British)
MP3 Hallmark

October 6, 1930

Brunswick Records, New York City
Nick Lucas (vocal, guitar)
Wasting My Love on You [E-33989]
10"-78 Brunswick 4959
10"-78 Brunswick 4959 (Australia)
Maybe It's Love [E-33990]
10"-78 Brunswick 4960
10"-78 Brunswick 4960X (Australia)
10"-78 Brunswick 01057 (British)

October 15, 1930

Brunswick Records, New York City
Nick Lucas (vocal, guitar)
Three Little Words [E-34017]
10"-78 Brunswick 4959
10"-78 Brunswick 4959 (Australia)
I'm Yours [E-34018]
10"-78 Brunswick 4960

November 15, 1930

Brunswick Records, New York City
Nick Lucas (vocal, guitar) and His Crooning Troubadours
You're Driving Me Crazy [E-35404]
10"-78 Brunswick 4987
10"-78 Brunswick 4987 (Argentina; as Me Estas Enloqueciendo)
10"-78 Brunswick 4987 (Australia)
10"-78 Brunswick 01055 (British)
10"-78 Brunswick A8982 (Germany)
10"-78 Brunswick A8986 (Germany)
12"-LP ASV AJA-5022 (British)
CASSETTE ASV ZC-AJA-5022 (British)
CASSETTE "Sounds of a Century" 1875-D
CD ASV CD-AJA-5329 (British)
CD Crystal Stream Audio IDCD81
CD "Sounds of a Century" 1975-D
MP3 Emerald Echoes
MP3 Hallmark
MP3 Vinyl Masters
I Miss a Little Miss (Who Misses Me in Sunny Tennessee) [E-35405]
10"-78 Brunswick 4987
10"-78 Brunswick 4987 (Argentina; as Extrano Una Amiguita)
10"-78 Brunswick 4987 (Australia)
10"-78 Brunswick 01055 (British)
10"-78 Brunswick A8986 (Germany)
CASSETTE "Sounds of a Century" 1975-D
CD Crystal Stream Audio IDCD81
CD "Sounds of a Century" 1875-D

December 20, 1930

Brunswick Records, New York City
Nick Lucas (vocal, guitar) and His Crooning Troubadours
Lady, Play Your Mandolin [E-35770]
10"-78 Brunswick 6013
10"-78 Brunswick 6013 (Australia)
10"-78 Brunswick 01081 (British)
10"-78 Brunswick A8982 (Germany)
CD ASV CD-AJA-5329 (British)
CD Flapper PAST-CD-7075
MP3 Emerald Echoes
Senora Toque Su Mandolina (Lady Play Your Mandolin) [E-35771]
10"-78 Brunswick 41272 (as Nick Lucas y Sus Trovadores)

Discography

Labels for Nick Lucas' 1931 Brunswick record "You're Driving Me Crazy"/"I Miss a Little Miss (Who Misses Me in Sunny Tennessee)" as issued in Argentina.

Say "Hello" to the Folks Back Home [E-35772]
10"-78 Brunswick 6013
10"-78 Brunswick 6013 (Australia)
10"-78 Brunswick 01081 (British)

January 31, 1931

Brunswick Records, New York City
Nick Lucas (vocal, guitar) and His Crooning Troubadours
You Didn't Have to Tell Me (I Knew It All the Time) [E-35967]
10"-78 Brunswick 6045
10"-78 Brunswick 6045 (Argentina; as No Tenias Que Haberme Dicho)
10"-78 Brunswick 6045 (Australia)
10"-78 Brunswick 01100 (British)
CD Crystal Stream Audio IDCD81
Hello! Beautiful [E-35968]
10"-78 Brunswick 6032X (Australia; as Nick Lucas and His Orchestra)
10"-78 Brunswick 6049
10"-78 Brunswick 01102 (British)
10"-78 Brunswick A9028 (Germany)
CD "Take Two" TT-418CD
When You Were the Blossom of Buttercup Lane and I Was Your Little Boy Blue [E-35969]
10"-78 Brunswick 6045
10"-78 Brunswick 6045 (Argentina; as Cuando Eras Tu Capullo, Del Ilorido Sendero)
10"-78 Brunswick 6045 (Australia)
10"-78 Brunswick 01100 (British)
CD Crystal Stream Audio IDCD81

February 6, 1931

Brunswick Records, New York City
Nick Lucas (guitar, vocal) and His Crooning Troubadours
Walkin' My Baby Back Home [E-36029]
10"-78 Brunswick 6048
10"-78 Brunswick 6059X (Australia)
10"-78 Brunswick 01119 (British)
CD Crystal Stream Audio IDCD81
Falling in Love Again [E-36030]
10"-78 Brunswick 6048
10"-78 Brunswick 6048X (Australia)
10"-78 Brunswick 01119 (British)
Running Between the Raindrops [E-36031]
10"-78 Brunswick 6049
10"-78 Brunswick 6049X (Australia)
10"-78 Brunswick 01102 (British)
10"-78 Brunswick A9028 (Germany)
CD Crystal Stream Audio IDCD81

March 29, 1931

Brunswick Records, New York City
Nick Lucas (vocal, guitar)
I Surrender Dear [E-36424]
10"-78 Unissued
Wabash Moon [E-36425]
10"-78 Brunswick 6089
10"-78 Brunswick 6090 (Australia)
10"-78 Brunswick 01138 (British)
10"-78 Brunswick A9078 (Germany)

April 9, 1931

Brunswick Records, New York City
Nick Lucas (vocal, guitar) and His Crooning Troubadours
Can't You Read Between the Lines? [E-36449]
   10"-78 Brunswick 6104
   10"-78 Brunswick 6104 (Australia)
Boy! Oh! Boy! Oh! Boy! I've Got It Bad [E-36450]
   10"-78 Brunswick 6096 (Australia)
   10"-78 Brunswick 6098
   10"-78 Brunswick 01141 (British)
   CD "Vocalist's Showcase 3"
Now You're in My Arms [E-36451]
   10"-78 Brunswick 6104
   10"-78 Brunswick 6104 (Australia)
Let's Get Friendly [E-36452]
   10"-78 Brunswick 6098
   10"-78 Brunswick 6098 (Australia)
   10"-78 Brunswick 01141 (British)
   CD "Vocalist's Showcase 3"
I Surrender, Dear [E-36453]
   10"-78 Brunswick 6089
   10"-78 Brunswick 6089 (Australia)
   10"-78 Brunswick 01138 (British)
   10"-78 Brunswick A9078 (Germany)

June 30, 1931

Brunswick Records, New York City
Nick Lucas (vocal, guitar) and His Crooning Troubadours
That's My Desire [E-36894]
   10"-78 Brunswick 6147
   10"-78 Brunswick 01190 (British)
   10"-78 Brunswick A9111 (Germany)
   CASSETTE "Sounds of a Century" 1875-D
   CD "Take Two" TT-508CD
   CD "Sounds of a Century" 1875-D
When the Moon Comes Over the Mountain [E-36895]
   10"-78 Brunswick 6147
   10"-78 Brunswick 01214 (British)
   10"-78 Brunswick A9111 (Germany)
   10"-78 Embassy E145 (Australia)
   10"-78 Panachord P12235 (British; as The Desmond Duo)
   CASSETTE "Sounds of a Century" 1875-B
   CD Crystal Stream Audio IDCD81
   CD "Sounds of a Century" 1875-B

October 2, 1931

Brunswick Records, New York City
Nick Lucas (vocal, guitar) with Victor Young and His Orchestra
Goodnight, Sweetheart [E-37237]
   10"-78 Brunswick 6195
   10"-78 Brunswick A9165 (Germany)
   12"-LP ASV AJA-5022 (British)
   CASSETTE ASV ZC-AJA-5022 (British)
   MP3 Hallmark

January 1932

Hit of the Week Records, New York City
Nick Lucas (vocal, guitar) and His Troubadours
An Evening in Caroline [1193-A]
   10"-78 Hit of the Week B-3-4
   12"-LP ASV AJA-5022 (British)
   CASSETTE ASV ZC-AJA-5022 (British)
   CD ASV CD-AJA-5329 (British)
   CD Crystal Stream Audio IDCD81
   CD Kipepeo Publishing
   CD "Sounds of a Century" 1875-A
   CD "Vocalist's Showcase 3"
   MP3 Emerald Echoes
   MP3 Hallmark
All of Me/Goodnight Ladies [1194-A]
   10"-78 Hit of the Week A-4-B-1
   12"-LP Broadway International BR-109
   CD ASV CD-AJA-5329 (British)
   CD Crystal Stream Audio IDCD81
   CD "Sounds of a Century" 1875-A
   CD "Vocalist's Showcase 3"
   MP3 Emerald Echoes
Note: "Goodnight Ladies" is paired with "All of Me" and does not include a vocal by Nick Lucas but instead is sung by an unbilled trio. "All of Me/Goodnight

Ladies" was issued on January 28, 1932, and "An Evening in Caroline" was released on February 18, 1932. The Hit of the Week recordings had music only on one side; the other side features a picture of Lucas.

December 6, 1932

Brunswick Records, New York City
Nick Lucas (guitar)
Picking the Guitar [B-12690]
10"-78 Brunswick 6508
10"-78 Brunswick 01433 (British)
10"-78 Columbia B.12690-A test pressing
10"-78 Regal Zonophone G22171 (Australia)
12"-LP Yazoo L-1057
CD Crystal Stream Audio IDCD81
Teasing the Frets [B-12691]
10"-78 Brunswick 6508
10"-78 Brunswick 01433 (British)
10"-78 Columbia B.12690-B (test pressing)
10"-78 Regal Zonophone G22171 (Australia)
12-LP Yazoo L-1057
CD Crystal Stream Audio IDCD81

December 21, 1932

Brunswick Records, New York City
Nick Lucas (vocal, guitar)
I'm Sure of Everything But You [B-12767]
10"-78 Brunswick 6459
10"-78 Brunswick 10437 (British)
CD Crystal Stream Audio IDCD81
CD "Vocalist's Showcase 3"
More Beautiful Than Ever [B-12768]
10"-78 Brunswick 6459
CD Crystal Stream Audio IDCD81
CD "Vocalist's Showcase 3"
Till Tomorrow [B-12769]
10"-78 Brunswick 6462
10"-78 Brunswick 01437 (British)
CD "Vocalist's Showcase 3"
I Called to Say Goodnight [B-12770]
10"-78 Brunswick 6462
10"-78 Brunswick 01465 (British)
CD "Vocalist's Showcase 3"

May 8, 1934

Brunswick Records, New York City
Nick Lucas (vocal, guitar) with Victor Young and His Orchestra
Love Thy Neighbor [15177–1]
10"-78 Banner 33061
10"-78 Melotone M-13026
10"-78 Perfect 13006
10"-78 Rex 8219
CASSETTE "Sounds of a Century" 1875-D
CD Crystal Stream Audio IDCD81
CD "Sounds of a Century" 1875-D
A Thousand Good Nights [15178–1]
10"-78 Banner 33061
10"-78 Melotone M-13026
10"-78 Perfect 13006
10"-78 Rex 8219
CASSETTE "Sounds of a Century" 1875-D
CD Crystal Stream Audio IDCE81
CD "Sounds of a Century" 1875-D
Carry Me Back to the Lone Prairie [15179]
10"-78 Brunswick M-13027
10"-78 Rex 8306
CD "Sounds of a Century" 1875-A
Goin' Home [15180]
10"-78 Melotone M-13027
CD "Sounds of a Century" 1875-A
REEL-TO-REEL Old Time Record Collectors Club [no number]

August 3, 1934

Brunswick Records, New York City
Nick Lucas (vocal, guitar) with Victor Young and His Orchestra
Moon Glow [15535–1]
10"-78 Banner 33124
10"-78 Melotone M-13091
10"-78 Oriole 2937
10"-78 Perfect 13025

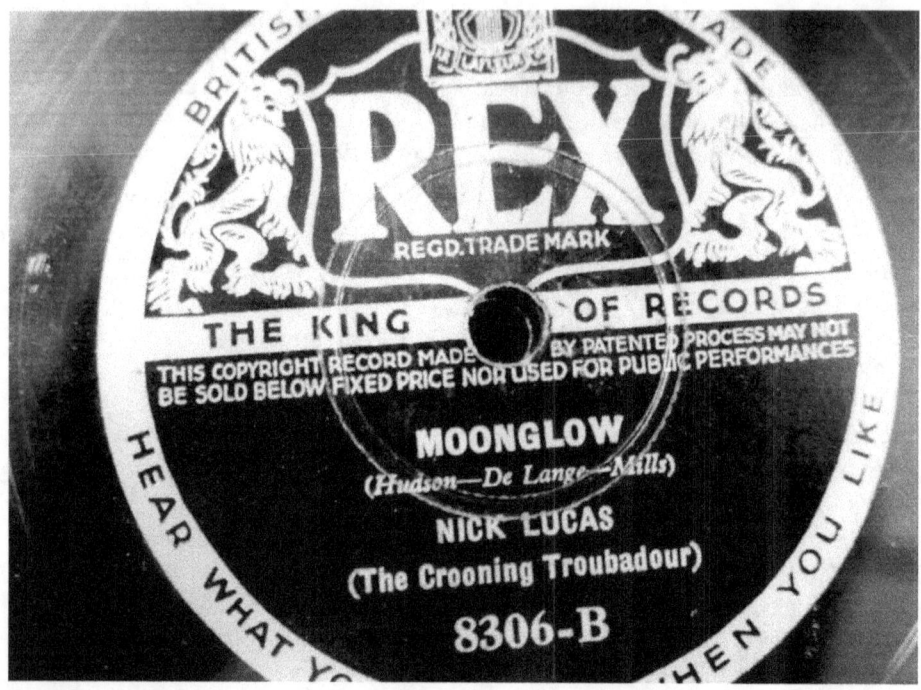

Label for the British release "Moonglow" by Nick Lucas on the Rex label in 1934.

10"-78 Rex 8306
CD Crystal Stream Audio IDCD81
CD "Sounds of a Century" 1875-A
For All We Know [15536]
10"-78 Banner 33124
10"-78 Melotone M-13091
10"-78 Oriole 2937
10"-78 Perfect 13025
CD Crystal Stream Audio IDCD81
CD Rivermont
CD "Sounds of a Century" 1875-A

April 8, 1936

Radio Broadcast (WABC); Hollywood Restaurant, New York City
Nick Lucas (vocal, guitar) with His Troubadours and Mimi Rollins* (vocal)
Doin' the Manhattan [instrumental]
10"-78 Universal Recording
Cling to Me
10"-78 Universal Recording
You*
10"-78 Universal Recording
There's Always a Happy Ending
10"-78 Universal Recording
Play It, Mr. Charlie [Guitar solo]
10"-78 Universal Recording
I'll Stand By
10"-78 Universal Recording
Mutiny in the Park*
10"-78 Universal Recording
I Want to Go Where You Go [Guitar solo]
10"-78 Universal Recording
My Blue Heaven
10"-78 Universal Recording
Note: The Universal Recording discs were not intended for commercial release.

circa 1936

C.P. MacGregor Transcription Company, Los Angeles, California
Nick Lucas (vocal, guitar)
It Looks Like Rain in Cherry Blossom Lane [MS-3067]
10"-78 C.P. MacGregor 1049
CASSETTE "Sounds of a Century" 1875-A

CD Melody Man MMCD-2606
CD "Sounds of a Century" 1875-A
You'll Never Get to Heaven [MS-3068]
10"-78 C.P. MacGregor 1050
CASSETTE "Sounds of a Century" 1875-A
CD Melody Man MMCD-2606
CD "Sounds of a Century" 1875-A
Till the Clock Strikes Three [MS-3071]
10"-78 C.P. MacGregor 1053
CD Melody Man MMCD-2606
The Moon Got in My Eyes [MS-3072]
10"-78 C.P. MacGregor 1054
CD Melody Man MMCD-2606
A Sailboat in the Moonlight [MS-3073]
10"-78 C.P. MacGregor 1055
CD Melody Man MMCD-2606
The Dream in My Heart [MS-3074]
10"-78 C.P. MacGregor 1056
CD Melody Man MMCD-2606
We Can't Go On This Way [MS-3075]
10"-78 C.P. MacGregor 1057
CD "Take Two" TT-425CD
Strangers in the Dark [MS-3076]
10"-78 C.P. MacGregor 1058
CD Melody Man MMCD-2606
Tiptoe Through the Tulips [MS-3077]
10"-78 C.P. MacGregor 1059
Side by Side [MS-3078]
10"-78 C.P. MacGregor 1060
Little Old Fashioned Music Box [MS-3079]
10"-78 C.P. MacGregor 1061
CD Melody Man MMCD-2606
The Miller's Daughter Marianne [MS-3080]
10"-78 C.P. MacGregor 1062
CD Melody Man MMCD-2606
Tomorrow Is Another Day [MS-3081]
10"-78 C.P. MacGregor 1063
CD Melody Man MMCD-2606
Gone with the Wind [MS-3082]
10"-78 C.P. MacGregor 1064
CD Melody Man MMCD-2606
My Cabin of Dreams [MS-A1799]
10"-78 C.P. MacGregor 1122
CD Melody Man MMCD-2606

When I Look at You [MS-3115]
10"-78 C.P. MacGregor 1196
CD Melody Man MMCD-2606
Pickin' the Guitar [MS-3116]
10"-78 C.P. MacGregor 1197
CD Melody Man MMCD-2606
Vieni, Vieni [MS-3117]
10"-78 C.P. MacGregor 1198
CD Melody Man MMCD-2606
You Can't Stop Me from Dreaming [MS-3118]
10"-78 C.P. MacGregor 1199
CD Melody Man MMCD-2606
In a Little Carolina Town [MS-3119]
10"-78 C.P. MacGregor 1200
CD Melody Man MMCD-2606
Please Pardon Us We're in Love [MS-3120]
10"-78 C.P. MacGregor 1201
CD Melody Man MMCD-2606

Note: The C.P. MacGregor transcriptions were made only for radio broadcast and not for commercial release.

circa late 1930s

Radio Broadcast, New York City (?)
Nick Lucas (vocal, guitar)
Our Love Will Flow
10"-78 Unissued Test Pressing
Teasin' the Frets [guitar solo]
10"-78 Unissued Test Pressing

November 22, 1939

Columbia Gramophone Company, Sydney, Australia
Nick Lucas (vocal, guitar) with Novelty Rhythm Accompaniment (Charles Lees, vibes [vibraharp]; Reg Lewis, piano; Reg Robinson, bass)
An Apple for the Teacher [CT-1728]
10"-78 Regal Zonophone G23898 (Australia)
12"-LP ASV AJA-5022 (British)
CASSETTE ASV ZC-AJA-5022 (British)
CD ASV CD-AJA-5329 (British)
CD Crystal Stream Audio IDCD81
MP3 Emerald Echoes

MP3 Hallmark
A Man and His Dream [CT-1729]
10"-78 Regal Zonophone G23898 (Australia)
12"-LP ASV AJA-5022 (British)
CASSETTE ASV ZC-AJA-5022 (British)
CD Crystal Stream Audio IDCD81
MP3 Hallmark
Go Fly a Kite [CT-1730]
10"-78 Regal Zonophone G23900 (Australia)
12"-LP ASV AJA-5022 (British)
CASSETTE ASV ZC-AJA-5022 (Australia)
CD ASV CD-AJA-5329 (British)
CD Crystal Stream Audio IDCD81
MP3 Emerald Echoes
Good Morning [CT-1731]
10"-78 Regal Zonophone G23900 (Australia)
12"-LP ASV AJA-5022 (British)
CASSETTE ASV ZC-AJA-5022 (British)
CD Crystal Stream Audio IDCD81
MP3 Hallmark
Over the Rainbow [CT-1732]
10"-78 Regal Zonophone G23899 (Australia)
12"-LP ASV AJA-5022 (British)
CASSETTE ASV ZC-AJA-5022 (British)
CD ASV CD-AJA-5329 (British)
CD Crystal Stream Audio IDCE81
MP3 Emerald Echoes
MP3 Hallmark
The Man with the Mandolin [CT-1733]
10"-78 Regal Zonophone G23899 (Australia)
12"-LP ASV AJA-5022 (British)
CASSETTE ASV ZC-AJA-5022 (British)
CD Crystal Stream Audio IDCD81
MP3 Hallmark
Note: On the Australian Regal Zonophone releases, the labels read "Nick Lucas, The Singing Guitarist."

1941

Radio Broadcast (*Kraft Music Hall*, NBC), Hollywood, California
Nick Lucas (vocal, guitar) with studio orchestra
Maria Elena
12"-LP Star-Tone ST-206

June 16, 1942

Compo Company, Montreal, Canada
Nick Lucas (vocal, guitar)
Side by Side [9949]
10"-78 Compo CT-5020
Note: This was one of an undetermined number of radio transcriptions recorded by Lucas for the Compo Company. Other titles are unknown since the company's ledgers for that period are apparently lost.

1944

Soundies Corporation of America; Hollywood, California
Nick Lucas (vocal, guitar) with orchestra
Tiptoe Through the Tulips
Side by Side
Goodnight, Wherever You Are
An Hour Never Passes
Note: The Soundies Corporation of America recordings were made as soundtracks for three-minute films played on jukeboxes and were not intended for commercial release.

July 21, 1944

Audio-Scriptions, Inc.; WABC Radio, New York City
Nick Lucas (vocal, guitar)
Tiptoe Through the Tulips
10"-78 Audio-Scriptions (no number)
Side by Side
10"-78 Audio-Scriptions (no number)

November 1944

Premier Records, St. Louis, Missouri
Nick Lucas (vocal, guitar) with Orchestra
Tiptoe Through the Tulips [20196]
10"-78 Premier 28992
Always [20198]
10"-78 Premier 28992

Note: The Premier Records masters were purchased by Mercury Records in the spring of 1946.

November 8, 1944

Republic Recording; Chicago, Illinois
Nick Lucas (vocal, guitar)
Radio Spot Announcements for Holsum Bread

December 1945

W.E. Long Company, Chicago, Illinois
Nick Lucas (vocal, guitar) with Billy Blair's Orchestra
Start with a Whistle in the Morning
Let's Start Off the Day Right
I Wish You a Happy Birthday
Let's Make Every Day Mother's Day
Let's Be on Time for Dinner Tonight
Note: Along with several other performers (Two-Ton Baker, Red Foley, Nancy Martin, Betty Maurer, Little Jackie Heller, the Murtagh Sisters), Lucas recorded the above songs for the syndicated *Program Themes* radio series; they were composed by Lola Hill and Delos Owen.

circa 1945

Sellers, Inc; Dallas, Texas
Nick Lucas (vocal, guitar)
My Blue Heaven
10"-78 Sellers G-5978
It's Been a Long, Long Time
10"-78 Sellers G-5978

circa 1945–46

C.P. MacGregor Transcription Company, Hollywood, California
Nick Lucas (vocal, guitar)
Sleepy Time Gal [Lucas USA #1]
16"-ET C.P. MacGregor CT-5013
16"-ET United Transcribed System [UTS] UTS-2094 (Canada)
CD Soundies SCD-4134
I'm Looking Over a Four Leaf Clover [Lucas USA #1]
16"-ET C.P. MacGregor CT-5013
16"-ET United Transcribed System [UTS] UTS-2094 (Canada)
CD Soundies SCD-4134
In a Little Spanish Town [Lucas USA #1]
16"-ET C.P. MacGregor CT-5013
16"-ET United Transcribed System [UTS] UTS-2094 (Canada)
CD Soundies SCD-4134
Three Little Words [Lucas USA #1]
16"-ET C.P. MacGregor CT-5013
16"-ET United Transcribed System [UTS] UTS-2094 (Canada)
CD Soundies SCD-4134
Oh, How I Miss You Tonight [Lucas USA #1]
16"-ET C.P. MacGregor CT-5013
16"-ET United Transcribed System [UTS] UTS-2094 (Canada)
CD Soundies SCD-4134
Always [Lucas USA #4]
16"-ET C.P. MacGregor CT-5016
16"-ET United Transcribed System [UTS] UTS-2095 (Canada)
CD Soundies SCD-4134
It Looks Like Rain in Cherry Blossom Lane [Lucas USA #4]
16"-ET C.P. MacGregor CT-5016
16"-ET United Transcribed System [UTS] UTS-2095 (Canada)
CD Soundies SCD-4134
I'll Get By [Lucas USA #4]
16"-ET C.P. MacGregor CT-5016
16"-ET United Transcribed System [UTS] UTS-2095 (Canada)
CD Soundies SCD-4134
The Song Is Ended [Lucas USA #4]
16"-ET C.P. MacGregor CT-5016
16"-ET United Transcribed System [UTS] UTS-2095 (Canada)
CD Soundies SCD-4134
Mexicali Rose [Lucas USA #4]
16"-ET C.P. MacGregor CT-5016
16"-ET United Transcribed System [UTS] UTS-2095 (Canada)
CD Soundies SCD-4134
Painting the Clouds with Sunshine (Lucas USA #9)

16"-ET C.P. MacGregor CT-5021
16"-ET United Transcribed System [UTS] UTS-2103 (Canada)
CD Soundies SCD-4134
Tangerine [Lucas USA #9]
16"-ET C.P. MacGregor CT-5021
16"-ET United Transcribed System [UTS] UTS-2103 (Canada)
CD Soundies SCD-4134
The Gay Ranchero [Lucas USA #9]
16"-ET C.P. MacGregor CT-5021
16"-ET United Transcribed System [UTS] UTS-2103 (Canada)
CD Soundies SCD-4134
Minnie the Mermaid [Lucas USA#9]
16"-ET C.P. MacGregor CT-5021
16"-ET United Transcribed System [UTS] UTS-2103 (Canada)
CD Soundies SCD-4134
Just Like a Melody Out of the Sky [Lucas USA #11]
16"-ET C.P. MacGregor CT-5023
16"-ET United Transcribed System [UTS] UTS-2105 (Canada)
You Are Everything I Love [Lucas USA #11]
16"-ET C.P. MacGregor CT-4023
16"-ET United Transcribed System [UTS] UTS-2105 (Canada)
CD Melody Man MMCD-2606
Among My Souvenirs [Lucas USA #11]
16"-ET C.P. MacGregor CT-4023
16"-ET United Transcribed System [UTS] UTS-2105 (Canada)
Charley My Boy [Lucas USA #11]
16"-ET C.P. MacGregor CT-4023
16"-ET United Transcribed System [UTS] UTS-2105 (Canada)
CD Melody Man MMCD-2606
(Here Am I) Brokenhearted [Lucas USA #11]
16"-ET C.P. MacGregor CT-4023
16"-ET United Transcribed System [UTS] UTS-2105 (Canada)

Note: The C.P. MacGregor transcriptions were made for radio broadcast and were not intended for commercial release.

The UTS Canadian issuances were circa 1952.

Spring 1946

Diamond Records, St. Louis, Missouri
Nick Lucas (vocal, guitar) and His Orchestra
Coax Me a Little Bit [A-5000]
10"-78 Diamond 2018
If I Had My Way [A-5001]
10"-78 Diamond 2018
What You Gonna Do? [A-5005X]
10"-78 Diamond 2019
Painting the Clouds with Sunshine (A-5004)
10"-78 Diamond 2019
Seems Like Old Times
10"-78 Diamond 2021
Give My Heart a Break
10"-78 Diamond 2021
My Blue Heaven [2024]
10"-78 Diamond 2022
Everyone Is Looking for the Rainbow [2022]
10"-78 2022

Note: Diamond 2021 was released in August 1946.

circa 1947

Radio Broadcast, New York City
Nick Lucas (vocal, guitar)
Tiptoe Through the Tulips
10"-78 Audiodisc 20196
Open Up That Door
10"-78 Audiodisc 20196

May 30, 1948

Radio Broadcast (CBS), New York City
Nick Lucas (vocal, guitar)
I'm Looking Over a Four Leaf Clover
10"-78 Frankay and Jackson Recording [no number]
Among My Souvenirs
10"-78 Frankay and Jackson Recording [no number]
My Blue Heaven

10"-78 Frankay and Jackson Recording [no number]
Tiptoe Through the Tulips
10"-78 Frankay and Jackson Recording [no number]
Bye Bye Blackbird
10"-78 Frankay and Jackson Recording [no number]
Seems Like Old Times
10"-78 Frankay and Jackson Recording [no number]

June 1948

Huckster Records, Hollywood, California
Nick Lucas (vocal, guitar) with orchestra
Tiptoe Through the Tulips [3491]
10"-78 Capitol 15242
10"-78 Huckster 1006
12"-LP Capitol TBO-1572
12"-LP Capitol T/ST-1221
12"-LP EMI VMP-1022 (British)
Side by Side [3492-3]
10"-78 Capitol 15242
10"-78 Huckster 1006
Bye Bye Blackbird [3496]
10"-78 Huckster
(Here Am I) Brokenhearted [3497]
10"-78 Unissued
Painting the Clouds with Sunshine (3498)
10"-78 Unissued
Brown Eyes, Why Are You Blue? [3499]
10"-78 Capitol Promotional
I Used to Love You (But It's All Over Now) [3500]
10"-78 Capitol Promotional
I Miss You Most of All (The Chair's in the Parlor) [3501]
10"-78 Huckster
Note: Capitol Records purchased the masters of the Huckster recordings on August 20, 1948, and assigned their matrix numbers. Capitol 15242 was released on October 11, 1948.

December 21, 1948

Capitol Records, Hollywood, California
Nick Lucas (vocal, guitar) with Ivan Ditmars, organ
Don't Gamble with Romance [3812]
10"-78 Capitol 15353
Tea Times on the Thames [3813]
10"-78 Capitol 15353
Note: Capitol 15353 was released on January 17, 1949.

February 1949

Teleways Transcriptions, Hollywood, California
Nick Lucas (vocal, guitar)
Note: In a series of radio transcriptions for Teleways Radio Productions, Lucas performed both the introductions and songs. The number of songs recorded and their titles are unknown.

April 15, 1949

Capitol Records, Hollywood, California
Nick Lucas (vocal, guitar) with Frank De Vol and His Orchestra
Bye Bye Blackbird [4201]
10"-78 Capitol 57-607
12"-LP Capitol TBO-1572
Don't Call Me Sweetheart Anymore [4202]
10"-78 Capitol 57-607
Note: Capitol 57-607 was released May 16, 1949.

November 1951

Snader Telescriptions; Hollywood, California
Nick Lucas (vocal, guitar) with orchestra and girl trio*
Bela Bimba [11601]
Mexicali Rose* [11602]
Walking My Baby Back Home [11603]
I Love the Sunshine of Your Smile* [11604]
Get Out Those Old Records* [11605]
Marie, Oh Marie [11606]

Looking at the World Thru Rose Colored Glasses [11607]

Note: The Snader Telescriptions recordings, made for television, were not intended for commercial release. One or more of the Snaders appear on the album "Diamond Jim Favorites" (Camay 3020); the titles are not known.

circa 1951

Boney Records, Kinston, North Carolina
Nick Lucas (vocal, guitar)
Tiptoe Through the Tulips
10"-78 Boney 1005
7"-45 Boney 1005
My Blue Heaven
10"-78 Boney 1005
7"-45 Boney 1005

October 20, 1952

Cavalier Records, San Francisco, California
Nick Lucas (vocal, guitar) with Jimmy Diamond and His Orchestra
Coquette [CAV-825-A]
10"-78 Cavalier CAV-825
10"-LP Cavalier LP-50033
12"-LP Cavalier CVLP-6007
Francine [CAV-824-B]
10"-78 Cavalier CAV-824
10"-LP Cavalier LP-50033
Francine [CAV-873B] [alternate take]
12"-LP Cavalier CVLP-6007
7"-45 Cavalier CAV-873
My Blue Heaven [CAV-824-A]
10"-78 Cavalier CAV-824
10"-LP Cavalier LP-50033

Label for Nick Lucas' 1951 record "My Blue Heaven" on Boney Records.

12"-LP Cavalier CVLP-6007
Teardrops [CAV-825-A]
10"-78 Cavalier CAV-825
10"-LP Cavalier LP-50033
12"-LP Cavalier CVLP-6007
Lady Be Good [CAV-826-B]
10"-78 Cavalier CAV-826
10"-LP Cavalier LP-50033
12"-LP Cavalier CVLP-6007
Painting the Clouds with Sunshine (CAV-823-B)
10"-78 Cavalier CAV-823
10"-LP Cavalier LP-50033
12"-LP Cavalier CVLP-6007
Til the End of Forever [CAV-826-A]
10"-78 Cavalier CAV-826
10"-LP Cavalier LP-50033
Tiptoe Through the Tulips [CAV-823-A]
10"-78 Cavalier CAV-823
10"-LP Cavalier LP-50033
12"-LP Cavalier CVLP-6007

Note: Cavalier CAV-825 was issued in March 1953; Cavalier CAV-826 was released in December 1953, and Cavalier CAV-873 was released in April 1957. Cavalier LP-50033 was issued in black, blue, gold, green, purple and red vinyl.

April 1953

Cavalier Records, San Francisco, California
Nick Lucas (vocal, guitar)
Title(s) Unknown

September 1953

Cavalier Records, San Francisco, California
Nick Lucas (vocal, guitar)
Title(s) Unknown

August 1954

Cavalier Records, San Francisco, California
Nick Lucas (vocal, guitar)
Sadie Thompson
10"-78 Unissued

Late 1954

Crown Records, Los Angeles, California
Nick Lucas (vocal, guitar, banjo) with orchestra directed by Maxwell Davis
Looking at the World Thru Rose Colored Glasses [JB-437]*
10"-78 Crown 141
7"-45 Crown 141
Did You Ever See a Dream Walking? [JB-438]
10"-78 Crown 141
7"-45 Crown 141
Note: Crown 141 was issued in February 1955.

January 1955

Crown Records, Los Angeles, California
Nick Lucas (vocal-guitar)
Prize of Gold
10"-78 Unissued

April 1, 1955

Accent Records, Hollywood, California
Nick Lucas (vocal, guitar) with Scott Seely Music
Bella Nonna (Little Grandmother) [1026-A]
10"-78 Accent AC-1026
7"-45 Accent AC-1026
CD Melody Man MMCD-2577
Paper Roses [1026-B]
10"-78 Accent AC-1026
7"-45 Accent AC-1026
CD Melody Man MMCD-2577
Note: Accent AC-1026 was issued in July 1955.

circa 1955

Bowery Records, Del Mar, California
Nick Lucas (vocal, guitar) with orchestra
Tiptoe Through the Tulips [303-A]
10"-78 Bowery GN-303
7"-45 Bowery 45-GN-303
Painting the Clouds with Sunshine (303-B)
10"-78 Bowery GN-303
7"-78 Bowery 45-GN-303

Note: Lucas believed that the Bowery single was a bootleg. It was released in May 1955 and some issuances of 45-GN-303 are in red vinyl.

September 3, 1955

Accent Records, Hollywood, California
Nick Lucas (vocal, guitar) with Scott Seely Music
Kind of Considerate [1030A]
10"-78 Accent AC-1030
7"-45 Accent AC-1030
CD Melody Man MMCD-2577
Kind and Considerate [1030B]
CD Melody Man MMCD-2577
Soldier's Guitar [1030A]
CD Melody Man MMCD-2577
Soldier's Guitar [1030B]
10"-78 Accent AC-1030
7"-45 Accent AC-1030
CD Melody Man MMCD-2577
Note: Accent AC-1030 was issued in November 1955.

December 15, 1955

Accent Records, Hollywood California
Nick Lucas (vocal, guitar) with Scott Seely Music
Pasta Cheech [1033]
10"-78 Accent AC-1033
7"-45 Accent AC-1033
CD Melody Man MMCD-2577
Not Guilty [1033–0]
10"-78 Accent AC-1033
7"-45 Accent AC-1033
CD Melody Man MMCD-2577
Note: Accent AC-1033 was issued in February 1956.

January 1957

Cavalier Records, San Francisco, California
Nick Lucas (guitar, vocal) with Jimmy Diamond and His Orchestra with Buddy Webster* (vocal duet)
Side by Side
12"-LP Cavalier CVLP-6007
Brown Eyes, Why Are You Blue?
12"-LP Cavalier CVLP-6007
Get Out Those Old Records* [CAV-873A]
12"-LP Cavalier CVLP-6007
7"-45 Cavalier CAV-873
Among My Souvenirs
12"-LP Cavalier CVLP-6007
I'll Get By
12"-LP Cavalier CVLP-6007
Note: Cavalier CAV-873 was issued in April 1957.

August 8, 1957

Decca Records, Los Angeles, California [Producer: Sonny Burke]
Nick Lucas (vocal, guitar) with orchestra
Painting the Clouds with Sunshine (L10, 431)
12"-LP Decca DL-8653
CD Calle Mayor VM-1273 (Spain)
CD Vintage Music VM-1273
Tiptoe Through the Tulips [L10, 432]
12"-LP Decca DL-8653
CD Calle Mayor VM-1273 (Spain)
CD Vintage Music VM-1273
Dancing with Tears in My Eyes [L10, 433]
12"-LP Decca DL-8653
CD Calle Mayor VM-1273 (Spain)
CD Vintage Music VM-1273
Just Like a Melody Out of the Sky [L10, 434]
12"-LP Decca DL-8653
CD Calle Mayor VM-1273 (Spain)
CD Vintage Music VM-1273

August 9, 1957

Decca Records, Los Angeles, California [Producer: Sonny Burke]
Nick Lucas (vocal, guitar) with orchestra
Moonbeam, Kiss Her for Me [L10, 441]
12"-LP Decca DL-8653
CD Calle Mayor VM-1273 (Spain)
CD Vintage Music VM-1273
I'll Get By [L10, 442]

12"-LP Decca DL-8653
CD Calle Mayor VM-1273 (Spain)
CD Vintage Music VM-1273
Together [L10, 443]
12"-LP Decca DL-8653
CD Calle Mayor VM-1273 (Spain)
CD Vintage Music VM-1273
Among My Souvenirs [L10, 444]
12"-LP Decca DL-8653
CD Calle Mayor VM-1273 (Spain)
CD Vintage Music VM-1273

August 12, 1957

Decca Records, Los Angeles, California [Producer: Sonny Burke]
Nick Lucas (vocal, guitar) with orchestra
Bye Bye Blackbird [L10, 449]
12"-LP Decca DL-8653
CD Calle Mayor VM-1273 (Spain)
CD Vintage Music VM-1273
Side by Side [L10, 450]
12"-LP Decca DL-8653
CD Calle Mayor VM-1273 (Spain)
CD Vintage Music VM-1273
Looking at the World Thru Rose Colored Glasses [L10, 451]
12"-LP Decca DL-8653
CD Calle Mayor VM-1273 (Spain)
CD Vintage Music VM-1273
My Best Girl [L10, 452]
12"-LP Decca DL-8653
CD Calle Mayor VM-1273 (Spain)
CD Vintage Music VM-1273
Dreamer of Dreams [L10, 453]
12"-LP Unissued

December 23, 1958

Radio Broadcast, New York City
Nick Lucas with Andy and Virginia
The Andy and Virginia Program [10393]
16"-ET Audio Disc 8092
Note: Lucas is interviewed on the syndicated radio show *The Andy and Virginia Program*.

April 1961

Decca Records, Los Angeles, California

Nick Lucas (vocal, guitar) and The Troubadours
Title(s) Unknown

January 5, 1964

Accent Records, Hollywood, California
Nick Lucas (vocal, guitar) with orchestra
Hello, Dolly [1117]
7"-45 Accent AC-1117
CD Melody Man MMCD-2577
Tiptoe Through the Tulips [1117–0]
7"-45 Accent AC-1117
CD Melody Man MMCD-2577

February 24, 1964

Accent Records, Hollywood, California
Nick Lucas (vocal, guitar)
While We Danced at the Mardi Gras
CD Melody Man MMCD-2577
Can't We Talk It Over?
CD Melody Man MMCD-2577

July 5, 1966

Accent Records, Hollywood, California
Nick Lucas (vocal, guitar, banjo*) with orchestra
Darling, I Love You [1206]
7"-45 Accent AC-1206
CD Melody Man MMCD-2577
It's Been a Good Life* [1206–0]
7"-45 Accent AC-1206
CD Melody Man MMCD-2577

December 3, 1967

Accent Records, Hollywood, California
Nick Lucas (vocal, guitar) with orchestra
Worryin' [1237]
7"-45 Accent AC-1237
CD Melody Man MMCD-2577
Brown Eyes, Why Are You Blue? [1237–0]
7"-45 Accent AC-1237
CD Melody Man MMCD-2577
I'm Blue for You [1239]
7"-45 Accent AC-1239
CD Melody Man MMCD-2577
Our San Diego [1239–0]

7"-45 Accent AC-1239
CD Melody Man MMCD-2577

October 5, 1968

Accent Records [Producers: Harry and Alice Ardern], Hollywood, California

Nick Lucas (vocal, guitar) with Scott Seely (piano) and Thurman Teague (acoustic bass)

Those Were the Days [5027–1]
12"-LP Accent ACS-5027
12"-LP Beacon SBEAB-4 (British)
12"-LP Regal SREG-30034 (New Zealand)
CD Melody Man MMCD-1493
Get Out Those Old Records [5027–1]
12"-LP Accent ACS-5027
12"-LP Beacon SBEAB-4 (British)
12"-LP Regal SREG-30034 (New Zealand)
CD Melody Man MMCD-1493
It Happened in Monterey [5027–1]
12"-LP Accent ACS-5027
12"-LP Beacon SBEAB-4 (British)
12"-LP Regal SREG-30034 (New Zealand)
CD Melody Man MMCD-1493
Somebody Stole My Gal [5027–1]
12"-LP Accent ACS-5027
12"-LP Beacon SBEAB-4 (British)
12"-LP Regal SREG-30034 (New Zealand)
CD Melody Man MMCD-1493
Darling, I Love You [5027–1]
12"-LP Accent ACS-5027
12"-LP Beacon SBEAB-4 (British)
12"-LP Regal SREG-30034 (New Zealand)
CD Melody Man MMCD-1493
My Blue Heaven [5027–1]
12"-LP Accent ACS-5027
12"-LP Beacon SBEAB-4 (British)
12"-LP Regal SREG-30034 (New Zealand)
CD Melody Man MMCD-1493
Tiptoe Through the Tulips [5027–2]
12"-LP Accent ACS-5027
12"-LP Beacon SBEAB-4 (British)
12"-LP Regal SREG-30034 (New Zealand)
CD Melody Man MMCD-1493
Baby Face [5027–2]
12"-LP Accent ACS-5027
12"-LP Beacon SBEAB-4 (British)
12"-LP Regal SREG-30034 (New Zealand)
CD Melody Man MMCD-1493
South of the Border [5027–2]
12"-LP Accent ACS-5027
12"-LP Beacon SBEAB-4 (British)
12"-LP Regal SREG-30034 (New Zealand)
CD Melody Man MMCD-1493
While We Danced at the Mardi Gras [5027–2]
12"-LP Accent ACS-5027
12"-LP Beacon SBEAB-4 (British)
12"-LP Regal SREG-30034 (New Zealand)
CD Melody Man MMCD-1493
Sleepy Time Gal [5027–2]
12"-LP Accent ACS-5027
12"-LP Beacon SBEAB-4 (British)
12"-LP Regal SREG-30034 (New Zealand)
CD Melody Man MMCD-1493
Zei Gezunt [5027–2]
12"-LP Accent ACS-5027
12"-LP Beacon SBEAB-4 (British)
12"-LP Regal SREG-30034 (New Zealand)
CD Melody Man MMCD-1493

April 16, 1969

Accent Records, Hollywood, California

Nick Lucas (vocal, guitar) with Robert E. Armstrong (piano), Vincent Terri (bass) and Clifford Eils (clarinet)

Painting the Clouds with Sunshine (5043-A)
12"-LP Accent ACS-5043
Dancing with Tears in My Eyes [5043-A]
12"-LP Accent ACS-5043
I'm Sitting on Top of the World [5043-A]

12"-LP Accent ACS-5043
In a Little Spanish Town [5043-A]
12"-LP Accent ACS-5043
I Want to Hold You in My Arms [5043-A]
12"-LP Accent ACS-5043
A Cup of Coffee, a Sandwich and You [5043-A]
12"-LP Accent ACS-5043
I'm Looking at the World Thru Rose Colored Glasses [5043-B]
12"-LP Accent ACS-5043
Lady Play Your Mandolin [5043-B]
12"-LP Accent ACS-5043
At Sundown [5043-B]
12"-LP Accent ACS-5043
Margie [5043-B]
12"-LP Accent ACS-5043
Lady Be Good [5043-B]
12"-LP Accent ACS-5043
It's Been a Good Life [5043-B]
12"-LP Accent ACS-5043
May I Have the Next Dream? [5043]
12"-LP Unissued

Spring 1969

Radio Broadcast, New York City
Nick Lucas interviewed Richard Lamparski
Whatever Became of...?
12"-LP Unknown label and number
Note: Lucas was interviewed on this syndicated radio program and selections from his Accent Records albums were played.

February 4, 1972

Private Recording, Hollywood, California
Lucas interviewed by Gary Williams
Tiptoe Through the Tulips
REEL-TO-REEL Old Time Record Collectors Club (no number)
Note: Lucas was interviewed by Gary Williams on this tape for members of the Old Time Record Collectors Club. An excerpt from the 1922 record "Pickin' the Guitar" was played along with the complete 1934 record "Goin' Home." Lucas closed the tape performing "Tiptoe Through the Tulips."

February 1974

Paramount Records, Los Angeles, California
Nick Lucas (vocal) with Nelson Riddle and His Orchestra
When You and I Were Seventeen
12"-LP Paramount PAS-3001
CASSETTE Paramount 8091–3001N
8-TRACK Paramount 8091–3001N
Five Foot Two, Eyes of Blue
12"-LP Paramount PAS-3001
CASSETTE Paramount 8091–3001N
8-TRACK Paramount 8–91–3001N
I'm Gonna Charleston Back to Charleston
12"-LP Paramount PAS-3001
CASSETTE Paramount 8091–3001N
8-TRACK Paramount 8–91–3001N

September 6, 1974

Accent Records, Hollywood, California
Nick Lucas (vocal, guitar) with orchestra
Tiptoe Through the Tulips [1322]
7"-45 Accent ACS-1322
CD Melody Man MMCD-2577
Silver Sails [1322–0]
7"-45 Accent ACS-1322
CD Melody Man MMCD-2577

September 29, 1974

Paramount Records, Hollywood, California
Nick Lucas (vocal) with studio orchestra
I Wished on the Moon
12"-LP London PS-912

March 21, 1975

Private Performance; Los Angeles, California
Nick Lucas (vocal, guitar) with Lee Donn (piano) and Gary Williams (guitar)
Anytime [S-1088]

Label for Nick Lucas' last recording of "Tiptoe Through the Tulips" on Accent Records in 1974.

12"-LP "Take Two" TT-1001-S
My Melancholy Baby [S-1088]
12"-LP "Take Two" TT-1001-S
Say It Isn't So [S-1088]
12"-LP "Take Two" TT-1001-S
What'll I Do? [S-1088]
12"-LP "Take Two" TT-1001-S
Pastime Number One [S-1088]
12"-LP "Take Two" TT-1001-S
Tie a Yellow Ribbon 'Round the Old Oak Tree [S-1088]
12"-LP "Take Two" TT-1001-S
Granada [S-1088]
12"-LP "Take Two" TT-1001-S
You're a Real Sweetheart
12"-LP "Take Two" TT-1001-S
I'll Get By [S-1089]
12"-LP "Take Two" TT-1001-S
I'm Looking at the World Thru Rose Colored Glasses [S-1089]
12"-LP "Take Two" TT-1001-S
Lady Play Your Mandolin [S-1089]
12"-LP "Take Two" TT-1001-S
In a Shanty in Old Shanty Town [S-1089]
12"-LP "Take Two" TT-1001-S
That Old Gang of Mine [S-1089]
12"-LP "Take Two" TT-1001-S
Femmena [S-1089]
12"-LP "Take Two" TT-1001-S
It's Been a Good Life [S-1089]
12"-LP "Take Two" TT-1001-S
Tiptoe Through the Tulips
12"-LP Unissued

July 23, 1975

Metro-Goldwyn-Mayer Studios [MGM Records]; Los Angeles, California
Nick Lucas (vocal) with studio orchestra
I'll See You in My Dreams [1926-2564-1]
We'll Make Hay While the Sun Shines [1926-2564-2]
My Blue Heaven [1926-2566-3]
Happy Days Are Here Again [1926-2566-4]
Ja Da [1926-2566-3]
Wang Wang Blues [1926-2569]
Note: The MGM recordings were included on the soundtrack of the motion picture *Hearts of the West* (MGM, 1975).

circa 1975

Radio Program; Anaheim, California
Lucas interviewed by Lynn Fairhurst.
Star Sound
12"-LP BBC Radio (no number)
CASSETTE BBC Radio (no number)
Note: Lucas was interviewed by Lynn Fairhurst, host of the British radio program *Sound Stage,* in Anaheim, California. In addition to the interview, the program included the 1929 Brunswick recording of "Tiptoe Through the Tulips" along with the songs ("When You and I Were Seventeen," "Five Foot Two, Eyes of Blue," "I'm Gonna Charleston Back to Charleston") from the soundtrack of *The Great Gatsby* (Paramount, 1974) and "I Wished on the Moon" from the soundtrack of *The Day of the Locust* (Paramount, 1974).

April 1976

Paramount Records, Los Angeles, California
Nick Lucas (vocal) with studio orchestra
To Be Loved by You
They're Playing Our Song (Won Ton Rag)
Note: These songs were recorded for the soundtrack of *Won Ton Ton, the Dog Who Saved Hollywood* (Paramount, 1976) but were not included on its soundtrack.

circa mid– to late 1970s

Accent Records, Hollywood, California
Nick Lucas (vocal, guitar)
Forever Yours
Do You Love Me?
They're Playing Our Song
The Astronaut Song
Never Lose Your Twinkle
Note: The above songs were recorded but never issued.

September 15, 1980

Private Recording, Los Angeles, California
Nick Lucas (vocal, guitar)
Angela
Note: The above recording was not intended for commercial release.

November 26, 1980

Accent Records, Rancho Mirage, California
Nick Lucas (vocal, guitar) with Scott Seely (piano)
Are You Lonesome Tonight?
CD Melody Man MCCD-2577
How Did You Have the Heart to Break My Heart?
CD Melody Man MCCD-2577

circa mid– to late 1981

Accent Records, Rancho Mirage, California
Nick Lucas (vocal, guitar) with Scott Seely (piano)
The Magic Waltz
CD Melody Man MMCD-2577

Single Records by Company

Accent

1026 Bella Nonna (Little Grandmother)/ Paper Roses
1030 Soldier's Guitar/Kind and Considerate
1033 Pasta Cheech/Not Guilty
1117 Hello, Dolly/Tiptoe Through the Tulips
1206 It's Been a Good Life/Darling, I Love You
1237 Brown Eyes, Why Are You Blue?/Worryin'
1239 Our San Diego/I'm Blue for You
1273 Looking at the World Thru Rose Colored Glasses/I'm Sitting on Top of the World
1274 A Cup of Coffee, a Sandwich and You/I Want to Hold You in My Arms
1322 Silver Sails/Tiptoe Through the Tulips

Banner

33061 Love Thy Neighbor/A Thousand Good Nights
33124 For All We Know/Moon Glow

Boney

105 Tiptoe Through the Tulips/My Blue Heaven

Bowery

GN-303 Tiptoe Through the Tulips/Painting the Clouds with Sunshine

Brunswick [United States and Canada]

2536 Pickin' the Guitar/Teasin' the Frets
2768 My Best Girl/Dreamer of Dreams
2769 Oh! Mabel
2803 Because They All Love You/Somebody Like You
2827 I've Named My Pillow After You/If I Can't Have You
2846 The Only Only One/When I Think of You
2906 Isn't She the Sweetest Thing?/By the Light of the Stars
2940 I Might Have Known/I'm Tired of Everything but You
2961 Brown Eyes, Why Are You Blue?/If You Hadn't Gone Away
2990 Sleepy Time Gal/I Found Someone to Love
3021 Forever and Ever with You/Smile a Little Bit
3052 A Cup of Coffee, a Sandwich and You/Whose Who Are You?
3088 Always/I Don't Believe It but Say It Again
3141 No Foolin'/My Bundle of Love
3184 Bye Bye Blackbird/Adorable
3185 I'm Glad I Found a Girl Like You [single sided record]
3229 Sleepy Head/How Many Times?
3283 Looking at the World Thru Rose Colored Glasses/Let Me Live and Love You Just For Tonight
3367 Because I Love You/When You're Lonely
3369 Previous/I'd Love to Call You Sweetheart
3370 I've Got the Girl/Hello, Bluebird
3433 In a Little Spanish Town/Put Your Arms Where They Belong
3439 I'm Looking Over a Four Leaf Clover/High, High, High Up in the Hills
3466 I'm Lonesome for a Girl Named Mary/Underneath the Weeping Willow
3492 Moonbeam! Kiss Her for Me/So Blue
3512 Side by Side/Why Should I Say I'm Sorry?
3518 Rosy Cheeks/Underneath the Stars with You
3602 Sing Me a Baby Song/(Here Am I) Brokenhearted
3614 I Can't Believe That You're in Love with Me/Sweet Someone
3684 Among My Souvenirs/(My) Blue Heaven
3736 The Song Is Ended/Kiss and Make Up
3749 Together/Keep Sweeping the Cobwebs Off the Moon
3773 My Ohio Home/Without You, Sweetheart
3850 Sunshine/I Still Love You
3853 Marcheta/I'm Waiting for Ships That Never Come In [release cancelled]
3925 It Must Be Love/I Can't Do Without You
3965 Just Like a Melody Out of the Sky/For Old Times' Sake
3966 When You Said Goodnight/You're a Real Sweetheart
3968 Marcheta/I'm Waiting for Ships That Never Come In
4016 Chiquita/Someday, Somewhere
4141 My Tonia/The Song I Love
4156 I'll Get By/How About Me?
4171 When the World Is at Rest/I'll Never Ask for More
4214 I'm Telling You/Some Rainy Day
4215 Old Timer/Heart O' Mine

4302 Coquette/I've Got a Feeling I'm Falling
4378 Singin' in the Rain/Your Mother and Mine
4390 When My Dreams Come True/Just Another Kiss
4418 Tiptoe Through the Tulips/Painting the Clouds with Sunshine
4464 My Song of the Nile/Ich Liebe Dich (I Love You)
4468 Where Are You Dream Girl?/Sweethearts' Holiday
4547 I Don't Want Your Kisses/Until the End
4834 Dancing with Tears in My Eyes/Telling It to the Daisies
4847 Singing a Song to the Stars/My Heart Belongs to the Girl Who Belongs to Somebody Else [release cancelled]
4860 Singing a Song to the Stars/My Heart Belongs to the Girl Who Belongs to Somebody Else
4896 Just a Little Closer/Don't Tell Her What's Happened to Me
4900 The Kiss Waltz/Go Home and Tell Your Mother
4954 Siboney
4959 Three Little Words/Wasting My Love on You
4960 Maybe It's Love/I'm Yours
4987 You're Driving Me Crazy/I Miss a Little Miss
6013 Lady Play Your Mandolin/Say "Hello" to the Folks Back Home
6045 You Didn't Have to Tell Me/When You Were the Blossom of Buttercup Lane and I Was Your Little Boy Blue
6048 Walkin' My Baby Back Home/Falling in Love Again
6049 Hello! Beautiful/Running Between the Raindrops
6089 Wabash Moon/I Surrender Dear
6098 Boy! Oh! Boy! Oh! Boy I've Got It Bad/Let's Get Friendly
6104 Can't You Read Between the Lines?/Now You're in My Arms
6147 That's My Desire/When the Moon Comes Over the Mountain
6195 Goodnight, Sweetheart
6459 I'm Sure Everything but You/More Beautiful Than Ever
6462 Til Tomorrow/I Called to Say Goodbye
6508 Pickin' the Guitar/Teasin' the Frets

Brunswick [Australia]

2768 My Best Girl/Dreamer of Dreams
2803 Because They All Love You/Somebody Like You
2827 I've Named My Pillow After You/If I Can't Have You
2846 When I Think of You/The Only, Only One
2906 Isn't She the Sweetest Thing?/By the Light of the Stars
2940 I Might Have Known/I'm Tired of Everything but You
2961 Brown Eyes, Why Are You Blue?/If You Hadn't Gone Away
2990 Sleepy Time Gal/I Found Somebody to Love
3021 Smile a Little Bit/Forever and Ever with You
3052 A Cup of Coffee, a Sandwich and You/Whose Who Are You?
3088 Always/I Don't Believe It—But Say It Again
3141 My Bundle of Love/No Foolin'
3184 Bye Bye Blackbird/Adorable
3229 Sleepy Head/How Many Times?
3283 I'm Looking at the World Thru Rose Colored Glasses/Let Me Live and Love You Just for Tonight
3367 Because I Love You/When You're Lonely
3369 I'd Love to Call You My Sweetheart/Precious
3370 Hello, Bluebird/I've Got the Girl
3433 In a Little Spanish Town/Put Your Arms Where They Belong
3439 I'm Looking Over a Four Leaf Clover/High, High, High Up in the Hills

3466 I'm Looking for a Girl Named Mary/ Underneath the Weeping Willow
3492 Moonbeam! Kiss Her for Me/So Blue
3512 Side by Side/Why Should I Say That I'm Sorry (When Nobody's Sorry for Me)?
3518 Rosy Cheeks/Underneath the Stars with You
3602 (Here Am I) Brokenhearted/Sing Me a Baby Song
3614 Sweet Someone/I Can't Believe That You're in Love with Me
3684 Among My Souvenirs/(My) Blue Heaven
2736 The Song Is Ended/Kiss and Make Up
3749 Together/Keep Sweeping the Cobwebs Off the Moon
3773 My Ohio Home/Without You Sweetheart
3850 Sunshine/I Still Love You
3925 It Must Be Love/I Can't Do Without You
3965 Just Like a Melody Out of the Sky/ For Old Times' Sake
3966 You're a Real Sweetheart/When You Said Goodnight (Did You Really Mean Goodbye)?
3968 Marcheta/I'm Waiting for Ships That Never Come In
4016 Chiquita/Someday, Somewhere
4141 My Tonia/The Song I Love
4156 I'll Get By/How About Me?
4171 When the World Is at Rest/I'll Never Ask for More
4214 Some Rainy Day/(You're Not Asking Me) I'm Telling You
4215 Old Timer/Heart O' Mine
4302 Coquette/I've Got a Feeling I'm Falling
4378 Singin' in the Rain/Your Mother and Mine
4390 When My Dreams Come True/Just Another Kiss
4418 Tiptoe Through the Tulips/Painting the Clouds with Sunshine
4464 My Song of the Nile/Ich Liebe Dich (I Love You)
4468 Where Are You Dream Girl?/ Sweetheart's Holiday
4547 Until the End/I Don't Want Your Kisses (If I Can't Have Your Love)
4834 Dancing with Tears in My Eyes/ Telling It to the Daisies
4860 Singing a Song to the Stars/My Heart Belongs to the Girl Who Belongs To Somebody Else
4896X Just a Little Closer/Don't Tell Her What Happened to Me
4900X Go Home and Tell Your Mother
4959 Three Little Words/Wasting My Love on You
4960X The Kiss Waltz/Maybe It's Love
4987 You're Driving Me Crazy/I Miss a Little Miss
6013 Lady, Play Your Mandolin/Say "Hello" To the Folks Back Home
6032X Hello, Beautiful
6045 You Didn't Have to Tell Me/When You Were the Blossom of Buttercup Lane and I Was Your Little Boy Blue
6048X Falling in Love Again
6049X Running Between the Raindrops
6059X Walking My Baby Back Home
6089 I Surrender Dear
6090 Wabash Moon
6096 Boy! Oh Boy! Oh Boy! I've Got It Bad
6098 Let's Get Friendly
6104 Now You're In My Arms/Can't You Read Between the Lines?

Brunswick [British]

2827 I've Named My Pillow After You/If I Can't Have You
2846 When I Think of You/The Only, Only One
2906 Isn't She the Sweetest Thing?/By the Light of the Stars
2940 I Might Have Known/I'm Tired of Everything but You
2961 Brown Eyes, Why Are You Blue?/If You Hadn't Gone Away
2990 Sleepy Time Gal/I Found Somebody to Love

3021 Smile a Little Bit/Forever and Ever with You
3052 A Cup of Coffee, a Sandwich and You/Whose Who Are You?
3088 Always/I Don't Believe It—But Say It Again
3141 My Bundle of Love/No Foolin'
3184 Bye Bye Blackbird/Adorable
3229 Sleepy Head/How Many Times?
3283 I'm Looking at the World Thru Rose Colored Glasses/Let Me Live and Love You Just for Tonight
3367 Because I Love You/When You're Lonely
3369 I'd Love to Call You My Sweetheart/Precious
3370 Hello, Bluebird/I've Got the Girl
3423 In a Little Spanish Town/Put Your Arms Where They Belong
3439 I'm Looking Over a Four Leaf Clover/High, High, High Up in the Hills
3466 I'm Looking for a Girl Named Mary/Underneath the Weeping Willow
3492 Moonbeam! Kiss Her for Me/So Blue
3512 Side by Side/Why Should I Say That's I'm Sorry (When Nobody's Sorry for Me)?
3518 Rosy Cheeks/Underneath the Stars with You
3602 (Here Am I) Brokenhearted/Sing Me a Baby Song
3614 Sweet Someone/I Can't Believe That You're in Love with Me
3684 Among My Souvenirs/(My) Blue Heaven
3736 The Song Is Ended/Kiss and Make Up
3773 My Ohio Home/Without You, Sweetheart
3850 Sunshine/I Still Love You
3914 I'll Get By/How About Me?
3925 It Must Be Love/I Can't Do Without You
3949 Some Rainy Day/Old Timer
3965 Just Like a Melody Out of the Sky/For Old Times' Sake
3966 You're a Real Sweetheart/When You Said Goodnight (Did You Really Mean Goodbye)?
3968 Marcheta/I'm Waiting for Ships That Never Come In
3998 Coquette/I've Got a Feeling I'm Falling
4016 Chiquita/Someday, Somewhere
4141 My Tonia/The Song I Love
4171 When the World Is at Rest/I'll Never Ask for More
5007 (You're Not Asking Me) I'm Telling You/Heart O'Mine
5048 Tiptoe Through the Tulips/Painting the Clouds with Sunshine
01012 Dancing with Tears in My Eyes/Telling It to the Daisies
01026 The Kiss Waltz/Go Home and Tell Your Mother
01030 Don't Tell Her What Happened to Me
01047 Siboney
01055 You're Driving Me Crazy/I Miss a Little Miss
01057 Maybe It's Love/Just a Little Closer
01081 Lady Play Your Mandolin/Say 'Hello' To the Folks Back Home
01100 You Didn't Have to Tell Me/When You Were the Blossom of Buttercup Lane and I Was Your Little Boy Blue
01102 Hello! Beautiful/Running Between the Raindrops
01119 Walkin' My Baby Back Home/Falling in Love Again
01138 Wabash Moon/I Surrender Dear
01141 Let's Get Friendly/Boy! Oh! Boy! Oh! Boy! I've Got It Bad
01190 That's My Desire
01214 When the Moon Comes Over the Mountain
01433 Pickin' the Guitar/Teasin' the Frets
01437 I'm Sure of Everything but You/Til Tomorrow
01465 I Called to Say Goodnight

Brunswick [Germany]

A432 In a Little Spanish Town/Put Your Arms Where They Belong

A446 Rosy Cheeks/Underneath the Stars with You
A473 (Here Am I) Brokenhearted/Sing Me a Baby Song
A492 Sweet Someone/I Can't Believe That You're In Love with Me
A7505 Side by Side/Why Should I Say That I'm Sorry (When Nobody's Sorry for Me)?
A7558 The Song Is Ended/Kiss and Make Up
A7572 Among My Souvenirs/(My) Blue Heaven
A8067 My Tonia/The Song I Love
A8130 Chiquita/Someday, Somewhere
A8289 Singin' in the Rain/Your Mother and Mine
A8300 Coquette/I've Got a Feeling I'm Falling
A8319 When My Dreams Come True/Just Another Kiss
A8322 Tiptoe Through the Tulips/Painting the Clouds with Sunshine
A8799 Dancing with Tears in My Eyes/Telling It to the Daisies
A8818 Singing a Song to the Stars/My Heart Belongs to the Girl Who Belongs to Somebody Else
A8902 Siboney
A8982 You're Driving Me Crazy/Lady, Play Your Mandolin
A8986 You're Driving Me Crazy/I Miss a Little Miss
A9028 Hello, Bluebird/Running Between the Raindrops
A9078 Wabash Moon/I Surrender, Dear
A9111 That's My Desire/When the Moon Comes Over the Mountain
A9165 Goodnight, Sweetheart

Capitol

15242 Tiptoe Through the Tulips/Side by Side
15353 Don't Gamble with Romance/Tea Time on the Thames
57–607 Bye Bye Blackbird/Don't Call Me Sweetheart Anymore

Cavalier

823 Tiptoe Through the Tulips/Painting the Clouds with Sunshine
824 My Blue Heaven/Francine
825 Teardrops/Coquette
826 Til the End of Forever/Lady Be Good
873 Francine/Get Out Those Old Records

Crown

141 Looking at the World Thru Rose Colored Glasses/Did You Ever See a Dream Walking?

Diamond

2018 If I Had My Way/Coax Me a Little Bit
2019 What Ya Gonna Do?/Painting the Clouds with Sunshine
2021 Seems Like Old Times/Give My Heart a Break
2022 My Blue Heaven/Everyone Is Looking for the Rainbow

Embassy

E-145 That's My Desire/When the Moon Comes Over the Mountain

Hit of the Week

A-4-B-1 All of Me/Goodnight Ladies
B-3–4 An Evening in Caroline

Huckster

1006 Tiptoe Through the Tulips/Side by Side

Melotone

MT-13026 Love Thy Neighbor/A Thousand Good Nights
MT-13027 Goin' Home/Carry Me Back to the Lone Prairie
MT-13091 For All We Know/Moon Glow

Oriole

2937 For All We Know/Moon Glow

Panachord

P12235 That's My Desire/When the Moon Comes Over the Mountain [as The Desmond Duo]

Pathe Actuelle

020794 Pickin' the Guitar/Teasin' the Frets
10392 Pickin' the Guitar/Teasin' the Frets

Perfect

11041 Picking the Guitar/Teasin' the Frets
13025 For All We Know/Moon Glow

Premier

28992 Tiptoe Through the Tulips/Always

Regal Zonophone (Australia)

G22191 Pickin' the Guitar/Teasin' the Frets
G23898 A Man and His Dream/An Apple for the Teacher
G23899 Over the Rainbow/The Man with the Mandolin
G23900 Good Morning/Go Fly a Kite

Rex

8219 Love Thy Neighbor/A Thousand Good Nights
8306 Moon Glow/Carry Me Back to the Lone Prairie

Silvertone

1207 Pickin' the Guitar/Teasin' the Frets

Record Albums and Tapes

"An Evening with Nick Lucas"

(Take Two TT-1001-S) 12"-LP [1982]

Anytime/My Melancholy Baby/Say It Isn't So/What'll I Do?/Pastime Number One/Tie a Yellow Ribbon 'Round the Old Oak Tree/Granada/You're a Real Sweetheart/I'll Get By/You're Driving Me Crazy/Looking at the World Thru Rose Colored Glasses/Lady Play Your Mandolin/In a Shanty in Old Shanty Town/That Old Gang of Mine/Femmena/It's Been a Good Life

"The Nick Lucas" Souvenir Album

(Accent ACS-5027) 12"-LP [1968]

Those Were the Days/Get Out Those Old Records/It Happened in Monterey/Somebody Stole My Gal/Darling, I Love You/My Blue Heaven/Tiptoe Through the Tulips/Baby Face/South of the Border/While We Danced at the Mardi Gras/Sleepy Time Gal/Zei Gezunt

Released in Great Britain as "Those Were the Days" (Beacon SBEAB-4) in 1969; released in New Zealand as "Those Were the Days" (Regal SREG-30034) in 1969.

"Painting the Clouds with Sunshine"

(Decca DL-8652) 12"-LP [1957]

Painting the Clouds with Sunshine/I'll Get By/Just Like a Melody Out of the Sky/Side by Side/Dancing with Tears in My Eyes/Tiptoe Through the Tulips/Looking at the World Thru Rose Colored Glasses/Together/Moonbeam, Kiss Her for Me/My Best Girl/Among My Souvenirs/Bye Bye Blackbird

"Rose Colored Glasses"

(Accent ACS-5043) 12"-LP [1969]

Painting the Clouds with Sunshine/Dancing with Tears in My Eyes/I'm Sitting on Top of the World/In a Little Spanish Town/I Want to Hold You in My Arms/A Cup of Coffee, a Sandwich and You/Looking at the World Thru Rose Colored Glasses/Lady Play Your Mandolin/At Sundown/Margie/Lady Be Good/It's Been a Good Life

"The Singing Troubadour"

(ASV Living Era AJA-5022) 12"-LP [1983; British]

You're Driving Me Crazy/Go Fly a

Kite/A Cup of Coffee, a Sandwich and You/ An Evening in Caroline/The Man with the Mandolin/Singin' in the Rain/Oh! Mabel!/I Might Have Known/Looking at the World Thru Rose Colored Glasses/Over the Rainbow/Good Morning!/Painting the Clouds with Sunshine/You Mother and Mine/A Man and His Dream/Siboney/An Apple for the Teacher/Bye Bye Blackbird/Oh! My Bundle of Love/I've Got the Girl/Goodnight, Sweetheart

[1924–31 Brunswick recordings, 1932 Hit of the Week recording and 1939 Regal Zonophone recordings; also on cassette (ZC-AJA-5022). Released on MP3 by Hallmark in 2010.

"Tiptoe Through the Tulips with Nick Lucas"

(Cavalier LP-50033) 10"-LP [1953]

Coquette/Francine/My Blue Heaven/Teardrops/Lady Be Good/Painting the Clouds with Sunshine/Til the End of Forever/Tiptoe Through the Tulips

"Tiptoe Through the Tulips with Nick Lucas"

(Cavalier CVLP-6007) 12"-LP [1957]

Tiptoe Through the Tulips/Side by Side/Brown Eyes, Why Are You Blue?/Coquette/Francine/Painting the Clouds with Sunshine/Get Out Those Old Records/Among My Souvenirs/My Blue Heaven/Teardrops/I'll Get By/Lady Be Good

Compact Discs [CDs]

"The Crooning Troubadour"

(Crystal Stream Audio IDCD81) [2002; Australia]

You're Driving Me Crazy/I Miss a Little Miss/You Didn't Have to Tell Me (I Knew It All the Time)/When You Were the Blossom of Buttercup Lane (And I Was Your Little Boy Blue)/Walkin' My Baby Back Home/Running Between the Raindrops/When the Moon Comes Over the Mountain/An Evening in Caroline/All of Me and Goodnight Ladies/Picking the Guitar/Teasing the Frets/I'm Sure of Everything but You/More Beautiful Than Ever/Love Thy Neighbor/A Thousand Good Nights/Moon Glow/For All We Know/An Apple for the Teacher/A Man and His Dream/Go Fly a Kite/Good Morning/Over the Rainbow/The Man with the Mandolin

(1930–1934 Brunswick Recordings; 1932 Hit of the Week Recordings; 1934 American Record Company [ARC] Recordings; 1939 Regal Zonophone Recordings)

"First and Last Accents"

(Melody Man MMCD-2577) [2007]

Paper Roses/Bella Nonna (Little Grandmother)/Kind and Considerate (Take One)/Kind and Considerate (False Start)/Kind and Considerate/Soldier's Guitar (Take One)/Soldier's Guitar/Not Guilty/Pasta Cheech/Can't We Talk It Over?/While We Danced at the Mardi Gras/Hello Dolly/Tiptoe Through the Tulips/It's Been a Good Life/Darling, I Love You/Worryin'/Brown Eyes, Why Are You Blue?/I'm Blue for You/Our San Diego/Silver Sails/Tiptoe Through the Tulips/How Could You Have the Heart to Break My Heart/Are You Lonesome Tonight?/The Magic Waltz

[1955–1981 Accent recordings]

"Golden Song Spotlight"

(Melody Man MMCD-2606) [2018]

Strangers in the Dark/A Sailboat in the Moonlight/The Dream of My Heart/Little Old Fashioned Music Box/The Miller's Daughter Marianne/Tomorrow Is Another Day/Gone with the Wind/When I Look at You/Vieni, Vieni/You Can't Stop Me From Dreaming/In a Little Carolina Town/Please Pardon Us We're In Love/It Looks Like Rain in Cherry Blossom Lane/Picking the Guitar/Wasting My Love on

You/You'll Never Get to Heaven/Till the Clock Strikes Three/The Moon Got in My Eyes/My Cabin of Dreams/You Are Everything I Love/Charley My Boy/Teasing the Frets

[1936 and 1945–1946 C.P. MacGregor Transcriptions]

"Looking Over a Four-Leaf Clover"

(Emerald Echoes [MP3]) [2016]

I'm Looking Over a Four-Leaf Clover/Painting the Clouds with Sunshine/A Cup of Coffee, a Sandwich and You/Always/Brown Eyes, Why Are You Blue?/My Best Girl/Pickin' the Guitar/Sleepy Time Gal/My Bundle of Love/Bye Bye Blackbird/Looking at the World Thru Rose Colored Glasses/Tiptoe Through the Tulips/So Blue/Side by Side/An Evening in Caroline/I'll Get By/Lady, Play Your Mandolin/My Blue Heaven/Singin' in the Rain/Without You Sweetheart/You're Driving Me Crazy/Over the Rainbow/Go Fly a Kite/An Apple for the Teacher/All of Me

[1924–1929 Brunswick, 1932 Hit of the Week and 1939 Regal Zonophone recordings]

"Nick Lucas #1"

("M.C. Productions Vintage Recording") [2011; CD-ROM]

I'm Tired of Everything But You/I Might Have Known/Brown Eyes, Why Are You Blue?/I You Hadn't Gone Away/Whose Who Are You?/A Cup of Coffee, a Sandwich and You/Always/I Don't Believe It But Say It Again/Looking at the World Thru Rose Colored Glasses/Let Me Live and Love You Just for Tonight/I'm Looking Over a Four Leaf Clover/High, High, High Up in the Hills/So Blue/Moonbeam Kiss Her for Me/Why Should I Say That I'm Sorry?/Side by Side/Here Am I Brokenhearted/Sing Me a Baby Song/I Can't Believe That You're in Love with Me/Sweet Someone/My Blue Heaven/Among My Souvenirs/The Song Is Ended/Kiss and Make Up

[1925–1927 Brunswick Recordings]

"Nick Lucas #2"

("M.C. Productions Vintage Recording") [2011; CD-ROM]

Sleepy Head/How Many Times?/Because I Love You/When You're Lonely/Put Your Arms Where They Belong/In a Little Spanish Town/Keep Sweeping Cobwebs Off the Moon/Together/Sunshine/I Still Love You/You're a Real Sweetheart/When You Said Good Night/Marcheta/I'm Waiting for Ships That Never Come In/How About Me?/I'll Get By/Some Rainy Day/I'm Telling You/Singin' in the Rain/Your Mother and Mine/Tiptoe Through the Tulips/Painting the Clouds with Sunshine/Somebody Like You/Because They All Love You

[1925–1929 Brunswick Recordings]

"Nick Lucas—1920's Jazz Vocals and Guitar, Encore 1; 1925–1926"

("Vocalist's Showcase")

Somebody Like You/Because They All Love You/Isn't She the Sweetest Thing/By the Light of the Stars/I'm Tired of Everything but You/By the Light of the Stars/If You Hadn't Gone Away/Brown Eyes, Why Are You Blue?/Smile a Little Bit, Smile/Forever and Ever with You/Always/I Don't Believe It but Say It Again/My Bundle of Love/No Foolin'/Sleepy Head/Looking at the World Thru Rose Colored Glasses/Let Me Live and Love You Just for Tonight/Precious/I'd Love to Call You Sweetheart

[1925–1926 Brunswick Recordings]

"Nick Lucas—1920's Jazz Vocals and Guitar, Encore 2; 1926–1927"

("Vocalist's Showcase")

I Got the Girl/Hello Bluebird/In a Little Spanish Town/Put Your Arms Where

They Belong/I'm Looking Over a Four Leaf Clover/High, High, High Up in the Hills/So Blue/Moonbeam Kiss Her for Me/Why Should I Say I'm Sorry?/Side by Side/Rosy Cheeks/Underneath the Stars/I Can't Believe That You're in Love with Me/Sweet Someone/My Blue Heaven/Among My Souvenirs/The Song Is Ended/Kiss and Make Up/Keep Sweeping the Cobwebs Off the Moon/Together

[1926–1927 Brunswick Recordings]

"Nick Lucas—1920's Jazz Vocals and Guitar, Encore 3; 1928–1932"

("Vocalist's Showcase")

It Must Be Love/I Can't Do Without You/You're a Real Sweetheart/When You Said Goodnight/My Song of the Nile/Ich Liebe Dich [I Love You]/Telling It to the Daisies/Dancing with Tears in My Eyes/Sing a Song to the Stars/The Kiss Waltz/Go Home and Tell Your Mother/Boy! Oh Boy! I've Got It Bad/Let's Get Friendly/All of Me/An Evening in Caroline/I'm Sure of Everything but You/More Beautiful Than Ever/I Called to Say Goodnight/Till Tomorrow

[1928–1932 Brunswick Recordings]

"Nick Lucas, Volume One"

("Sounds of a Century" 1875-A)

Always/Bye Bye Blackbird/Looking at the World Thru Rose Colored Glasses/Side by Side/Among My Souvenirs/The Song I Love/Painting the Clouds with Sunshine/All of Me/It Looks Like Rain in Orange Blossom Lane/Carry Me Back to the Lone Prairie/Hello Bluebird/I'm Looking Over a Four Leaf Clover/Just Like a Melody Out of the Sky/Singin' in the Rain/Tiptoe Through the Tulips/An Evening in Caroline/ You'll Never Get to Heaven/For All We Know/Moonglow/Goin' Home

[1926–1934 Brunswick, Hit of the Week and C.P. MacGregor recordings; also released on cassette]

"Nick Lucas, Volume Two"

("Sounds of a Century" 1875-B)

Pickin' the Guitar/My Best Girl/Isn't She the Sweetest Thing?/I'm Tired of Everything but You/Smile a Little Bit/Let Me Sing of Love/When You're Lonely/I'd Love to Call You Sweetheart/I Can't Believe That You're in Love with Me/You're a Real Sweetheart/I'm Looking for a Girl Named Mary/Moonbeam! Kiss Her for Me/Why Should I Say I'm Sorry/For Old Times Sake/Marcheta/Someday Somewhere/My Tonia/When the World Is at Rest/(You're Not Asking Me) I'm Telling You/When the Moon Comes Over the Mountain

[1922–1931 Brunswick recordings; also released on cassette]

"Nick Lucas, Volume Three"

("Sounds of a Century" 1875-C)

Teasin' the Frets/Dreamer of Dreams/I Might Have Known/Adorable/Because I Love You/Precious/I've Got the Girl/So Blue/Rosy Cheeks/(Here Am I) Brokenhearted/By the Light of the Stars/Forever and Ever with You/I Don't Believe It—But Say It Again/Sleepy Head/High, High, High Up in the Hills/Underneath the Weeping Willow/Underneath the Stars with You/Sing Me a Baby Song/Sweet Someone/When You Said Goodnight—Did You Really Mean Goodbye?

[1923–1928 Brunswick recordings; also released on cassette]

"Nick Lucas, Volume Four"

("Sounds of a Century" 1875-D)

Some Rainy Day/I'm Waiting for Ships That Never Come In/Chiquita/I'll Never Ask for More/Your Mother and Mine/You're Driving Me Crazy/That's My Desire/I Miss a Little Miss/Singing a Song to the Stars/Love Thy Neighbor/

My Ohio Home/Without You, Sweetheart/Sunshine/I Still Love You/How About Me?/I'll Get By/Heart O'Mine/Old Timer/My Heart Belongs to the Girl Who Belongs to Somebody Else/A Thousand Goodnights

[1927–1931 Brunswick and 1934 Melotone recordings; also released on cassette]

"Painting the Clouds with Sunshine"

(Soundies SCD-1434) [2001; CD]

Painting the Clouds with Sunshine/Tangerine/Gay Ranchero/Minnie the Mermaid/Sleepy Time Gal/I'm Looking Over a Four Leaf Clover/In a Little Spanish Town/Three Little Words/Oh, How I Miss You Tonight/Always/It Looks Like Rain in Cherry Blossom Lane/I'll Get By/The Song Is Ended/Mexicali Rose/Tiptoe Through the Tulips/Painting the Clouds with Sunshine (reprise)

[1945–1946 C.P. MacGregor transcriptions and two songs from the soundtrack of *The Gold Diggers of Broadway* (Warner Bros., 1929)]

"Singing Troubadour"

(Hallmark [MP3] [2010])

You're Driving Me Crazy/ Go Fly a Kite/A Cup of Coffee, a Sandwich and You/An Evening in Caroline/The Man with the Mandolin/Singin' in the Rain/Oh! Mabel!/I Might Have Known/Looking at the World Thru Rose Colored Glasses/Over the Rainbow/Good Morning/Painting the Clouds with Sunshine/Your Mother and Mine/A Man and His Dream/Siboney/An Apple for the Teacher/Bye Bye Blackbird/Oh! My Bundle of Love/I've Got the Girl/Goodnight Sweetheart

(1924–1929 Brunswick, 1932 Hit of the Week and 1939 Regal Zonophone recordings. MP3 reissue of the 1983 British long playing album "The Singing Troubadour" [ASV Living Era AJA-5022])

"The Singing Troubadour"

(Vintage Music VM-1273) [2015]

Painting the Clouds with Sunshine/Together/Looking at the World Thru Rose Colored Glasses/I'll Get By/Just Like a Melody Out of the Sky/Tiptoe Through the Tulips with Me/Side by Side/My Best Girl/Dancing with Tears in My Eyes/Moonbeam, Kiss Her for Me/Bye Bye Blackbird/Among My Souvenirs

[Compact disc re-release of Decca DL-8653; issued in Spain in 2017 on Calle Mayor VM-1273]

"Souvenir Album"

(Melody Man MMCD-1493) [2006]

Those Were the Days/Get Out Those Old Records/It Happened in Monterey/Somebody Stole My Gal/Darling, I Love You/My Blue Heaven/Tiptoe Through the Tulips/Baby Face/South of the Border/While We Dance at the Mardi Gras/Sleepy Time Gal/Zei Gezunt

[Reissue of Accent ACS-5027]

"Tiptoe Through the Tulips"

(ASV Living Era CD-AJA-5329) [2000; British]

Tiptoe Through the Tulips/Painting the Clouds with Sunshine/Pickin' the Guitar/My Best Girl/Brown Eyes, Why Are You Blue?/Sleepy Time Gal/A Cup of Coffee, a Sandwich and You/Always/My Bundle of Love/Bye Bye Blackbird/Looking at the World Thru Rose Colored Glasses/I'm Looking Over a Four Leaf Clover/So Blue/Side by Side/My Blue Heaven/Without You, Sweetheart/I'll Get By/Singin' in the Rain/You're Driving Me Crazy/Lady, Play Your Mandolin/An Evening in Caroline/All of Me/An Apple for the Teacher/Go Fly a Kite/Over the Rainbow

[1923–1930 Brunswick, 1932 Hit of the Week and 1939 Regal Zonophone recordings]

Compilation Albums and Compact Discs

"Art Deco Vocal Jazz of the 30s"
(Vintage Music VM-1448) CD [2013]
Painting the Clouds with Sunshine/Just Like a Melody Out of the Sky/Bye Bye Blackbird
[Also available on MP3]

"Best of the Roaring Twenties"
(Stardust [MP3]) [2013]
I'd Love to Call You My Sweetheart

"Camp!"
(Capitol T/ST-1221) 12"-LP [1967]
Tiptoe Through the Tulips

"Chart Stoppers of the '20s"
(Emerald Echoes [MP3]) [2015]
Tiptoe Through the Tulips

"The Crooners, Vol. 2"
("Sounds of a Century") CD and Cassette
I'd Love to Call You My Sweetheart

"Day of the Locust"
(London PS-912) 12"-LP [1975]
I Wished on the Moon

"Diamond Jim Favorites"
(Camay CA-3020) 12"-LP [1963]
Selection(s) unknown; from Snader Telescriptions

"Echoes from the 1920s: 40 Vintage Jazz Age Recordings"
(Take Two TT-509CD) CD [2000]
I'd Love to Call You My Sweetheart

"An Evening in Caroline"
(Kipepeo Publishing) CD [2015]
An Evening in Caroline

"Favorites of the Roaring Twenties"
(Take Two TT-502CD) CD [1998]
Tiptoe Through the Tulips

"The First Crooners, Volume One: The Twenties"
(Take Two TT-411) CD [1994]
The Song I Love

"The First Crooners, Volume Two: 1930–1934"
(Take Two TT-418CD) CD [1996]
Hello! Beautiful

"The First Crooners, Volume Three: 1935–1940"
(Take Two TT-425CD) CD [1999]
We Can't Go on This Way

"Great Crooners"
(Sony Music Special Products A26545) CD [1996]
Always

"The Great Gatsby"
(Paramount PAS-2-3001) 12"-LPs [1974]
Five Foot Two, Eyes of Blue/I'm Gonna Charleston Back to Charleston/When You and I Were Seventeen
[Also issued on cassette (Paramount 8091-3001N) and 8-Track tape (Paramount 8091-3001N)]

"Hits of 1925"
(K-Tel [MP3] [2013])
Brown Eyes, Why Are You Blue?

"Hits of '25"
(Ingrooves [MP3] [2017])
Brown Eyes, Why Are You Blue?

"Hits of '25—Yes Sir, That's My Baby"
(ASV CD-AJA-5525) CD [2006; British]
Brown Eyes, Why Are You Blue?

"Hits of '26"
(Ingrooves [MP3]) [2017]
Always/Sleepy Time Gal

"Hits of '26"
(K-Tel [MP3]) [2013]
Always/Sleepy Time Gal

"Irving Caesar"
(Flapper PAST-CD-7075) CD [1995; British]
Lady Play Your Mandolin

"Legendary Entertainers"
(Pro-Arte/Fanfare/Intersound CDD-483) CD [1989]
Tiptoe Through the Tulips

"Legends of the Musical Stage"
(Take Two TT-104) 12"-LP [1980]
Tiptoe Through the Tulips
[Reissued in 1983 as Legends of the Musical Stage: Rare Soundtrack Recordings 1928–1930" (Sandy Hook SH-2076)]

"Lost Films: Trailers from the First Years of Sound"
(Take Two TT-110) 12"-LP [1984]
Tiptoe Through the Tulips/Painting the Clouds with Sunshine/In a Kitchenette

"Marion Harris—Look for the Silver Lining"
(Emerald Echoes [MP3]) [2016]
I'll See You in My Dreams

"100 Hits Vintage No. 5"
(Vintage Music [MP3]) [2013]
I'm Looking at the World Thru Rose Colored Glasses

"Paper Hits: Hit of the Week Recordings, Volume Two"
(Broadway Intermission BR-109) 12"-LP [1983]
All of Me

"Pioneers of the Jazz Guitar"
(Yazoo L-1057) 12"-LP [1981]
Pickin' the Guitar/Teasin' the Frets

"Radio Crooners, Disc One"
(Music & Memories 131722/RCA Special Products BMG Direct Marketing DMC-2-1111-1) CD [1993]
Tiptoe Through the Tulips

"The Roaring Twenties"
(AAO Music) CD [2013]
Tiptoe Through the Tulips

"The Roaring Twenties"
(Compendia [MP3]) [1997]
Tiptoe Through the Tulips

"The Roaring Twenties"
(EMI VMP-1022) 12"-LP [1977]
Tiptoe Through the Tulips

"The Roaring Twenties"
(Pro Jazz) CD [1991]
Tiptoe Through the Tulips

"Runnin' Wild: The Original Sounds of the Jazz Age"
(ASV AJA-5017) 12"-LP [1983; British]
How Many Times?

"Shake It and Break It"
(Capitol TBO-1572) 12"-LPs [1961]
Tiptoe Through the Tulips/Bye Bye Blackbird

"Singing Troubadours on the Air"
(Star-Tone St-206) 12"-LP [1983]
Maria Elena

"Songs of Harry Woods"
(Emerald Echoes [MP3]) [2016]
I'm Looking Over a Four-Leaf Clover

"Speakeasy Music of the 1920s"

(Vinyl Masters [MP3]) [2013]
You're Driving Me Crazy

"Ted Fio Rito & His Orchestra—Never Been Blue 1922–1942"

(Transatlantic Radio TR-0021) CD [2003]
Copenhagen

"Those Wonderful Thirties, Volume One"

(Decca DEA-7–1) 12"-LPs [1969]
Tiptoe Through the Tulips

"Vintage Summer, Volume 2"

(Vintage Music [MP3]) [2013]
Looking at the World Thru Rose Colored Glasses

"Voices of Romance from the 1930s"

(Take Two [TT-508CD] CD [2002])
That's My Desire

Streaming

The following Nick Lucas albums and compilations are offered by various international streaming services.

"The Big Broadcast, Volume 8: Jazz and Popular Music of the 1920s and 1930s"

(Rivermont) [2013]
How Many Times?

"Cheerful Little Earful"

(Circle) [2013]
Walkin' My Baby Back Home

"The Essential 1920s Collection, Volume 2"

(Suburban Squire) [2014]
I'm Looking Over a Four Leaf Clover/Tiptoe Through the Tulips

"Fabulous Thirties"

(Sharp Edge) [2014]
Tiptoe Through the Tulips

"Freedom's Front Door: Music of the Ellis Island Era 1900–1930"

(Soundies) [2004]
I'm Looking Over a Four Leaf Clover

"The Great Gatsby"

(Vintage Masters) [2012]
Tiptoe Through the Tulips

"Hits of Nick Lucas"

(Black & Partners LLC) [2014]
All of Me/An Evening in Caroline/Can't You Read Between the Lines/Falling in Love Again/Hello Beautiful/I Called to Say Goodnight/I Miss a Little Miss/I'm Sure of Everything but You/I Surrender Dear/Lady, Play You Mandolin/More Beautiful Than Ever/Running Between the Raindrops/Say Hello to the Folks Back Home/That's My Desire/Till Tomorrow/Walkin' My Baby Back Home/When the Moon Comes Over the Mountain/You Didn't Have to Tell Me/You're Driving Me Crazy

Also available as "Essential Hits" (Solid Blue Group S.L.) [2014]

"Mad for Pop Music Through the Years, Volume One"

(Suburban Squire) [2014]
I'm Looking Over a Four Leaf Clover

"Mad for Pop Music Through the Years, Volume Five"

(Suburban Squire) [2014]
Tiptoe Through the Tulips

"Plenty of 20s Classics, Volume Five"

(Wyte Myce) [2015]
Sleepy Time Gal

"The Roots of Steampunk 1903–1929"

(Essential World Masters) [2012]
Tiptoe Through the Tulips

"Tiptoe Through the Tulips— The Best of Nick Lucas"

(Master Classics) [2013]

Tiptoe Through the Tulips/Painting the Clouds with Sunshine/Singin' in the Rain/Always/In a Little Spanish Town/The Song Is Ended/Bye Bye Blackbird/An Apple for the Teacher/Lady, Play Your Mandolin/The Gay Ranchero/A Cup of Coffee, a Sandwich and You/Three Little Words/Mexicali Rose/So Blue/It Looks Like Rain in Apple Blossom Lane/An Evening in Caroline/My Best Girl/You're Driving Me Crazy/I'll Get By/Brown Eyes, Why Are You Blue?/Over the Rainbow/Looking at the World Thru Rose Colored Glasses/Go Fly a Kite/Oh, How I Miss You Tonight/Tangerine/My Blue Heaven/Side by Side/Sleepy Time Gal/All of Me/Without You Sweetheart/I'm Looking Over a Four Leaf Clover/Minnie the Mermaid

"Top 100 Hits—1920, Volume One"

(Oldies but Goodies) [2015]
Tiptoe Through the Tulips

Songbooks and Song Folios

The following is a list and the contents (when known) of songbooks and song folios compiled by Lucas. Several of the songbooks were republished into the 1970s. Songs composed by Lucas are noted with an asterisk (*) and those arranged by him are shown with a double asterisk (**).

Songbooks

The Gem Collection of Plectrum Guitar Solos
(Nicomede Music Company, Altoona, Pennsylvania; 1940)

Althean/The Gondolier/Gliding Along on My Guitar/The Student/My Love For You, Dear Guitar/The Singing Guitar/Marching with My Guitar/Pupil's Delight/At the Grasshopper's Ball/Teasing the Basses/Novelette Waltz/Memories: Medley Overture/Home, How Can I Forget Thee/Blue Mountain/Simplicity.

Let's Play Together for Plectrum Guitar
(Nicomede Music Company, Altoona, Pennsylvania)

The Mastertone Guitar Method
(Robbins Music Corporation, New York City; 1929) [Edited by Nick Lucas, Carson Robison, Andy Sanella and Eddie Lang]

Home Sweet Home/One Ahead March/Jingle Waltz/Silver Fox Polka/Echo Waltz/Old Black Joe/Hobo March/Guessing Waltz/Moonbeam Mazurka/Surprise Waltz/The Wobbler March/Take It Easy/Bellmore March/Sweet Genevieve/Bellair Waltz/The Campus Drag/Oh Dem a-Golden Slippers/Doin' Things/Without You Sweetheart/Among My Souvenirs

Morris's Modern Method for Tenor Banjo
(Nicomede Music Company, Altoona, Pennsylvania; 1935)

Written in 1922 by William (Banjo Bill) Morris, this three-volume songbook was revised by Lucas in 1935.

Nick Lucas Chord, Rhythm and Fill-In Book for Guitar (or Guitar-Banjo)
(Nicomede Music Company, Altoona, Pennsylvania; 1934)

Virginny's Calling Me Back/Just a Cottage/Old Folks at Home

Nick Lucas Collection of Neapolitan Love Songs
(Robbins Music Corporation, New York City; 1935)

A Happy Heart [Funiculi-Funicula]/Celeste Aida (Heavenly Aida)/Chiribiribee [Ciribiribin]/Come Back to Sorrento [Torna a Surriento]/Come to the Sea [Vieni Sul Mar]/Down Her Soft Cheek a Pearly Tear [Una Furtiva Lagrima]/Farewell Dear Napoli [Addio Alla Bella Napoli]/French Pins ['E Spingole Frangese!]/Here in the Twilight [Santa Lucia]/La Spagnola (Maid of Spain)/Mandolinata/Margarita/Oh Marie [Maria, Maria!]/O Lola [Siciliana]/O Sole Mio/On Venice Waters [Gondolier Waltz]/Romance of Nadir (Pearl Fishers) [Romanza di Nadir]/Serenade of Olden Days [Serenata Medioevale]/Serenade of the Roses [A Serenata de' 'e Rose]/The French Girl ['A Frangesa]/The Rose [La Rosa]/'Tis Not True! [Non e Ver~]/The New Moon [Luna Nova]/Vesti La Giubba (from Pagliacci)/Voice of Night [Voce'e Notte]/Woman Is Fickle [Donna de Mobile]

Cover of the 1935 songbook *Nick Lucas Collection of Neapolitan Love Songs.*

Nick Lucas' Comic Songs for Ukulele & Guitar
(Robbins-Engel, Inc., New York City; 1926)

Gid-dy-up Napoleon/Please Don't Dog Me 'Round/Ev'ry Once in a While/Sing It

Again/Tra La-La-La-La/What's Better Than That/Wait for the Wagon/If I Can't Have You All to Myself/Ve-Vum-Ve/Too Much Trouble

The Nick Lucas Guitar Method for Pick Playing
(Nicomede Music Company, Altoona, Pennsylvania; 1930)

The Dutch Girl/Long, Long Ago/Minor Waltz/America/Broken Chord Studies/Blue Moon/Triplets/Happy Rastus*/There Is Music in the Air/The Spanish Cavalier/Tremolo Studies/Old Black Joe/At the Races/Veno Fox Trot/Fascinating Waltz/Benjamin Blues/ Set Them Up/Rudy Fox Trot/Margaret Waltz/You Played with My Heart/Varsity Blues*/Flappers Trot*/Crazy Quilt*/Hot Steps/Little Rose/Gold Diggers*/Warm Breezes*/Cholla*/Drag Your Feet*/Bootlegger's Blues*

The Nick Lucas Guitar Method for Plectrum Playing (Nicomede Music Company, Altoona, Pennsylvania; 1940) [3 volumes]

Bobby Shafto March/Little Star March/Pastime on Open Strings/Big Boy/Hail! Hail! The Gang's All Here/Billy Boy March/Polly Wolly March/Viking/Long, Long Ago March/The Taps/Aloha Oe/The Assembly/Onward, Christian Soldiers**/Home, Sweet Home/Happy Land/Puzzle Tune/The Peasant March*/Longfellow/Midway/Bass Solo/It's Three-Four Time/The Dot Girl/Football/Screen Girl*/Our School*/At Work/Our Teacher**/Come Along*/The Circus Man/Study on Sixteenth Notes/Cider Barrel**/Dream Girl/Old Black Joe**/Etude/Honey Bee**/Duet in C Major/Big Bass Solo/The Elevator Girl/Speedboat/Bombay/Over the Ocean**/There's Music in the Air/Sharpshooters March/Sally in Her Alley/The Sailor/Chromatic Polka/Benjamin Blues/Rainbow Waltz/Primo Waltz/The March King*/Gaiety Waltz*/Ever So Good*/Battle Axe/Jazz King/Rudy/Moonlight Serenade/Aeroplane March/At the Races/Cannon Ball/Buy a Broom*/The Dancer*/Dancing Girls*

Note: This three-book set is a different version of the trio of volumes listed below as **The Nick Lucas Plectrum Guitar Method**.

The Nick Lucas Hawaiian Guitar Method
(Nicomede Music Company, Altoona, Pennsylvania; 1931)

Please Find My Name/Dusty Skies/Vibrato Waltz/A Little Action/Dreaming/That Hawaiian Girl/Kalina Waltz/The Slide/Neath the Coppery Lantern Moon/Old Folks at Home/Swing Waltz/Hawaiian Waters/Sweet Marie/Honolulu Bound/Kua Lua/Hawaiian Highway March/Natona Waltz/Beautiful Hawaiian Moon/America/Beautiful Hawaii/Scarlet Sage/The Sunset Evening Prayer/Hawaiian Sunset/Hula Lu Waltz/On the Sands of Waikiki/Won't You Come Back to Me/Wally, Wally

The Nick Lucas Hawaiian Guitar Method, Volume Two
(Nicomede Music Company, Altoona, Pennsylvania; 1932)

Hula Polka, Hawaiian Melody/Counter Marching**/On Trial/Dreamy Days/Technical Studies/Guitarella*/Catching On/Melody/Etude in D/Temptation Mazurka*/Melodious Etude/Korei Waltz/Waltz Etude/Aloha Oe/Night Shadows*/The Strutters March*/

The Crooners/Serenade in D/Sand Dance/Waltz Melody in Bb/In the Flats/Across the Bars/Amusement in F Major/Moonlight on the Beach*/Hawaiian Feathers*/ Footlights/ Luakolo/Gliding Waters/Amusement/Dainty Lady Waltz/The Whirligig/Rudy**/Etudes in E Major and E Minor/El Toreador*/On the Beach Together*/Etude in C/Starlight Serenade—Con Moto/One Two Three***/ Lingering/Massa's in the Cold, Cold Ground**/ Hawaiian Rose March/In Argentine*/Gypsy Dance/Santa Lucia**/Hula Dance/Spanish Waltz/Lucien/Happy Days March*

The Nick Lucas Hawaiian Guitar Method, Volume Two
(Nicomede Music Company, Altoona, Pennsylvania; 1940)
[revised edition]

Dreamy Days/A Study in Hawaii/Counter Marching/On Trial/Guitarella*/The Slide/ Catching On/Actual Notation/Korei Waltz/The Whirligig/Night Shadows Reverie/The Circus Man/March Melody/Aloha Oe**/Won't You Come Back to Me?/Moonlight on the Beach*/Sand Dance/Footlights/Santa Lucia**/Chimes at Waikiki/One Two Three Four**/ Dainty Lady Waltz/On the Beach Together*/Melodious Etude/Gliding Waters/The Strutters March*/The Land of Beautiful Waters/Staccato/ Lingering/El Toreador*/Massa's in the Cold, Cold Ground/Pop Goes the Weasel/ Cowboy Joe**/Moku Manu Hula/Sweet Hawaiian Dreams/Moonbeams/My Hawaiian Belle/Temptation Mazurka*/Gypsy Dance/ Rudy**/Somebody Taka Da Watch/Spanish Waltz/Hula Dance/Lucien/In Argentine*

The Nick Lucas Hawaiian Guitar Method, Volume Three
(Nicomede Music Company, Altoona, Pennsylvania; 1940)

We Meet Again at School/Steel Angels/Arpeggio in E Minor/Love at Hilo/Honolulu Mix-up/Do You Regret/Oalee Waltz/Laughing Waters*/You Played with My Heart/A Frolic on the Island/Love in Hawaii/Just a Cottage/On the Hawaiian Mountains*/Hawaiian Winds/Kona/Troops on Review/Sunrise on Oahu*/Betty Jane/Please Find My Name**/Silent Night/Walking on Sands of Honolulu/Blue/Dance of the Surf/ Hawaiian Pineapple Blues/Island Dream Girl/My Island Hula/The Magic South Sea/ Marcia Waltz*/Happy Days March*/O Kavai*/Miss Anola*/Harmonic Mazurka*/Nocturne/Galit Serenade*/Queen of Hawaii*/League of Nations**

The Nick Lucas Plectrum Guitar Method, Volume One
(Nicomede Music Company, Altoona, Pennsylvania; 1935)

Hail! Hail! the Gang's All Here/Billy Boy March/Polly Wolly March/Viking/Long, Long Ago March/The Taps/Aloha Oe/Onward Christian Soldiers**/Home, Sweet Home/ The Peasant March*/Screen Girl*/Our School**/At Work/Our Teacher**/Come Along*/I Lost My Name/The Circus Man*/Find My Name**/Cider Barrel**/Dream Girl/Old Black Joe**/Honey Bee*/Duet in C Major/The Test March*/The Elevator Girl**/Bombay/Over the Ocean**/Sally in Her Alley/The Cannonade*/Row Your Boat/Little Actress**/Benjamin Blues/The March King*/Gaiety Waltz*/Ever Go Good*/Battle Axe/Jazz King/Rudy/ Moonlight Serenade/Aeroplane March/At the Races/Cannon Ball/Buy a Broom**/The Dancer*/Dancing Lights*

Also called **Nick Lucas Guitar Method for Plectrum Playing, Volume One**.

The Nick Lucas Plectrum Guitar Method, Volume Two
(Nicomede Music Company, Altoona, Pennsylvania; 1935)

The Bear Dance/Merry Go Round/Asia Minor/Amusement in E Minor/Grenadine*/The Streamliner/Roller Skating/The Spanish Cavalier/Over the Waves/Love Song/Veno/Broken Chords/Always Dancing/Syncopated Bill/It's Chord Time/Kitty Clyde*/That Red Head Girl*/Burlesque*/The Lantern Dance*/Maxine*/Happy Rastus*/Orchestra Style Obligato/That Clever Waltz*/Ball Room Schottische/On the Clouds*/A Little Bit of Irish/Race Track/Castilian Waltz*/You Played with My Heart/Let's Have Fun/A Little Tango/Pamela Waltz*/Winding, Winding/Margaret/A Blue Melody*/Flappers Trot*/Crazy Quilt*/Drag Your Feet*/Tickling the Strings*/Gold Diggers*/La Contessa*

Also called **Nick Lucas Guitar Method for Plectrum Playing, Volume Two**.

In the May 1932 issue of *B.M.G.*, a monthly British magazine devoted to the banjo, mandolin and guitar, A. de Vekey reviewed this songbook:

> This is a welcome follow on the first Book by this well-known writer. It is a work of some 64 pages, containing a number of solos, duets and studies in all keys, together with a mass of information for plectrum guitarists, harmony hits, study in artificial harmonics, how to read from banjo tenor parts, special orchestra accompaniments, introducing breaks, cross rhythm, etc.; embellishments, playing from piano copy, movable six-string chord studies, and many other interesting features. A work I can recommend, for it covers practically everything for the plectrum guitarist.

The Nick Lucas Plectrum Guitar Method, Volume Three
(Nicomede Music Company, Altoona, Pennsylvania; 1935)

Bright Is the Day*/Our Pride*/Calvary**/The Fascinating Waltz/The Old Grey Mare**/The Top Guard/Dream of Love/Just a Cottage**/Eccentric Guitar Duet/Song Without Words**/Cochita Waltz*/The Swing Boys*/This Is the Night*/Bootlegger's Blues*/She Came from Spain*/My Dear Student*/Radio Waves Waltz*/Cholla*/Warm Breezes*/Betty Jane**/The Moonlight Dance*/Visions*/Varsity Blues*/The Siamese Twins/Moonlight Dreams/Silver Star/The Flyers*/Irish Rose O'Mine**/White Plumes*/El Choclo**/Plectrola*/Cionchina/The Firefly*/The Foot Disturber*/Flights of Melody*

Note: The three volumes comprising **The Nick Lucas Plectrum Guitar Method** were re-published by Mills Music Company, New York City.

The Nick Lucas Progressive Foundation for Plectrum Playing
(Nicomede Music Company, Altoona; Pennsylvania; 1938)

Song Folios

The Crown Folio of Guitar Solos (Plectrum Style)
(Nicomede Music Company, Altoona, Pennsylvania; 1932)

Marche Triumph/Idle Hours/Little Coquette/Jolly Fellows/Marche Orientale/Danse E'spagnole/My Ideal/Dainty Fingers/Frolics of Spring/Artist's Choice/Cupid's Caprice/Polish Dance No. 1/La Petite Spagnola

Note: All the songs in this folio were composed by Edward Ferrucci and arranged for guitar by Lucas.

The Gem Dance Folio for 1926:
Selections from the Season's Most Popular Successes
(Shapiro, Bernstein & Company, New York City; 1926)

If You Hadn't Gone Away/If I Can't Have You

The Imperial Folio for Hawaiian Guitar
(Nicomede Music Company, Altoona, Pennsylvania; 1935)

Ho Hi Lio March/Rigoletto/My Bonnie/Aloha Oe/Marching Thru Georgia/Home, Can I Forget Thee/Listen to the Mocking Bird/Il Trovatore/Spanish Cavalier/Old Black Joe/Peanut Song/Old Folks at Home

The Keystone Folio for the Guitar (Plectrum Style)
(Nicomede Music Company, Altoona, Pennsylvania; 1932)

Massa's in De Cold Ground/Over the Waves/Old Black Joe/Home Sweet Home/Onward Christian Soldiers/Rosalie**/Listen to the Mocking Bird/Aloha Oe/Drink to Me Only with Thine Eyes**/Brown Jug**/Melodious Melodies [Jingle Bells/ Rosalind]**/Parting

Let's Play Together for Hawaiian Guitar
(Nicomede Music Company, Altoona, Pennsylvania; 1936) [Arranged by Nick Lucas]

Thirty-eight songs, including Twinkle, Twinkle, Little Star/Hail! Hail! The Gang's All Here/Silent Night/My Bonnie Lies Over the Ocean/Old MacDonald Had a Farm/Goodnight Ladies/Santa Lucia/The Star Spangled Banner/Oh Where Has My Little Dog Gone

The Liberty Folio of Guitar Solos (Pick Style)
(Nicomede Music Company, Altoona, Pennsylvania; 1931)

Imitation Fandango/At the Mark/Lenora Waltz/Evelyn Waltz/Waving Plumes/The Little Princess/Comin' Thro'/Never Mind/In Blossom Time/The Red Arrow/Little Frolic/Something New

The National Folio for the Hawaiian Guitar (Plectrum Style)
(Nicomede Music Company, Altoona, Pennsylvania; 1935)

The Junior Waltz/My Alabama Moon/One Two Three Four/The Serenaders/You Played with My Heart/You Told Me of Love/On Wings of Glory/Tickling Waves Waltz/Veno Fox Trot/Chocoletta

Also issued in two parts: **Book One**: Hawaiian Guitar Solo/Second Hawaiian

Cover of Nick Lucas' *The Keystone Folio for the Guitar* (1932).

Guitar and Ukulele/Symbols; **Book Two**: Hawaiian Guitar Obligato/Hawaiian Guitar Accompaniment (Symbols)/Spanish Guitar Accompaniment/Mando-Bass.

Nick Lucas De Luxe Plectrum Guitar Solos
(Nicomede Music Company, Altoona, Pennsylvania, 1935)

Picking the Guitar/Teasing the Frets

Nick Lucas Plectrum Guitar Solos
(Nicomede Music Company, Altoona, Pennsylvania; 1935)

Beautiful Dreamland/Silk Stockings/Some Blues/Shake That Guitar/The Broadside/Wyoming Joe/Toda Va Bien/With You My Guitar/Guitar Melody/A Telephone Call
Note: These songs were later issued individually for Spanish Guitar by Mills Music.

The Premier Folio of Guitar Solos and Duets
(Nicomede Music Company, Altoona, Pennsylvania; 1935)

Ben Bolt/Wait for the Wagon/Home Sweet Home/Upidee/Nealstead Waltz/The Gold Tip/Just a Cottage/My Yankee Girl/Gibson Beauty March/Prohibition/Tickling Waves

Six Original Nick Lucas Guitar Solos
(Nicomede Music Company, Altoona, Pennsylvania, 1931)

Notes of Joy/The Ghost Is Coming/The Gypsy Moth/Says Which!/Guitar Antics/Hot Air

The Waikiki Folio for the Hawaiian Guitar
(Nicomede Music Company, Altoona, Pennsylvania; 1935)

To You/Sweet Chiming Bells/Laugh Feet Laugh/Onward Waltz/Melody in D/Song Without Words/Let's Go/Carlota/Echo Answers/Serenade Waltz
Also issued in two parts: **Book One:** Hawaiian Guitar Solo/Second Hawaiian Guitar & Ukulele/Symbols; **Book Two:** Hawaiian Guitar Obligato/Hawaiian Guitar Accompaniment (Symbols)/Spanish Guitar Accompaniment/Mando-Bass.

Solo Song Folios

Nick Lucas Fascinating Plectrum Guitar Solos
(Nicomede Music Company, Altoona, Pennsylvania; 1936)

With You and My Guitar*

Nick Lucas Fascinating Plectrum Guitar Solos
(Nicomede Music Company, Altoona, Pennsylvania; 1936)

The Broadside*

Songs

The following are songs composed by Nick Lucas were not done for his songbooks and song folios.

I Found Somebody to Love (1925; with Sam H. Stept)
I Might Have Known (1925; with Sam H. Stept)
I Tip My Heart to You (1954)
If I Can't Have You (1925)
It's Been a Good Life (1966; credited to David Garvin)
I've Named My Pillow After You (1925; with Fred Rose and Billy Waldron)
Let Me Live and Love You Just for Tonight (1926; with Sam H. Stept)
The Magic Waltz (1981; with Scott Seely)
Underneath the Stars with You (1927; with Sam H. Stept)
When You're Lonely (1926; with Willard Thompson)

Sheet Music

The following is sheet music that features Lucas' picture on the cover. An asterisk (*) denotes the songs recorded by Lucas.

And Still They Fall in Love (1929)
Angry (1925)
Blue Kentucky Moon (1931)
By the Light of the Stars* (1925)
Cherie Chilly-Pom-Pom-Pee (1928)
Clouds (1935)
Doodle-Doo-Doo (1924)
Dream Time (1936)
Dreamer of Dreams* (1925)
Everyone in Town Loves Little Mary Brown (1931)
Go to Bed (1929)
The Gold Diggers of Broadway Selection (1929)
Goody Goody (1936)
Here Am I—Brokenhearted* (1927)
Here Comes the Sun (1930)
How I Love That Girl! (1924)
I Saw Stars (1934)
I'd Love to Call You My Sweetheart* (1926)
If I Can't Have You (1925) [name only as composer]
I'll Close My Eyes to Everyone Else (1934)
I'm in Love (1929)
I'm Looking for a Girl Named Mary* (1926)
In a Kitchenette (1929)
In a Little Spanish Town* (1927)
In the Quiet of an Autumn Night (1934)
It Happened to Me (1931)
It Must Be Love!* (1928)
I've Got an Invitation to a Dance (1934)
Just Once Too Often (1934)
Lady Play Your Mandolin* (1931)
The Last Waltz with You (Was the Sweetest Waltz of All) (1925)
Linger Awhile (1923) [listed as Nick Lucos]
Little Black Buddie (1924)

Sheet music for "Lady, Play Your Mandolin" (1931), introduced by Nick Lucas.

Loneliness Calls (1944)
Lonely Moonlight Troubadour (1933)
Lonely Troubadour (1929)
Looking at the World Thru Rose Colored Glasses* (1926)
Lost in a Fog (1934)
Lucky Kentucky (1924)
Mechanical Man (1929)
The Midnight Waltz (1925) [Nick Lucas is pictured with the Oriole Orchestra]
Moonlight and You (1924)
My Sweetie Turned Me Down (1925)
Oh How I Miss You Tonight (1925)
Oh, What a Thrill (1931)
Painting the Clouds with Sunshine* (1929)
Red Hot Henry Brown (1924)
Red Sails in the Sunset (1935)
Silver Sails* (1974)
Sleepy Time Gal* (1926)
Soldier's Guitar* (1955)
Susie Song (1924)
Sweet Someone* (1927)
Sweetie Pie (1934)
There's Yes Yes in Your Eyes (1924)
This Is My Love Song (1931)
This Side of Paradise (1930)
A Thousand Goodnights* (1934)
Tiny Little Fingerprints (1925)
Tiptoe Through the Tulips* (1929)
Too Many Parties and Too Many Pals (1925)
Underneath the Stars with You* (1927)
What Will I Do Without You (1929)
When Ever You Are Near (1926)
When You're Lonely* (1926)
Where the Red, Red Roses Grow (1926)
While We Danced at the Mardi Gras* (1931)
Who's Who Are You?* (1925)
Winter Wonderland (1934)
The Wooden Soldier and the China Doll (1931)
Yankee Rose (1936)
Yearning Just for You (1925)

1931 sheet music for "While We Danced at the Mardi Gras" picturing Nick Lucas.

Filmography

The theatrical motion pictures in which Lucas appeared or sang on the soundtrack.

Lonesome (Universal, 1928) 7 reels

Production Supervisor: Carl Laemmle, Jr. Director: Paul Fejos. Screenplay: Edward T. Lowe. Dialogue-Titles: Tom Reed. Story: Mann Page. Photography: Gilbert Warrenton. Editor: Frank Atkinson.

CAST: Barbara Kent (Mary), Glenn Tryon (John), Fay Holderness (Flashy Woman), Gustav Partos (Romancer), Eddie Phillips (The Sport).

Universal released two versions of *Lonesome*, one silent and the other with sound effects and a talking sequence, in the summer of 1928. (It was the studio's first feature film with dialogue.) Lucas can be heard in the latter version singing "Always," which he recorded for Brunswick Records in 1927. This romantic drama tells of a love-starved couple, switchboard operator Mary (Barbara Kent) and drill press operator John (Glenn Tryon), who meet at a beach and immediately fall in love. While on a roller coaster they get separated and valiantly try to find each other only to discover they live in the same New York City boardinghouse and are reunited when the young man plays Nick's recording.

Reviews:

Exhibitor's Herald: "It is an unusually fine picture and an attraction that will be heard from."

Film Daily: "Worthwhile mainly because of excellent direction. Story slight but human and appealing. A different picture for intelligent audiences."

The Film Spectator: "It is a simple little thing ... and probably will be a financial failure, as it is not the type of picture to appeal very strongly to the average audience ... a pretty good piece of work."

Filmograph: "A splendid symphony of the screen. The film is going to ranked as one of the best of the year."

Harrison's Reports: "This is an unusual picture. The plot is very simple, but the mood of the story is so vivid that a deep impression is left on one's mind, an impression that lasts long after one has seen the picture."

Photoplay: "[A] good human interest story.... Lots of trick camera work but, on the whole, worth your while."

Variety: "Save for two or three dialog sequences ... it's just an ordinary sound picture, average in story and badly synchronized.... Some of the photography and the basic appeal of the theme saves it for a time, but for the main *Lonesome* drags and ultimately peters out."

My Tonia (Synchro Song Film, 1929) and *Woman Disputed, I Love You* (Synchro Song Film, 1929)

There is little information on these three-minute short subjects released to theaters in the spring of 1929. *My Tonia* was the theme song of the first all-talking western, Fox's *In Old Arizona* (1929); Lucas also recorded it for Brunswick Records. *Woman Disputed, I Love You* was from the 1928 United Artists release *Woman Disputed*. According to advertising, Syncho Song Films were "[s]et before our eyes on the screen in beautiful exotic surroundings. The words of each song unfolds before your audience while being sung by the greatest artists in the country." Synchro Song Film was patented by Universal Optical Corporation of Providence, Rhode Island.

The Gold Diggers of Broadway trailer (Warner Bros., 1929)
One Reel [3070]

CAST: Conway Tearle, Nick Lucas, Ann Pennington, Winnie Lightner, Lawrence Gray, Helen Foster, William Bakewell, Nancy Welford, Gertrude Short, Lilyan Tashman (Themselves).

To advertise *The Gold Diggers of Broadway* (q.v.) in theaters, Warner Bros. produced a trailer that includes footage of stars from the film performing specifically for this one-reeler. Conway Tearle served as master of ceremonies and introduced the various players who discuss their roles in the film or perform music from the picture. The first performer to be introduced is Lucas, who briefly talks about his appearance in the film and then sings abbreviated versions of "Tiptoe Through the Tulips," "In a Kitchenette" and "Painting the Clouds with Sunshine." Ann Pennington does a brief dance number to "Tiptoe Through the Tulips," Winnie Lightner sings part of "Mechanical Man" and Nancy Welford does a bit of "Song of the Gold Diggers." The trailer closes with a production number from the film built around "Song of the Gold Diggers." Although this trailer is no longer extant, the soundtrack exists.

The Gold Diggers of Broadway (Warner Bros., 1929)
98 minutes; Color

Producer: Darryl F. Zanuck. Director: Roy Del Ruth. Story: Robert Lord, from the play *The Gold Diggers* by Avery Hopwood. Photography: Barney McGill and Ray Rennahan. Editor: William Holmes. Staging: Larry Ceballos. Music and Lyrics: Al Dubin and Joe Burke. Titles: De Leon Anthony. Costumes: Earl Luick. Orchestra: Louis Silvers. Assistant Director: D. Ross Lederman. Technicians: L. Geib, F.N. Murphy, M. Parker and V. Vance.

CAST: Conway Tearle (Stephen Lee), Nancy Welford (Jerry), Ann Pennington (Ann Collins), Winnie Lightner (Mabel), Lilyan Tashman (Eleanor), Nick Lucas (Nick), William Bakewell (Wally), Helen Foster (Violet), Albert Gran (Blake), Gertrude Short (Topsy), Lawrence Grant (Wealthy Man), Neely Edwards (Stage Manager), Julia Swayne Gordon (Cissy Gray), Lee Moran (Dance Director), Armand Kaliz (Barney Barnett), George Raft (Dancer).

Issued in the fall of 1929, *The Gold Diggers of Broadway* was a remake of *The Gold Diggers* (Warner Bros., 1923) and was Lucas' feature film debut. Highlighted by Technicolor (called Natural Color in the film's advertising) and a bevy of catchy tunes, the movie's plot had a wealthy man (Conway Tearle) trying to break up his nephew's (William Bakewell) romance with a chorus girl (Helen Foster), only to fall in love with her friend (Nancy Welford). As entertainer Nick, Lucas was highlighted in two lavish production numbers centered around the songs "Painting the Clouds with Sunshine" and "Tiptoe Through the Tulips." He also sang "In a Kitchenette," "Go to Bed" and "What Will I Do Without You?" Other songs in the film included "The Song of the Gold Diggers," "Mechanical Man," "Keeping the Wolf from the Door," "And Still They Fall in Love" and "Poison Kiss of That Spaniard." The film's tremendous financial success was the impetus for Warner Bros.' successful "Gold Diggers" musicals of the 1930s. Only a few minutes of footage from *The Gold Diggers of Broadway* survives today (although the soundtrack is extant) with one segment showcasing Nick Lucas singing "Tiptoe Through the Tulips."

Reviews:

The Billboard: "[D]espite a weak story, [it] is by far the best thing thus far produced in the talkie era. It's a howl for laughs and a beauty for music and color, with just enough dancing to make any audience happy ... [The] story runs smoothly and photography is clear, except for ensemble shots, and well focused."

The Brooklyn (New York) *Citizen*: "[It] combines an exceptional cast with a story that jingles with smart dialogue throughout to make it one of the outstanding singing and talking screen production of the last two years."

Exhibitors Herald: "Here is a 100 percent production, if ever there was one. Beautiful settings that will hold you spellbound, rare comedy, all the singing is good especially that of Nick Lucas.... The whole cast is exceptionally good, and the color is perfect. We cannot find enough appropriate adjectives in Webster's to describe this properly. It must be seen and heard to be appreciated."

Film Daily: "Built for the mob entertainment. Has beautiful color. Pleasant enough story. Good music.... The story is punctuated by backstage stuff, many musical comedy numbers in which Winnie Lightner holds first place with Nick Lucas in second and Nancy Welford some considerable distance behind."

Harrison's Reports: "There is no plot in *The Gold Diggers of Broadway*; or, whatever plot there is, it is flimsy. But this plot is inconsequential; it is the beautiful colors, which are enhanced by brilliant camera work, the melodious music, the dancing and the singing and the occasional joke 'cracking,' that counts in this picture. Some of the scenes are enchanting; they mingle color and lively music... [It] does credit to the motion picture art."

Hutchinson (Kansas) *News:* "Nick Lucas sings most of these songs and those who enjoy his voice over the radio will find it even more to their liking when they see him singing them on the screen."

Los Angeles (California) *Evening Express*: "[It] is in keeping with the festal spirit of celebration of new ownership. Its buoyant comedy, spectacular prismatic photography and good performances combined to give the house a send-off that could hardly be bettered."

Motion Picture News: "Rest assured that you can't go wrong on this picture. It will get real money anywhere, anytime and audiences will go away loving it."

Movie Age: "Here is another all-color musical extravaganza of the screen that Warners can feel proud of.... Nick Lucas registers with his crooning voice, though altogether he is a little too much in evidence."

New Movie Magazine: "[L]ively and jazzy.... Winnie Lightner contributes a lot of noisy comedy, Nick Lucas sings a great deal. Little Ann Pennington is wasted on a tiny bit. The color photography is well above average in this film. Everybody works hard to put this across and very probably you will like it."

New York Daily Mirror: "A lulu. Broadway doesn't top the entertainment value packed into this snappy, beautiful song-and-dance movie."

New York Evening Journal: "[G]ood entertainment... [I]f the story moves a bit slowly, the picture offers plenty of musical and dance features ... it's all very eye-filling and lavish."

New York Graphic: "Warners have dressed the 'gimme' artists in atmospheric effects that exceed in pretensions and beauty anything which has yet appeared in the talking pictures. They provide a musical score that contains at least two hits."

New York Herald-Tribune: "[It] is distressingly lacking in zest or freshness. As a production, though, it does have definite values.... The chorus numbers are well staged and all of the musical comedy sections are properly lavish and lively."

New York Morning Telegraph: "Running in and out of this story and bringing to it enough comedy and melody to insure it a long run on Broadway and box-office success wherever it is shown, are Winnie Lightner and Nick Lucas."

Photoplay: "Two things stand out about this gay picture. One is the startling beauty of its all–Technicolor treatment. The other is the fact it has two catchy tunes."

Picture Play Magazine: "[I]t is entirely in color and this, together with the dialogue, singing, and dancing, will put the picture over with those who are easily diverted by entertainment of the lightest sort."

Screenland: "Don't miss this show! It is the best amusement of the month... [It] offers a full measure of evening's entertainment; but it seems short. It is gay and rollicking; spontaneous and unforced. It is a feast of beauty. Dazzling scenes in color. Comedy scenes, as funny as you have ever seen. Love scenes with a nice naturalness. And tinkling tunes of the type that will send you whistling out of the theatre."

Variety: "Lots of color—Technicolor—lots of comedy, girls, songs, music, dancing, production and Winnie Lightner with Nick Lucas the main warbler.... That's going to send the picture into the money class.... A very good entertainment on the screen ... splendidly photographed and recorded...."

The Winnipeg (Winnipeg, Manitoba, Canada) *Tribune*: "[T]he picture overshadows the play from every angle. It is gorgeous, glittering and always entertaining.... The ensembles are colorful and the chorus numbers delightfully tuneful."

The Show of Shows (Warner Bros., 1929) 128 minutes; Part-Color

Producer: Darryl F. Zanuck. Director: John G. Adolfi. Special Material: Frank Fay and J. Keirn Brennan. Photography: Barney McGill. Dance Director: Larry Ceballos.

Sound: George R. Groves. Songs: Ned Washington, Herb Magidson, Michael Cleary, Ray Perkins, M.K. Jerome, Herman Ruby, Al Dubin, Joe Burke, J. Keirn Brennan, Joe Goodwin, Gus Edwards, Arthur Freed, Nacio Herb Brown, Al Bryan, Ed Ward, Joe Young, Sam Lewis, Jean Schwartz, Bernie Seaman, Marvin Smolev, Rube Bloom, Perry Bradford and Jimmy Johnson.

Cast: "Chinese Fantasy" Sequence: Nick Lucas (Chinese Prince), Myrna Loy (Chinese Princess); Rest of Cast: Frank Fay (Master of Ceremonies), William Courtenay (Minister), H.B. Warner (Victim), Hobart Bosworth (Executioner), Marian Nixon, Sally O'Neill, Myrna Loy, Alice Day, Patsy Ruth Miller (Florodora Sextette), Ben Turpin (Waiter), Heinie Conklin (Ice Man), Lupino Lane (Street Cleaner), Lee Moran (Plumber), Bert Roach (Father), Lloyd Hamilton (Hansom Cabby), Noah Beery, Tully Marshall, Wheeler Oakman, Bull Montana, Kalla Pasha, Anders Randolf, Philo McCullough, Otto Matiesen, Jack Curtis (Pirates), Johnny Arthur (Hero), Carmel Myers, Ruth Clifford, Sally Eilers, Viola Dana, Shirley Mason, Ethlyne Clair, Frances Lee, Julanne Johnston (Ladies), Douglas Fairbanks, Jr. (Ambrose), Chester Conklin (Traffic Cop), Grant Withers, William Collier, Jr., Jack Mulhall, Chester Morris, William Bakewell (Boys), Lois Wilson, Gertrude Olmstead, Pauline Garon, Edna Murphy, Jacqueline Logan (Girls), Monte Blue (Condemned Man), Albert Gran, Noah Beery, Lloyd Hamilton, Tully Marshall, Kalla Pasha, Lee Moran (Soldiers), Armida, John Barrymore, Richard Barthelmess, Sally Blane, Irene Bordoni, Anthony Bushell, Marion Byron, Georges Carpentier, James Clemmons, Betty Compson, Dolores Costello, Helene Costello, Marceline Day, Louise Fazenda, Alexander Gray, Beatrice Lillie, Winnie Lightner, Hariette Lake [Ann Sothern], Lila Lee, Ted Lewis, Nick Lucas, Molly O'Day, Rin-Tin-Tin, E.J. Radcliffe, Sid Silvers, Sojin, Lola Vendrill, Ada Mae Vaughn, Alberta Vaughan, Ted Williams Adagio Dancers, Alice White, Loretta Young (Themselves).

Frank Fay is the master of ceremonies for this all-star revue with 77 stars and 21 minutes of Technicolor, including the "Chinese Fantasy" sequence headlined by Lucas and Myrna Loy. Introduced by Rin-Tin-Tin with a series of barks, this intricate production number has Chinese prince Lucas crooning "Li-Po-Li" to his lovely princess (Loy); the song is about a bandit. It was written by Al Bryan and Ed Ward. As Lucas serenades Loy, dozens of chorines in Chinese costumes dance around them. The sequence is very charming and holds up well today, though more for Nick's singing and Myrna's dancing than for the production number itself. Also in a blackout sequence, Lucas engages in comedy patter with Frank Fay and sings "Lady Luck" and "The Only Song I Know."

The Show of Shows, costing over $800,000, was previewed late in 1929 but did not go into general release until the spring of 1930. Lucas also appears in the *Show of Shows* trailer, in scenes from the film.

Reviews:

The Billboard: "It is spectacular, brilliant, chameleonic and kaleidoscopic.... But in spite of the lavishness the production is totally lacking in comedy and novelty."

Film Daily: "A Pageant of color splendidly interspersed with musical numbers.... It's box office anywhere. A record breaker cast.... Drags at times."

Harrison's Reports: "Those who like musical comedy plays should enjoy *The Show of Shows*. Those who seek dramatic entertainment, may not enjoy it so well. The picture has been produced most lavishly, the color scenes are beautiful, and the songs melodious. But there is no plot.... The sound reproduction is only fair, the talking being mostly dull."

Motion Picture News: "This is the greatest show on earth."

Photoplay: "You'll be too busy enjoying yourself to count all the celebs in this super-revue.... And besides there are stunning stage effects and dance routines, gorgeous Technicolor, and millions of laughs."

Picture Play Magazine: "The most gorgeous and varied and interesting of all the revues—that's a conservative estimate of *The Show of Shows*. Entirely in Technicolor it has everything to justify its title, with more well-known names than have ever been crowded into a single picture, and more originality and charm than have heretofore been captured by screen musicals."

Reading (Pennsylvania) *Times* (January 2, 1930): "*The Show of Shows* is without doubt the most pretentious of all productions of either stage or screen.... Myrna Loy, Nick Lucas and an Oriental chorus do an iridescent Chinese fantasy...."

Organloguing the Hits with Nick Lucas, the Crooning Troubadour (Master Art Products, 1933) 9 minutes

Executive Producer: E. Schwartz. Director: Neil McGuire. Photography: Dave Kasson. Songs: Hoagy Carmichael, Johnny Mercer, Will Jason, Val Burton and Buddy Pepper.

CAST: Nick Lucas, Herbert Rawlinson, Lew White (Themselves).

This was the first of two one-reel musical shorts Lucas headlined for Master Art Products (the second was *Home Again*, listed below). It has silent screen matinee idol Herbert Rawlinson as master of ceremonies and series regular Lew White playing the organ. A facet of the series has the lyrics of a song (or two) shown on the screen for an audience sing along. Lucas performed "Lazy Bones," "Lyin' in the Hay Wagon" and "Isn't This a Night for Love."

Home Again (Master Art Products, 1933) 8 minutes

CAST: Nick Lucas, Lew White, Kelvin Keech (Themselves).

The second Master Art Products short starring Lucas (the first was *Organloguing the Hits with Nick Lucas*, above). Nick performs the title tune.

On the Air and Off (Universal, 1933) 19 minutes

Director: Lynn Shores. Story: Ballard MacDonald. Songs: Ballard MacDonald and Milton Schwartzwald.

CAST: Nick Lucas, Adelaide Hall, Leon Belasco, Hizi Koyke, Eddie Garr, the Bovard Sisters and Murray, Kelvin Keech, Lord Oliver Wakefield, Sam Liebert.

The first of Universal's Menotone (Vaudeville on Film) musical shorts, this two-reel musical is about a salesman who tries to get a board of directors to advertise its soap product on a radio program. Lucas appears as himself as the star of a radio show and sings "Lonely Moonlight Troubadour."

Reviews:

Motion Picture Daily: "[P]lenty of laughs."

Variety: "It employs a large and capable cast headed by Nick Lucas. While it has missed opportunities to be better than it is, entertaining capacity of the subject is sufficient to insure its favorable audience reaction.... Considerable comedy relief goes with the singing, musical and other type numbers which are worked into the short as through broadcast."

What This Country Needs
(Warner Bros.–Vitaphone, 1934) 21 minutes

Director: Roy Mack. Story: Eddie Moran and A. Dorian Otvas.
CAST: Nick Lucas, Janet Reader, The Presser Girls.

A theatrical firm that has lost all of its theaters to banks decides what the nation needs is a new type of bank, a musical one. The whole affair turns out to be a dream. Lucas sings "Tiptoe Through the Tulips," "How Can You Lose?" and "It Happened in Spain."

Reviews:

Exhibitors' opinions: "One of the best short subjects we have played.... You'll be glad you played it" and "Entertaining musical with several clever numbers."

Variety (as *The Country Needs*): "Nick Lucas gives his name to this musical, though he plays no more important a part than the others.... Silly but has some laughs and plenty of production values. Lucas croons a couple but the numbers are not outstanding. Good filler."

This Is the Life (20th Century–Fox, 1935)
63- and 67-minute versions

Associate Producer: Joseph Engel. Director: Marshall Neilan. Screenplay: Lamar Trotti and Arthur Horman. Story: Gene Towne and Graham Baker. Photography: Daniel B. Clark. Editor: Fred Allen. Music Director: David Buttolph. Songs: Sam H. Stept and Sidney Clare. Dance Stager: Fanchon. Art Directors: Duncan Cramer and Walter Koessler. Sound: W.D. Flick. Gowns: Helen Myron.

CAST: Jane Withers (Geraldine Revier), John McGuire (Michael Grant), Sally Blane (Helen Davis), Sidney Toler (Professor Lafcadio F. Breckenridge), Gloria Roy (Diane Revier), Gordon Westcott (Ed Revier), Francis Ford (Sticky Jones), Emma Dunn (Mrs. Davis), Harry C. Bradley (Minister), Emmett Vogan (Inspector), Fred Kelsey (Kansas City Police Chief), Selmer Jackson (Mr. Walters), Oscar Apfel (Department of Justice Head), Robert Graves (San Francisco Police Chief), Charles Wilson (Theater Manager), Harry Dunkinson (Mailman), James T. Mack (Doorman), Dell Henderson (Chicago Commissioner), Harrison Greene (Boy's Father), Tony Merlo (Waiter), Jack Walters (Malibu Gateman), Jack Kennedy (Denver Chief of Police), Rudolph Cameron (Booking Agent), Harry Strang (Chauffeur), Tom London, Pat O'Malley (Highway Patrolmen), J.P. McGowan, Bert Bracken, Harvey Perry, Chick Collins (Hobos).

Lucas, Fritzi Brunette, Ralf Harolde and Jayne Hovig appeared in the original version of *This Is the Life* but the film was released in various versions with running times varying from 63 to 67 minutes, so their footage were apparently deleted in some showings.

Intended to star Shirley Temple, this comedy-drama with songs has Jane Withers as an overworked vaudeville child star who befriends a man (John McGuire) who is on the run from the law for a crime he didn't commit. They end up getting involved with two hucksters (Sidney Toler, Francis Ford) before an eventual happy resolution. Sam H. Stept, Lucas' former co-writer and recording pianist, provided the lyrics for the trio of songs in the film: "I Got a New Kind of Rhythm," "Fresh from the Country" and "Sunday and Me."

Reviews:
Film Daily: "Here is a simple story stuffed with hokum, but so well directed, so well acted in every part, so well woven with pathos and belly laughs that it can't miss for popular appeal.... This picture is tailor made for the family trade."

Harrison's Reports: "Fairly good ... suitable for all."

Motion Picture Daily: "Keynoted by wholesome family appeal ... a pleasing comedy drama."

Nick Lucas and His Troubadours (Warner Bros.–Vitaphone, 1936) 9 minutes

Director: Joseph Henaberry.

CAST: Nick Lucas, Marion Wilkins and Jack Walters, Kay Kernan, Nick Lucas' Troubadours.

The second of Lucas' three Warner Bros.–Vitaphone musical shorts, this one-reel outing presents him and his band performing several tunes: "Tiptoe Through the Tulips," "Doin' the Manhattan," "Castanet," "Goody Goody," "Negre Consentida" and "Sing an Old Fashioned Song." For this one-reel entry in Vitaphone's "Melody Masters" series, filming began on February 22, 1936, at Brooklyn's Vitaphone Studios. Warner Bros. reissued it in 1938 as *Nick Lucas and His Band*.

Vitaphone Headliners (Warner Bros.–Vitaphone, 1936) 10 minutes

Directors: Roy Mack and Joseph Henaberry.

CAST: Nick Lucas, The Four Mullen Sisters, Eddie Stuart, O'Donnell and Blair.

In his final Warner Bros.–Vitaphone musical short, Lucas appears in a clown costume and sings "Broken Hearted Troubadour." The sequence was reused in the compilation short *Big Time Revue* (q.v.) 11 years later.

Review:
Motion Picture Daily: "A collection of second-rate vaudeville acts aid and hinder this piece of film to some extent by their ordinary performances and the method of presentation."

Yankee Doodle Home (Columbia, 1939) 13 minutes

Producer-Director: Arthur Dreifuss. Associate Producer: William C. Kent. Story: Sam Shayon and Buddy Burston. Photography: George Webber. Music: Al Lewis, Allie Wrubel, Al Sherman, Buddy Burston and Harry Cohan.

CAST: Nick Lucas (Nick), Vince Barnett (Vince), The Mullen Sisters (The Three Blue Notes), Fred Hillebrand (Boss), Jean Walters (Secretary), Nathaniel Shilkret and His Orchestra.

The fourth outing in Fanchon and Marco's "Music Hall Vanities" series, this one-reel short cast Lucas and Vince Barnett as songwriters fired by their boss (Fred Hillebrand) in deference to the wishes of a foreign producer. Barnett masquerades as the rival and Nick sings their composition "The Great American Home," winning them back their positions. The Mullen Sisters perform "Keep on Singing a Song" and Jean Walters sings a tune about being a good secretary.

Reviews:

Billboard: "A top-notch musical tinged with an air of patriotism by virtue of a clever song dealing with loyal Americans of foreign extraction and capably sung by Nick Lucas."

Motion Picture Herald: "[H]umorous and entertaining."

Congamania (Universal, 1940) 17 minutes

Associate Producer: Will Cowan. Director: Larry Ceballos. Dialogue: Stanley Rubin. Photography: William Sickner. Editor: Irving Birnbaum. Music Director: Charles Previn. Orchestrator: Milton Rosen. Sound: Bernard B. Brown.

CAST: Nick Lucas, Nina Orla, Jose Cansino Dancers, The Theodores, Peggy Carrol, Pepe Guizar, The Flores Brothers, Eddie Durante and His Band.

Larry Ceballos, dance director for *The Gold Diggers of Broadway* and *The Show of Shows* (qq.v.), helmed this two-reel musical, centered on the popular Conga dance fad and taking place at the Casa Longa night club. The highlight is Lucas performing "In a Little Spanish Town," a song he recorded for Brunswick Records in 1927.

Reviews:

Boxoffice: "There is a fair amount of entertainment in the form of dancing, singing, and the like."

Film Daily: "A cast of top entertainers…. The music is hot and tuneful and subject as a whole is smooth and entertaining."

Motion Picture Daily: "This is a diversified and entertaining musical that is likely to prove a strong attraction to those afflicted with the title ailment…. Nick Lucas and Eddie Durante and his orchestra are the more popular of the entertainers."

Showmen's Trade Review: "[T]he subject is lively and entertaining."

Goodnight, Wherever You Are (Soundies Corporation of America, 1944) 3 minutes

Producer-Director: William Forest Crouch.

CAST: Nick Lucas (Himself).

The setting is a broadcast studio with Lucas at the microphone performing the title song. The scenes changes a few times and two girls, a sailor and a soldier are each shown separately as they listen to the song. This was the first of Lucas' four short films for Soundies Corporation of America. They were not shown theatrically but instead on special jukeboxes. All four were later reissued on 16mm by Castle Films.

An Hour Never Passes (Soundies Corporation of America, 1944) 3 minutes

Producer-Director: William Forest Crouch.
CAST: Nick Lucas (Himself).
Lucas sings "An Hour Never Passes" to a pretty brunette as they stand on the steps in front of a house. Another couple is seen listening to the song.

Side by Side (Soundies Corporation of America, 1944) 3 minutes

Producer-Director: William Forest Crouch.
CAST: Nick Lucas (Himself).
Lucas performs "Side by Side" as he strolls around a park where several young couples are seated. They listen to Nick sing and the film ends with a close-up of him finishing the song. "Side by Side" was a best-selling record for him on Brunswick Records in 1927.

Tiptoe Through the Tulips with Me (Soundies Corporation of America, 1944) 3 minutes

Producer-Director: William Forest Crouch.
CAST: Nick Lucas (Himself).
In a garden setting at night, Lucas serenades a lovely girl on a balcony with the title song, a recreation of his hit Brunswick record from 1929. A couple is seated on a bench below the balcony; during the song, the girl dances to the music. As she finishes, the young lady from the balcony comes into the garden and dances around a tulip bed and sits on a bench with Nick as he concludes "Tiptoe Through the Tulips."
This short was included in the Castle Films compilation *Rhythm in Rhapsody*.

Big Time Revue (Warner Bros., 1947) 10 minutes

Producer: Gordon Hollingshead. Photography: Edwin DuPar. Editor: Rex Steele.
CAST: Nick Lucas, Eddie Peabody, Aunt Jemima [Tess Gardella], The Rio Brothers, Chaz Chase, Pat Rooney, Sr., Pat Rooney, Jr. (Themselves).
A "Melody Master Band" short, this one-reeler is made up of footage from earlier Vitaphone releases and was designed as a tribute to vaudeville and its famous stars. Lucas, as a Pagliacci character, appears in footage from 1936's *Vitaphone Headliners* (q.v.) singing "Broken Hearted Troubadour."
Review:
Motion Picture Daily: "[It] contrasts the vaudeville of yesteryear with that of today."

Disc Jockey (Allied Artists, 1951) 77 minutes

Producer: Maurice Duke. Director: Will Jason. Story and Screenplay: Clark E. Reynolds. Photography: Harry Neumann. Editor: Otho Lovering. Music Director: Russ Morgan. Assistant Music Director: Richard Hazard. Art Director: Dave Milton. Sound:

Tom Lambert. Assistant to Producer: Tony Roberts. Production Manager: Allen K. Wood. Set Decorator: Otto Siegel. Set Continuity: Ilona Vas. Makeup: Lou Filippi. Hair Stylist: Fritzi La Bar. Wardrobe: Courtney Haslam and Ether Krebs. Assistant Director: Edward Morey, Jr.

CAST: Ginny Simms (Vickie Peters), Tom Drake (Johnny), Jane Nigh (Marion), Michael O'Shea (Mike Richards), Jerome Cowan (Fritz Marley), Lenny Kent (Happy O'Shea), Herb Jeffries (H.J. Ball), Nick Lucas, Russ Morgan, Tommy Dorsey, Sarah Vaughan, George Shearing, The Weavers, Foy Willing and the Riders of the Purple Sage, Ben Pollack, Red Nichols, Red Norvo, Joe Venuti, Jack Fina, Vito Musso (Themselves), Gertrude Astor, Harry Tyler (Diners), Tom Dugan (Bartender), George Chandler (Public Relations Man), Tristram Coffin (Pioneer Disc Jockey), Martin Block, Paul Dixon, Ed Hubbard, Ernie Simon, Ed McKenzie, Dick Gilbert, Bill Gordon, Gil Newsome, Norman Prescott, Sherman Feller, Ed Gallagher, Larry Wilson, Paul Brenner, Doug Arthur, Les Malloy, Jimmy Murray, Bob Kennedy, Joe Allison, Paul Masterson, Bill Anson, Gene Norman, Joe Adams, Maurice Hart, Don Bell, Bob Clayton, Bruce Hayes, Bea Kalmus, Tom Mercein, Art Pallaius, Bob Poole, Fred Robbins (Disc Jockeys).

In this musical comedy, a disc jockey (Michael O'Shea) tries to keep his job by proving to a candy sponsor (Jerome Cowan) that his profession is not passé. Through his secretary's (Jane Nigh) talent agent boyfriend (Tom Drake), he meets an aspiring singer (Ginny Simms) and tries to promote her to stardom. Among his efforts on her behalf is the enlistment of several recording artists and 31 of the country's top disc jockeys. In a tribute to the early days of radio, Lucas sings "Let's Meander Through the Meadow."

Reviews:

Harrison's Reports: "The value of this picture ... will depend almost entirely on the names that appear in it and on the songs that are played and sung, for the story is very weak."

Motion Picture Daily: "[I]t delivers what is promised, a tremendous lot of music, plus a story that is adequate to the purpose of tying it all together."

Variety: "On the exploitation basis of the numerous recording artists, each of whom has his and her own followers, plus the guest appearance of 28 [sic] deejays from scattered sections of the country…[it] seems headed for tidy returns at the boxoffice."

Hollywood Without Makeup
(Filmaster Productions, 1963) 50 minutes

Producer-Photography: Ken Murray. Directors: Rudy Behlmer and Loring D'Usseau. Screenplay: Royal Foster. Additional Photography: Lew Ayres and Cary Grant. Editor: Reg Browne. Negative Editors: James Brock and Bud Thompson. Music: George Stoll. Music Editor: Robert Ives. Orchestrator: Leo Arnaud, Robert Van Epps and Albert Sendry. Music Research: Bernard Brody. Sound: Franklin Milton. Second Unit Directors: Frances Heflin, Shirley Boone, Betty Lou Murray and Helen Rackin.

CAST: Ken Murray, Eddie Albert, June Allyson, George K. Arthur, Mary Astor, Lew Ayres, Max Baer, Lucille Ball, Richard Barthelmess, Rex Bell, Edgar Bergen, Sally Blane, Humphrey Bogart, John Boles, Pat Boone, Eddie Borden, Hobart Bosworth, Clara Bow, William Boyd, Fannie Brice, Paul Brinkman, Paul Brooks, Joe E. Brown,

Johnny Mack Brown, Virginia Bruce, Rory Calhoun, Leo Carrillo, Charles Chaplin, Lew Cody, Claudette Colbert, William Collier, Jr., Russ Columbo, Gary Cooper, Jackie Cooper, Jeanne Crain, Robert Cummings, Linda Darnell, Marion Davies, Joan Davis, Olivia de Havilland, Dolores Del Rio, Cecil B. DeMille, Jack Dempsey, Walt Disney, Kirk Douglas, Marie Dressler, Josephine Dunn, Irene Dunne, Stuart Erwin, Ruth Etting, Douglas Fairbanks, Douglas Fairbanks, Jr., Charles Farrell, Todd Fisher, Errol Flynn, Joan Fontaine, Glenn Ford, Clark Gable, Maria Franklin Gable, Greta Garbo, Reginald Gardiner, Amadeo Giannini, Hoot Gibson, John Gilbert, Cary Grant, Alan Hale, Oliver Hardy, William Randolph Hearst, Van Heflin, Jean Hersholt, William Holden, Bob Hope, Hedda Hopper, Walter Huston, Sam Jaffe, Van Johnson, Buck Jones, Arthur Lake, Patricia Lake, Hope Lange, Charles Laughton, Carole Lombard, Nick Lucas, William Lundigan, Fred MacMurray, Jayne Mansfield, George Marshall, Herbert Marshall, The Marx Brothers (Chico, Groucho, Harpo), Joel McCrea, Victor McLaglen, Adolphe Menjou, Mayo Methot, Tom Mix, Marilyn Monroe, Frank Morgan, Wayne Morris, Betty Lou Murray, Janie Murray, Pamela Ann Murray, Martha O'Driscoll, Tony Owen, Jean Parker, Louella Parsons, Mary Pickford, Dick Powell, Ellen Powell, Tyrone Power, George Raft, Gregory Ratoff, Donna Reed, Debbie Reynolds, Charles "Buddy" Rogers, Charles Ruggles, Albert Schweitzer, George Seaton, Norma Shearer, George Stevens, Lewis Stone, Margaret Sullavan, Robert Taylor, William T. "Bill" Tilden, George Tobias, Tony (horse), Spencer Tracy, Helen Twelvetrees, Lupe Velez, Jimmy Wakely, John Wayne, Johnny Weissmuller, Mae West, Claire Windsor, Robert Woolsey, Jane Wyman (Themselves).

A compilation of home movie footage shot mostly by Ken Murray, augmented by footage from other private collections, including those of Lew Ayres and Cary Grant. Lucas is seen briefly with Murray in footage shot at Paramount in 1931 as they watch a go-kart race between Jackie Cooper and Groucho and Harpo Marx that is officiated by Carole Lombard and Charles Laughton.

The Great Gatsby (Paramount, 1974) 144 minutes

Producer: David Merrick. Associate Producer: Hank Moonjean. Director: Jack Clayton. Screenplay: Francis Ford Coppola, from the novel by F. Scott Fitzgerald. Photography: Douglas Slocombe. Editor: Tom Priestley. Music: Nelson Riddle. Art Directors: Robert Laing and Eugene Rudolf.

CAST: Robert Redford (Jay Gatsby), Mia Farrow (Daisy Buchanan), Bruce Dern (Tom Buchanan), Karen Black (Myrtle Wilson), Scott Wilson (George Wilson), Sam Waterston (Nick Carraway), Lois Chiles (Jordan Baker), Howard Da Silva (Meyer Wolfsheim), Roberts Blossom (Mr. Gatz), Edward Herrmann (Klipspringer), Elliott Sullivan (Wilson's Friend), John Devlin (Gatsby's Bodyguard), Tom Ewell (Mourner), Janet and Louise Arters (Twins).

Lavish, but somewhat dull, screen adaptation of F. Scott Fitzgerald's novel, filmed previously in 1926 and 1949. This drama, a nice recreation of Long Island society in the Roaring Twenties, centers on a rich man (Robert Redford) who has everything he wants except the woman (Mia Farrow) he loves. To add authenticity to the music score (which won an Academy Award), Lucas (uncredited) sang "When You and I Were Seventeen." He also performed "Five Foot Two, Eyes of Blue" and "I'm Gonna Charleston

Back to Charleston" on the film's soundtrack album. Although critically panned, *The Great Gatsby* grossed $14.2 million.

The Day of the Locust (Paramount, 1974) 144 minutes

Producer: Jerome Hellman. Associate Producer–Unit Production Manager: Sheldon Schrager. Director: John Schlesinger. Screenplay: Waldo Salt, from the novel by Nathanael West. Photography: Conrad Hall. Editor: Jim Clark. Music: John Barry. Art Director: John Lloyd. Sound: Tommy Overton. Production Designer: Richard MacDonald. Costumes: Ann Roth. Special Effects: Tim Smyth. Sets: George Hopkins. Special Photographic Effects: Albert Whitlock. Makeup: Del Armstrong. Hair Stylist: Lynn Del. Gaffer: Richard Martens. Wardrobe: Robert de Mora and Tony Scaano. Key Grip: Danny Jordan. Property Master: Allan Gordon. Stunt Coordinator: Phil Adams. Script Supervisor: Karen Wookey. Production Associate: Michael Childers. Dance Supervisor: Marge Champion. Assistant Director: Tim Zinneman.

CAST: Karen Black (Faye), Donald Sutherland (Homer), Burgess Meredith (Harry), William Atherton (Tod), Geraldine Page (Big Sister), Richard A. Dysart (Claude Estee), Bo Hopkins (Earl Shoop), Pepe Serna (Miguel), Lelia Goldoni (Mary Dove), Billy Barty (Adore), Gloria LeRoy (Mrs. Loomis), Jane Hoffman (Mrs. Oldlesh), Norman Leavitt (Mr. Oldlesh), Madge Kennedy (Mrs. Johnson), Natalie Schafer (Audrey Jennings), Nita Talbot (Joan), Gloria Strook (Alice Estee), Alvin Childress (Butler), Angela Greene, Byron Paul, Abbey Greshler, Roger Price, Virginia Baker, Robert Oliver Ragland (Guests), Gyl Roland, Ann Coleman (Girls), Paul Stewart (Helverston), John Hillerman (Ned Grote), William Castle (Director), David Ladd, Dennis Dugan, Robert Pine, Jerry Fogel (Apprentices), Paul Jabara (Entertainer), Bill Baldwin (Announcer), Dick Powell, Jr. (Dick Powell), Nicholas Cortland (Projectionist), Ina Gould, Florence Lake (Lee Sisters), Margaret Willey, John War Eagle (The Gingos), Fred Scheiweiller, Wally Rose (Assistant Directors), Grainger Hines (French Lieutenant), De Forest Covan (Shoe Shine Boy), Michael Quinn (Major Domo), Bob Holt (Tour Guide), Queenie Smith (Palsied Woman), Margaret Jenkins (Choral Director), Jonathan Kidd (Mortician), Kenny Solms (Chapel Boy), Wally Berns (Theater Manager), Nick Lucas, Louis Armstrong, Lotte Lehmann, Pamela Myers, Jimmie Grier and His Orchestra, Grey Gordon and His Toc Toc Rhythm, Michael Dees (Musical Artists).

This R-rated melodrama of Hollywood in the 1930s tells of the futile career attempt of a young starlet (Karen Black) and how a studio artist (William Atherton) seeks her affections. As in *The Great Gatsby* (q.v.), Lucas recreates the era, this time with his rendition of "I Wished on the Moon," heard via radio. Burgess Meredith was nominated for an Academy Award as Best Supporting Actor for his performance as Black's father, a vaudevillian who never made it to the top.

Review:

Los Angeles Times: "Few movies, ever, are such obvious and sustained labors of love. The logistics are mind-boggling, and no expense was spared. It is almost embarrassing to be unable to react more enthusiastically to a film for which such hopes seemed possible. With its flaws, it is a better and more admirable film than most. In the end, its patient, painstaking, accurate literality is the film's undoing. *The Day of the Locust* was an assertion of style; the movie is a recreation."

Hearts of the West (MGM, 1975) 102 minutes

Producer: Tony Bill. Director: Howard Zieff. Screenplay: Rob Thompson. Photography: Mario Tosi. Editor: Edward Warchilka. Music: Ken Lauber. Music Editor: Bill Saracino. Art Director: Robert Luthardt.

CAST: Jeff Bridges (Lewis Tater), Andy Griffith (Howard Pike), Donald Pleasence (A.J. Neitz), Blythe Danner (Miss Trout), Alan Arkin (Kessler), Richard B. Shull (Fat Man), Herbert Edelman (Polo), Alex Rocco (Earl), Frank Cady (Pa Tater), Anthony James (Lean Man), Burt Gilliam (Lester), Matt Clark (Jackson), Candy Azzara (Waitress), Marie Windsor (Nevada Hotel Clerk), Dub Taylor (Ticket Agent), Anthony Holland (Beach Guest), Jane Dulo (Mrs. Stern), Nick Lucas, Merle Travis, Roger Patterson (Musical Artists).

A very pleasant nostalgic comedy, *Hearts of the West* tells the story of low-budget Western moviemaking by Poverty Row film companies in the 1930s. Jeff Bridges plays a struggling young writer who comes to Hollywood and becomes involved with the lower strata of filmmaking and becomes a star. Andy Griffith gives a superb performance as a has-been cowboy movie hero. Again Lucas' vocals are used to revive the 1930s and on the soundtrack he sings the film's title theme, "I'll See You in My Dreams," plus "Happy Days Are Here Again," "Ja Da," "My Blue Heaven," "Wang Wang Blues" and "We'll Make Hay While the Sun Shines."

Zelig (Orion Pictures, 1983) 79 minutes

Producer: Robert Greenhut. Executive Producer: Jack Rollins. Associate Producers: Charles H. Jaffe and Michael Peyser. Director-Screenplay: Woody Allen. Photography: Gordon Willis. Editor: Susan E. Morse. Music: Dick Hyman. Music Recording Engineer: Roy B. Yokelson. Art Director: Speed Hopkins. Sound: Marjorie Deutsch. Set Decorators: Les Bloom and Janet Rosenbloom. Production Designer: Mel Bourne. Costumes: Santo Loquasto. Makeup: Fern Buchner. Production Manager: Michael Peyser. Unit Manager: Ezr Swerdlow.

CAST: Woody Allen (Leonard Zelig), Mia Farrow (Dr. Eudora Nesbitt Fletcher), Garrett Brown (Actor Zelig), Sol Lomita (Martin Geist), Mary Louise Wilson (Sister Ruth), Stephanie Farrow (Meryl Fletcher), Dimitri Vassilopoulos (Martinez), John Buckwalter (Dr. Sindell), Paul Nevens (Dr. Brisky), Michael Jeter, Gale Hansen (Freshmen), Peter McRobbie (Rally Speaker), Will Holt (Rally Chancellor), Deborah Rush (Lita Fox), Jeanine Jackson (Helen Gray), Bernie Herold (Carter Dean), Sharon Ferrol (Miss Baker), Richard Litt (Charles Koslow), Edward McPhillips (Scotsman), Marvin Chatinover, Stanley Swerlove, Howard Erskine, George Hamlin, Will Hussong, Richard Whiting, Ralph Bell (Doctors). Eli Resnik (Man in Park), Robert Iglesis (Barber Customer), Ed Herlihy (Pathe News Announcer's Voice), Patrick Hogan (Narrator).

Using vintage newsreels and records, director-writer-star Woody Allen fashioned a tongue-in-cheek look at the fad-crazy Roaring Twenties and plays a character who becomes a national idol by associating with the famous, via archive footage. Among the recordings used to recreate the era is Lucas' 1930 rendition of "I'll Get By," which is wrongly listed on the film's credits as by Ben Bernie.

Fragments: Surviving Pieces of Lost Films
(Flicker Alley, 2011) 110 minutes

Producers: Randy Haberkamp and Jeffry Masino. Editors: Pat Fitzgerald and Daniel Brantley. Music-Sound: Michael Mortilla. Archive Footage: Tommy Jose Stather.

CAST: Mike Mashon, Michael Pogrzelsi, Heather Linville (Hosts).

This documentary presents surviving clips from silent and early sound productions otherwise lost. Lucas appears in the two reels from *The Gold Diggers of Broadway*.

Radio

Lucas either starred or was a recurring regular to the following radio programs. Songs performed by him are given for some broadcasts.

Brunswick Hour of Music (WGN, Chicago, 1928–29)

Lucas was one of several Brunswick recording artists featured in this half-hour weekly program that debuted on February 9, 1928. Other performers heard on the series were bandleaders Vincent Lopez and Ben Bernie along with Al Jolson, Marion Harris and Lee Sims.

RKO Hour (NBC, 1929)

Lucas made regular appearances on this Tuesday night one-hour program that featured Leo Reisman's orchestra.

January 21, 1929: The Song I Love/How About Me?
September 3, 1929: Kiss in the Garden

Brunswick Brevities (syndicated, 1929–30)

This 30-minute program was made up of transcribed Brunswick recordings and featured a different star each week. Its 26 episodes appeared on 32 radio stations nationwide. Lucas was one of the Brunswick artists participating in the series along with Al Jolson, Belle Baker, Ray Miller, Zelma O'Neal, Mario Chamlee and the orchestras of Ben Bernie, Hal Kemp, Red Nichols and Abe Lyman. The series was broadcast from August 1929 to May 1930.

RKO Theatre of the Air (NBC, 1930–32)

A follow-up to *RKO Hour*, this series was hosted by William Hanley and featured star performers who played the Keith-Orpheum vaudeville circuit.

December 5, 1930: Three Little Words/You're Driving Me Crazy
February 6, 1931: Napoli/Hello Beautiful/You Didn't Have to Tell Me

June 26, 1931: When the Moon Comes Over the Mountain/I Surrender Dear/It Must Be True
August 28, 1931: I Can't Write the Words/Picking the Guitar
January 15, 1932: Have You Forgotten Waikiki/Isle of Golden Dreams
February 5, 1932: You're My Everything/While We Danced at the Mardi Gras
July 11, 1932: Give Her a Kiss for Me/When You're Alone Try to Remember Me
July 18, 1932: The Song Is Ended/All of Me

The Ludwig Baumann Hour (NBC, 1930–32)

Lucas was a regular guest artist on this one-hour variety program along with Ruth Etting, Russ Columbo, the Mills Brothers, Gus Van, the Boswell Sisters, Vaughn De Leath, George Jessel, Will Osborne, Everett Marshall and Georgie Price.
November 30, 1930: Thinking of You, Dear/Here Comes the Sun

Nick Lucas (NBC, 1931–32)

Nick Lucas headlined this 15-minute music program that was broadcast nationally on NBC, originating on station WEAF in New York City. The show was done mainly on Wednesday, Thursday and Saturday nights at 7 p.m. and was sponsored by Campbell Soup. Freddie Rich and His Orchestra provided musical accompaniment. The series was broadcast from August 31, 1931, to January 31, 1932, and its theme song was "Lady, Play Your Mandolin."

September 2, 1931: It's the Girl/Parisian Lover/My Best Girl/Why Did It Have to Be Me?
September 6, 1931: There's a Ring Around the Moon/Without You/Lady Luck/Just Between the Two of Us
September 16, 1931: Blue Lady/Guilty/Don't Be Mad at Me/My Blue Heaven
September 17, 1931: Each Little Kiss/You're My Only Sweetheart/Honey Baby/Lady, Play Your Mandolin
December 3, 1931: You Didn't Know the Music/Say It Again
January 16, 1932: I'm Only Guessin'/Starlight/Just So/High, High, High Up in the Hills
January 23, 1932: Mary, I Love You/Oh, What a Thrill/Kiss by Kiss

Nick Lucas (KOB, Albuquerque, New Mexico, 1932–1933)

A 15-minute series made up of Lucas recordings.

Nick Lucas (CBS, 1934–35)

In his second starring network radio program, Lucas appeared on CBS with broadcasts originating on station WABC in New York City. The quarter-hour episodes were on each Wednesday at 11 p.m. and Friday at 6:30 p.m., later changed to 7 p.m. In early July, the show was on Monday at 7:15 p.m. while remaining in its Wednesday 11 p.m. slot. Freddie Rich and His Orchestra provided the background music. The show debuted on March 21, 1934, and ran until June 16, 1935. An asterisk (*) denotes songs performed by Freddie Rich and His Orchestra.

- March 21, 1934: Let's Fall in Love/Old Spinning Wheel/You Oughta Be in Pictures/Smoke Gets in Your Eyes/Tiptoe Through the Tulips/In a Kitchenette/Painting the Clouds with Sunshine
- March 28, 1934: Over Somebody Else's Shoulder/Champagne Waltz/Waiting at the Gate for Katie/Love Locked Out/Siboney
- March 30, 1934: Over Somebody Else's Shoulder/Champagne Waltz/Waiting at the Gate for Katie*/Love Locked Out/Siboney
- April 6, 1934: Lady, Play Your Mandolin/Carioca/In a Shelter from a Shower/A Thousand Goodnights/A Cup of Coffee, a Sandwich and You
- April 11, 1934: Play to Me, Gypsy/If I Love Again/I Hate Myself/Ill Wind/Singing in the Rain
- April 13, 1934: Lady, Play Your Mandolin (Theme)/Orchids in the Moonlight/Emaline/Butterfingers*/Boulevard of Broken Dreams/Bye Bye Blackbird
- April 20, 1934: Lady, Play Your Mandolin/Neighbors/Somebody Cares for You/As Long as I Live/Goin' To Heaven on a Mule/I'm Looking at the World Thru Rose Colored Glasses
- April 25, 1934: You Oughta Be in Pictures/Carry Me Back to the Lone Prairie/Your Love/Cocktails for Two/Paradise
- April 27, 1934: There Goes My Heart/I Wonder Who's with You Tonight?/Nasty Man/Little Dutch Mill/Marcheta
- May 1, 1934: Carioca/Your Love/Love Thy Neighbor/Painting the Clouds with Sunshine
- May 4, 1934: I've Had My Moments/Champagne Waltz/Let's Dress for Dinner/Why Do I Dream These Dreams?/Spain
- May 6, 1934: Old Covered Bridge/She Reminds Me of You/How Do I Know It's Saturday*/Play to Me, Gypsy/O Sole Mio
- May 9, 1934: Old Water Mill/How Do I Know It's Saturday?/Why Don't You Practice What You Preach?/A Thousand Goodnights/Home on the Range
- May 11, 1934: Pagan Love Song
- May 16, 1934: Over Somebody Else's Shoulder/Prairie Lullaby/Let's Dress For Dinner/Little Dutch Mill/I Love You
- May 18, 1934: I Ain't Lazy, I'm Just Dreaming/Little Man, You've Had a Busy Day/Just a Perfect Night for Love/Love Your Neighbor/The Last Roundup
- May 20, 1934: Hold My Hand/Why Didn't I Sleep Last Night?/Baby Take a Bow*/Carry Me Back to the Lone Prairie/You're a Real Sweetheart
- May 23, 1934: Call of the Rockies/Love Me/Because It's Love*/Goodnight, Lovely Little Lady/The Song Is Ended
- May 25, 1934: Lady, Play Your Mandolin/Fair and Warmer/No More Heartaches, No More Tears/Broadway's Gone Hill Billy*/Cocktails for Two/Among My Souvenirs
- May 27, 1934: Call of the Rockies/Love Me/Goodnight, Lovely Lady/The Song Is Ended

June 1, 1934: Fair and Warmer/When a Woman Loves a Man/Fare Thee Well/Let's Dress for Dinner/You're My Everything
June 2, 1934: I Wish I Were Twins/How Can't It Be a Beautiful Day?/I'm Glad I Waited*/I'll String Along with You/Moonbeam, Kiss Her for Me
June 13, 1934: I've Had My Moments/Don't Let Your Love Go Wrong/So Help Me/Side by Side/My Dear*
June 15, 1934: Fare Thee Well/Mission Bells at Sundown/Everything Is Peaches Neath the Old Apple Tree/Boulevard of Broken Dreams/Who
June 18, 1934: Au Revoir/Thank You for a Lovely Evening/Hots Dogs and Sarsaparilla*/As Far as I'm Concerned/When You Were the Blossom of Buttercup Lane and I Was Your Little Boy Blue
June 20, 1934: Hold My Hand/Mighty Thankful/Why Don't You Practice What You Preach?/When a Woman Loves a Man/In a Kitchenette
June 22, 1934: All I Do Is Dream of You/It Doesn't Cost a Thing to Dream/Swing on Mississippi*/Over Somebody Else's Shoulder/Sleepy Time Gal
June 24, 1934: I'm Dancing with the Girl of My Dreams/As Far as I'm Concerned/So Help Me*/Little Dutch Mill/In a Little Spanish Town
June 27, 1934: Yes Sir, I Love Your Daughter/Your Love/I Got a Warm Spot in My Heart for You*/Sleepy Head/I'll Get By
June 29, 1934: I've Had My Moments/Love Me/My Dear/So Help Me/Side by Side
July 3, 1934: Hey, Sailor/Easy Come, Easy Go/A Little Church Around the Corner/Without That Certain Thing/America, I Love You
July 11, 1934: Dancing, Dreaming/Spellbound/Steak and Potatoes*/Cocktails For Two/I Want to Go Where You Go
July 23, 1934: Fare Thee Well/I Never Had a Chance/How's About Tomorrow Night?/Sleepy Head/Walking My Baby Back Home
July 25, 1934: Moonlight Parade/Straight from the Shoulder/Kissing Games/And I Still Do/So Blue
August 1, 1934: Take a Lesson from the Lark/Nothing Ever Happens to Me/What's Mine Is Yours*/With My Eyes Wide Open I'm Dreaming
August 4, 1934: My Hat's on the Side of My Head/Sweet Organ Man/So/I Only Have Eyes for You/Oh, Marie
August 15, 1934: Straight from the Shoulder/I'd Give Anything Under the Sun/The Moon Was Yellow/Did You Ever See a Dream Walking?/La Cucaracha*
August 20, 1934: Lone Prairie/Mission Bells at Sundown/Then I'll Be Tired of You/Siboney
August 22, 1934: Pardon My Southern Accent/Don't You Remember Me?/Love in Bloom*/For All We Know/The Very Thought of You
August 25, 1934: What's Mine Is Yours/Many Thanks for the Dance/Nothing Ever Happens to Me/Just Like a Melody Out of the Sky
August 26, 1934: I Saw the Stars/New England in the Rain/What's Mine Is Yours*/Dust on the Moon/By the Light of the Stars
August 29, 1934: Take a Lesson from the Lark/Moonglow/She Never Knew He Lived Next Door*/Love in Bloom/Stardust
September 5, 1934: I'm Hummin', I'm Whistlin', I'm Singin'/I'm Lonesome for You, Caroline/Dust on the Moon/I Only Have Eyes for You/Toot Toot Tootsie

September 9, 1934: So You're Not Gonna Kiss Me/Butterfly/I Saw Stars/Street Organ Man/No, No Nora

September 12, 1934: I'm in Love/I'm Sorry I Lost You/The Lights Are Low*/The Moon Was Yellow/Japanese Sandman

September 26, 1934: Yearning/Stars Fell on Alabama/Lonesome for You, Caroline/Lady, Play Your Mandolin

January 30, 1935: After All/When the Church Bells Toll/Isle of Capri/Go Home and Tell Your Mother

February 21, 1935: After All/Solitude/It's Unbelievable/My Dream Is in My Arms/Mary Lou

March 7, 1935: Fare Thee Well, Annabelle/I'm Lost for Words/I'm Keeping Those Keepsakes You Gave Me/I Got a Kick Out of You/Gypsy Fiddles

Columbia Variety Hour (CBS, 1934–35)

In addition to his 15-minute CBS program, Lucas was also a regular on the network's mid-afternoon Tuesday program *Columbia Variety Hour*, along with the orchestras of Freddie Rich and Mark Warnow. Also featured were Loretta Lee, Vera Van, Johnny Green and Fray and Braggiotti.

Nick Lucas and His Orchestra (CBS, 1936)

In 1936, Nick Lucas and His Troubadours did a 15-minute CBS series that featured vocalist Mimi Rollins. It was broadcast three times a week from the Hollywood Café in New York City, from January into April, then twice a week (Wednesday, Saturday) until the end of the year.

April 8, 1936: Doin' the Manhattan (Instrumental)/Cling to Me/You (Mimi Rollins)/There's Always a Happy Ending/Play It, Mr. Charlie (Guitar Solo)/I'll Stand By/Mutiny in the Park (Mimi Rollins)/I Want to Go Where You Go (Guitar Solo)/My Blue Heaven

Watch the Fun Go By (CBS, 1937–38/NBC, 1938–39)

Lucas was a regular vocalist on this 30-minute CBS variety program sponsored by the Ford Motor Company. It was broadcast each Tuesday night during 1937–38 and on Monday night the next season when it became *Al Pearce and His Gang* on NBC, sponsored by Grape Nuts cereal. Other regulars were Arlene Harris, Bill Comstock, Monroe Upton and the Larry Marsh and Carl Hoff orchestras. Lucas left the cast on April 27, 1937, for a three-month tour, and returned on January 11, 1938.

May 4, 1937: Was It Rain?
July 20, 1937: We Can't Go on Like This
August 17, 1937: First Time I Met You
August 24, 1937: Til the Clock Strikes Three

September 21, 1937: The Lady Who Couldn't Be Kissed
February 20, 1939: Bye Bye Blackbird

Nick Lucas Sings (syndicated, 1937–1939)

This 15-minute program was made up of electrical transcription recordings. Among the stations carrying the program were KFYO in Lubbock, Texas, KPDN in Pampa, Texas, KRBC in Abilene, Texas, KRLH in Odessa, Texas, KROW in Oakland, California, KSUB in Cedar City, Utah, WBAX in Wilkes-Barre, Pennsylvania, WGRM in Grenada, Mississippi, KLD in Ogden, Utah, WSIX in Nashville, Tennessee, and WJJD in Madison, Wisconsin.

Nick Lucas (Australian Broadcasting Commission, 1939)

While appearing in Australia in 1939, Lucas starred in this 6 a.m. radio program broadcast weekdays for several weeks. Its theme song was "Good Morning," a song he recorded at the time for Regal Zonophone. The program originated from 3LO Broadcasting Station in Melbourne.

September 20, 1939: Wishing/Music, Maestro, Please/Mexicali Rose

Lucas appeared regularly on several other radio programs while in Melbourne, including *After Dinner Show* and *All Star Variety*, along with shows featuring the bands of Harry Bloom and Jim Davidson. He also appeared on radio programs while working the Tivoli theatres in Brisbane and Sydney.

Nick Lucas (Mutual-Don Lee, 1940)

This 15-minute series broadcast over station KORE in Eugene, Oregon, among others, was probably radio transcriptions.

Nick Lucas—Voice of Memory (CJRC, Winnipeg, Ontario, Canada, 1942–1943)

Broadcast in 1942 and 1943, this 15-minute series was radio transcriptions made in Toronto for Masons United Advertising Agency. The program was syndicated on 47 stations throughout Canada.

Nick Lucas Show (CKCO, Ottawa, Canada, 1944–1945)

Broadcast over Ottawa's radio station CKCO, this musical program was on the air from March 1944 to February 1945, weekdays from 9:45 to 10 a.m. It was probably made up of the Masons' transcription recordings.

Nick Lucas (Mutual-Don Lee, 1945)

A second Mutual–Don Lee 15-minute series by Lucas was broadcast over station KORE in Eugene, Oregon; again, probably radio transcriptions.

Program Themes (syndicated, 1946)

Lucas recorded the songs "Start with a Whistle in the Morning," "Let's Start Off the Day Right," "I Wish You a Happy Birthday," "Let's Make Every Day Mother's Day" and "Let's Be on Time for Dinner Tonight" for this five-minute series, made by the W.E. Long Company of Chicago. The tunes were used to introduce shows on the 400 radio stations that purchased them.

The Nick Lucas Show (Teleways Radio Transcriptions, 1949)

A 15-minute, five-days-a-week syndicated series with Lucas introducing and performing hit songs of the past recorded on electrical transcriptions. Among the stations carrying the program was WFOW in Madison, Wisconsin, in 1950.

Saturday Night at the Shamrock (ABC, 1951) 30 minutes

In 1951, Lucas headlined this musical program telecast from the Shamrock Hotel in Austin, Texas.

February 17, 1951: Seems Like Old Times/Get Out Those Old Records/I'm Looking Over a Four Leaf Clover/My Melancholy Baby/Bye Bye Blackbird/Tiptoe Through the Tulips

Nick Lucas Show (KWIN, Medford, Oregon, 1953)

Broadcast Monday through Friday from 4:30 to 4:45 p.m., this musical program was on the air in the fall of 1953 and was probably made up of radio transcriptions.

* * *

The following is a select list of radio programs on which Lucas appeared; in some cases, the songs he performed are listed. From 1924 until 1981, Lucas was on hundreds of national and local radio programs:

(July 29, 1924–February 24, 1925; WEBH, Chicago, Illinois) [numerous appearances]
Chicago Theatre Revue Radio Artists Night (December 13, 1924; WMAQ, Chicago)
Nick Lucas, Guitar and Songs (March 11, 13 and 15, 1925; WJZ, New York City)
The Home Electric Company Program (April 7, 1925; WIAS, Burlington, Massachusetts)

Nick Lucas, Guitar (May 12, 1925; WNYC, New York City)
Nick Lucas, Guitar and Songs (May 13–May 25, 1925; WJZ, New York City)
Nick Lucas, Guitar and Songs (May 19 and 20, 1925; WEAF, New York City)
Indianapolis Radio Exposition (September 20, 1925; WFBM, Indianapolis, Indiana)
Nick Lucas, Tenor & Guitar (February 15, 1926; WJZ, New York City)
Nick Lucas (November 8, 1926; BBC, London, England)
Nick Lucas, Guitar & Songs (January 29, 1927; WEAF, New York City)
Rivoli Theatre Broadcast (March 8, 1927; WFBR, Chicago)
Majestic Theatre Hour (May 16, 1927; CBS)
Nick Lucas (August 12, 1927; KGO, Oakland, California)
Nick Lucas, Strumming Troubadour (September 16, 1927; KGO, Oakland, California)
Nick Lucas (September 23, 1927; KGO, Oakland, California)
Nick Lucas (December 19 and 21, 1927; WMBS, Harrisburg, Pennsylvania)
Indianapolis Radio Reference Fund (March 1, 1928; WFBM, Indianapolis, Indiana)
Grand Ole Opry (1928; WSM, Nashville, Tennessee) [several shows]
Nick Lucas (March 5 and 6, 1928; WSM, Nashville, Tennessee)
Nick Lucas, the Crooning Troubadour (September 4, 1928; WSM, Nashville, Tennessee)
Nick Lucas (October 1, 9 and 11, 1928; WFAA, Dallas, Texas)
Nick Lucas, the Crooning Troubadour (March 4, 1929; N.S.W. Broadcasting, 2SKY, Sydney, Australia) [recordings]
Nick Lucas, Crooning Troubadour (May 9, 1929; KFI, Los Angeles, California)
Nick Lucas (July 12, 1929; WMCA, New York City): Tiptoe Through the Tulips/Painting the Clouds with Sunshine
Nick Lucas, Recording Artist (February 21, 1930; WFBM, Indianapolis, Indiana)
Nick Lucas, the Crooning Troubadour (March 21, 1930; WCAU, Philadelphia, Pennsylvania)
Nick Lucas (April 22 and 23, 1930; WRAW, Reading, Pennsylvania)
Philco Radio Hour (August 14, 1930; CBS)
Wise Shoe Program (September 23, 1930; CBS)
Nestle's Chocolateers (November 7, 1930; NBC): Three Little Words/Picking the Guitar/Maybe It's Love
Major Bowes' Capitol Family (November 20, 1930; NBC): Lady, Play Your Mandolin
Major Bowes' Capitol Family (December 13, 1930; NBC)
Chase and Sanborn Hour (January 4, 1931; NBC): When You Were the Blossom of Buttercup Lane and I Was Your Little Boy Blue/You're Driving Me Crazy/Lady, Play Your Mandolin/For You
Vitality Personalities (April 26, 1931; CBS)
Vitality Personalities (August 28, 1931; CBS): That's My Desire/Tiptoe Through the Tulips
Nick Lucas (December 17, 1931; WEAF, New York City): One More Kiss and Good Night
Christmas Season Songs (December 23, 1931; NBC)
Voice of Broadway with Louis Sobol (January 31, 1932; WOR)
Dea Cole Second Anniversary Program (April 13, 1932; WLW, Cincinnati, Ohio)

Nick Lucas, Crooner (May 1, 1932; KMOX, St. Louis, Missouri)
Nick Lucas (June 22, 1932; KYA, Santa Rosa, California)
Adela Rogers Hyland interview (July 1932; NBC)
Nick Lucas, the Crooning Troubadour (August 5, 1932; KWWG, Brownsville, Texas)
Nick Lucas, Tenor & Guitarist (August 25, 1932; NBC)
The Weekend Hour (August 26, 1932; CBS): Tiptoe Through the Tulips/Marcheta
Nick Lucas, Songs (November 4, 1932; WBBC, Brooklyn, New York)
Nick Lucas (January 7, 1933; KOB, Albuquerque, New Mexico)
Hal Kemp's Parade of Melodies (April 29, 1933; CBS)
Nick Lucas, Guest Artist (April 30, 1933; WGN, Chicago, Illinois)
Columbia University Glee Club (June 12, 1933; WOR, New York City)
Fire Department Benefit Show (November 18, 1933; WBAX, Wilkes-Barre, Pennsylvania)
Nick Lucas (November 25, 1933; CBS)
Voice of Columbia (June 2, 1934; CBS): Siboney
Columbia Variety Hour (November 19, 1934; CBS)
Keep Smiling (December 18, 1934; KREG, Santa Ana, California): Marcheta/I'm Waiting for Ship That Never Come In
Kate Smith New-Star Revue (January 7, 1935; CBS)
Stoopnagle and Budd (March 15, 1935; CBS): Isle of Capri
Detroit Federation of Musicians' Thanksgiving Ball (November 29, 1935; WJBK, Detroit, Michigan)
Shell Chateau (January 30, 1937; NBC): Serenade in the Night/Hits Medley
Buddy Clark Program (November 11, 1937; CBS)
Jack Oakie's College (November 30, 1937; CBS)
Theatre Stars (March 2, 1938; CKRC, Winnipeg, Manitoba, Canada)
Nick Lucas Songs (March 3, 1938; CBS)
(March 21, 1938; WCKY, Cincinnati, Ohio): Tiptoe Through the Tulips
Spunkey's Super Hits (April 20, 1938; KFRO, Longview, Texas): Chiquita
Hal Kemp's Parade of Melodies (April 29, 1938; CBS)
Rudy Vallee's Royal Gelatin Hour (1939; NBC)
Interview with Nick Lucas (August 12, 1939; Australian Broadcasting Commission, 3AR, Melbourne, Australia)
(September 4, 1939; Australian Broadcasting Commission, 2BL, Melbourne, Australia)
All Star Variety (September 6, 1939; Australian Broadcasting Commission, 2FC, Melbourne, Australia)
Nick Lucas, Guitarist (September 13, 1939; Australian Broadcasting Commission, 3AR, Melbourne, Australia)
(November 3, 1939; Australian Broadcasting Commission; Sydney, Australia)
Kraft Music Hall (1941; NBC): Maria Elena
Remember (1943; Mutual): Side by Side/Tiptoe Through the Tulips
Service Serenade (January 1944; WXYZ, Detroit/Michigan Network)
(July 21, 1944; WABC, New York City): Tiptoe Through the Tulips/Side by Side
Welcome Home (December 25, 1944; WEBR, Buffalo, New York)
Mother's Day Tribute (May 11, 1945; WEBR, Buffalo, New York)

Showtime (October 14, 1945; WFAA, Dallas, Texas): Painting the Clouds with Sunshine/It's a Beautiful Day
Roundup Time (circa 1946; syndicated): Be My Life's Companion/Side by Side
Hobby Lobby (May 30, 1946; CBS): I'm Looking Over a Four Leaf Clover/Among My Souvenirs/My Blue Heaven/Tiptoe Through the Tulips/Bye Bye Blackbird/Seems Like Old Times
Vaudeville Isn't Dead (October 23, 1946; WNEW, New York City)
Time on My Hands (December 11, 1946; KDYL, Salt Lake City, Utah)
Eddie Albert (July 2, 1947; ABC): Tiptoe Through the Tulips/I'm Looking at the World Thru Rose Colored Glasses
All Star Western Theatre (April 3, 1948; syndicated): Seems Like Old Times/I'm Looking Over a Four Leaf Clover/Among My Souvenirs/Bye Bye Blackbird/Tiptoe Through the Tulips
All Star Western Theatre (June 12, 1948; syndicated)
Song Shop (December 10, 1950, NBC)
Jane Pickens (1952; NBC): Love Thy Neighbor
The Joe Reichman Show (July 28, 1952; WFAA, Dallas, Texas): Tiptoe Through the Tulips
The Joe Reichman Show (November 1952; WFAA, Dallas, Texas) [five appearances]
Bud's Bandwagon (April 13, 1953; syndicated): Side by Side
The Jim Hawthorne Show (April 30, 1953; KNX, Los Angeles, California): Lady Be Good/Painting the Clouds with Sunshine
The Jimmy Wakely Show (April 6, 1958; CBS)
Turn Back the Clock (1958–60; syndicated) [31 programs]
The Andy and Virginia Show (December 23, 1958; syndicated)
Chester Unlimited (January 6, 1967; KNX, Los Angeles, California)
Whatever Became Of…? (1968; syndicated)
The Great Old Days of Radio (August 25, 1968; KABC, Los Angeles, California): Tiptoe Through the Tulips/Mexicali Rose/Margie
The Wally George Show (1970s, KIEV, Los Angeles) [numerous appearances]
The Robert Q. Lewis Show (April 4, 1972; KFI, Los Angeles, California)
The Sam Yorty Show (1973–75, KGBS, Los Angeles) [numerous appearances]
The Bert Nelson Show (November 1979, Melbourne, Australia)
The Carolyn Churchman Show (May 1980; WFBM; Indianapolis, Indiana)
America's Popular Music (Information Unknown): Bye Bye Blackbird/Painting the Clouds with Sunshine
G.I. Jive (information unknown): Side by Side
Keeper (information unknown): Lady Be Good

Television

The following is a selected list of Lucas' television appearances, followed by the song(s) he performed. Between 1939 and 1981, Lucas appeared on scores of local and national TV shows.

Experimental broadcast (May 31, 1939; Station W2XBS [NBC], New York City)
The Ken Murray Show (January 7, 1950; CBS)
The Toast of the Town (January 1950; CBS)
Music in the Morgan Manner (July 15, 1950; ABC)
The Kate Smith Show (May 25, 1951; NBC)
Carl Cotner and Gang (June 10, 1952; KTTV-TV, Los Angeles, California)
You Asked for It (1952; ABC-TV): Seems Like Old Times/Tiptoe Through the Tulips/ Painting the Clouds with Sunshine/My Melancholy Baby/Bye Bye Blackbird
Von Sheridan's Guest Book (August 1, 1952; WFAA-TV, Dallas, Texas)
The Narcotics Pushers (1953; Wigmar Productions; pilot episode)
The Paul Coates Show (January 9, 1953; KNXT-TV, Hollywood California)
The Gypsy (May 5, 1953; KTLA-TV, Los Angeles, California)
Ladies' Choice (July 28, 1953; WFAA-TV, Dallas, Texas)
The Bandstand Review (February 13, 1954; KTLA-TV, Los Angeles, California)
The Liberace Show (1954; syndicated): Tiptoe Through the Tulips
Hollywood's Best (January 8, 1955; KRCA-TV, Hollywood, California)
Hollywood's Best (June 8, 1955; KRCA-TV; Hollywood, California)
Strictly Informal (September 20, 1955; KTLA-TV, Los Angeles, California)
Magazine with Jerry Haynes (February 6, 1956; WFAA-TV, Dallas, Texas)
The Tonight Show (April 16, 1957; NBC)
Top Tunes (June 20, 1957; WSTV-TV, Chicago, Illinois)
The Big Record (January 15, 1958; CBS): Painting the Clouds with Sunshine/Tiptoe Through the Tulips
Del Courtney Showcase (March 23, 1958; KPIX-TV, San Francisco, California)
Hi-Fi Vision (April 1, 1958; KTLA-TV, Los Angeles, California)
Country America (April 19, 1958; KABC-TV, Los Angeles, California)
Panorama Pacific (April 30, 1963, KTLA-TV, Los Angeles, California)
Lamplighter Playhouse (October 1963; KCHU-TV, San Bernardino, California)
Hollywood and the Stars [episode: "The Fabulous Musicals"] (November 18, 1963; NBC) [archive footage]
Art Linkletter's House Party (February 27, 1964; NBC)
The Lawrence Welk Show (November 28, 1964; ABC)

The Lawrence Welk Show (January 27, 1965; ABC)
The Lawrence Welk Show (February 27, 1965; ABC): Looking at the World Thru Rose Colored Glasses/Hey, Mr. Banjo (w. Buddy Merrill and Neil Le Vang)
The Lawrence Welk Show (May 1, 1965; ABC): Painting the Clouds with Sunshine/Down Yonder/Swanee
Art Linkletter's House Party (May 5, 1965; NBC)
The Lawrence Welk Show (May 22, 1965; ABC)
Melody Ranch (July 10, 1965; KTLA-TV, Los Angeles, California)
Social Security in Action (October 3, 1965; KCOP-TV, Los Angeles, California)
Art Linkletter's House Party (February 11, 1966; NBC)
Social Security (July 3, 1966; KTTV-TV, Los Angeles, California)
Mr. Blackwell's Hollywood (October 20, 1967; KCOP-TV, Los Angeles, California)
Melody Ranch (July 13, 1968; KTLA-TV, Los Angeles, California)
Melody Ranch (August 28, 1968; KTLA-TV, Los Angeles, California)
The Tonight Show (September 18, 1969; NBC): Margie/Maria Elena/Somebody Stole My Gal/Tiptoe Through the Tulips (duet with Tiny Tim)
The Tonight Show (December 17, 1969; NBC): Painting the Clouds with Sunshine/Tiptoe Through the Tulips
The Merv Griffin Show (June 26, 1972; syndicated): Tiptoe Through the Tulips
Vaudeville (January 19, 1975; syndicated): Tiptoe Through the Tulips/Painting the Clouds with Sunshine/Five Foot Two, Eyes of Blue
Vaudeville (August 22, 1975; syndicated)
The Sam Yorty Show (1975–79, KCOP-TV, Los Angeles, California)
All You Need Is Love (1977; London Weekend Television)
Murphy's America (1977; Irish TV/RTE)
Variety Club Telethon '77 (May 14, 1977; KTLA-TV, Los Angeles, California)
The Wally George Show (1979–81, KCOP-TV, Los Angeles, California)
Rose Bowl Parade (January 1, 1980; syndicated)
The Merv Griffin Show (February 17, 1981; syndicated): Tiptoe Through the Tulips
The Nelson Riddle Show (1981; PBS): What'll I Do?/Five Foot Two, Eyes of Blue
The Walking Dead [episode "Start to Finish"] (November 29, 2015; American Movie Classics): Tiptoe Through the Tulips [recording]

Stage Shows

The Crowded Hour (March–April 1919; Park Square Theatre, Boston, Massachusetts, and Teck Theatre, Buffalo, New York)

Writers: Edgar Selwyn and Channing Pollock. Orchestra Director: George Paul Wegler.

CAST: Florence Johns (Peggy Lawrence), Eugenie Gei (Martha), Emile J. De Varney (Captain Reni Soulier), Alan Dinehart (Billy Laidlaw), Hale Norecross (Matt Wilde), William Keighley (Lieutenant Caswell), Frederick Kerr (Dr. Beauchamps/Veteran), Raymond Sinclair (Lieutenant Bailey), Jean Evans (Vivian), Andre Cholin (Jackson/Apolla), Alison Bradshaw (Dorothy Wayne), E.H. Gillespie (Lieutenant Williams/Charley), Marion Barney (Grace Laidlaw), George Lesoir (Captain Dalton), C.P. Bird (Captain Epstein), Jack Browning (Captain Walcott), Emile Cop (General Dubois), Eugene Cochet (Grandmere Buvaise), Simone Cochet, Betty Cochet (Granddaughters), "The Three Chums": Nick Lucas (Merrick), James Miller (Davis), Gill Mack (Nevins); Harry Webster (Wills), Eugene Geinova (Telephone Operator), Emile Chipelian (General).

Making his professional stage debut, Lucas appeared as a member of the Signal Corps and, as one of the Three Chums, he sang "Buffalo Boys Come Back." This was in a road company edition of the play that appeared on Broadway in 1918–19 starring Willette Kershaw with support from Jane Cowl, Orme Caldara, Georges Flateau, Henry Stephenson, Cyril Raymond, Christine Norman, Franklyn Ardell and Jules Epailly. The play depicted how its characters' lives were changed by the World War.

Reviews:

The Buffalo (New York) *Times* [Deshler Welch]: "I was not the only man who wept in the Teck Theatre last night. I would like to have gone into a telephone box and howled. Most of the people had their first visualization of war desperation, suffering and madness, and participated very largely in it themselves for *The Crowded Hour* ran in the very heights of realism."

Munsey's Magazine: "There is melodrama enough in *The Crowded Hour* to outfit an entire Third Avenue of the old days, but happily none of it is crude, if properly played… [I]t is a really big war play."

Sweetheart of Dixie (April–May 1925; Grand Central Theatre, St. Louis, Missouri)

Producer-Director-Writer: Larry Conley.

CAST: Nick Lucas, James Dunn, Thelma White, the Keller Sisters, Ed Lynch, Kendall Capps, Taylor, Parsons and Hawks, Dorothy Johnson.

Lucas was featured in this one-hour musical comedy production in a flash act performing a trio of songs as well as accompanying Ed Lynch and the Keller Sisters.

Sweetheart Time (January 19, 1926–May 27, 1926; Imperial Theatre, New York City; 143 performances)

Producer: Rufus LeMaire. Director: William Collier. Book: Harry B. Smith. Music: Walter Donaldson and Joseph Meyer. Lyrics: Ballard MacDonald and Irving Caesar. Music Orchestrators: Stephen Jones and Maurice De Packh. Music Director: John L. McManus. Choreography: Larry Ceballos. Costume Designer: Charles LeMaire. Scenic Designers: Karl O. Amend and Nicholas Yellenti.

CAST: Mary Milburn (Violet Stevenson), Eddie Buzzell (Dion Woodbury), Fred Leslie (Lord Hector Raybrook), Marion Saki (Marian Stevenson), Al Sexton (Roy Henderson), Marie Nordstrom (Mrs. Stevenson), George LeMaire (Dr. Ralph Galesby), Nick Lucas (Song Specialty), M. Marcel Rousseau (Alphonse), Dorothy McNulty [Peggy Singleton], Bob Gordon, Harry King (Dancers), Bobbie Breslaw (Bobbie), Wilmer Bentley (Griggs), Laine Blaire (Nina), Dorothy Brown (Dorothy), Bob Callahan (Walter), Rita Del Marga (Carlita), Harry Kelly (Detective James), Starke Patterson (Jeffries), Alice Wood (Alice), Betty Wright (Betty), Bessie Katemova (Bessie), Dorothy Van Alst, Aida Winston, Ann Hardman, Nelda Snow, Beverly Maude, Loretta Rehm, Adele Hari, Mary Hoover, Alice Monroe, Nellie McCarthy, Peggy Thayer, Margaret Olson (Young Ladies of the Ensemble).

Lucas appeared in the second act of this boy-meets-girl musical comedy and introduced the song "Sleepy Time Gal."

Reviews:

The Billboard: "[T]he producer and his aides have passed up most of the comedy possibilities contained in the script and spotted dancing specialties in their places. There are solo dances, duets and ensembles, extensive in variety and breathless with speed, and the numbers are liable to pop out unexpectedly at any time, from anywhere and by anyone. And all of them are good."

New York American: "A gorgeous dancing show."

New York Herald-Tribune: "Danced, talked, posed and sang its way into the bosom of an audience of rapt firstnighters."

New York Telegram: "Has all the earmarks of a glib, prattling, prancing summer show."

Variety: "[Rufus] LeMaire seems to have produced a lively, likable musical...."

Show Girl (July 2, 1929–October 5, 1929; Ziegfeld Theatre, New York City; 111 performances)

Producer: Florenz Ziegfeld, Jr. Director-Material: William Anthony McGuire. Novel: J.P. McEvoy. Music: George Gershwin. Lyrics: Ira Gershwin, Gus Kahn, Thomas Malie, Sidney Skolsky, W.H. Farrell and Jimmy Durante. Additional Music: W.H. Farrell and Jimmy Durante. Songs: J. Little. Music Director: William Daly. Orchestra Director: William Daly. Dances: Bobby Connolly. Ballets: Albertina Rasch. Settings: Joseph Urban. Costumes: John W. Harkrider.

Cast: Ruby Keeler (Dixie Dugan), Nick Lucas (Rudy), Jimmy Durante (Snozzle/Somber Eyes), Eddie Foy, Jr. (Denny Kerrigan), Harriet Hoctor (Ballerina), Barbara Newberry (Virginia Witherby/Sunshine), Duke Ellington's Cotton Club Orchestra (Musicians), Frank McHugh (Jimmy Doyle), Noel Francis (Peggy Ritz), Lou Clayton (Gypsy), Eddie Jackson (Deacon/Tony Morato), Austin Fairman (John Milton), Joseph Macauley (Alvarez Romero), Calvin Thomas (Colonel Witherby/Roy Collins), Althea Heinle (Estelle), Matthew Smith (Captain Robert Adams), Blaine Cordner (Steve), Andy Jochim (Kenneth Boles/Mr. Wright), Wanda Stevenson (Bessie), Doris Carson (Raquel), Howard Morgan (Matt Brown), Caryl Bergman (Anna/Sylvia), Kathryn Hereford (Bobby), Mary Charles (Aunt Jennie/Gladys), Maurine Holmes (Hazel), Sadie Duff (Mrs. Dugan), The Albertina Rasch Dancers.

In *Show Girl*, Lucas introduced "Liza" and also performed his latest Brunswick record, "Singin' in the Rain/You're Mother and Mine." He left after nine performances.

Reviews:

The Billboard: "[It] is the weakest attraction that impresario [Florenz Ziegfeld] has brought to Broadway in recent years. It is a distinct disappointment. William Anthony McGuire's adaptation is weak, disjointed and empty; George Gershwin's score is limpid and uninspired. Indeed, it is only the master touch of Ziegfeld in mounting the show that rates it a place above the average."

Brooklyn (New York) *Times Union*: "Florenz Ziegfeld added one more lavish musical play to his long and impressive lists of accomplishments... [It] gave every evidence of being a suitable successor to the other words and music works that have preceded it... [The players] render fine assistance, as does Duke Ellington's Cotton Club Orchestra in several scenes and Nick Lucas, who sings to guitar accompaniment."

Variety: "This splendidly Ziegfeld produced musical comedy is just a good summer show. It's far and away from a smash.... Main trouble appears to be music and the lack of it in a popular way."

The Silver Screen (September 1941; Wiltshire Bowl, Los Angeles, California; 10 performances)

Producers: John Murray Anderson and Hugh Anderson. Music Director: Franz Steininger. Choreography: Larry Cebellos. Business Manager: Sam Weisenthal.

Cast: Nick Lucas, Bryant Washburn, Betty Compson, Clara Kimball Young, Betty Blythe, The Original Keystone Kops [Chester Conklin, Hank Mann, Snub Pollard], Tom Patricola, Clyde Cook, Al Herman, Gitta Alper, Cynda Glenn, Grace Pozzi and Igor, Jack Holland, The Mangeans, The Silver Screen Juveniles, The Four Rosebuds, Darryl Hargis' Orchestra.

Billed as "a musical glamorama of the movies," this production took a nostalgic look at film history with Lucas singing songs from early sound films. *Variety* (September 17, 1941) noted, "Nick Lucas, although not of the films strictly speaking, caught the sitters basking in the glow of the not-so-golden days and had them pleading for more of the heart-tuggers he strummed and sung years ago for gramophones." The production, which also doubled as a night club revue, had only a brief run due, mainly to its high ($10) ticket fee plus a hefty cover charge.

Ken Murray's Blackouts (1947–49; El Capital Theatre, Hollywood, California)

Producer-Director: Ken Murray.
CAST: Ken Murray, Marie Wilson, Nick Lucas, Jack Mulhall, The Elderly Lovelies.

Lucas joined the cast of the long-running West Coast production *Ken Murray's Blackouts* and remained with it for two years as the featured vocalist. It closed in 1949.

Blackouts of 1949 (September 6–October 15, 1949; Ziegfeld Theatre, New York City; 51 performances)

Presenter: David Siegel. Producer-Director-Book-Conception: Ken Murray. Music-Lyrics: Charles Henderson and Royal Foster. Special Dialogue and Comedy: Royal Foster. Music Director: Bert Shefter. Music Arranger: Alexander Courage. Scenic Designer: Ben Tipton. Gowns: Betty Colburn Kreisel.
CAST: Ken Murray, Nick Lucas, Jack Mulhall, Owen McGiveney, Pat Williams, Shelton Brooks, Crystal White, Dot Remy, Danny Alexander, Peg Leg Bates, Alphonse Berge, George Burton, Mabel Butterworth, Milton Charleston, Danny Duncan, Harris and Shore, Hightower and Ross, Irene Kaye, Al Mardo, Charles Nelson, D'Vaughn Pershing, Elizabeth Walters, Joe Wong, Les Zoris.

Ken Murray transferred his popular West Coast revue to Broadway in the fall of 1949 but it did not do well. Lucas, who appeared in the show from 1947 to 1949 at the El Capitan Theatre in Hollywood, continued with the production, singing a variety of tunes.

Reviews:
Brooklyn Daily Eagle [George Currie]: "If exuberant life, lively acts and a steady stream of asides by the master of ceremonies that have a resemblance to ad libbing means a good show, the *Ken Murray's Blackouts of 1949* … should be marked down as a 'knockout.' …It is hard to recollect anything Mr. Murray has overlooked in this fun and frolic…. He presents an amusing and enjoyable evening."

Louis Sobol—"Voice of Broadway" (September 16, 1949): "The theatrical season bowed in with Ken Murray's *Blackouts* bringing to town some beautiful girls, some familiar acts, a few atrociously vulgar blackouts and a handful of old timers, including Jack Mulhall, once a silent film star; Nick Lucas, guitarist and minstrel, and Owen McGiveney, the quick-change fellow who plays the assorted characters in the 'Oliver Twist' sketch wearing himself and the audience out, there is much that is highly diverting in the *Blackouts*, notably George Burton and his trained live birds, and Lucas—and a girl lovely to look at, Pat Williams, who replaced Marie Wilson. Also Ken Murray himself in his droller moods. But the flash blackouts are obnoxious and unfunny—and so is some of the dialogue."

Blackouts of 1966 (1966; Cal-Neva Lodge, Lake Tahoe, Nevada/ Las Vegas, Nevada, and other locales)

Producer: David Siegel. Staging-Choreography: Jerry Franks.

CAST: Nick Lucas, Matty Melneck's Orchestra, Sammy Wolfe, Yonely, Helena Savoy.

Lucas headlined this musical revue that ran from July 15–31, 1966, in Lake Tahoe, Nevada, before going to other venues.

A 1970s publicity photograph of Nick Lucas.

Bibliography

Books and Articles

Burton, Jack. *The Blue Book of Tin Pan Alley*. New York: Century House, 1962.

Dorn, Norman K. "Nick Lucas: A Lively Legend is Show Biz's Original Crooner." *San Francisco (California) Examiner & Chronicle*. November 9, 1975.

Evans, Philip R., and Larry F. Kiner, with William Trumbauer. *Tram: The Frank Trumbauer Story*. Metuchen, NJ: Scarecrow Press, 1994.

Fidler, Jimmie. "Inside Hollywood." *The Monroe (Louisiana) News-Star*. March 27, 1953.

Foster, Joan. "Nick Lucas Strikes Nostalgic Note." *St. Louis (Missouri) Globe-Democrat*. January 15, 1959.

Friedwald, Will. *A Biographical Guide to the Great Jazz and Pop Singers*. New York: Pantheon Books, 2010.

Gans, Tom, and Mary Anne Gans. *Guitars*. N.p.: Paddington Press, 1977.

Hickerson, Jay. *The New, Revised Ultimate History of Network Radio Programming and Guide to All Circulating Shows*. Hamden, CT: Jay Hickerson, 1997.

Hoover, Will. *Picks! The Colorful Saga of Vintage Celluloid Guitar Plectrums*. San Francisco, CA: Miller Freeman Books, 1995.

Humphrey, Mark. "The New Fangled Guitar Sound of 1922." *Los Angeles Free Weekly*. August 21, 1981.

_____. "Nick Lucas: The Artist Behind the Name." *Frets*. August 1980.

Kinkle, Roger. D. *The Complete Encyclopedia of Popular Music and Jazz 1900–1950* (4 volumes). New Rochelle, NY: Arlington House, 1974.

Kovach, Ted. "Grandpa Nick Lucas Set for Crooner Comeback." *Valley Times* (North Hollywood, CA), April 5, 1952.

Kuehne, Antoinette. "Nick Lucas Impresses by Frankness of Personality." *The Daily Texan*. October 14, 1928.

Laird, Ross. *Brunswick Records: A Discography of Recordings, 1916–1931* (4 volumes). Westport, CT: Greenwood Press, 2001.

Lamparski, Richard. *Whatever Became Of...? Fourth Series*. New York: Crown, 1973.

"Lucas Can't Quit While He's Ahead." *Dallas (Texas) Morning News*. February 7, 1956.

Lucas, Nick. "Inside Hollywood—Clean Entertainment." *Monroe (Louisiana) Morning World*. September 27, 1953. (Distributed by McNaughton Syndicate, Inc.)

_____. *The Keystone Folio for the Guitar (Plectrum Method)*. Altoona, PA: Nicomede Music Co., 1932.

_____. *Nick Lucas Collection of Neapolitan Love Songs*. New York: Robins Music Corporation, 1935.

_____. *The Nick Lucas Guitar Method for Pick Playing*. Altoona, PA: Nicomede Music Co., 1930.

_____. *The Nick Lucas Hawaiian Guitar Method*. Altoona, PA: Nicomede Music Co., 1932.

_____. *The Nick Lucas Hawaiian Guitar Method, Vol. 2*. Altoona, PA: Nicomede Music Co., 1932.

_____. *The Nick Lucas Hawaiian Guitar Method, Vol. 3*. Altoona, PA: Nicomede Music Co., 1940.

_____. *The Nick Lucas Plectrum Guitar Method*. Altoona, PA: Nicomede Music Co., 1935.

_____. *The Nick Lucas Plectrum Guitar Method, Vol. 2*. Altoona, PA: Nicomede Music Co., 1935.

_____. *The Nick Lucas Plectrum Guitar Method, Vol. 3*. Altoona, PA: Nicomede Music Co., 1935.

_____. "Singer Relates Early Experience—Hard Work Feature Success." *Oakland (California) Tribune*. September 2, 1926.

McCarty, Bob. "Across the Board." *The Sacramento (California) Union*. November 25, 1963.

Newman, Marshall. "The Nick Lucas Special." *Acoustic Guitar*. December 1998.

"Nick Lucas Tends to Business and Collects Reward." *Dallas (Texas) Morning News*. October 1, 1928.

"Nick Lucas—The Singing Troubador." *Italian Tribune*. December 4, 1981.

Obrecht, James. "The First Star of Recorded Guitar: Nick Lucas." *Guitar Player* December 1980.

_____. "Nick Lucas: A Conversation with the Crooning Troubadour." *Victrola and 78 Journal*. Winter 1994.

Parish, James Robert, and Michael R. Pitts. *Hollywood Songsters: A Biographical Dictionary*. New York: Garland Publishing, 1991.

_____, and _____. *Hollywood Songsters: Singers Who Act and Actors Who Sing, 2nd Edition* (2 volumes). New York: Routledge, 2002.

Phillips, Perry. "Night Sounds." *Oakland (California) Tribune*. December 14, 1962.

Pisano, Dorothy. "Nick Lucas Began as a Street Singer." *Dallas* (Texas) *Morning News*. October 21, 1928.
Pitts, Michael R. "An Interview with Nick Lucas." *Screen Thrills*. Number 6, 1978.
_____. "Nick Lucas on Film, Stage, Radio and Records." *Classic Images*. January 1984.
_____. "Nick Lucas: The Singing Troubadour." *Focus on Film*. Number 20, Spring 1975.
_____. "Nick Lucas." *American National Biography Online*. 2000.
_____. "Nostalgia Reigns as Lucas Returns." *Anderson* (Indiana) *Herald*. March 5, 1978.
_____. "Pop Singers on the Screen." *Film Fan Monthly*. October, 1970.
_____. "The Recording Career of Nick Lucas." *RTS Music Gazette*. May-June-July, 1978.
Pitts, Michael R., and Frank Hoffman, Dick Carty and Jim Bedoian. *The Rise of the Crooners*. Lanham, MD: The Scarecrow Press, 2002.
Pitts, Michael R., and Louis H. Harrison. *Hollywood on Record: The Film Stars' Discography*. Metuchen, NJ: The Scarecrow Press, 1978.
Pollock, Bill. "Lucas 'Tiptoes' Through the Mayfair." *Los Angeles* (California) *Herald-Examiner*. April 28, 1974.
"Radio Helped Nick Lucas Find Himself." *Santa Ana* (California) *Register*. September 13, 1927.
Raffetto, Francis. "After Dark: Down Memory Lane with Lucas." *Dallas* (Texas) *Morning News*. March 9, 1966.
Rust, Brian. *The American Dance Band Discography 1917–1942* (2 volumes). New Rochelle, NY: Arlington House, 1975.
_____, with Allen G. Debus. *The Complete Entertainment Discography from the Mid-1890s to 1942*. New Rochelle, NY: Arlington House, 1973.
Scott, Vernon. "Nick Lucas: The Original Troubadour Still Singing at 83." *Philadelphia* (Pennsylvania) *Times Herald*. April 22, 1981.
Sennett, Ted. *Warner Bros. Presents*. New Rochelle, NY: Arlington House, 1971.
Simcross, Lynn. "Tiptoeing Through a Comeback." *Los Angeles* (California) *Times*. August 5, 1975.
Sisley, Geoff. "A Gallery of Guitarists: Nick Lucas." *B.M.G.*, July 1935.
Slide, Anthony. *The Vaudevillians: A Dictionary of Vaudeville Performers*. Westport, CT: Arlington House.
Smith, Jack. "The Nick of Time." *Los Angeles* (California) *Times*. May 9, 1979.
Smith, Joyce. "After 50 Years of Song, Nick Lucas Still Strumming Strong." *The Enterprise* (Riverside, California). May 24, 1978.
Spelvin, George. "The Gentle Art of Crooning: Nick Lucas Says It Came from the Cradle." *Dallas* (Texas) *Morning News*. September 30, 1928.
Townsend, Dorothy. "Nick Lucas, 84, Famed as Singing Troubadour, Dies." *Los Angeles* (California) *Times*. July 31, 1982.
Variety Radio Directory 1937–38. New York City: Variety, Inc. 1937.
Wakeman, R.J., with Tim Gracyk. "Brunswick's 'Light-Ray' and Panatrope Era—and Beyond." *Victrola and 78 Journal*. Autumn 1998.
Webb, Graham. *Encyclopedia of American Short Films, 1926–1959*. Jefferson, NC: McFarland, 2020.
Wheeler, Tom. *American Guitars: An Illustrated History*. New York: Harper Perennial, 1990.
Whitford, Eldon, and David Vinopal and Dan Erlewine. *Gibson's Fabulous Flat-Top Guitars: An Illustrated History & Guide*. San Francisco: GPI Books, 1994.
Who's Who on the Air 1932. New York: Ludwig Baumann Company, 1932.
Willing, Sharon Lee. *No One to Cry To*. Tucson, AZ: Wheatmark, 2006.
The Witmark Theme Song Dance Folio No. 2. New York: M. Witmark & Sons., 1930.
Zoppi, Tony. "Dallas After Dark." *Dallas* (Texas) *Morning News*. June 28, 1954.

Newspapers

The Age (Melbourne, Australia)
Altoona (Pennsylvania) *Tribune*
Amarillo (Texas) *Daily News*
Ames (Iowa) *Daily Tribune*
Anderson (Indiana) *Herald*
Angola (New York) *Record*
Austin (Texas) *Daily Texan*
Bakersfield (California) *Californian*
Bridgeport (Connecticut) *Telegram*
Brooklyn (New York) *Citizen*
Brooklyn (New York) *Times Union*
Buffalo (New York) *Courier-Express*
Burlington (Iowa) *Gazette*
Capital (Madison, Wisconsin) *Times*
Chicago (Illinois) *Sun Times*
Cleveland (Ohio) *News*
County Sun (San Bernardino, California)
Daily Standard (Red Branch, New Jersey)
Daily Texan (Austin, Texas)
Daily Times (Chattanooga, Tennessee)
Dallas (Texas) *Morning News*
Dayton (Ohio) *Herald*
Decatur (Illinois) *Herald*
Emporia (Kansas) *Gazette*
The Enterprise (Riverside, California)
Fitchburg (Massachusetts) *Sentinel*
Forest Park (Illinois) *Review*
Fort Wayne (Indiana) *Journal-Gazette*
Franklin County (Missouri) *Tribune*
Frederick (Maryland) *News Post*
Galveston (Texas) *Daily News*
Gazette and Daily (York, Pennsylvania)
Globe-Democrat (St. Louis, Missouri)
Greeley (Colorado) *Daily Tribune*
Harrisburg (Pennsylvania) *Evening News*
Harrisburg (Pennsylvania) *Telegraph*
Hollywood (California) *Independent*
Indianapolis (Indiana) *Star*
Indianapolis (Indiana) *Times*
Italian Tribune (Newark, New Jersey)
Kansas City (Missouri) *Times*

Knickerbocker (Albany, New York) *News*
Knoxville (Tennessee) *News-Sentinel*
Los Angeles (California) *Examiner*
Los Angeles (California) *Free Weekly*
Los Angeles (California) *Herald-Examiner*
Los Angeles (California) *Times*
Mobile (Alabama) *Journal*
Monroe (Louisiana) *Morning World*
Monroe (Louisiana) *News Star*
Nashville (Tennessee) *Banner*
Naugatuk (Connecticut) *Daily News*
Nebraska State Journal (Lincoln, Nebraska)
Nevada State Journal (Reno, Nevada)
New York Daily News
New York Evening Graphic
New York Evening-Telegram
New York Graphic
New York Herald Tribune
New York Sun
New York Times
New York World
Oakland (California) *Tribune*
Oklahoma News (Oklahoma City, Oklahoma)
Omaha (Nebraska) *Bee-News*
Outlook (Alexandria City, Alabama)
Pasadena (California) *Independent*
Pasadena (California) *Post*
Philadelphia (Pennsylvania) *Times Herald*
Plain Speaker (Hazelton, Pennsylvania)
Reading (Pennsylvania) *Times*
Redlands (California) *Daily Fact*
Reno (Nevada) *Evening Gazette*
Rocky Mountain News (Denver, Colorado)
Sacramento (California) *Union*
St. Louis (Missouri) *Globe-Democrat*
Salt Lake City (Utah) *Tribune*
San Antonio (Texas) *Light*
San Francisco (California) *Examiner & Chronicle*
San Mateo (California) *Standard*
Santa Ana (California) *Register*
Santa Ana (California) *Speaker*
Scranton (Pennsylvania) *Republican*
Sioux City (Iowa) *Journal*
Standard-Speaker (Hazelton, Pennsylvania)
Sydney (Australia) *Morning Herald*
Sylacauga (Alabama) *Advance*
Terre Haute (Indiana) *Tribune*
Times (San Mateo, California)
Times Journal (Selma, Alabama)
Times Mirror (Warren, Pennsylvania)
Times Standard (Eureka, California)
Trenton (New Jersey) *Evening News*
Ukiah (California) *News*

Valley News (Van Nuys, California)
Valley Times (North Hollywood, California)
Vancouver (Canada) *Sun*
Vancouver (Canada) *World*
Washington (D.C.) *Times*
Wilkes-Barre (Pennsylvania) *Times Leader/Evening News*
Winnipeg (Canada) *Tribune*

Periodicals

Acoustic Guitar
The Big Reel
(The) Billboard
B.M.G.
Casting Call
Classic Images
Daily Variety
Exhibitor's Herald
Film Daily
Film Fan Monthly
Focus on Film
Frets
Guitar Player
Hollywood Reporter
Music Trade Journal
Music Trade Review
Nostalgia Digest
Phonograph Monthly Review
Photoplay
Radio Daily
Radio Dial
Radio Mirror
Radio Stars
RTS Music Gazette
Screen Thrills
Talking Machine World
Variety
Vaudeville News & New York Star
Victrola & 78 Journal

Websites

Fulton History (https://fultonhistory.com)
Internet Movie Database (www.imdb.com)
Media History Digital Library (www.archive.org)
Newspaper Archive (www.newspaperarchive.com)
Newspapers.com (www.newspapers.com)
Nick Lucas.com (www.nicklucas.com)
World Radio History (worldhistoryradio.com)
YouTube (www.youtube.com)

Index

Aberlach, Jules 93
Accent Records 103, 111, 113, 114, 119, 169, 170–175
Adams, Stanley 103
Adorable 145
Agnew, Charlie 8
Ahern, Will 115
Al Pearce and His Gang 73, 223
The All American Revue 81
All of Me/Goodnight Ladies 62, 160, 161
All Star Western Theatre 92
Allen, Woody 216
Alper, Gitta 83
Always 26, 45, 90, 144, 164, 165, 203
Among My Souvenirs 2, 38, 150, 166, 170, 171
Amos 'n' Andy 13
Anderson, John Murray 82
The Andrews Sisters 115
The Andy and Virginia Program 171
Angela 175
The Anglo-Persians 158
Anthony, Ralph 74
Apex Records 11
An Apple for the Teacher 163
Arbuckle, Roscoe "Fatty" 53
Ardell, Franklyn 231
Arden, Phil 99
Arden, Toni 103
Are You Lonesome Tonight? 126, 175
Armstrong, Robert E. 172
Arnold, Eddy 93, 104
Ash, Paul 65
Ashley, Lord 27
Astaire, Adele 27
Astaire, Fred 27
At Sundown 173
Atherton, William 117, 215
Atkins, Chet 128
Austin, Gene 1, 15, 37, 111
Autry, Gene 2, 55. 84, 92, 93, 104, 109, 117, 128
Ayres, Lew 214

Baby Face 172
Bailey, Mildred 85
Bailey's Lucky Seven 11, 130–140
Baker, Belle 43, 47, 54, 55, 56, 219

Baker, Two Ton 165
Bakewell, William 48, 204, 205
Ballew, Smith 1
Banner Records 176
Banta, Frank 11, 132–135
Bara, Theda 77
Barnett, Vince 211
Barrymore, Ethel 61
Barrymore, John 53
Baruch, Andre 73
Bauer, Franklyn 1
Baxter, Warner 45
Beacon Records 114
Because I Love You 27, 146
Because They All Love You 17, 18, 22, 141
Beckman, Jack 93
Beery, Wallace 61
Bela Bimba 94, 167
Bell, Archie 60
The Bell Sisters 97
Bella Nona (Little Grandmother) 103, 169
Bellson, Lou 106
Bennett, Tony 1
Benny, Jack 43, 45, 101
Bergen, Edgar 122
Berle, Jack 126
Berle, Milton 119, 126
Berlin, Irving 62
Bernard, Al 140–141
Bernie, Ben 37, 47, 54, 56, 73, 77, 216, 219
Beside a Lazy Stream All the World is Mine 23
Big Time Revue 72, 210, 212
Birth of a Song 101
Bissell, Leonard 77, 112
Bissell, Leonard, Jr. 112
Bissell, Mark Lucas 112
Bissell, Nicholas W. 112
Black, Frank 23
Black, Karen 118, 215
The Blackouts of 1949 93, 234
The Blackouts of 1966 111, 235
Blake, Norman 33
Blalock, Richard 107
Blondie of the Follies 64
Bloom, Harry 79, 224
Bloom, Rube 11
Bloomfield, Fred 90
Boles, John 1

Bond, Johnny 92, 109
Boney Records 95, 168, 176
Boone, Pat 115
Boswell, Connee 76
The Boswell Sisters 61, 220
Boutelje, Phil 134
Bowery Records 169–170, 176
Boy! Oh! Boy! Oh! Boy! I've Got It Bad 160
Boyd, William 99
Bratton, David 57, 63
Brian, Mary 61
Bridges, Jeff 119, 216
Brito, Phil 1
Britton, Milt 86
Broadway Hit Parade 73
Broken Hearted Troubadour 72, 210, 212
Brown, Les 110
Brown Eyes, Why Are You Blue 21, 22, 111, 143, 167, 170, 171
Brunette, Fritzi 209
Brunswick-Balke-Collender Company 14, 21–22
Brunswick Brevities 54, 219
Brunswick Hour of Music 37, 219
Brunswick Panatrope 21–22
Brunswick Records 10, 14, 15, 21–27, 38, 39, 45, 50, 54, 55, 56, 59, 72, 140–162, 176–180, 203, 211, 219
Bryan, Al 207
Buchanan, Jack 25, 27
Buck and Bubbles 115
Budginer, Victoria 113, 114
Burbig, Henry 64
Burk, Jim 93
Burke, Joe 47
Burke, Larry 59
Burke, Sonny 103, 170
Burtnell, Earl 56
Butera, Sam 110
Buttram, Pat 93, 111
Buzzell, Eddie 22
By the Light of the Stars 21, 23, 142
Bye Bye Blackbird 1, 30, 91, 92, 145, 167, 171
Byrd, Robert 55

Caesar, Irving 22
Café de Paris 25, 27, 28, 29
Cagney, James 109

Index

Caldra, Orme 231
Campbell, Frank 21, 31
Campbell, Glen 128
Campbell, William 126
The Campbell Program 61
Canova, Annie 78
Canova, Judy 78
Canova, Zeke 78
Can't We Talk It Over 171
Can't You Read Between the Lines? 160
Capitol Records 91, 92, 93, 100, 167, 180
The Cardinal Dance Orchestra 11
Cardinal Records 11
Carillon, George 98
Carmelita Sisters of the Sacred Heart 115
Carnera, Primo 2
Carpenter, Ken 113
Carroll, John 90
Carry Me Back to the Lone Prairie 72, 161
Carson, Johnny 7, 113, 114
Castanet 210
Cavalier Records 98, 99, 100–101, 102, 103, 168–169, 170, 180
Ceballos, Larry 211
The Cell Block Seven 99
Challenger, Connie 122
Chamlee, Mario 54, 219
Chandler, A.B. "Happy" 75
Chaplin, Charles 53
Chaplin, Lita Grey 53, 57
Chaplin, Sydney 53
Charley My Boy 166
Chatterton, Ruth 59
Checker, Chubby 115
Chevie, Howard 106
Chiquita 152–153
Chissell, Noble "Kid" 122, 124
Cifrodella, Angelo 7
Cifordella, Antonette 7
Cifordella, Catherine *see* Lucas, Catherine
Cifordella, Christina 7
Cifordella, Columba 7
Cifordella, Nicholas 7
Cifordella, Rose 7
Clayton, Lou 44
Clooney, Rosemary 111
Coast-to-Coast Agency 86
Coax Me a Little Bit 166
Coburn, Charles 90
Cody, Lew 53, 61
College Scandal 70
Collins, Ted 61
Colonna, Jerry 110
Columbia Variety Hour 223
Columbo, Russ 58, 220
Como, Perry 1
Compo Company 164
Compson, Betty 83
Comstock, Bill 223
Congamania 211
Conklin, Chester 83
Conley, Larry 19
Connaught, Prince Arthur of 27

Connaught, Princess of 27
Contino, Dick 96
Cook, Clyde 83
Cook, Captain Frederick Albert 13
Cook, Joe 76
Cooper, Bud 23
Cooper, Jackie 214
Cooper, Jerry 1
Coquette 2, 100, 101, 154–155, 168
Cornell, Don 1
Coslow, Sam 87
Costello, Charlie *see* Palloy, Charlie
Costi, Maria 99
Cotton, Carolina 93
Count Your Blessings 107
Cowan, Jerome 213
Cowan, Lynn 93
Cowl, Jane 231
C.P. MacGregor Transcription Company 73, 91, 162–163, 165–166
Criswell (Jaron King Criswell) 111, 116, 118
Criswell Predicts 111, 116, 118
The Crooning Troubadour (CD) 182
Crosby, Bing 1, 2, 30, 61, 62, 102, 103
Cross, Leo H. 91
The Crowded Hour 8, 231
The Crown Folio of Guitar Solos (Plectrum Style) 195–196
Crown Records 169, 180
Crown Theatrical Agency 99
Cuando Eras tu Capullo, del Ilorido Sendero 159
Cugat, Xavier 67
A Cup of Coffee, a Sandwich and You 25, 144, 173
Curtis, Billy 93

Dahl, Arlene 109
Dalhart, Vernon 15
Damone, Vic 1
Dana, Bill 112
Dancing with Tears in My Eyes 2, 55, 56, 157, 170, 172
D'Andrea, Luigi 58
Daniels, Bebe 61
Danner, Blythe 119
Darling, I Love You 171, 172
Datsun Automobiles 118
Davidson, Jim 79, 224
Davies, Marion 64
Davis, Maxwell 169
Davis, Sammy, Jr. 101, 103
Dawn, Alice 85
Day of the Locust 118, 120, 175, 187
Dean, Eddie 92, 104, 128
de Bosari, Count Anthony 27
De Carlo, Yvonne 112
The De Castro Sisters 110
Decca Records 103, 170–171
Dee, Lenny 103
De Leath, Vaughn 220
Dempsey, Jack 2, 124

Denny, William 13
The Denny Beckner Revue 94
De Vol, Frank 91, 112, 167
Diamond, Jimmy 168, 170
Diamond Records 89, 90, 166, 180
Did You Ever See a Dream Walking? 169
Diplomat Novelty Orchestra 11
Diplomat Orchestra 11
Disc Jockey 95, 212–213
Ditmars, Ivan 167
The Dixie Stars 140–141
Doherty, James 23
Doin' the Manhattan 210
Don Marlowe's Vanities 111
The Don Parker Trio 11, 131–135
Donahue, Al 83
Donaldson, Walter 22
Donn, Lee 173
Don't Call Me Sweetheart Anymore 92, 167
Don't Gamble with Romance 92, 167
Don't Tell Her What's Happened to Me 157
Dooley, Jed 93
D'Orsay, Fifi 15
Dorsey, Jimmy 11, 71
Dorsey, Tommy 11, 71
Drake, James A. 24
Drake, Tom 213
Dreamer of Dreams 14, 141, 171
Dubin, Al 47
Duchin, Eddy 75
Duncan, Vivian 116
Dunn, Dewey 91, 92
Dunn, James 19, 232
Dunne, Irene 22
Dunstedter, Eddie 90
Durand, Frank 70
Durante, Jimmy 82, 44, 45, 115, 126, 130, 131
Durium Corporation 62
Dylan, Bob 33

Earl Fuller's Jazz Band 9, 130
Ebsen, Buddy 122
Eckstine, Billy 110
Edgewater Beach Hotel 12, 13
Edison, Thomas A. 1, 5
Edison Bell Winner 11
Edwards, Cliff "Ukulele Ike" 11, 15, 47, 134, 135
Edwards, Gus 92
Edwards, Mrs. Gus 92
Eils, Clifford 172
Einstein, Albert 61
Ellington, Duke 44
Ellis, Seger 1
Embassy Records 180
English, Harry 44
Epailly, Jules 231
Erickson, Leif 106
Erlewine, Dan 32
Ernie Farrow's Wallace Brothers Circus 105
Estabrook, Howard 105
Etting, Ruth 220

Index

Even Steven 106
An Evening in Caroline 62, 160, 161
An Evening with Nick Lucas (LP) 181
Everyone Is Looking for the Rainbow 166

Fair Follies 101
Fairhurst, Lynn 175
Falling in Love Again 159
Fanchon and Marco 78, 84
Farrow, Ernie 105
Farrow, Mia 117, 214
Fay, Frank 34, 207
Fejos, Paul 45
Femmena 175
Ferrucci, Edward 196
Fetchit, Stepin 88
Fiddler, Jimmie 99, 100, 101
Fields, Arthur 11
Fields, Gracie 29
Fiestacades of 1952 97
Fio Rito, Ted 7, 8, 9, 12, 14, 106, 115, 139, 140, 141
First and Last Accents (CD) 182
Fisher, Freddie 81
Fitzgerald, F. Scott 214
Fitzgerald, Leo 15, 17, 18, 25, 30, 46, 50, 52, 71, 79
Five Aces of Syncopation 9
Five Foot Two, Eyes of Blue 117, 127, 173, 175, 214
Flateau, Georges 231
Foley, Red 165
For All We Know 72, 162
For Old Times' Sake 152
Foray, June 112
Ford, Francis 210
Foster, Helen 48
The Four Aces 103
Fox, Bernard 122
Fox, Roy 156
Foy, Eddie, Jr 44, 119.
Fragments: Surviving Pieces of Lost Films 217
Franchi, Sergio 1
Francine 103, 168
Francis, Connie 38
The Frank Lucas Chord-Rhythm and Fill-In Book For Accordion 93
Frankay and Jackson Recording 166–167
Fray and Braggiotti 223
The Frederick Brothers 89
Freeman, Norine 76
Fuller, Earl 9, 130
Fun Unlimited 99, 102
Fyffe, Will 43

Gale, Sunny 102
Galento, Tony 2, 76, 116, 124
Gans, Mary Anne 32
Gans, Tom 32
Garvin, David 111, 199
The Gay Ranchero 166
Gaylord, Chester 1

The Gem Collection of Plectrum Guitar Solos 191
The Gem Folio for 1926: Selected from the Season's Most Popular Successes 196
General Amusement Corporation 84
Gennett Records 11, 130–140
George, Wally 116, 126
Gerity, Julia 9
Gershwin, George 10, 44, 130
Gershwin, Ira 44
Get Out Those Old Records 94, 103, 167, 170, 172
Gibson, Frank 20
Gibson Guitar Company 20–21, 31–33, 54, 69
Gibson Guitar Hall of Fame 127
Gilbert, Paul 112
Gillam, Art 15
Give My Heart a Break 166
Glenn, Cynthia 83
Gluck, Henry 138
Go Fly a Kite 164
Go Home and Tell Your Mother 158
Go to Bed 155, 205
Godfrey, Arthur 112
Goin' Home 72, 161, 173
The Gold Diggers 46
The Gold Diggers of Broadway 1, 46–50, 78, 99, 155, 204–206, 211, 217
The Gold Diggers of Broadway Trailer 155, 204
Golden Song Spotlight (CD) 182–183
Goldstone, Duke 94
Gone with the Wind 163
Good Morning 79, 164, 224
Goodnight Sweetheart 61, 160
Goodnight, Wherever You Are 87, 164, 211
Goody Goody 210
Grable, Betty 106
Granada 174
Grande, Vincent 133
Grant, Cary 214
Grant, Earl 103
Grant, Lawrence 204, 205
The Great American Home 78, 211
The Great Gatsby (1974) 117, 118, 127, 175, 187, 214–125
The Great Old Days of Radio 112
Green, Johnny 223
Greene, Eddie 104
Greer, Jimmie 76
Griffin, Merv 115, 127
Griffith, Andy 119, 216
Grogan, Oscar 1
Groves, Hy 14

Haenschem, Walter "Gus" 16, 24, 144
Hall, Wendell 15
Hallett, Mal 11
Halperin, Sammy 7

Hanapi, Mikiel 151
Hanley, William 219
The Happiness Boys (Billy Jones & Ernie Hare) 37, 47
Happy Days Are Here Again 119–120, 216
Harding, Ann 61
Hare, Earnest "Ernie" 11, 137
Harolde, Ralf 209
Harp, Darryl 83
Harris, Arlene 223
Harris, Marion 15, 37, 56, 141, 219
Harris, Phil 75
Havana Casino Revue 69
Heart o' Mine 154
Hearts of the West 119, 174, 216
Heidt, Horace 102
Hellenberg, John 138
Heller, Little Jackie 165
Hello! Beautiful 59, 159
Hello Bluebird 146
Hello Dolly 111, 171
(Here Am I) Brokenhearted 2, 38, 149, 166, 167
Herman, Woody 108, 110
Hibbler, Al 103
Hickman, Walter D. 17, 19, 21, 26, 37, 38, 60, 64
High, High, High Up In the Hills 31
Highetta, Philip 3
Hill, Lois 165
Hit-of-the-Week Records 62, 160–161, 180
Hits of 1937 75
Hittin' the Ceiling 155
Hoff, Carl 223
Hoffman, Harold J. 70
Holland, Jack 83
Hollywood Without Makeup 213–214
Holman, Libby 56
Holsum Bread Radio Spots 88, 165
Home Again 64, 208
The Hoosier Hot Shots 99
Hoover, Herbert 61
Hoover, Richard 33
Hoover, Will 58
Hope, Bob 65, 90, 102, 110
Hopper, Hedda 96
Hopwood, Avery 46
An Hour Never Passes 87, 164, 212
Hovig, Jayne 209
How About Me? 153, 154
How Can I Lose? 209
How Did You Have the Heart to Break My Heart 126, 175
How Many Times 26, 27
Howell, Beatrice 65
Hucksters Records 90, 91, 100, 167, 180
Hulme, Freddy 140
Humphrey, Mark 4, 33
Humphries, Captain Robin 27, 28, 29
Hunt-McCafferty Productions 100

Index

Hunter, Kim 112
Hutton, Betty 77
Hylton, Jack 29

I Called to Say Goodnight 72, 161
I Can't Believe That You're in Love with Me 150
I Can't Do Without You 152
I Don't Believe It—But Say It Again 26, 144, 145
I Don't Want Your Kisses (If I Can't Have Your Love) 156
I Found Somebody to Love 142, 199
I Love the Sunshine of Your Smile 94, 167
I Might Have Known 21, 23, 142, 199
I Miss a Little Miss (Who Misses Me in Sunny Tennessee) 55, 59, 158, 159
I Miss You Most of All (The Chair's in the Parlor) 167
I Still Love You 152
I Surrender Dear 159, 160
I Tip My Heart To You 102, 199
I Used to Love You (But It's All Over Now) 167
I Want to Hold You in My Arms 173
I Wished on the Moon 118, 173, 175, 215
Ich Liebe Dich (I Love You) 156
I'd Love to Call You My Sweetheart 26, 146
If I Can't Have You 23, 39, 141, 199
If I Had My Way 166
If You Hadn't Gone Away 21, 142
I'll Get By 2, 153, 165, 170, 174, 216
I'll Never Ask for More 153
I'll See You in My Dreams 120, 174, 216
I'm Blue for You 111, 171
I'm Glad I Found a Girl Like You 145
I'm Gonna Charleston Back to Charleston 117, 173, 175, 214
I'm Looking for a Girl Named Mary 147
I'm Looking Over a Four Leaf Clover 2, 31, 38, 147, 165, 166
I'm Sitting on Top of the World 172
I'm Sure of Everything But You 72, 161
I'm Tired of Everything But You 21, 142, 143
I'm Waiting for Ships That Never Come In 2, 151–152
I'm Yours 158
In a Kitchenette 47, 49, 155, 204, 205
In a Little Spanish Town 2, 38, 146, 147, 165, 173, 211
In a Shanty in Old Shanty Town 174
In Old Arizona 45
Iroquis Club 6, 7

Isn't She the Sweetest Thing? 21, 23, 142
Isn't This a Night for Love 208
It Happened in Monterey 172
It Happened in Spain 209
It Looks Like Rain in Cherry Blossom Lane 162, 165
It Must Be Love 152
It's Been a Good Life 111, 171, 173, 174, 199
It's Been a Long, Long Time 165
I've Found the Girl 146
I've Got a Feeling I'm Falling 2, 154
I've Named My Pillow After You 22, 23, 142, 199
Ives, Burl 103
The Imperial Folio for Hawaiian Guitar 196

Ja Da 120, 174, 216
Jackson, Eddie 44
James, Harry 110
James, Lewis 138
The Jazz Derby Revue 19
Jernberg, George 140
Jesse James 74
Jessel, George 122, 220
Johnson, Chic 34
Johnson, Erskine 105
Johnson's Café 6
Jolson, Al 15, 37, 44, 45, 54, 55, 56, 61, 219
Jones, Billy 137, 138
Jones, Isham 56
Jones, Janice 108
Jostyn, Jay 113
Joy, Jimmy 99
Joy, Leatrice 47
Joyce, Jimmie 68
Jubliesta 76
Just a Little Closer 157
Just Another Kiss 155
Just Like a Melody Out of the Sky 2, 38, 152, 166, 170

Kahn, Gus 94
Kahn, Otto 28
Kalcheim, Jack 89
Kapp, Jack 56
Kassell, Barney 128
Katzman, Louis 56, 158
Kaufman, Irving 11, 137, 138
Kay, Beatrice 77, 105, 115
Keaton, Buster 43, 61
Keeler, Ruby 44, 45
Keep Sweeping the Cobwebs Off the Moon 151
The Keller Sisters 19, 212
Kellner, George 106
The Kelso Brothers 65
Kemp, Hal 54, 219
The Ken Murray Show 93
Ken Murray's Blackouts 90, 91, 92, 93, 109, 234
Kengle, Dorothy 74
Kennedy, John F. 110
Kent, Barbara 203

The Kentucky Five 7, 8
Kerr, Lady Innes 28
Keyes, Nelson 27
The Keystone Folio For Guitar 196, 197
Kind and Considerate 103, 170
The King Sisters 110
Kiss and Makeup 151
The Kiss Waltz 157–158
Kit Kat Club (London) 28, 29
Knowles, Patric 106
Krueger, Benny 8, 130, 131, 132, 135, 137, 138, 141
Kuehne, Antoinette 41

Labato, Paddy 97
Lady Be Good 100, 173
Lady Luck 50, 157, 169, 207
Lady Play Your Mandolin 2, 55, 59, 158, 173, 174, 201, 220
Laine, Frankie 1, 46, 61, 107
Lambert, Harold "Scrappy" 23, 55
Lamparski, Richard 113, 173
Lane, Lillian 90
Lang, Eddie 10, 57
Lanin, Sam 11–12, 130–140
Largay, Raymond 93
Laugh-In 113
Laughton, Charles 214
The Lawrence Welk Show 109
Lazy Bones 208
Lee, Don 225
Lee, Loretta 223
Lee, Phil 120
Lees, Charlie 163
Le Maire, Rufus 22
Leonard, Jack 113
Leslie, Lou 9
Let Me Live and Love You Just for Tonight 23, 25, 26, 27, 145, 199
Let's Get Friendly 59
Let's Meander Through the Meadow 95, 213
Let's Play Together for Hawaiian Guitar 196
Let's Play Together for Plectrum Guitar 191
Lewis, Forrest 113
Lewis, Patti 106
Lewis, Reg 163
Lewis, Ted 9, 43, 47, 55, 61, 130
Levy, Jules, Jr. 138
Li-Po-Li 50, 157
Liberace 96
Liberace, George 117
The Liberty Folio for Guitar Solos 196
Lightner, Winnie 47, 49, 204, 205
Linkletter, Art 96
Little, Big Tiny 110
Little, Little Jack 15, 47, 55, 73
Liza 44, 233
Loeb, Bill 97
Lombard, Carole 214
Lombardo, Carmen 1
London Records 118
Lonely Moonlight Troubadour 208

Lonesome 45, 203–204
Long, Huey 2, 61
Looking at the World Thru Rose Colored Glasses 1, 25, 26, 27, 30, 114, 146, 168, 169, 171, 173, 174, 202
Lopez, Vincent 8, 9, 37, 47, 77, 219
Lorraine, Allie 108
Lou Leslie's Blackouts 9
Love Thy Neighbor 72, 161
Lovejoy, Carl 17
Loy, Myrna 50, 51, 52, 202
Lucanese, Anthony 3, 7, 124, 127
Lucanese, Bella (Carmelia) Ermiania 3, 67
Lucanese, Frank *see* Lucas, Frank
Lucanese, Librato "Libby" 3, 4, 5, 7, 67, 124, 127
Lucanese, Nicolina 3
Lucanese, Otto Maria 3, 30
Lucanese, Theresa (Tessie) 3, 124
Lucas, Catherine (Cifrodella) 6, 7–8, 9, 29, 33, 77, 78, 89, 107, 109, 112, 114, 127
Lucas, Emily (Bissell) 8, 9, 29, 77, 112, 127
Lucas, Frank 3, 4, 5, 7, 10, 30, 62, 93, 131
Lucas, Leona 62
Lucas, Lib *see* Lucanese, Librato "Libby"
Lucas Novelty Quartet 10, 131
Lucas Ukulele Trio 10, 131, 132
Luddy, Barbara 113
The Ludwig Baumann Hour 57, 220
Lyin' In the Hay Wagon 208
Lyman, Abe 54, 56, 73, 219
Lynch, Ed 19, 232
Lynn, Judy 110
Lytell, Jimmy 135, 137, 138

MacDonald, Eugene 13
MacGregor, C.P. 73, 91, 107, 109, 162–163, 165, 183, 185
Mack, Gill 8
Mack, Roy 19
MacPherson, Virginia 95
Madalane 102
The Magic Waltz 126, 175, 199
Malone, Gia 110
Mammone, Wingy 85
A Man and His Dream 164
The Man with the Mandolin 164
Manango, Don 140
The Mangeans 83
Mann, Hank 83
Mantz, Paul 90
Marcellino, Muzzy 106
Marcheta 151, 152
Margie 173
Maria Elena 164
Marie, Ah Marie 95, 167
Marie and Antoinette 65
Marlowe, Don 111
Marsh, Larry 223
Marshall, Everett 220

Martin, Dean 1
Martin, Dick 113, 122
Martin, Nancy 165
Martino, Al 1
Marvin, Johnny J, 15
Marx, Groucho 214
Marx, Harpo 214
Masons United Advertising Agency 84, 85, 224
Master Art Products 64, 208
The Mastertone Guitar Method 57
Matthews, Hal 140
Maurer, Betty 165
May I Have the Next Dream? 173
Maybe It's Love 158
Mayes, Mutt 140
Mayfair Music Hall 20, 118, 119, 121, 122, 125
Mays, Harry 23
McCaffrey, William 18
McDonald, Grace 89
McGuire, John 210
McMillan, Dr. Donald Baxter 13
McMurray, Loring 131, 138
McNulty, Dorothy 22
McRae, Carmen 103
Melody Ranch 109
Melotone Records 59, 180
Melrose Records 90
Melton, James 67
Mercury Records 165
Meredith, Burgess 215
The Merry Macs 113
The Merv Griffin Show 115, 127
Mexicali Rose 95, 165, 167
Milburn, Mary 22
Miles, Harry 83
Miller, Jack 1
Miller, Ray 54, 219
The Mills Brothers 61, 78, 103, 220
Mills Music 58
Milt Deutch Agency 98
Minnie the Mermaid 166
Mr. Blackwell's Hollywood 112
Mitchum, Robert 93
Mix, Mabel 99
Mix, Tom 63, 65, 99
Mole, Miff 11, 137
Moon Glow 72, 161, 162
The Moon Got in My Eyes 163
Moonbeam! Kiss Her for Me 38, 148, 170
More Beautiful Than Ever 72, 161
Moreland, Mantan 114
Morgan, Dennis 90
Morgan, Freddie 112
Morgan, Helen 61
Morris, William (Banjo Bill) 191
Morrison, Harold 112
Morris's Modern Method for Tenor Banjo 191
Mother Margarita Maria 115, 121–122
Mulhall, Jack 109
The Mullen Sisters 211
Muni, Paul 61

Murphy, George 65
Murphy's Hollywood 122
Murray, Ken 43, 47, 57, 90, 93, 122, 214, 234
Murray, Mae 43, 61
Murray, Tom 43
The Murtagh Sisters 165
My Best Girl 14, 22, 30, 141, 142, 171
My Blue Heaven 30, 95, 120, 150–151, 165, 166, 168, 172, 174, 216
My Bundle of Love 145
My Cabin of Dreams 163
My Heart Belongs to the Girl Who Belongs to Somebody Else 55, 56, 157
My Melancholy Baby 174
My Ohio Home 2, 151
My Song of the Nile 156
My Tonia 45, 46, 153, 204

Nagel, Conrad 61
Naish, J. Carrol 99
Napoleon, Phil 131–132, 135, 136–137, 138
The Narcotics Pushers 98
Naset, Clayton 110
The National Folio for the Hawaiian Guitar 196–197
Negre Consentida 210
Neill, Frank 78
Nelson, Ozzie 1, 56
Nestles Chocolateers 226
New Year's Revue 82
Newman, Marshall 33
Nichols, Red 11, 56
Nick Lucas (radio) 220–225
Nick Lucas and His Band 210
Nick Lucas and His Crooning Troubadours 158, 159, 160
Nick Lucas and His Guitar 106
Nick Lucas and His Orchestra 72, 213
Nick Lucas and His Troubadours 71–73, 108, 160, 210, 223
The Nick Lucas Chord, Rhythm and Fill-In Book 192
Nick Lucas Collection of Neopolitan Love Songs 58, 192
Nick Lucas' Comic Songs for Ukulele and Guitar 20, 192–193
Nick Lucas De Luxe Plectrum Guitar Solos 197
Nick Lucas Fascinating Plectrum Guitar Solos 198
Nick Lucas Guitar Picks 58
The Nick Lucas Guitar Method for Pick Playing 57, 193
The Nick Lucas Guitar Method for Pick Playing, Volume Two 57
The Nick Lucas Guitar Method for Plectrum Playing 193, 194
The Nick Lucas Guitar Method for Plectrum Playing, Volume Two 195
The Nick Lucas Hawaiian Guitar Method 193
The Nick Lucas Hawaiian Guitar Method, Volume Two 193–194

Index

The Nick Lucas Hawaiian Guitar Method, Volume Three 194
Nick Lucas—1920's Jazz Vocals and Guitar Encore, Volumes 1-3 183–184
The Nick Lucas Plectrum Guitar Method 194–195
Nick Lucas Plectrum Guitar Solos 198
The Nick Lucas Progressive Foundation For Plectrum Playing 195
The Nick Lucas Revue 99, 105
A Nick Lucas Serenade 97
The Nick Lucas Shape (Guitar Pick) 58
The Nick Lucas Souvenir Album (LP) 113–114, 181, 185
Nick Lucas Special (Guitar) 31–33, 44, 69
Nick Lucas, the Singing Troubadour (radio) 85
Nick Lucas, Voice of Memory (radio) 85, 224
Nick Lucas, Volume 1-4 (CDs) 184–185
Nick Lucas' Ukulele Trio 131, 132
Nicomede, Joseph W. (Joe) 57, 58
Nicomede Music Company 57, 58
Nigh, Jane 213
A Night at the Orpheum 115
No Foolin' 145
Norman, Christine 231
Norman, Lucille 107
Not Guilty 103, 170
Novis, Donald 69
Now You're in My Arms 160

Obrecht, James 6
O'Brian, Jack 119
O'Connor, Donald 122
O'Connor, Kitty 23
O'Dea, Sunnie 79
Oh How I Miss You Tonight 165
Oh! Mabel 14, 141
Ohman, Phil 141
O'Keefe, Jimmy 56
Old Timer 154
Oliver, Susan 112
Olsen, George 73
Olsen, Ole 34
On the Air and Off 64–65, 208–209
The Only, Only One 142
The Only Song I Know 50, 156, 207
Organloguing the Hits with Nick Lucas, the Crooning Troubadour 64, 208
The Original Dixieland Jazz Band 9
Oriole Records 180
Oriole (Terrace) Orchestra 12, 14, 140, 141
Osborne, Will 220
O'Shea, Michael 213
Our San Diego 111, 171
Over the Rainbow 79, 164
Owen, Delos 165

Paget, Lord Victor 27
Painting the Clouds (CD) 185
Painting the Clouds with Sunshine (LP) 103, 181
Painting the Clouds with Sunshine (song) 1, 46, 48, 49, 50, 56, 129, 155, 165, 166, 167, 169, 170, 172
Palala's Hawaiians 23
Palloy, Charlie 58
Palmer, Peter 112
Palmieri, Antonio 30
Palmieri, Maria 30
Panachord Records 181
Panelli, Charlie 135, 138
Paper Roses 103, 169
Papile, Frank 140
Paramount Pictures 118, 121
Paramount Records 118
Paris, Frank 142
Parker, Don 11, 131–135
Parker, Col. Tom 1, 104, 115
Parsons, Louella O. 46
Parton, Dolly 127
Pasta Cheech 103, 170
Pastime Number One 174
Pathe Actuelle Records 10, 181
Paul, Anthony "Tony" 4, 5, 20, 34, 78
The Pavilion Players 11
Peabody, Eddie 34, 97
Pearce, Al 73, 74, 75, 77, 223
Peary, Hal (Harold) 113
Peking Café 8
Pennington, Ann 204, 205
Perfect Records 181
Pickin' the Guitar 10, 72, 134, 139, 161, 163, 173
Pisano, Dorothy 7, 34, 41, 128
The Platinum Blonde Revue 77
Pollard, Snub 83
Poltha, Don 112
Ponselle, Rosa 68
Powell, Dick 1
Pozzi, Grace and Igor 83
Precious 26
The Premier Folio of Guitar Solos and Duets 198
Premier Records 90, 181
Presley, Elvis 1, 104, 115
Price, Georgie 220
Prima, Louis 110
Prince of Wales (Edward VIII) 2, 27, 28
Prize of Gold 169
Program Themes 89, 165, 225
Pryor, Roger 77
Puchta, Charlie 140
Purviance, Edna 53
Put Your Arms Where They Belong 146

Quantrell, Frank 9, 153
Queen of Spain (Princess Ena Windsor) 2, 28

Raft, George 68
Rainger, Ralph 8
Ranson, Jo 62, 63

Rapee, Erno 62
Rapp, Barney 69
Rawlinson, Herbert 208
Ray, Johnnie 38
Raye, Martha 122
Raymond, Cyril 231
RCM Company 87
Reagan, Ronald 112
Redford, Robert 117, 214
Reese, Della 110
Reeves, Horace 28
Regal Zonophone Records 163–164, 181
Regent Orchestra 11
Reinherz, Sid 144
Reisenweber's Café 7
Reisman, Leo 219
Renard, Jacques 69
Republic Recording 165
Rex Records 181
Rhythm in Rhapsody 212
Rich, Freddie 67, 73, 220, 221, 223
Richman, Harry 55, 56, 57
Riddle, Nelson 117, 127, 173
Rin-Tin-Tin 207
Ripley's Believe It or Not 12
Ritter, Tex 46
The RKO Hour 43, 57, 219
RKO Theatre of the Air 219–220
Robbins-Engel, Inc. 20
Robbins Music Corporation 57, 58
Robertson, Dale 106
Robertson, Dick 1, 55
Robey, George 78
Robinson, Bill 34, 68
Robinson, Reg 163
Robinson, Russel 140–141
Robison, Carson 57
Rodino, Peter 2
Rogers, Charles "Buddy" 115, 116
Rogers, Ginger 61, 116
Rollins, Lillian 135
Rollins, Mimi 72, 223
Rooney, Pat 34
Roosevelt, Franklin D. 87
Roosevelt, James 87
Rose Colored Glasses (LP) 114, 181
Rose, Fred 23, 141, 199
Rose Marie 67
Roseland Ballroom 11
Roselli, Jimmy 1
Rosenberg, Murray 63, 71
Rosenbloom, Maxie 102
Rosini, Paul 75
Rossi, Steve 1
Rosy Cheeks 149
Roth, Jack 135, 137, 138
Rowan, Dan 113
Royal, John 18
Rubin, Benny 115, 122
Rubinoff, David 39, 148, 151, 152
Ruby, Jack 110
Running Between the Raindrops 159
Russo, Danny 12, 14, 140, 141

Sadie Thompson 169
A Sailboat in the Moonlight 163

Index

Salemme, Louis 9
The Sam Yorty Show 116
Sanders, Scott 79
Sandler, Tony 110
Sannella, Andy 57
The Santa Cruz (California) Guitar Company 33
Santrey, Henry 43
Sardi, Al 9
Saturday Night at the Shamrock 45, 95, 225
Say "Hello" to the Folks Back Home 159
Say It Isn't So 174
Schlesinger, John 118
Schmidt, Lucien 144
Scott, Vernon 126, 127
Seely, Scott 103, 111, 169, 170, 172, 175, 199
Seems Like Old Times 166, 167
Sellers, Inc. 165
Selznick, David O. 38
Sennett, Ted 50
Senora Toque Su Mandolina 158
Sergeant York 50
Sharpe, Gus 133
Short, Gertrude 204, 205
Show Girl 44–45, 119, 232-233
The Show of Shows 1, 50–52, 55, 109, 157, 206–208, 211
Shriner, Herb 79, 112
Siboney 158
Side By Side (film) 87
Side By Side (song) 30, 91, 92, 148, 163, 164, 167, 170, 171, 212
Signorelli, Frank 137, 138
Silver Sails 119, 173, 202
The Silver Screen 82, 233–234
Silvertone Records 181
Silvers, Phil 122
Sims, Ginny 113, 213
Sims, Lee 37, 219
Sinatra, Frank 1, 30
Since You Went Away 38
Sing a Little Love Song 155
Sing an Old Fashioned Love Song 210
Sing Me a Baby Song 149
Singin' in the Rain 45, 156, 233
Singing a Song to the Stars 55, 56, 157
The Singing Troubadour (CD) 185
The Singing Troubadour (LP) 181–182
Singleton, Penny 22
Sisley, Geoff 70
Six Original Nick Lucas Guitar Solos 198
Skelton, Red 94
Slavin, Slick (Trustin Howard) 106
Sleepy Head 26, 27, 145
Sleepy Time Gal 1, 22, 23, 144, 165, 172, 202, 232
Small, Danny 23
Small, Paul 1
Smile a Little Bit 144
Smith, Jack 113

Smith, Kate 47, 61, 96
Smith, "Whispering" Jack 15, 37
Snader Telescriptions 94–95, 167, 168, 211–212
Snow, Hank 104
So Blue 148
Soanes, Wade 44, 64
Sobol, Louis 234
Society for the Preservation of Variety Arts 125
Soldier's Guitar 103, 170
Some Rainy Day 153
Somebody Like You 17, 18, 141
Somebody Stole My Gal 172
Someday, Somewhere 152
The Song I Love 153
The Song Is Ended (But the Melody Lingers On) 2, 38, 151, 165
Sothern, Ann 77
Sound Stage 175
Soundies Corporation of America 87, 164
South of the Border 172
Spevlin, George 40
Spinosa, Tony 100
Spitalny, Phil 56, 62
Star Sound 30, 119
Starr, Kay 84, 85
Starr Records 11
Stasio, Frank 74
Steel, John 75
Stein, Jules 153
Stephens, Laraine 99
Stephenson, Henry 231
Stept, Sam H. (Sammy) 23, 39, 145, 146, 148, 199, 210
Stevens, April 106
Stokowski, Leopold 68
Stone, Ezra 113
Stone, Lewis 61
Stuarti, Enzo 1
Sullivan, Ed 93, 115
Sunshine 151
The Sunshine of Your Smile 94
Sweet Someone 150, 202
Sweetheart of Dixie 19, 231–232
Sweetheart Time 19, 22, 24, 232
Sweetheart's Holiday 113
Swenson, Karl 113
Synchro Sound Film 153, 204

Tangerine 166
Tashman, Lilyan 204, 205
Taylor, Robert 83
Tea Time on the Thames 92, 167
Teague, Thurman 172
Teal, Ray 65
Teardrops 100, 169
Tearle, Conway 48, 204, 205
Teasing the Frets 10, 72, 134, 139, 161, 163
Teleways Radio Productions 93, 167
Teleways Transcriptions 93, 167, 225
Telling It To the Daisies 55, 56
Temple, Shirley 210
The Tennessee Two 138

Terhune, Max 103
Terri, Vincent 172
Tetley, Walter 113
Texas Tommy 75
That Old Gang of Mine 174
That's My Desire 61, 160
They're Playing Our Song (The Won Ton Rag) 121, 175
This Is Show Business 116
This Is the Life 209–210
Thompson, Bill 113
Thompson, Hank 93
Thompson, Willard 23, 199
Thor Brooks Productions 105
Those Were the Days 114, 172, 181
A Thousand Goodnights 72, 161, 202
Three Cheers 80
The Three Chums 8, 231
Three Little Words 2, 158, 165
The Three Vagrants 5
Ticket to Adventure 105
Tie a Yellow Ribbon 'Round the Old Oak Tree 174
Til the Clock Strikes Three 163
Til the End of Forever 100, 169
Till Tomorrow 72
Tiny Tim (Herbert Kauhry) 24, 113, 114, 121
Tiptoe Through the Tulips (film) 87
Tiptoe Through the Tulips (song) 1, 47–48, 49, 50, 51, 56, 67, 72, 90, 91, 111, 114, 115, 123, 126, 127, 155–156, 163, 164, 166–175, 182, 185, 202, 204, 205, 209, 210, 212
Tiptoe Through the Tulips with Nick Lucas (LP) 100, 101, 103
The Toast of the Town 93
To Be Loved By You 121, 175
Todd, Dick 1
Together 38, 171
Toler, Sidney 210
The Tonight Show 113, 114
Tournament of Roses Parade (1980) 126
The Townaires 106
Trailer to the Gold Diggers of Broadway 204
Trask, Walter 115
Travis, Merle 2, 10, 92, 128
Treacher, Arthur 92–93
Tremayne, Les 113
The Troubadour Production Company 106
Truex, Ernest 61
Trumbauer, Frank 9
Tryon, Glenn 203
Tucker, Sophie 9, 34, 43, 47, 77

Underneath the Stars with You 23, 30, 149, 199, 202
Underneath the Weeping Willow 147–148
Unfaithful 59
United Transcribed System (UTS) 91
Upton, Monroe 223

USO (United Service Organization) 88

Vale, Jerry 1
Vallee, Rudy 1, 2, 30, 47, 58, 62, 77, 115, 116, 122
Van, Gus 220
Van, Vera 223
Van and Schneck 47
Variety Arts Theatre 122
Vaudeville 119
Vaudeville Lives 122
Venuti, Joe 84, 85
Vernon Country Club Orchestra 9–10, 11, 130
The Vernon Trio 10, 44, 130
Vieni, Vieni 163
Vinopal, David 22
Vitaphone Headliners 72, 210, 212

Wabash Moon 159
The Waikiki Folio for the Hawaiian Guitar 198
Wakely, Jimmy 92, 95
Walbon, Cliff 104
Waldo, Janet 113
Waldron, Billy 23, 100
Walker, Mickey 124
Walker, Ralph 140
Walking My Baby Back Home 2, 59, 95, 159, 167
Wallace Brothers Circus 105
Walsh, Raoul 45
Walters, Jean 211
The Waltons 55
Wang Wang Blues 120, 174, 216
Ward, Ed 207
Waring, Fred 62
Waring's Pennsylvanians 47
Warnow, Mark 223
Warren, Harry 103
Washburn, Bryant 83
Wasting My Love On You 158
Watch the Fun Go By 93, 223–224
Waters, Ethel 34
Wayne, John 89, 90
Weaver, Doodles 126
Weaver, Ned 113

WEBH Radio 13–14, 225
Webster, Buddy 170
Weidoft, Rudy 138
Welford, Nancy 48, 99, 204, 205
Welk, Lawrence 109
We'll Make Hay While the Sun Shines 120, 174, 216
West, Mae 115
Westcott, Helen 99
Westmore, Ern 98
Westport Records 11
What This Country Needs 67, 209
What Will I Do Without You 155, 205
What Ya Gonna Do? 89, 166
Whatever Became of. . .? 173
What'll I Do 117, 127, 174
Wheeler, Bert 15
Wheeler, Tom 22
When I Think of You 141
When My Dreams Come True 156
When the Moon Comes Over the Mountain 61, 160
When the World Is at Rest 153
When You and I Were Seventeen 117, 173, 175, 214
When You Said Goodnight (Did You Really Mean Goodbye?) 54, 152
When You Were the Blossom of Buttercup Lane and I Was Your Little Boy Blue 159
When You're Lonely 23, 27, 146, 199, 202
While We Danced at the Mardi Gras 171, 172, 202
White, Lew 39, 64, 152, 208
White, Thelma 19, 232
Whiteman, Paul 7, 9, 29, 73
Whitford, Eldon 32
Whiting, Richard 18
Whitmer, Ken 64
Who's Who Are You? 144, 202
Why Should I Say I'm Sorry (When Nobody's Sorry for Me) 148, 149
The Wiere Brothers 119
Williams, Bob 97

Williams, Gary 173
The Williams Sisters 45
Willing, Foy 92
Wilson, Earl 109
Wilson, Marie 90, 93
Winter Olympic Revue 108
Wirges, William F. 39, 149, 150, 151, 152, 153
Withers, Jane 210
Without You, Sweetheart 151
Woman Disputed 46
Woman Disputed, I Love You 46, 153, 204
Won Ton Ton, The Dog Who Saved Hollywood 121, 175
Woolsey, Robert 15
Worryin' 111, 171
Wuerl, Jack 140

Yankee Doodle Home 78, 210–211
Yorty, Sam 2, 116
You Are Everything I Love 166
You Didn't Have to Tell Me (I Knew It All the Time) 159
Young, Clara Kimball 83
Young, Margaret 18
Young, Ralph 110
Young, Victor 61, 72, 160, 161
Youngman, Henny 77, 90
Your Mother and Mine 45, 156, 233
You're a Real Sweetheart 54, 174
You're Driving Me Crazy 2, 55, 59, 158, 159
(You're Not Asking Me) I'm Telling You 153

Zaharias, Babe 81
Zaharias, George 81
Zanuck, Darryl F. 46, 47, 48, 50
Zei Gezunt 172
Zelig 216
Zieff, Howard 119
Ziegfeld, Florenz 44, 45
The Ziegler Sisters 7, 8
Zig, Joe 9
Zoppi, Tony 101, 102, 109, 110
Zumba 117

www.ingramcontent.com/pod-product-compliance
Lightning Source LLC
Chambersburg PA
CBHW080802300426
44114CB00020B/2805